Unfinished Conquest

Other Works by Victor Perera

The Conversion (a Novel)

The Loch Ness Monster Watchers

The Last Lords of Palenque: The Lacandon Mayas of the Mexican Rain Forest (with Robert D. Bruce)

Rites: A Guatemalan Boyhood

Testimony: Death of a Guatemalan Village, by Victor Montejo (Editor and translator)

Unfinished Conquest

The Guatemalan Tragedy

Victor Perera

Photographs by Daniel Chauche

UNIVERSITY OF CALIFORNIA PRESS
Berkeley • Los Angeles • London

Contents

Acknowledgments

Of the six years that I have worked on this book, seven months of each year on the average were spent in Guatemala. From my base in Antigua, where most of the book was written, I made numerous excursions to the Maya highlands and to Petén. I owe a special debt of gratitude to the late William R. Swezey, whose passing in June 1989 weighs heavily on us all.

I am indebted for support in periods of adversity to my agents, Gloria Loomis, Nicole Aragi, and Kendra Taylor, to Ana Livingston Paddock, and to other friends and colleagues too numerous to mention. The steady and capable stewardship of my editors, Naomi Schneider and Barbara Ras, eased the travails of preparing this work for publication.

I am also indebted to the Djerassi Foundation, the Virginia Center for the Creative Arts, and the Blue Mountain Center for granting me residencies to work on *Unfinished Conquest*. The last phases of preparation were also aided by the generous assistance of a Lila Wallace-Reader's Digest Grant. And I thank *The New Yorker* and the late William Shawn for a stipend that permitted me to travel to the Ixil Triangle in 1986 and 1987.

Portions of this book have appeared, in somewhat different form, in the *New York Times Magazine*, *Antioch Review*, *The Nation*, *Mother Jones*, the *New York Review of Books*, and *Grassroots Development*.

Preface

In the fall of 1985 I returned to Guatemala, my country of birth, as an observer to the first open and fraud-free presidential elections in twenty years. The solid victory of Christian Democrat Vinicio Cerezo Arévalo in the second round bore with it the voters' hopes for a respite in the decades-long war between the army and leftist insurgents that left tens of thousands of Guatemalans dead or disappeared and a million more displaced from their homes.

In his inaugural address, President Cerezo exhorted intellectuals, journalists, and other professionals to return from exile and help to fortify the country's democratic *apertura,* or opening. Although I did not consider myself an exile, having lived in the States voluntarily from the age of twelve, my infrequent return visits had been furtive and brief. In spring of 1971 I had reported for the *New York Times Magazine* on the nasty counterinsurgency war General Carlos Arana Osorio was waging with U.S. military assistance in the eastern provinces under the Vietnam-era rubric "Pacification Campaign." The article evidently nettled President Arana, for his press secretary warned my uncle that I would be chopped into mincemeat *("lo vamos a hacer picadilla")* if I attempted to set foot in the country again. Needless to say, I took the warning very much to heart and stayed clear of Guatemala for the remainder of Arana's presidency.

During the five years of Vinicio Cerezo's shaky civilian rule, I resided in the old colonial capital of Antigua, a half hour's drive from

Guatemala City and two to five hours from the highland Mayan communities described in this book. Sadly, I had to witness the progressive unraveling of Cerezo's democratic renewal as Guatemala's unredeemed, violent history cast a pall over his presidency and over his successor's as well. My base was the Hotel Aurora, a converted Spanish colonial residence that had been my family's weekend retreat when I was a boy.

In Antigua I found myself reliving painful episodes from my early years, some of which I've laid down in a recent memoir. Since being declared a national monument in the mid-forties, Antigua, with its rococo church and convent ruins I once played in unmolested, has become overrun with foreign tourists and hippies. Antigua, which was the Spanish throne's administrative capital for Chiapas and Central America, has a colorful five-hundred-year-long history crisscrossed with natural and unnatural calamities. The previous colonial capital, which lay two miles south of Antigua in the valley of Almolonga, was destroyed a mere fourteen years after its founding in 1527 by a massive flood and mud slide from the nearby Agua volcano. The opulent Renaissance and Baroque capitals that arose consecutively in what is now Antigua were each destroyed by catastrophic earthquakes in the seventeenth and eighteenth centuries. The stately remnants of Antigua's churches, convents, and monasteries were further damaged by the earthquake of February 1976.

In the rose garden patio of the Hotel Aurora, which survived the 1976 quake virtually intact, I sit by the same eighteenth-century fountain I tried to clamber over when I was two and searching for goldfish. And I wander the same pillared corridors, draped with sprays of bougainvillea and honeysuckle, where I once chased after birds and lizards. From a neighboring terrace I beheld for the first time the awesome symmetry of Agua volcano, which looms over Antigua like an immense and sullen sentinel. In the safe haven of the Aurora I had nursed the wounds inflicted by the murder of my seventeen-year-old Maya nursemaid, Chata, who was stabbed seven times by her jealous lover only a block away from my kindergarten. And here I also brooded on the five white-tunicked Lacandón Mayas I encountered in dictator Jorge Ubico's national fair. The Lacandones, who had shoulder-length matted hair and sad, beautiful eyes that made their gender a mystery, had been smuggled into the country from their home in the Chiapas rain forest. At the fair, they were put on display inside a chicken-wire enclosure for the amusement of Ubico's satraps and his loyal subjects, among them, my tender, impressionable self.

At the Aurora I have explored the hidden links between these and other seemingly unconnected events from my first decade of life. At first I felt as if I were returning to the hotel like a thief drawn irresistibly to the scene of his crime. But my obsession is not so readily categorized. To my gratified surprise, the heirs of Hotel Aurora extended to me the same warm welcome the original *dueña* gave my parents four decades ago. The cook, waiters, and chambermaids are descended from the hired help who attended my family, and they are as conversant with Antigua folklore and traditions as their predecessors were.

When I was five, our chambermaid María Luisa would sneak me into the cathedral and urge me to pray to the crucified Christ to save my heathen Jewish soul. In the evenings, she would tell me hair-raising stories of *brujería,* or witchcraft, and of the elaborate depravities committed in centuries past by nuns and monks of the Capuchinas and Merced convents, who rendezvoused in dank underground passageways. Nearly a half-century later María Luisa's nephew Roberto assures me, while serving breakfast, that the secret tunnels are still used for illicit purposes by the convent's present occupants. And today I read in the newspapers of a house in Antigua used for hiding kidnapped children, who would then be sold to wealthy childless couples abroad. The couple who ran the house said they had been afraid to turn in the kidnapper, a cousin to a former military president, "because she is a witch."

Antigua conserves its ancient wounds and dark tales more jealously than any Old World city I know. And with an alchemy that mystifies foreign visitors, Catholic Antigua also conserves balm for its wounds and magic antidotes against the dark witchery of its past. Antigua is the home of Hermano Pedro of Bethancourt, the Franciscan lay brother from Spain's Canary Island of Tenerife who founded the Bethlehemite order and hospital in the seventeenth century. Hermano Pedro was beatified in 1980 in recognition of his now legendary labors to heal the sick and feed the destitute. His followers had hoped that Pope John Paul II would canonize Hermano Pedro during his pastoral visit to the Americas in October 1992. Brother Pedro is Antigua's authentic saint. Thousands of his devotees have covered the walls of his grave site with crutches, braces, appendage-shaped amulets, photographs, and children's drawings that testify to his miraculous healing powers. The alloy of morbidity in these humble offerings would have troubled Hermano Pedro not at all. Among the cult objects displayed in a museum in back of the church is a human skull he kept in his cell to meditate on life's transiency, and he regularly mortified his flesh with twenty lashes. When Hermano Pedro died, the calluses on his knees and elbows from a lifetime of ascetic devotion were cut up into fragments and preserved as holy relics.

In October 1990 Hermano Pedro's remains were removed from their simple wall niche and placed in a sumptuous sculpted crypt, in anticipation of His Holiness's visit. No miracles attended the exhumation of Hermano Pedro, but his skeleton was found nearly entire. The thin, delicate bones belonged to a man not much more than five feet tall, and just over a hundred pounds in weight; the small yet sturdy skull seemed the twin of the one he had contemplated in his cell.

In October 1984, shortly before my return to Guatemala, I was invited on a speaking tour of Scotland by the Edinburgh office of Amnesty International. I was in Glasgow when a Catholic priest and two catechists with Guatemala's Justice and Peace Committee spoke at a local union hall. The youngest of the three Guatemalans touring northern European industrial cities was a Mayan woman who wore the patterned blue wraparound skirt and white blouse of Alta Verapaz. After bowing from the waist and greeting each of the rugged miners and the others in her native Quekchí, "Marina" spoke in a clear, unfaltering Spanish of the massacre she had witnessed in her village outside Cobán. In excruciating detail, she described the silent arrival of the platoon of soldiers, the efficient manner in which they rounded up the villagers in the square, separating the men from the women and children. After stabbing women and infants with their bayonets, they raped several younger women, who pleaded in vain for mercy. Then the soldiers systematically tortured a dozen men they accused of being guerrilla collaborators and shot them point blank with their Galil rifles. Before departing, the soldiers set fire to every home in the village, including Marina's.

The Scots audience listened to Marina's testimony in awed silence. Many among them were veterans of world wars and bitter mining strikes and had suffered economic hardship as well; none of them had heard anything like this before.

After her presentation I approached Marina and told her about the murder of my nursemaid, Chata, who had been a native of Cobán like herself.

She gazed at me with her soft dark eyes, and touched my shoulder. "As a Guatemalan, you know that I could not tell them the full truth of what is being done to our people, for fear no one would believe me. How could I tell them of watching a soldier bayonet my aunt in the stomach, rip out her four-month-old fetus, and smash it against a house post? How could I speak to them of our children waking up screaming in the middle of the night, beyond comforting, and of our nightly prayers to God for justice in our land? And how should we seek justice, by arming ourselves?" Fixing me with her clear gaze, unclouded by tears, Marina said: "I have looked in the eyes of the soldier who raped and stabbed my aunt and killed her unborn child, and I know he is a child of the Mayas who lives in Christ, as I am. Is it for me to pass judgment on him? Is it not for the soldier, driven by his superiors to commit these senseless atrocities, to seek forgiveness? What would happen to my soul if I had lifted a stone to kill this soldier; would I not have become the same as he? Would not the violence instilled in him have won over me as well? These are the questions I ask myself. You know as well as I do how important it is that we tell the story of our people, so that the army officers who ordered the massacres will not have the final say." Without another word, Marina shook my hand, bundled up in her borrowed down coat, and slipped out with her colleagues into the frigid northern night.

These past years have led me to Marina's understanding that the violence visited on her village has in one way or another been visited on millions of other Guatemalans, myself included. This book tells a part of that story.

MEXICO

Uaxactún

Tikal

Piedras
Negras

El Naranjo   Dos Aguadas

BELIZE

Yaxchilán

Flores

La Libertad   San Francisco

EL PETÉN

Poptún

Gulfo de
Honduras

IXCÁN

Sebol

San Mateo Ixtatán   Barillas   EL
                                        QUICHÉ   ALTA VERAPAZ
San Miguel Acatán
                      Soloma   IZABAL
HUEHUETENANGO   Chajul   Cahabon
Todos Santos   Nebaj   San Juan   San Cristóbal
Ixtahuacán   Chiantla   Cotzal   Cobán   Panzós
                                  Cunén   Uspantán   Pancajche
       Huehuetenango   Sacapulas
SAN   BAJA VERAPAZ
MARCOS   Santa Cruz   San Pedro   Rabinal
            del Quiché   Jocopilas   Salamá   ZACAPA
TOTONI-   Chichicastenango San Miguel   San
CAPÁN   Chicaj   EL   Cristóbal
              SOLOLÁ   San Martín   PROGRESO
                         Iximché   Jilotepéque
              San Pedro   Comalapa   Guatemala   San Luis   Chiquimula
              La Laguna   Tecpán   City   Jilotepeque   CHIQUIMULA   HONDURAS
                          Patzún   Antigua   Jalapa   Esquipulas
              Santiago   GUATEMALA   JALAPA
              Atitlán
              Tequisate
                         Santa Lucia   Cuilapa
                         Cotzumalguapa   JUTIAPA
                         ESCUINTLA   SANTA
                                Iztapa   ROSA
              SACATEPÉQUEZ
                                San José   EL
              CHIMALTENANGO   SALVADOR

OCEANO
PACIFICO

CUBA
MEXICO BELIZE JAMAICA
              GUATEMALA
              HONDURAS
EL
SALVADOR
NICARAGUA   Zona del
COSTA RICA   Canal
       PANAMA

QUEZALTENANGO

RETALHULEU

SUCHITEPÉQUEZ

Introduction

"And as I observed their ill will toward the service of his
Majesty, and for the good benefit of this country, I burned
them and ordered that the city be burned to its foundation."
Pedro de Alvarado, letter to Carlos V of Spain

One month after the conquistador of Guatemala, Cortés's blond captain Pedro de Alvarado, was crushed under a horse during a campaign
in Nochiztlán, Mexico, rainwater spilled over the crater of majestic
Agua volcano and flooded the newly founded capital of Santiago de
los Caballeros de Guatemala. Among the hundreds of Spaniards buried by the mud slides and the ensuing earthquake was the grieving
widow of Pedro de Alvarado, who had dubbed herself "Doña Beatriz
the Unlucky." The opening chapter of the Conquest of Guatemala
ended as it began, in a violent convulsion.

Five hundred years before the arrival of the Spaniards, the Mayas
who built the great temples at Tikal, Palenque, and Yaxchilán abandoned their cities for reasons that continue to mystify scholars. They
left behind the majestic shells of what was probably the most advanced civilization to have ever flourished on the American continent.
Only fragments of their achievements in mathematics, philosophy,
astronomy, and calendrical science survived at the time of first contact
with the European invaders. Many of those fragments went up in
flames in the infamous auto-da-fé celebrated in 1562 by Yucatán's
Bishop Diego de Landa in the plaza of Maní. As the climax to his
personal and unauthorized inquisition into Indian heresy, Landa
burned possibly hundreds of hieroglyphic Mayan books and codices,
which he denounced as "superstitions and falsehoods of the devil."

1

A remnant of what may have been the Mayas' equivalent to the *Iliad* and the *Odyssey* surfaced in highland Guatemala in the sixteenth century as the *Popol Vuh,* or "Book of Council." Composed in Quiché Maya and rendered in the Spanish alphabet, the *Popol Vuh* recounts the migrations of the Quichés' ancestors to Guatemala from their ancient capital of Tula in the Mexican highlands. Another, perhaps older section of the *Popol Vuh* recounts the adventures of the heroic wizard twins, Hunahpú and Xbalanqué, who defeat the Death Lords of the Maya underworld, Xibalbá, and initiate the present cycle of creation. A growing body of evidence suggests that the twins' epic encounters inspired the symbolic chthonic journeys undertaken by the *Ahauob,* the philosopher kings of the classical Maya era.

After the ancient Mayan sites were abandoned, many of the survivors dispersed to what is today Mexico's Yucatán Peninsula, while others made their way to the highlands of Chiapas and Guatemala, dividing into the thirty or so warring kingdoms of the post-classic Maya era. Today's twenty-one Mayan linguistic communities, headed by the Quichés, the Cakchiquels, the Tz'utujils, the Mams, and the Quekchís, are descended from the warring kingdoms of the post-classic Mayas.

At the time of first contact with the Europeans, the highlands of Guatemala were rent by internal dissensions caused by the break-up of the powerful Quiché empire, whose king, Quicab the Great, had ruled over approximately 26,000 square kilometers of high plains, or *altiplano,* and collected tribute from more than one million subjects.

Captain Pedro de Alvarado was commissioned by his commander Hernán Cortés to explore the territories making up present-day Guatemala and to "endeavor with the greatest care to bring the people to peace without war and to preach matters concerning our holy faith." In the performance of his commission the mercurial, rapacious Alvarado strayed so far from his commander's behest that his Indian name, Tonatiuh, meaning "sun"—a reference to his blond hair and beard—has become synonymous with the bloodiest chapter in the Conquest of the Americas.

In 1523 Captain Alvarado climbed to the altiplano from the Pacific with 120 horsemen, 300 foot soldiers, and several hundred Mexican auxiliaries from Cholula and Tlaxcala. They were accompanied by two priests, Juan Godínez and Juan Díaz. Alvarado's expedition met scant resistance until it reached the plains near present-day Quezal-tenango (Xelahú), where it was met by a large army of Quichés led by their king, Tecún Umán, grandson of Quicab the Great. Had the Quichés persuaded their neighboring Cakchiquels and Tz'utujils to join them in repelling the Spaniards, the Conquest might have had a different and more complicated denouement. But the Cakchiquels still smarted from decades of harsh treatment by the Quichés, who had exacted exorbitant tributes, and both nations were distrusted by the Tz'utujils, who had fought bitterly to defend their territories on Lake Atitlán. Alvarado cleverly exploited these animosities to divide and conquer the altiplano.

The Quiché warriors, who greatly outnumbered the invading Span-iards, gave a good account of themselves, fighting the armored foot soldiers toe-to-toe with obsidian-tipped arrows, lances, spears, and leather shields. The Maya warriors feared the Spanish mastiffs and the cavalry far more than their steel weapons or their light artillery. In the Spaniards' version, the sight of man and horse merged in a single terrifying beast persuaded many of the Quichés—as it had the Aztecs before them—that they were locked in battle with superhuman beings. According to a colonial Quiché document cited by Victoria Bricker [1981], Tecún Umán was a great sorcerer who "flew up like an eagle" and vanquished Alvarado when he thrust his lance at his mount, beheading it in one stroke. But the unscathed Alvarado instead passed his own steel lance through the heart of Tecún Umán. With the Quiché king lying mortally wounded on the ground, the battle was soon decided in the Spaniards' favor. The sight of the noble Tecún Umán covered in quetzal feathers and crowns of gold, silver, and precious stones profoundly moved Alvarado, according to the Quiché documents. In a gesture of deference toward his adversary, Alvarado stopped his mastiffs from tearing apart the fallen monarch and re-turned the body to his subjects for burial. Alvarado named the site of battle Quezaltenango in honor of Tecún Umán.

Alvarado's own chronicle drily reports the death of "one of the four lords of Utatlán who was captain-general of this realm." The conquistador's ruthlessness would reassert itself in his next encounter with the Quichés, when they attempted to lure the Spaniards into their fortress capital of Gumarcaah (Utatlán) and ambush them. Sens-ing a trap, Alvarado stopped his troops at the entrance to the citadel.

He ordered the capture of the Quiché kings and nobles, strung them up to high posts, and burned them alive, ignoring their pleas for mercy.

The defeat of the Quichés was followed by Alvarado's betrayal of the Cakchiquels, whom he first befriended and recruited to brutally subdue their enemies, the Tz'utujils. Having disposed of the Cakchiquels' enemies, Alvarado founded the first Spanish colonial capital beside the Cakchiquel's citadel at Iximché, near present-day Tecpán. Wasting no time, he ordered their kings to hand over one thousand leaves of gold weighing fifteen *pesos* each. Stunned by the abrupt turn in Tonatiuh's amicable disposition, the Cakchiquels balked, pleading with him to lower the tribute. Infuriated by their demurral, Alvarado threatened to hang and burn the kings if they did not meet his demands in full within five days. "Woe to you if you do not bring it!" he shouted. "I know my heart!"

Alvarado's execution of Cakchiquel nobles and his numerous other abuses recorded in the *Annals of the Cakchiquels* provoked the first uprising against Spanish domination. The Cakchiquels fled to the mountains, where for four years they engaged in an early form of guerrilla warfare against the Spaniards. They dug pits with pointed stakes that caused the death of many horses. But the conquering Spaniards would not be denied. Alvarado captured the rebel Cakchiquel kings one by one and hung them in the central plaza. After quelling the rebellion the Spaniards concluded that Iximché was no longer safe; they set fire to the majestic temples, palaces, and courtyards and relocated their ill-fated capital of Santiago de los Caballeros to the valley of Almolonga.

In the following years Alvarado and his lieutenants subdued each of the remaining Mayan kingdoms of the altiplano, conducting further massacres and stifling all resistance with their habitual brutality. The last to be brought under Spanish domination was the Kingdom of Tayasal, situated in the northern forests of Petén, which was not secured until 1697.

Estimates of the numbers of Mayas killed by the Spaniards vary widely. In his *Very Brief History of the Destruction of the Indies,* published shortly after Alvarado's death, Friar Bartolomé de las Casas accused him of killing 5 million Indians and "committing enormities sufficient to fill a particular volume, so many were the slaughters, violences, injuries, butcheries, and beastly desolations." Although the substance of las Casas's denunciation is beyond dispute, modern scholars calculate that no more than 2 million Mayas inhabited Guatemala at the time of first contact. As many as 750,000 may have died from plague, violence, and other Conquest-related causes in the first decades after the Spaniards arrived. Another million Mayas had died of European diseases by the middle of the seventeenth century. For all the righteous indignation of the saintly Friar de las Casas, the truth is that smallpox, yellow fever, influenza, diphtheria, and a host of other diseases unknown to the New World killed several times more Mayas than the most sanguinary of conquistadores ever intended to.

Las Casas lived long enough to witness the establishment of the social hierarchy that persists in Guatemala to the present day: European (*criollo*) landowners and generals dominating the mixed-blood (*ladino*) administrators and officers, who in turn oppress the lowly Mayan campesinos, often through Indian intermediaries in the guise of labor contractors, pastors, army sergeants, and municipal officers. The Spaniards named their Indian proxies—most of whom were former *caciques* or chieftains—*principales,* and set them above their fellows by extending them privileges and favors they denied to their communities. This was an early example of a continuing practice by the ruling criollo and ladino establishment to eradicate the Mayas' identity by co-opting and "ladinicizing" their leaders.

Despite the concerted efforts of criollos and ladinos, the Mayas have safeguarded many of their ancient customs by assimilating them with Iberian Catholicism into a system of syncretic beliefs and rituals they call *costumbre.* The main repository of costumbre is the *cofradía,* or brotherhood, that has endured in many highland Mayan communities for over 450 years. The original cofradías imported from Spain were craft and labor guilds, governed by a patron saint or virgin. The Mayas transformed them into religious sodalities that practiced animal sacrifices and pre-Columbian prayer ceremonies under the guise of Catholic saint-worship. Cofradías in the more remote communities still have shamans who observe the traditional Maya calendar. These "day-keepers" call on the powers inherent in each of the twenty name-days in order to heal the sick, invoke beneficent spirits, and—in extreme cases—cast spells on their enemies.

One year after Volcán Agua devastated Santiago and the Almolonga Valley in 1541, the Spanish capital was moved to what is now Antigua, Guatemala, in the valley of Panchoy. The move inaugurated the three-hundred-year colonial era, whose rigid hierarchical structures, feudal patterns of land ownership, and ruthless exploitation of Mayan communities persist, in modified form, to the present day.

In the territory governed by the city of Santiago, the sixteenth-century colonial capital of Guatemala, the task of converting the hundreds of thousands of Indian subjects was divided among the Franciscan, Dominican, and Mercedarian missions, while the conquered lands were carved up by Alvarado's officers into vast estates, or *haciendas*. Indigo, cochineal, and cacao were cultivated in the humid lowlands and highland foothills, while cattle ranching predominated in the temperate highlands and the dry Oriente. The labor to work these estates was provided by royal grants or *encomiendas,* which gave the *hacendado* full title to the Indian serfs living on the estate.

The practice of encomienda dated from the *Reconquista* in Spain, when the victorious Spaniards recruited vanquished Moors as serfs to work their Andalusian haciendas. Even so staunch a defender of Indian rights as Friar Bartolomé de las Casas was an *encomendero* for a time, during his sojourn in Cuba. The encomenderos' peons not only had to work without pay but also had to render tribute to their masters in the form of produce, poultry, and woven goods.

Las Casas was instrumental in the abolition of the encomiendas. In 1537 he prevailed on Carlos V to introduce a more humane treatment of his Indian subjects by gathering them around mission churches, where they would receive proper religious instruction. Las Casas's revolutionary precept that Indians were not inferior by nature but were instead "infants of the faith" made a deep impression on Carlos V. In 1542 the monarch incorporated las Casas's ideas into a more humane code of New Laws for the Spanish colonies. Las Casas put his precepts to work in the formerly war-torn regions of the eastern highlands, where he pacified the Quekchí Mayas with the introduction of Dominican missions. These eastern highland regions came to be known as Verapaz, lands of True Peace. Four hundred and fifty years later the military's war of counterinsurgency caught up with Baja and Alta Verapaz, killing several thousand of its Mayan residents and turning tens of thousands of others into refugees.

Las Casas's sworn enemies, the intemperate conquistadores and their immediate descendants, used their influence in court to ensure that the New Laws would be short-lived. After the death of las Casas the encomiendas were replaced by *repartimiento,* a system of forced labor that included a negligible wage.

To facilitate the Catholic missions' labor of converting the Mayas, as well as to provide additional serfs and tribute, the scattered communities outside the encomiendas were concentrated together through a process called *congregación*. After the first uprisings by abused laborers and tribute slaves a second congregación was aimed at breaking communal bonds by gathering the rebels from dispersed regions into closely supervised *pueblos indios*. This strategy would serve as an inspiration for the model village program introduced by the Guatemalan military in the 1980s to pacify insurgent highland Mayan communities in the Ixil Triangle, the Ixcán, and other "Zones of Conflict." In both cases, the forced nucleation of idiosyncratic Mayan communities not only undermined their cultural identity but also inflicted severe economic and environmental hardships.

Severo Martínez and other historians have written of the centuries-long tug of war for political influence and privilege between the peninsular Spaniards loyal to the throne and the *criollos,* or New World Spaniards, whose Indian mistresses birthed the first mixed-breed *ladinos*. Beneath the ladinos in status were the Indian *principales* chosen to keep order and collect tribute from the lowly peasants, who were and continue to be the most cruelly exploited native underclass in the Americas. (Colonial Mayas accepted las Casas's term *naturales* in place of the criollos' demeaning *indio, mozo,* and *peón. Naturales* is still widely used among highland Mayas.)

With occasional alterations, this hierarchical infrastructure remained in place throughout the colonial era, and with some twentieth-century refinements it continues to be operative. About three hundred large landowning families still represent the criollo interests, now in growing competition with an influential business and industrial elite. Along the Pacific coast, where coffee remained Guatemala's chief export crop for over a century, sugarcane, bananas, cotton, and, more recently, cardamom have replaced the colonial plantations of indigo, cochineal, and cacao. These large landholders (*latifundistas*) represent less than 2 percent of Guatemala's population but control over 65 percent of the arable land.

The traditional ladino role is now embodied by the army officer class and by the expanding middle class whose breadwinners fill white- and blue-collar occupations. Today's Maya principales tend to be more independent than their colonial forebears; they are often small landowners, tradesmen, municipal officers, and more recently the mayors of small towns and villages throughout the upper highlands.

The fortunes of the campesinos who worked as tenant farmers and manual laborers remained remarkably unchanged for over three and a half centuries—as attested to in the writings of travelers Thomas Gage, John Lloyd Stephens, Jackson Steward Lincoln, among others.

The system of encomienda and congregación was porous enough to allow hundreds of Mayan communities to go on farming their *milpas,* or cornfields, and to retain ownership of ancestral lands. In these remote outposts, the cultivation of corn remained a sacrament that linked the Maya farmer to his gods. The preparation and planting of a milpa, in times of plenty as well as in times of want, is at the heart of the Maya's conception of himself. This situation would change in the second half of the nineteenth century, after a sustained peasant rebellion against colonial and post-independence structures and institutions. The uprising was headed by the mestizo, or mixed-breed, cacique Rafael Carrera, whose invasions of fincas and assaults on the capital with hordes of Maya campesinos brought the criollos and ladinos face to face with their worst fears. These fears appeared to be substantiated when Carrera seized control of the government in 1840 and ruled the country directly and through puppet presidents during the next three decades.

Carrera was tamed to some degree by his alliance with the conservative Catholic church, and his thirty-year dominance left the landowning elites shaken but unmoved. The most radical change in Mayan communal land tenure came about a decade after Carrera's passing with the ascendancy of the self-styled Liberal Reformer, Justo Rufino Barrios. Beginning in the late 1870s, Barrios passed debt-peonage statutes and abolished hundreds of Mayan land titles in order to create an army of seasonal laborers for the huge coffee fincas that were springing up along Guatemala's Pacific piedmont. In 1884 alone, more than one hundred thousand acres of Maya-owned municipal lands passed into private hands. Hundreds of thousands of indigenous farmers who had never traveled more than a few kilometers from their milpas were conscripted to work in the coastal fincas as coffee pickers and peons.

Guatemala's agricultural elite has good reason to commemorate Justo Rufino Barrios as their great benefactor, and Guatemala's Mayan communities have equal reason to revile the memory of their greatest scourge after Pedro de Alvarado. The "Liberal Reformer's" lasting legacy was a thriving coffee-centered economy that controlled 14 percent of the world trade by 1905 and accounted for 85 percent of Guatemala's annual export revenues. Barrios's undermining of the milpa-based Mayan culture proved just as enduring. By the 1920s the growing taste for coffee in North America and Europe created the first millionaire fortunes in Guatemala at the same time that land-poverty became institutionalized in the Mayan highlands. Barrios's statutes remained on the books until 1934, when the "benevolent dictator" Jorge Ubico replaced them with vagrancy laws that obligated all campesinos owning less than three *manzanas* (two hectares) to do manual labor for a minimum of one hundred days a year. This assured plantation owners vast reserves of migrant laborers for their coffee and sugar harvests. Paradoxically, the new vagrancy statutes also planted the seeds of Mayan resistance; in the mid-nineteen-fifties, they led to the formation of the first peasant unions under presidents Arévalo and Arbenz.

Many historians now regard Barrios and the rise of the coffee fincas as the second chapter of the conquest and exploitation of Guatemala's indigenous population. The third and potentially final chapter may have begun in the late seventies with the massive counterinsurgency campaign mounted by the first of three military presidents, Romeo Lucas García. The total cost of the war that began in the early sixties with the rise of the first guerrilla organizations is now calculated at 120,000 Guatemalans killed, and another 46,000 disappeared and unaccounted for. (The transitive verb *"desaparecer"* [to disappear] originated in Guatemala.)

Although the leftist guerrillas who incited the most bloody military reprisals in Central America's history probably never numbered more than seventy-five hundred trained militants, they succeeded in recruiting close to half a million peasant supporters in the western and central highlands and in the northern department of El Petén. Had the three main guerrilla organizations, the Guerrilla Army of the Poor (EGP), the Revolutionary Organization of People in Arms (ORPA), and the Rebel Armed Forces (FAR), been able to coordinate and arm their enormous followings, this would have been a far different story. In 1982 these three organizations banded together with the military arm of the Guatemalan Workers Party (PGT) to form the Guatemalan National Revolutionary Union (URNG); but by then the guerrillas' best opportunities had already passed. Everyone underestimated the tenacity and ruthlessness of the ladino military officer class, which had been tempered by five centuries of subservience to criollo landowning elites.

The first real prospect of an end to Guatemala's war arose with the Esquipulas Peace negotiations held in Guatemala in 1986 and 1987 under the auspices of President Cerezo. The five Central American presidents signed agreements that disarmed the Contras in Nicaragua and provided the framework for peace negotiations between government and guerrilla leaders in El Salvador and Guatemala. (In 1987 Costa Rica's former president Oscar Arias received the Nobel Peace Prize for his skillful diplomacy.) In 1991 the Farabundo Martí National Liberation Front and President Alfredo Cristiani signed a peace accord in El Salvador that is not yet fully implemented. Guatemala's military and government representatives have engaged in ongoing negotiations with leaders of the URNG for the past three years. Despite sporadic signs of progress, negotiations have repeatedly stalled over the issue of accountability for human rights violations and the prosecution of the war.

2

More than any other country in the Central American isthmus, Guatemala sits on the cusp of interlocking contradictions. At 9.5 million, Guatemala is the most populous of the six Central American republics, the richest in natural resources, and it attracts the most investment dollars from the United States and the large multinational corporations in Europe and the Far East. And yet its Maya majority of nearly

5 million has the lowest per capita income in the region. (A study published in 1991 by the National Institute of Statistics revealed that 90 percent of highland residents live in conditions of extreme poverty.) Guatemala is the Central American country closest to our borders, yet it is by far the most neglected by the U.S. media. After the overthrow of democratically elected Jacobo Arbenz in 1954, a curtain of silence descended over Guatemala. The country and its war, which has lasted more than thirty years, have remained largely invisible, even to North Americans who defy the State Department's negative travel advisories and fly to the Mayan ruins of Tikal or visit the artisans' markets of Atitlán and Chichicastenango.

An important part of this story is the role played by Israel, Taiwan, Argentina, and other arms dealers who replaced the United States for four crucial years as suppliers of weapons and technical assistance to the Guatemalan military. In 1977 Guatemala stopped importing arms from the United States in anticipation of a credit ban from President Jimmy Carter, who deplored Guatemala's abysmal record of human rights abuse. Direct U.S. military aid began again in the early eighties, under Ronald Reagan.

One major result of the war is a shift in the power balance that has created a new landowning elite among military officers, who are proclaiming themselves the victors of a war that has by no means ended.

A remarkable product of Guatemala's war is the rise of a Protestant evangelical movement imported from the United States, which has already converted over one-third of Guatemala's nominally Catholic indigenous population. The early Protestant missions in Guatemala allied themselves with authoritarian Liberal governments, beginning with that of Justo Rufino Barrios. Until the rise of the communist specter in the early 1950s, the impact of these traditional Protestant churches on the Catholic Mayan communities had been negligible. The century-long influx of missionaries from traditional Protestant churches as well as the newer fundamentalist and Pentecostal sects crested into flood tide following the devastating earthquake of February 1976, which left over 27,000 dead and hundreds of thousands injured and homeless. The large majority of the quake victims lived in the highland Mayan departments of Chimaltenango and Quiché, which had borne the brunt of Alvarado's cruelty. Beginning in the late 1970s, these two departments would also become the prime targets of Alvarado's descendants, the criollo and mestizo generals who planned Guatemala's counterinsurgency strategy in the Mayan highlands.

The evangelicals who came to Guatemala to comfort and rehabilitate the survivors of the earthquake remained behind to convert them. Hundreds of temples associated with churches like the Central American Mission, Elim, Assemblies of God, and the Nazarenes rose from the rubble of Catholic churches leveled by the big quake. Mayan communities disillusioned with their priests' offers of heavenly rewards flocked to the new sects, drawn by promises of redemption through prayer, puritanical temperance, and individual enterprise. In the areas the army calls Zones of Conflict, thousands of survivors were drawn to the exorcistic rituals and millennialist prophecies of the Pentecostals, whose histrionic services placated their fears and helped them forget the loss of their relatives.

As the war widened under evangelical General Efraín Ríos Montt, who seized the presidency in a bloodless palace coup in March 1982, the agendas of many evangelical missions expanded to include wider geopolitical objectives. Ríos Montt's own Church of the Word, an offshoot of the California-based Gospel Outreach, planned to secure the countryside for a military occupation friendly to the United States. Evangelical groups like Full Gospel Businessmen's Fellowship became bulwarks of the Reagan Doctrine and waged holy war against the "diabolical" tenets of Marxism-Leninism and Liberation Theology. Many evangelicals openly boasted that Guatemala was to be the bridgehead for a Protestant takeover of Latin America, to be completed in time for Christ's Second Coming at the end of the millennium.

Once again, as in the early years of the Spanish Conquest, when three missionary Catholic orders competed for the salvation of Indian souls, war and religious conversion worked hand in glove to effect a profound transformation of the native Mayan culture. The devil of idol worship had been replaced by the devil of communism and Marxist theology. To the long-suffering descendants of the Mayas, who believed in interrelated time segments of *tuns* and *katuns* that recur in predetermined cycles, the wheel had turned full circle, and only the masks on the white faces had changed.

Once each year over the past four and a half centuries, highland residents have celebrated their patron saint feast days with a Dance of the Conquest. Hand-picked villagers stoke themselves with cheap rum and deck themselves out in the burgundy and green velvet finery of sixteenth-century Spaniards. In some versions of the dance, a participant will wear a brown or black-tinted mask of Tecún Umán. The charade is topped off by subtly crafted rose-and-cream wooden masks with blond beards and mustaches. For hours on end, the masked villagers move back and forth, shaking gourd rattles as they high-step and gyrate in random configuration to the strains of a marimba, tirelessly reenacting their ancestors'—and their own—defeat and humiliation.

In this book, I will focus on four highland regions where guerrilla insurgency, military counterinsurgency, and evangelical conversion had the most dramatic impact on traditional Mayan patterns of subsistence—the Ixil Triangle, Atitlán, Huehuetenango, and Chimaltenango. A separate section deals with the northern lowland region of Petén, where the Rebel Armed Forces have been concentrated. The radical transformation of these communities has taken on the character of a third conquest, whose full parameters are only now becoming apparent. Because the transformation of these areas—and of Guatemala itself—by the most underreported war of recent times is multifaceted, its story will be told in a layered format of journalistic reportage, personal narrative, oral testimony, and ethnographic investigation.

With the resurgence of a native Maya movement in Guatemala, marked by congressional approval of a standardized Maya alphabet and the more recent ratification of the Academy of Mayan Languages, the colonial pejorative *indio* (Indian) has, justifiably, fallen into disrepute. The award of the 1992 Nobel Peace Prize to the Quiché-Maya human rights activist Rigoberta Menchú has cast further opprobrium on colonial terminology and on the term *indio,* in particular. As a general rule, *Indian* will refer only to newly Christianized and colonial Mayas, and *Maya* or *Mayan* will refer to that pre-Columbian civilization as well as to the renaissant indigenous communities that are its direct descendants.

PART I

1

Guatemala City

"We are the children of garbage. But we are also human, and
we will win in the end."

Guatemala City dump-dweller

Marta Verónica, known as "La Flaca" for her tensile thinness, has
survived in Guatemala City's municipal dump since she was three
years old. She lives with her husband, a shoe salesman who makes
$8 a week, and their eight-year-old son in a lean-to, a *champa* put
together with old pinewood sidings, worn plastic sheets, bent cardboard, and burlap. In a slightly larger tin-roofed hovel next door lives
Marta Verónica's mother, Isabela, known familiarly as Chavela, who
moved to Guatemala City from the ladino region of Jalapa. Marta
Verónica's father, a highland native who had given up his Mayan
identity, lived with her mother for three years, until he died of pneumonia. Since then, Chavela has lived in the dump with a succession
of male companions, all of whom she has outlived.

The small shantytown of around fifty hovels sits on the edge of a
vast expanse of refuse that has grown fivefold in the past fifteen years,
as the capital's population has grown to nearly two and a half million.
Of the 1,200 tons of garbage dumped here every day, 900 comes from
residential neighborhoods. A major factor in Guatemala City's growth
is the ongoing war in Guatemala's highlands between the army's counterinsurgency units and four guerrilla organizations; the war has killed
approximately 65,000 Guatemalans of Mayan descent since 1978 and
has forced over 1 million more to flee their homes. Paradoxically,
another factor behind the mass peasant movements is a surge in population. Demographers calculate that it took over four centuries—

until 1950—for Guatemala's indigenous communities to recover their pre-Conquest population of around 2 million. Since the 1950s, the Mayas have doubled their numbers to nearly 5 million, placing added stress on their lands. At the present rate of population growth, their numbers could double again by the first decade of the next century.

Since 1980, as many as 500,000 highland Mayas displaced by the violence and by acute land shortages have made their way to Guatemala City. This exodus followed on the heels of an estimated quarter-million Mayas who fled to the capital in the wake of the 1976 earthquake. Between 1975 and 1987, the city's population more than tripled, from 675,000 to over 2.3 million, making it the most populous capital between Mexico City and Bogotá.

The majority of the displaced who arrive in the city every day seek anonymity in one of the sprawling shantytowns that have sprung up along the edges of ravines where they are vulnerable to mudslides and earthquakes. Thousands of these refugees scratch out a meager existence as part- or full-time scavengers in the municipal dump, or *basurero*, officially known by the euphemism "sanitary landfill."

On a good day, La Flaca can make five to seven quetzales—less than $1.50—collecting scrap cardboard, glass bottles, and plastic bags, which she sells to recyclers at the going rate of five *centavos* (or less than one U.S. cent) a pound.

As I gaze over the mobs of scavengers picking through the mountains of rotting detritus for edible discards or some valuable find like a necklace, a magnet, a broken watch, I ask La Flaca how her way of life has changed in the thirty years she has been here.

"The basurero used to be smaller," she says, "and we all knew one another and respected one another's turf. In some ways it was harder than now: there were fewer materials that could be sold, and people were less careless with their valuables; a silver-plated necklace or a bracelet was a real find then. But there was not as much theft or *envidia* [malicious envy] as there is now, and we all worked hard and helped one another stay alive. Now, look at it."

Again I pass my eyes over the fantastic landscape, taking in the hordes of circling black buzzards and the clouds of flies, the thick smoke rising from smoldering trash fires that release a sour smell of organic putrefaction and chemical waste. On rainy days, when the

wind blows from the northeast, the stench is a soiled finger stuck in
the back of your throat.

At the center of a huge trash pile, as in a dream, I make out two
local ragpickers hassling a Mayan woman in brightly woven native
dress for a bolt of colored cloth. The smoke and the pervasive stench
seem to leach the sky of all color, much as the pre-monsoon heat
and dust storms blot out the sky over northern India. At nightfall,
the basurero recalls the candescent *ghats* along the Ganges, where
hundreds of Hindu faithful are cremated every day. What is lacking
here is a saving sense of ceremony, a Vedic epiphany or received gospel
to sweeten the bitter pill of social inequity. Most of the scavengers
are only nominally Christian, and they do not believe in reincarnation.

At the northern edge of the visible dump a four-hundred-foot drop
marks the *barranco,* or winding ravine, down which the unused garbage is pushed by the bulldozers. Within La Flaca's lifetime, the
basurero has moved north by approximately one kilometer, as landfill
and concrete mixed with mountains of waste creep up the canyon
walls.

In the middle distance, I make out the larger tombstones of the
Cementerio General, which spread right to the edge of the ravine.
There, in the Jewish section, half a dozen of my relatives are buried.
Most of the deceased are kept in full-length coffins for about six
years. The remains are then placed in smaller boxes and moved to
wall niches, where the rent is more affordable. If the survivors default
on the rental, the bones may be removed from the boxes and thrown
into a central ossuary; or the coffins may be placed on the edge of
the barranco for six months. If no payment is made, they are pushed
over the side and tumble down to the bottom of the ravine where
the coffins rot or break open. In another two or three years, as the
dump creeps inexorably northward, the spilled human vestiges and
the decomposing refuse will mingle in a pestilential confluence.

A dozen yellow vehicles, from an electronic dump truck donated
by Germany to mule-drawn garbage scows, empty their contents into
a sea of raw slop; bulldozers shove the fresh garbage into enormous
mounds of compost, which with no soil to fertilize makes nothing
grow. On closer inspection, I see three cornstalks with healthy tassels

poking through the refuse at the rim of the precipice. And just as improbably a leafy banana tree grows behind one of the shanties. Archaeologists digging here centuries from now may believe they've uncovered a huge aboriginal kitchen or midden.

Here it's every creature for itself. The ubiquitous black turkey buzzards—*zopilotes*—have only a few seconds' jump on the human scavengers who swarm in to pick through the fresh deliveries. The scavengers come from everywhere in the highlands, the humid coast, the ladino eastern provinces. A Cakchiquel speaker from Comalapa with a huge moth caterpillar crawling unperturbed on his collar scratches for food in the same trash bin as a sugarcane cutter from the Pacific coast. When I ask him why he left his highland home, the Comalapense assures me the living is much better here. "*La milpa ya no da,*" he says—the cornfield doesn't yield anymore. The war's disruption of traditional agriculture together with depletion of the soil from the campesinos' overreliance on chemical fertilizers has contributed to the peasant exodus to the city.

The basurero is one of Guatemala's more egalitarian institutions: a newly arrived Mayan refugee and a ladino bachelor of arts down on his luck compete for survival on equal terms. The college graduate comes from Antigua and is a father of four. He explains to me in cultured tones that he can make as much as fifteen quetzales a day collecting glass bottles and cardboard, or twice what he would make slaving away in a factory. Although his income estimate sounds inflated to me, I do not contest it; we exchange business cards and I ask him to look me up in the Hotel Aurora.

"The change began fifteen years ago," La Flaca explains, "when the supermarkets and the large refineries began discarding large quantities of plastic containers, and there was money to be made from collecting them. People come from everywhere, and there is no respect for anyone. Last month I found a gold-plated necklace—the most valuable find I'd made in years. I wore it for only an hour before someone almost broke my neck trying to yank it away. The next day I sold it for twenty quetzales, because it was too dangerous to keep."

I ask La Flaca what the greatest risks are in her profession.

"Crime," she says without hesitation. "Now there are no rules, and people steal from you or kill you for something worth only a few quetzales. Before, we all knew one another, and our only enemy was a guard who kicked us out unless we gave him a share of our finds. Now people kill one another for nothing. A friend I've known from childhood was carved up in her home and set on fire because she rebuked someone for stealing. And two months ago, men armed with machetes attacked a family of four. The mother was so badly cut up she was crippled and went back to her home in Sololá. There are no more rules. The hunger and desperation are too great, and there are too many of us."

As we speak, her mother is gathering large stacks of cardboard in her backyard. Marta Verónica's latest stepfather works alongside her but cannot keep up with Chavela's nimble hands. In my several visits to the dump, I have yet to find her idle; and she always wears her baseball cap at exactly the same, slightly skewed angle.

Despite La Flaca's concern over the rising violence in the basurero, most people here die of respiratory diseases, severe malnutrition, and drug or alcohol addiction, or they suffocate under tons of debris when they stumble and fall under a bulldozer. The zopilotes rarely lack fresh carrion. In the late seventies, when the death squad killings were at their height, the basurero competed with rivers, volcano craters, and clandestine cemeteries as disposal sites for tortured and mutilated corpses.

The basurero is also a place of extraordinary resilience, of ingenious strategies for survival. During her thirty years' residence in the dump, La Flaca has endured afflictions and diseases that would have decimated an army. When faced with adversity, the instinct among dump-dwellers is to band together. In the past year, the Guatemala City municipality announced its intention to raze the shantytown "for reasons of hygiene." Fifty-seven of the eight hundred families residing in the dump formed an ad hoc committee to apply for legal title to their lots. They hope to erect residences of cement block, wood, or corrugated tin with proper ventilation to prevent the poisoning of their children by methane and other toxic gases. They have also applied for running water, electricity, a health clinic, and a school.

Most basurero rats have a flair for play and improvisation. A half-deflated ball pulled out of the muck ignites an intense soccer game among young and older men, who summon up unsuspected skills that seem immune to the ravages of hunger. The Comalapense refugee is right: there is a better chance for survival here than in many of the violence-wracked highland villages I have visited, and conditions are even worse in the refugee camps.

The thousands of scavengers who wrest a bare subsistence from the basurero live the shadow lives of the rich whose scraps they collect, consume, or recycle. A broken umbrella becomes an excuse for a sensuous stroll down a dimly remembered boulevard. Discarded LP's with yesterday's hit tunes are replayed on imaginary stereos. A throwaway piece of costume jewelry is worn for a night and then sold to feed a family for a week. Magnets are sold to Salvadorans as magic charms that attract good fortune. A twisted brass trumpet played deftly by a twelve-year-old sets off a New Orleans Mardi Gras stomp. Jazz, Hollywood, baseball, half-eaten Big Macs in plastic containers, TV reruns in shop windows are most of what they know of gringo culture, refracted through the glittering shards of a thousand spent and shattered dreams.

The most contented residents of the dump, judging by their appearance, are a small herd of gold-bristled hogs their owner sets loose every morning to root in the garbage. I watch them snuggled together after gorging themselves all morning, snorting aloud in pig-heavenly chorus. La Flaca tells me that on rare occasions one of them will be run over by a truck or bulldozer, and a pig roast will turn the basurero into a night-long fiesta. Their owner then withdraws his hogs for a few days, but they always come back.

I am continually surprised by the number of men dressed in old and worn camouflage fatigues. It is impossible to know how many of them have been guerrilla militants or sympathizers and how many are army veterans. In Guatemala's war of counterinsurgency, both sides frequently don each other's uniforms to test the campesinos' allegiance.

I approach a light-bearded young man from the ladino town of Zaragoza, in the Mayan province of Chimaltenango. He wears olive fatigues and tells me he served time in the army after he was picked up drunk by a transport during the town fiesta along with two dozen other revelers. The army replenishes its ranks with routine sweeps of towns and villages during their patron saint's feast day, or *fiesta patronal;* the single men between sixteen and thirty serve three months to a year. Armando and the others awoke in the army barracks of Chimaltenango, uniformed in army olive, with dummy rifles in their hands. After three months of basic training, the army placed Armando on reserve and returned him provisionally to civilian life. As a soldier he made the equivalent of $15 a month. He had been sent on dangerous patrols and saw combat three times. Once, the patrol ahead of his was ambushed by guerrillas and half the men were killed. Armando was lucky and got out alive, but he was emotionally traumatized. Two army helicopters buzzed the basurero as we spoke, and Armando tensed up until they went by. "They're on the lookout," he said, eyes bulging with fear. "They don't like us to wear our fatigues when we're out of the service."

Armando assured me he made more money collecting cardboard and plastic than he did from his army paycheck; moreover, he is his own man. He said he had met two of his former officers working in the basurero, a retired lieutenant colonel reduced to scavenging to pay his debts and an alcoholic former sergeant. Armando's mother and two brothers are living a few blocks from the dump, also scraping out a living from scavenging. Only his better-off uncles remained behind in Zaragoza, and they occasionally send his mother a few quetzales.

It is surprising how durable blood ties can be in the basurero. There may be no honor among scavengers any more, but there is always family. La Flaca sent her kid to school, but he goofed off. "*Es de febrero,*" she explains. "He was born in February and is temperamental. Sometimes he studies, sometimes not." He was born in a plastic and cardboard *champa,* redolent of the sickly sweet smell of fermenting garbage. He sees me taking notes and asks if I am collecting names. "G-E-R-S-O-N," he calls out proudly, as if intoning a potent rune.

"Smile for the man, it is your destiny," a father urges his three-year-old son, whom my associate Daniel Chauche is photographing. Scavengers are fatalistic, like most Guatemalans. They believe in the evil eye and ward off *brujería,* or witchcraft, from near and far by consulting curanderos. I asked La Flaca if there were evangelicals among the scavengers, and she replied, "A few. But most of us are Catholic and pagan."

When I inform the father that I want to tell the story of the people who live in the dump, because it too is Guatemala, he readily assents. He has been interviewed before. He counts journalists among his friends. He has heard of San Francisco, California. "I hope my older son, who is learning to read and write, will visit your country one day," he says, "and study how people live there." His mulatto wife, Juana, a sturdy woman of about thirty who seems to do most of the work, tells me she buys milk and potable water for her two older children and corn flour for their tortillas on the five quetzales they earn between them. Juana invites me inside her champa for lukewarm coffee. The smell of decomposition makes me gag, and the flies are so thick I can only stay a few moments. Later she sits erect and round atop a stack of cardboard to breastfeed her youngest.

(When I visit the couple nine months later, I learn that Juana's husband, or "life companion" as she called him, had recently died after choking on his own vomit. She has joined the swollen ranks of widowed mothers who manage, against odds that are unimaginable to most Westerners, to make do for herself and her children. To the durable women of the basurero, "compañeros de vida" are frail, transient beings that drift through their lives like shadows, leaving nothing behind but their seed.)

In the headquarters of the dump-dwellers' committee, I meet another widowed mother, Rosa, a rail-thin, quietly articulate fifty-year-old who has borne eleven children, five of whom are still alive. Her oldest son, an auto mechanic who was her chief provider, was run over and killed by his employer's bodyguards following an argument over money. Rosa, an official of the committee, confesses her shame for accepting a sixty-quetzal bribe to keep silent. "I am not a vindictive person by nature," Rosa says, in her soft-spoken, thoughtful manner. "But I am an enemy of injustice. If I had the money, I would take out a contract on my son's killers. That would be my only consolation."

Five teenagers between twelve and twenty hang out in a lean-to that doubles as the basurero's clubhouse. Their thirdhand T-shirts reflect an atlas of exotic logos, from the Miami Dolphins to Star Trek to the University of California, an odd favorite. They chortle when I ask if they are members of a *mara,* or youth gang, of the kind that has been terrorizing Guatemala City with increasing fearlessness and impunity. But the maras—whose membership has skyrocketed to three thousand or more—attract disaffected kids from the middle classes who dropped out of the best schools and in normal times would have grown up to be lawyers and businessmen. These basurero rats have known no other way of life. Insufficient protein has dulled their aggressiveness. Or, more than likely, they have been sniffing glue or paint thinner—the cocaine of the poor—which can burn out a brain far quicker. They docilely agree to our taking their picture as they suck on plastic bags of half-fermented sugar candy that may be their main meal of the day. The basurero rats form part of an estimated five thousand children between the ages of five and eighteen who live in the city's streets. Most of them go through life with no conception of a "normal" childhood. (Their images of adulthood, on the other hand, are colored by exposure to Stallone, Schwarzenegger, and Chuck Norris in cheap video shacks.) In the summer of 1990 an Amnesty International report raised the alarm over the escalating abuse of street kids by the police, who are resorting to extreme measures—including extrajudicial executions—against youths they regard as delinquents or those who may have witnessed police malfeasance. Guatemala shares with Brazil the distinction of having death squadrons that specialize in torturing and killing children.

In common with Brazil, Honduras, Haiti, and many other third-world countries, Guatemala is in the front lines of an undeclared war the world is waging against its children. Eight of every ten Guatemalan children are undernourished, and infant mortality in the Mayan highlands is the highest in the Western Hemisphere. According to a study by UNICEF, over one billion children in the world suffer from acute malnutrition. One hundred million are expected to die by the end of the decade of hunger and third-world diseases that could be prevented with the equivalent of a single day's military spending by each country. Guatemala contributes its share to these statistics, with its bloated military budget and its nonexistent health services for the poor.

On a return visit I interview the president of the Committee for the Acquisition of Urban Lots in the Garbage Dump, a dignified ex-farmer from the coast with the impressive name of Guillermo Valencia Mexicanos. Don Guillermo, a mestizo who taught himself to read and write at the age of eighteen, has lived in the dump with his wife for several years. He makes the equivalent of around two and a half dollars a day by collecting plastic and cardboard with a flashlight after nightfall.

"Most of the scavengers arrive at dawn and leave before sunset," he explains. "After dark there is less competition as well as less envidia." He adds that his wife is delicate and hates to quarrel over turf or a trinket with the new breed of scavengers, who are aggressive and heartless and have no sense of propriety. During the day Don Guillermo sorts and sells his cache, as well as carrying out his duties as committee president. He is especially proud of a new health center he has set up with the collaboration of foreign missionaries. The *puesto de salud* is a cardboard and tin shanty with two rickety chairs and a table (a sign outside the door reads "Protect your Environment"). Despite its appearance, it serves a more practical function than the enormous, sterile modern hospitals I would visit in the highlands. Those white elephants have no medicines, equipment, or patients and are empty showcases of the venality of recent military presidents and their contractors.

I am impressed by the quiet poise of Don Guillermo and the six other mestizo and Mayan committee officers who drop in during our interview. Like some of the new Mayan mayors I would meet in highland municipalities, they have learned to operate effectively within the limitations of their office. Don Guillermo sighs and shakes his head when I ask if they had thought of organizing the basurero community to demand a minimum price for recyclable materials. The swelling numbers of scavengers had recently pushed down the prices for cardboard and plastic from three to an outrageous one centavo a pound, a fraction of a U.S. penny.

"My jurisdiction is limited to the fifty-seven families that are members of the committee," he said. "During the day, it is anarchy. Over one thousand people show up to comb through the garbage, and everyone has to look after himself."

His eyes sparked with interest when I mentioned a new and inexpensive device being tried out by UNICEF that compacts scrap paper into bricks of fuel.

"That would solve one of our principal problems, which is the scarcity of firewood," Don Guillermo said, promising to look into it. He then showed me a diagram of one of the proposed housing units that would replace the condemned hovels. It was a rudimentary structure, like a child's house of lego blocks, with two periscope-shaped vents he called "respirators."

Don Guillermo then showed me the stack of fifty-six applications for new dwellings he had collected and surprised me by lamenting that the only hold-out was La Flaca, whose husband had not troubled to fill out an application or hand in the required I.D.

"Marta Verónica's husband calls himself a shoe salesman, but all he does is sniff cobbler's glue and live off his wife and mother-in-law. I would appreciate it if you would have a talk with Verónica, as they are prolonging our hardship by holding up the applications."

With a sinking heart, I went in search of La Flaca, and instead found her mother, Chavela, sorting a fresh garbage pile. In her matter-of-fact voice, she told me that her son-in-law was a wife beater and addict who had brought the family down.

As Chavela spoke in a flat, unemotional voice, I looked across the wasteland toward the newly arrived trucks, where La Flaca would be rummaging for some fresh find that would turn their luck for the better, one more time. After three or four minutes that stretched interminably, a thin figure detached itself from the gray mass of scavengers and moved toward us, with fluid energy and resolve. The red baseball cap leaped out of the leached, shimmering background, and then I made out the green apron and the rubber boots, rising and falling above the muck as she strode confidently between mounds of picked garbage and smoldering trash fires. In one hand she held two pieces of rusted lead piping, in the other what looked like a large wooden model schooner. La Flaca smiled radiantly when she saw me with her mother, and then in her apron pocket I spied the telltale plastic bottle with yellow-green shoemaker's glue and the black eye on her lean, smudged face.

Nine months later I found La Flaca's mother with a new live-in companion, working as hard as ever to make ends meet. Mountains of stacked cardboard rose in Chavela's backyard, because prices had dropped below one cent a pound and she was waiting for them to

rise again. La Flaca, who was visiting a friend, was slacking off more
and more, Chavela said, in her matter-of-fact voice. Her son-in-law's
drug habit had reduced him practically to a vegetable, and she did
not expect him to live out the year. As she told me this, her baseball
cap slightly askew as always, Chavela's hands moved uninterruptedly,
sorting tin cans and glass bottles into separate piles. An oily soup was
brewing in a large tin can on a grill set atop two bricks outside her
champa. The kindling consisted of plastic bags, scrap wood, and an
old leather shoe.

At the committee headquarters, I learn that Don Guillermo Mexicanos has had a good turn of fortune. He and his wife have saved
enough money so they no longer have to scavenge. He is now a
middleman who buys scrap from his neighbors, which he sells to the
recycling plants at a reasonable profit. He says he tries to set a good
example by paying twice what other middlemen do, and I believe
him.

Don Guillermo is in buoyant spirits. After a year-long silence, Guatemala City's Mayor Alvaro Arzú Irigoyen, a presidential candidate,
has finally acted on the dump-dwellers' application and agreed to
install a water line and electricity. In applying for title to their lots,
Don Guillermo discovered that the basurero sits on land donated to
the municipality in 1961 by a wealthy landowner. Dialma Mini Feltrín
de Smith, a member of the prominent Castillo family, learned of the
committee's application and recommended they be permitted tenancy
on the land, rent-free, for an indefinite period. The municipality consented, and committee members were free to build more permanent
residences. Two modest shacks of corrugated tin and pinewood sidings had already gone up. Several weeks earlier a gringo missionary,
Father William Allard, had erected a small Catholic chapel next to
the committee's headquarters. He furnished it with icons, an altar,
and a blackboard, so that the chapel alternates as a schoolroom and
medical dispensary. Nearby, two evangelical chapels had also gone
up, and local pastors were making the rounds to announce Christ's
imminent return. The scavengers' shantytown was turning into an
urban hamlet.

These victories for the dump-dwellers had not come easily. Don
Guillermo's face darkened as he reported on the anonymous threats

he received last July, shortly after he filed the applications. He had gone into hiding after three burly men in plainclothes drove up after nightfall and asked to see "El Presidente" about some lots he had requested. The committee officers filed a formal denunciation with the government-appointed Attorney of Human Rights. They described the vehicle with dark-tinted windshield and the men who had knocked on Don Guillermo's champa at 10:00 P.M. Within days, the threatening visits stopped. Don Guillermo and his vice-president, Miguel Angel Osorio, remain convinced that their interviews with human rights observers, foreign journalists, and priests were largely responsible for the authorities' change in attitude. "And of course," he added, "it is an election year, and the politicians want to be seen as sensitive to the needs of the poor. A year ago, when Mayor Arzú passed this way with his entourage, he stared at us as if we were creatures from another planet."

Don Guillermo informed us of plans by the municipality to convert a section of the basurero into a sports complex and children's park. A large parcel had already been cleared for the playground. A new prefabricated concrete divider insulated the park area from the garbage dump and the residents' hovels. But resourceful basurero rats lost no time in punching holes in the wall and using the slabs of cement to prop up their champas.

Don Guillermo described the project as a mixed blessing, at best. "They plan to get rid of us by gradually taking away our livelihood," he said. "First, they turn a part of the basurero into a park and put up a wall to keep us out of sight. Now we hear rumors that Japanese technicians have been contracted to bring their recycling equipment here. Our blessed dump will be a laboratory for testing the latest garbage-converting technology." Don Guillermo's eyes narrow, and his voice acquires an edge. "We are being dragged against our will into the twenty-first century, even as we are forced to go on living like oppressed Indians from the time of the Conquest. Well, if they displace us, they will have to find us another source of livelihood; otherwise, many of us will turn to theft or violent crime. What other alternative will we have?"

In mid July 1990, five hundred squatter families invaded eight square blocks of leveled landfill in the municipal dump. Two weeks

later, the anti-riot police evicted the squatters by force, inflicting a
number of injuries. The invaders included several hundred residents
whose hovels had been razed by the bulldozers or who could no
longer afford the rents in the surrounding neighborhoods. The next
day, two hundred of the evicted families set up lean-tos and pickets
outside the office of the government-appointed Attorney of Human
Rights. The press picked up their story, highlighting their demands
for shelter. Most of the squatters asked for small lots within com-
muting distance of the dump, their only source of livelihood.

The dump-dwellers' representatives spoke in a familiar mix of hyperbole and gallows eloquence: "After the basurero, where can we
go? . . . We are children of garbage, but we remain human. . . . We
have lost a battle, but we will win the war." The dump takeover
turned out to be only the first in a wave of land invasions by thousands
of dispossessed Guatemalans.

By the end of the week, the squatters' persistence and the sympathetic press coverage persuaded the National Bank, the Housing
Minister, and the Attorney of Human Rights to meet together to look
for living sites within the city's perimeter. But the meeting broke up
with no tangible results other than a vague proposal for a socioeconomic study of the dump-dwellers' living requirements.

That same week I visited Don Guillermo Mexicanos and was relieved to learn the eviction order had not affected the families of the
Dump-Dwellers' Committee. Two months earlier, the army had taken
part in the inauguration of the water spigot, after defraying part of
the cost of its installation. Ribbons had been cut, speeches on civic
responsibility had been delivered, and the army officer persuaded a
bemused Father Allard to bless the water spigot and celebrate mass.
The dwellers had also been promised sewage disposal and building
materials for their new homes. But the electric company had dragged
its feet in putting up power lines, although the lampposts for the
children's playground were already in place.

An upbeat Don Guillermo showed me the receipts for the water
meter and the spigot, paid for by forty-seven families. He lamented
that seven members of the original committee had defaulted on their
payments after disseminating nasty rumors. *Envidia,* malicious envy,
had reared its ugly head, as it inevitably does in deprived Guatemalan

communities whenever a windfall appears to be in the offing. Despite baseless accusations that he had received payoffs from the water department and the army, Don Guillermo remained firmly in charge. More worrisome were the persistent rumors that Japanese technicians were laying the pipes for a methane gas conversion facility, for which the "children's park" was a convenient facade.

Don Guillermo pointed across the bulldozed area to the first of ten thousand eucalyptus and rubber trees publicized as the "green lung" for the playground. Less than a hundred yards away behind the concrete divider, two dozen vehicles dumped raw refuse near the edge of the ravine. Several hundred scavengers and flocks of black buzzards were clustered together in the refuse, which exhaled a barely tolerable stench of chemical and fermenting organic waste. How could small children be expected to play in this infernal setting?

I asked Don Guillermo, "What happens after the Japanese install their equipment and start converting the toxic gases? Won't they try to get rid of you?"

"We have more allies now, and we are determined to use every means possible to fight eviction. We have the legal documents to back our claim, and the help of local lawyers and the Catholic church, not to mention the gringo missionaries. The municipality is committed to giving us fifty lots and sewage disposal. However, it's true that until we put up our dwellings, we will remain vulnerable."

In the small Catholic chapel, Father Bill Allard was whitewashing the walls. Allard, a genial Kentuckian of about fifty-five, was optimistic that the dump-dwellers would be allowed to stay on in Landívar 2, as they had formally named their settlement. "The attention from the press and from foreign do-gooders has apparently persuaded the government to let them stay on. As long as they put up permanent-looking dwellings before the park is completed, they should be O.K."

Ironically, the best hope for the forty-seven families appears to be the army's decision to turn their shantytown into a showcase of military patronage. This "model village" lacked the darker connotations of its counterparts in the highland Zones of Conflict, whose residents undergo strict military indoctrination and have to take part in costly and dangerous civil defense patrols. In an election year these durable, compost-bred children of garbage were still a long way from winning the war, but they had gained some breathing room.

2

A hundred yards behind the shanties begin the upscale residences of the older refugees, those who have saved enough to move into adobe or cement-block structures. These subdivisions of the basurero have upbeat names like Eureka, Green Mansion, Fields, Tractors. We head for the largest of these communities, *El Nuevo Amanecer*, the New Dawn, where my associate Daniel Chauche has photographs to deliver.

On the way we look in on several of the large shacks that serve as collection centers for the recyclable refuse. Each shack has its own specialty—plastic bags and containers, rags and cardboard, corrugated metal, glass bottles, firewood, and tin cans—each with its own hired help to clean, polish, wash, straighten, or pound the scrap materials into mint condition. The buyers for the processing plants enter singly or in pairs and move silently, loading the materials—for which they pay prearranged prices—onto their trucks and vans.

The owner of one of the collection shacks invites me to a cup of coffee, and I brim over with praise for his profession. I tell him, as I had attempted to tell La Flaca and several other scavengers, that they are rendering an invaluable service to the larger community; I explain that their work places them on a rung of ecological sophistication comparable to that of the Chinese and well above that of most developed countries. I predict that his profession is the wave of the future, since as many as a billion people worldwide are expected to live from recycling scrap refuse before the end of the century. The industrial world will soon be divided between waste makers and waste collectors, with nothing in between. In the United States, I say, citizens discard more food per capita than people in the third world consume, and their pet cats eat better than most Guatemalans. North Americans no longer know what to do with their overstock of pesticides, cigarettes, nuclear waste, except to dump them on their southern neighbors' doorsteps. Even now, I go on, a new underclass is emerging to replace the peasant farmers who worked the rich landowners' fields; these new peasant waste collectors will ensure that the affluent do not drown us all in their garbage.

The owner smiles and nods his head, but I'm not sure he knows what to make of my exposition. When I recast it in simpler, more graphic terms, he finally appears to understand.

"That is very interesting," grins the proprietor, wearing a New York Yankees cap, "but I am just trying to make a few quetzales."

I don't have the heart to tell him that when the Japanese technicians take over, he will be among the first to be out of a job.

The extended Caxtop family, Mayas from the highlands who moved to the capital over a decade ago, numbers about thirty members, less than half of whom still make their living directly from the basurero. The Caxtops live on the outer edges of the dump in New Dawn. As we enter the narrow alleyway that leads to their tin-roofed and wooden-sided home, we pass a branching electric utility pole so thickly clustered with yellow plastic sacks hung out to dry, it looks like some African or Australian tree in full exotic bloom.

Doña Micaela, the youthful matriarch of the family, greets Daniel like a long-lost black-sheep nephew, chiding him for his absence and for not bringing the photographs he'd promised to deliver "in just a few days." She is dressed in the yellow and red embroidered blouse and striped blue ankle-length *corte*, or wraparound skirt, of San Pedro Sacatepéquez. Like the rest of the Mayan women I saw in the basurero, Doña Micaela prides herself on keeping her clothes immaculately clean.

Harmony is restored after Daniel distributes prints of the family he'd taken months before. In a matter of minutes, all but three of the thirty Caxtops in the picture congregate to ogle and exclaim over their likenesses. People seem to materialize out of nowhere: from babes in arms to elderly patriarchs, corpulent cousins in undershirts, and maiden aunts who had been visiting neighbors. The consensus is that Daniel "es un buen fotógrafo," and several orders for more copies are placed on the spot.

Later we sit in the cramped patio next to the washing fountain, where several women continue to scrub plastic bags. Since Daniel is traveling with his wife, Jayne, and small daughter and I have a blonde companion, Judith, we are subjected by Doña Micaela to a familiar interrogation: who is married to whom, how many children, how many cars in the States, what kind of house, and is life really better there than in Guatemala?

When our turn comes, I ask her why the family left San Pedro

Sacatepéquez, and Doña Micaela replies unhesitantly, "Oh, because it's much better here, of course."

"You mean more money to be made?"

"Oh yes, much more opportunity, and less *chismes* [gossip]. Here we are much freer to live as we want to without worrying about the neighbors' criticism or envy. And there are more jobs: two of my sons are salesmen, another is a driver, another is studying in secondary school."

When I ask if they still speak their native Cakchiquel, Doña Micaela replies, "We grown-ups still do, but the children don't want to learn, because they get into fights in school if they speak our tongue."

"Does that mean they will grow up as ladinos?"

My question seems to strike Doña Micaela as funny; she bursts into laugher, saying that she hopes her children will grow up into *gringuitos* just like ourselves and have lots of money and several cars and a home in California.

As we soon learn, the Caxtops don't have to travel very far to find ladino role models. In the middle of our conversation a stereo next door erupts full blast into a Rod Stewart melody, "Do Ya Think I'm Sexy." A curtain parts and a neatly groomed young man emerges to invite us into his home. He is bare-chested and wears polyester blue pants. Ernesto, one of Doña Micaela's older sons, has married into a ladino family from Guatemala City.

Behind the cloth curtain we enter another world. The wooden sidings give way to cinderblock walls, the washing fountain and out-house to a sink and toilet. Next to the stereo is a large-screen TV, above which are pinned color photographs of relatives at various ceremonies—school graduation, first communion, weddings, and military academy promotions. On the bed to our left, two teenaged girls with their hair in rollers are shaving their legs and painting their toenails. The ladino in-laws' home is darker, and no larger or more amenable than the Caxtops' sprawling residence, but it lies across an invisible divider that separates a Mayan home from one plugged into the ladino consumer society.

We thank Ernesto and return with a sigh of relief to Doña Micaela's warm if rougher-hewn hospitality. Anticipating my next question she says with another cheerful laugh, "My sons appreciate the TV and the stereo and some of their other gadgets, but we don't have to become like our in-laws in order to have them."

In the fall, the Municipal Parks Department announced they had broken ground in the basurero on a $250,000 project, named St. Francis of Assisi, that would provide beautification, sanitation, and recreation facilities for the capital's most disadvantaged neighborhoods. Japanese technicians had indeed begun the installation of pipes under the compacted landfill to serve as safety valves for methane and other toxic gases. The Director of Parks, Carmen Pokorny, expressed particular satisfaction that the planned sports complex and playground would do away with the garbage recycling practices that posed a major health hazard to residents of the capital.

In September 1992, the first thirty-one dwellings of a projected 150 were presented to the dump-dwellers by a consortium headed by Wendy de Berger, the wife of Guatemala City Mayor Oscar Berger. The new units are provided with running water, drainage, and electricity.

A block and a half from Nuevo Amanecer and three blocks from the cemetery live Francisco Morales Santos and his wife, Isabel Ruíz, a writer and painter who are among Guatemala's most respected artists. Both have Mayan grandparents, and Francisco grew up as the child of resident peons on a coffee finca near Antigua. A long poem of Francisco's, which I have translated, is called "With Irate Hand"; it deftly pillories middle-class complacency and writers who sell out for money and official recognition. Isabel's paintings, which have been exhibited in Mexico City's Museum of Modern Art, are brilliant abstract expressionist satires of ladino culture in whose depths float redeeming Mayan images, such as a glyph or a royal mask.

With their three children they occupy a small apartment that has been their home for more than a dozen years, since well before the neighborhood was invaded by criminal elements, among them the dangerous new heroin and cocaine dealers. Although Francisco and Isabel's income from books, gallery exhibitions, and occasional teaching is modest, they make enough to be able to move out of the neighborhood if they chose to. During a brief visit with "Paco" and Isabel, I ask them why they have not thought of moving to a safer part of town, nearer their children's schools. They smile in unison to the familiar question, and Paco gives the practiced reply: "We both work well in this culturally dense neighborhood, and the risks help us maintain a balance between our rage and our hopes. To move now would be anticlimactic."

Within weeks of my visit with Francisco and Isabel a youth gang calling itself Deadend (*Callejón*) began to terrorize the neighborhood. At the same time, the influx of drug money drove rentals up beyond the range of genteel poverty. Angry and disgusted, Francisco and his family now plan to move to a small town on the road to Antigua.

3

After our visit to the basurero we stopped to wash and eat lunch in one of the *pollo camperos,* a chain of chicken restaurants that compares favorably with Colonel Sanders and McDonald's. Daniel's wife, Jayne, a Nebraskan, had never seen the inside of a synagogue; she asked if I would take her to the old Maguen David temple on *séptima avenida,* where my father had initiated me into the Jewish religion. I hesitated at first, since my writings had made me something of a pariah in the Guatemalan Sephardi community. I did not want to provoke a confrontation on hallowed ground that would further darken my reputation.

The drive to the synagogue took us past the Parque Central, the Palacio Nacional, and the house I had lived in as a child. I was ten at the time of the 1944 revolution that overthrew the dapper, iron-willed dictator General Jorge Ubico. Every year on his birthday, President Ubico would ride the length of *sexta avenida* on a caparisoned black stallion. Although he sided with the Allies in the Second World War and nationalized all German-owned coffee plantations, Ubico harbored a not-so-secret admiration for Adolf Hitler. "I am like Hitler," he boasted once, after putting into effect his infamous Fugitive Decree (*Ley Fuga*). "I execute first and ask questions later."

The October Revolution against the general who replaced Ubico—Federico Ponce—was led by college students, labor leaders, and white-collar professionals, and it was far more violent than the revolt that deposed Ubico five months earlier. The sound of mortar shells and bullets landing on our tin roof at two in the morning woke me into the absolute certainty that the apocalypse was at hand. Nothing impressed me more during the remainder of that awful night than my father's steady nerves and quiet determination. Refusing to panic, he acquired heroic dimensions in my eyes by moving us calmly to the windowless laundry room in back of the house; and then, at dawn, he shepherded us into the gray debris-covered streets on our way to Aunt Margo's house, several blocks east in a safer part of town.

That memory of my father returned as we approached the forbidding old synagogue with its tall black metal gates and the bas-relief Hebrew Decalogue displayed high above the main entrance. The last time I had been to the synagogue, shortly after the earthquake of 1976, there were still cracks on the walls, and for years afterward the Ten Commandments had been shorn of their imperious *lo*'s, or shalt-not's, whose letters had fallen off. "Put other gods before me— covet thy neighbor's wife—take the Lord's name in vain—" read the truncated commandments, sadly reflecting the decline of religious observance in the Sephardi community. Although the Decalogue has long since been restored to its Mosaic integrity, the other, delinquent version hovers kabbalistically nearby, invisible to the untrained eye.

We rang the bell three times before a chubby-faced boy answered the door. It was the afternoon of the Sabbath, but the boy—who turned out to be not a Jew but a Sabbath *goy*—told us the worshipers had already left. His mother showed up seconds later, pleased to show us around. The main prayer hall was closed for remodeling, so the services were held in the ballroom in the rear, where we used to receive sponge cake and *burrecas*, or cheese turnovers, as reward for attending Sabbath services. When I asked the woman how long the reconstruction had been going on, she became vague, hinting that shortages in contributions had slowed down the work. "Everything is too expensive now," she said, "and that is why there is no rabbi. The congregation can't afford one."

I very much doubted the truth of this; if anything, the hundred or so remaining Sephardi families were far wealthier now than they had been during my childhood, when synagogue attendance was at its height and a full-time imported rabbi was de rigueur. The rise in affluence had not translated into synagogue attendance.

Upon entering the main prayer hall, I was astonished by its size.
Instead of seeming shrunken, as I had expected, its emptiness made
it seem like a vast mausoleum. The stained-glass windows were as I
remembered: biblical scenes of deer and flowers and fruit trees—no
people. In the corner of one window was etched the name of my
Uncle Jacobo, who died when I was five. Three years later my father
had bought a ritual honor for me. I carried the Torah for the first
time, quaking in my boots for fear of dropping the scroll and pro-
faning holy writ.

The gentile woman who served as caretaker took us into the ballroom where the ark had been temporarily moved for Sabbath services.
Instinctively I looked for my father's large throne-like chair and found
it at once, right in front of the *bimah*, or raised altar, where it had
always been. "Salomon Perera—1938" it read. He was a founding
member. Next to his were the chairs of his younger brother, my uncle
Isidoro, and Jacobo—husband of Aunt Margo—all dead now. In 1960
my parents returned to their birthplace in Jerusalem, where my father
died a few months later. My mother, who never liked Guatemala and
who favored the earthy fourteenth-century Judeo-Spanish over contemporary Spanish, lived on in Ramat Gan, outside Tel Aviv, the last
surviving family member of her generation. She died and was buried
in Tel Aviv in June 1990, at eighty-five. Her last words to me were,
"Dices las verdades, tienes que pagar." You tell truths, you must pay.

Uncle Isidoro, the patriarchal figure who had loomed over my
childhood with his athletic prowess and blustery bravado, had died
only recently, after drifting into senile dementia at the age of seventy
or so; his condition had no doubt been aggravated by the grisly ac-
cidental death in 1971 of his older son, Jaime, who was torn in half
by the propeller of the fishing skiff he had been out in with some
friends. Jaime, a supporter of the candidacy of military strongman
Carlos Arana Osorio, was an ultraconservative businessman. During
a visit to the States in 1964 he deplored candidate Barry Goldwater's
platform as "too liberal" and dumbfounded my friends by insisting
that laissez-faire capitalism had not yet been given a fair trial in the
free world. In Guatemala City he often carried a hand grenade in his
pocket because of kidnapping threats from leftist guerrillas. Soon after
Jaime's death a number of prominent Jewish businessmen were in
fact kidnapped and held for ransom; in 1980 Abie Habie, a family

friend and the president of the Chamber of Commerce, was machine-gunned in the parking lot behind his office by militants of the Guatemalan Communist Workers' Party. That murder and the kidnappings hastened the decline of the Jewish community, as dozens of wealthy families fled the country with their capital. About seven to eight hundred Jews remain in Guatemala, three hundred less than during my childhood. Although reduced in numbers, they remain a microcosm of Guatemala's upper middle class.

All this family history passed through my memory as I sat down on my father's chair and recited the prayer for the dead—Kaddish— for the first time in years. The date and place of burial of each of my relatives were marked on a little notebook on the altar, and they appeared also on the memorial plaque near the exit. My father's generation had been the pioneers who made their living as ambulant peddlers shortly after the downfall of Estrada Cabrera, the dictator immortalized by Nobel Prize winner Miguel Angel Asturias in his novel *El Señor Presidente*. Many Sephardim had left behind Talmud study, medical school, or a cobbler's trade in Jerusalem or Smirna or Aleppo. When the State of Israel was founded, they salved their survivor's guilt by outdoing each other in generous contributions to the Jewish National Fund, whose fundraisers regularly visited Guatemala.

The engraved names of that Perera generation now dominate the empty hallways and hidden corners of the synagogue more palpably than they did during their lifetimes. The patriarchs are gone, but their legacy lives on in their widows and heirs.

On our way out, the caretaker pressed in my palm a cold burreca she had baked that morning, so that—she said—I might remember what it had been like.

2

La Violencia

"You may say that 1966 was the start of our civil war and
the beginning of our brutalization."

Guatemalan lawyer

Although I was born and raised in Guatemala, it was not until I
returned in 1971 after a twelve-year absence that I became aware of
the full extent of the tragedy that was befalling my native country. I
had been a college junior in June 1954, when the left-leaning, democratically elected government of Jacobo Arbenz Guzmán was overthrown by Colonel Carlos Castillo Armas and a ragtag army of three
hundred irregulars armed and equipped by Allen Dulles's C.I.A. In
the McCarthy climate of the mid-fifties, it was not surprising that the
presence of Communist Party members in Arbenz's government
would alarm Washington; but Arbenz had gone further by expanding
a far-reaching program of social and economic reforms launched by
his predecessor, "Spiritual Socialist" Juan José Arévalo. The hub of
Arbenz's program was the Agrarian Reform Act of 1952. In exchange
for long-term bonds large uncultivated holdings of the United Fruit
Company and other big landowners were expropriated by the government and redistributed to landless peasants on a tenancy basis.

To the powerful landowners and ultraconservative army officers
who remain the backbone of the Guatemalan right, the overthrow
of Arbenz and the dismantling of his reform program represented a
smashing victory over communism, which was gaining a foothold in
the Americas. The left and center sectors—university professors and
students, union leaders, liberal lawyers, and white-collar workers—
viewed Arbenz's overthrow as the Yankee-inspired bludgeoning of an

40

internal social revolution. Among Castillo Armas's first official acts, once a controversial election confirmed him in office, was the abolition of all labor unions and the return to United Fruit of the untilled lands expropriated by Arbenz.

The overthrow of Arbenz marked the end of two decades of good working relations between the United States and Latin America and rang down the curtain on the Good Neighbor Policy inaugurated by Franklin Delano Roosevelt in 1932. June 1954 also heralded the ascendancy of the C.I.A. as a major instrument of U.S. policy in the Americas. The clandestine wars on Cuba, Chile, Nicaragua, and Panama derive their inspiration, in varying degrees, from the C.I.A.'s role in ousting Arbenz from Guatemala.

In 1959 I had visited Guatemala on summer vacation from graduate studies in Ann Arbor. An uneasy calm prevailed under President Miguel Ydígoras Fuentes, who had succeeded Castillo Armas after his assassination by a palace guard. Earlier that year Fidel Castro's July 26 rebels had seized Havana, and soon afterward rural guerrillas became active in Guatemala. Since both Castro and Che Guevara had received part of their political education in Guatemala during Arbenz's presidency, their formative influence on Guatemala's guerrilla organizations amounts to a repayment of an ideological debt.

Ydígoras Fuentes did not take the guerrillas very seriously, and neither, as I recall, did most Guatemalans. My father, a liberal businessman, dismissed them as romantic young army officers and university students—"weekend guerrillas"—who played at Robin Hood to enlist impressionable peasants. In the early sixties the rebels grew in strength and formed two disciplined paramilitary organizations, the November 13 Movement (M.R.-13) and the Rebel Armed Forces (FAR), led by Luis Turcios Lima. By 1965 the two groups had formed guerrilla *focos*, or nuclei, in the western provinces and in San Marcos department to the west. Although together they probably never manned more than five hundred trained, hard-core rebels, M.R.-13 and FAR had potentially large support from campesinos who recalled the promises made by Arévalo and Arbenz.

In October 1966, Colonel Carlos Arana Osorio, commander of the Zacapa military district, launched a counterinsurgency campaign with the support of one thousand U.S. Green Berets and vigilante death squadrons composed largely of ranchers and off-duty police units. The campaign was to cost eight thousand lives in two years, including those of students and professors, labor leaders, and journalists; in the eastern provinces, hundreds of innocent peasants lost their homes and families in Vietnam-style search-and-destroy operations. The survivors of the guerrilla focos dispersed to the capital and larger towns. They formed Latin America's first urban guerrilla cells, whose terrorist operations culminated with the kidnapping and assassination of the U.S. and German ambassadors. For the first time, the guerrilla movement was taken seriously, and the government set into motion the well-oiled machinery of counterinsurgency and state terror that was to grow, two decades later, to gargantuan dimensions. In 1970 Carlos Arana Osorio, the butcher of Zacapa, had been elected president and unleashed a second wave of terror against rural and urban insurgent movements. The United States once again did its share by training 32,000 Guatemalan policemen through the Agency of International Development (AID) and its public safety program. Together with the paramilitary death squadrons that continued to operate in the capital and in the countryside, Arana's second pacification campaign accounted for approximately 15,000 killed or disappeared during his first three years in office.

My return to Guatemala in 1971 on a magazine assignment affected me profoundly. The landscape gripped me as it never had in childhood; my sense of time became so telescoped I felt I was reliving in six weeks the twelve years I had been abroad. And the light, the healing sunlight of Antigua, Chichicastenango, Atitlán, filtered through the rainbow loom of the Mayan weavers like the renewal of a covenant which back north I'd begun to fear humankind had irreparably broken. I was to fall in love again with my native country, only to discover that unwittingly I had become its enemy.

The country was enjoying an unprecedented prosperity, very little of which trickled down below the middle class. Beneath the economic boom ran an undercurrent of despair that was almost palpable. I spoke with hundreds of Guatemalans in an effort to understand what had been happening to the country during my long absence. My conversations with government officials and former classmates usually began with stories of personal success or failure or with Rotarian boasts about Guatemala's mineral resources and glorious weather or its remarkably stable currency. A businessman just back from the States would brag that there was no runaway inflation or industrial pollution in Guatemala, no drug epidemics or women's liberation. But always, in the end, the conversation would turn to La Violencia, and the verdict was nearly always the same: The situation is rotten. *Ya no se compone.* It is beyond repair.

2

Again and again, in trying to come to terms with the country's precipitous decline, I bumped up against Guatemalan fatalism. *Chapin* (that is, native Guatemalan) fatalism is contagious, omnipresent, and is as rooted in the soul of its people as the canyons and volcanoes that animate the landscape. Most ladinos and Mayas will agree that the stark social and economic inequalities between the two communities fuel the mercurial swings in the nation's outlook. Guatemala has an illiteracy rate of 75 percent—90 to 95 percent in the highlands— that is second highest in the hemisphere, after Haiti. Its infant mortality rate is officially 64 out of 1,000, but in actuality nearly half the Mayan children die before the age of five—a statistic that competes with Haiti's for the highest in the Western Hemisphere. The steady erosion of Guatemala's currency—the quetzal—in the early eighties and the 38 percent inflation registered in 1985 aggravated an already intolerable situation for Guatemala's Mayan majority.

Chapin fatalism is more than a mental outlook; it is a life-style, an obsession that makes the well-heeled cynicism of Washington, D.C., and Wall Street seem lightweight and bloodless by comparison. It is manifest in the numbed, dry-eyed faces of relatives who have lost a loved one through kidnapping or assassination and who obstinately refuse to notify the authorities because they fear one side as much as the other. It is in the bemused smile of an opposition leader as he tells you that he knows he has been condemned to death. (In some social and intellectual circles you gain status according to the number of "death lists" you get on.) Above all, the fatalism is in the proverbs. In Chapin parlance the glass is always half empty, the door, partway closed. "Eyes that don't see, heart that doesn't feel," a high government official explains, refusing to discuss the killings. "*A saber*," shrugs the wealthy industrialist's gardener when questioned about the fresh corpse—his employer's—dug up in the snapdragon bed. "*A saber*" (Who knows? Don't ask me.) is the wary Maya's reply to all queries from inquisitive ladinos and foreigners. *A saber* should be made the national motto.

The violence permeates the middle and upper middle classes as well. Among my relatives and friends, a Calvinistic acceptance of the blackest proclivities in human nature is coupled with a brand of machismo that consists in going about your daily business unflinching and unmoved as the bullets fly about you and the country's elite annihilate one another, either firsthand or through the convenience of paid killers. Too many Guatemalans have become silent accomplices to terror. The difference between them and the "good Germans" of World War II is that a Guatemalan *knows* the mere act of witnessing can cost you your life.

More and more of my acquaintances—otherwise sane doctors and lawyers—speak of *mala saña,* a fury in the marrow that surpasses the *mala sangre,* or bad blood, that accounted for the vendetta murders of a decade ago. *Mala saña* makes no political distinctions. Like a swelling tide, it carries everyone in its wake: conservatives and liberals, military and civilians, Mayas and ladinos. If a vengeful god had devised the cruelest punishment imaginable for a strayed and faithless host, it might well have been mala saña.

The communication breakdown that accompanies La Violencia converts the threat of assassination into a warped form of discourse. An anonymous death threat may not only deliver a straightforward message, such as "I don't like you" or "I hate your political views," it may also convey an explicit warning, such as "Don't you talk to me in that tone of voice again" or even "Stop messing with that woman." In March 1993 a death threat faxed to the Journalists' Association listed twenty-four critics of the government, most of them journalists.

Another inevitable result of the violence is a cheapening of human values to a degree I have encountered nowhere else in my extensive travels. It is hard to describe the chill one feels on hearing one's close relative dismiss the brutal assassination of a crippled law professor, calling him a "guerrilla brain," and thereby reducing him to some nonhuman abstraction. Even in the aftermath of the cold war, a psychopathology remains entrenched among the rich and powerful that twists all ideological meaning out of the words *communist* and *subversive,* so that they become arbitrary weapons used to snuff out all opponents, both real and presumed.

In the political arena, the clearest representative of this attitude is Mario Sandoval Alarcón, head of the ultraright Movement of National Liberation (MLN), which calls itself the "party of organized violence." Sandoval Alarcón, a self-proclaimed fascist, boasts of having modeled his views on those of the Spanish Falange. He is widely credited with masterminding the Mano Blanca death squadrons responsible for at least eight thousand murders in the late sixties and early seventies. Alarcón, a shadowy godfather figure who still commands respect in ultranationalist movements throughout Latin America, is also credited with passing his methods on to various protégés, most notably among them the late Roberto D'Aubuisson of El Salvador's anticommunist ARENA party. There is compelling evidence that Sandoval Alarcón received regular funding from the C.I.A. after 1953, when the MLN was founded as part of the U.S.-backed machinery to unseat Arbenz.

Mano is believed to have been behind the cowardly assassination of the moderate leftist law professor and congressional opposition leader Adolfo Mijangos López on January 13, 1971. Mijangos was machine-gunned in his wheelchair in broad daylight as he left his downtown office. A few weeks later I interviewed four of his colleagues and disciples, each of whom insisted—with a chilling brightness in his eyes—that he was number one on the ultraright's death lists after the elimination of Mijangos.

Among them was lawyer Francisco Villagrán Kramer, a Lincolnesque figure of forty-five who lived constantly in and out of hiding and who would later become vice president under Romeo Lucas García. In 1981 Villagrán Kramer fled to the United States before his term ran out. Appearing before Congress he declared, "Death or exile is the fate of those who would work for justice in Guatemala." (A similar declaration was made by journalist Irma Flaquer less than a year earlier, just prior to her own disappearance for witnessing and reporting on the abduction of twenty-seven labor union leaders, all of whom still remain unaccounted for.)

I also met with the popular mayor of Guatemala City, Manuel Colom Argueta, who had lowered the city-hall flag to half mast in Mijangos's honor and called for a government crackdown on the death squadrons. At a party some weeks later I met briefly with the charismatic Social Democratic leader Alberto Fuentes Mohr. Both these friends of Mijangos were assassinated two months apart in 1979, shortly after they declared themselves candidates for president. Veteran observers still mourn the loss of Colom Argueta and Fuentes Mohr as the two most qualified presidential prospects to have emerged in Guatemala since Juan José Arévalo.

As the crime statistics soar, the line between politically motivated kidnappings and assassinations and purely delinquent crimes becomes increasingly blurred. And in the absence of a reliable press, every kidnapping and assassination acquires four or five interpretations: the official government version, the left-wing and right-wing versions, and the versions convenient to the various private sectors. The *auto-secuestro*, or self-kidnapping, is one of the odd products of the violence. When the liberal former minister of the treasury was kidnapped before the 1970 elections, the left accused him of auto-secuestro to throw the election to Arana Osorio, while the right accused him of the same tactic to "embarrass the government." When the Group of Mutual Support (GAM) gathered strength in the early 1980s, it pressed the government for an accounting of three thousand of their relatives who had disappeared. President Oscar Humberto Mejía Víctores accused them of arranging the auto-secuestro of their loved ones, who—Mejía claimed—would reappear as trained guerrillas in Cuba or the Soviet Union.

In November 1989 New Mexico-born Dianna Ortiz, an Ursuline nun, was kidnapped from a religious retreat in Antigua by two plainclothes policemen who brutally raped and tortured her before she managed to escape. When Archbishop Penados del Barrio and U.S. church authorities pressed for a formal investigation of the incident, both Defense Minister Héctor Gramajo and Interior Minister General Villatoro Morales insisted Ortiz had arranged an auto-secuestro with her lesbian lover. Astonishingly, although Gramajo later retracted his accusation in the face of painstakingly gathered evidence—a doctor counted 111 cigarette burns on Ortiz's back—General Morales stood by the self-kidnapping story after he left office. To its shame, the U.S. Embassy went along with the auto-secuestro version, complaining that Ortiz, in her distraught condition, had not consented to an interview before she fled the country. (One year after her kidnapping, Sister Dianna Ortiz rendered a full account of her horrendous experience on ABC television. She filed legal suit against the Guatemalan government, but although church authorities in Guatemala and the United States continue to press for a full investigation, Dianna Ortiz's kidnappers are yet to be identified and no formal charges have been filed.)

Another gambit used in coverups of criminal activity by official forces has been the "crime of passion" charge. That one resurfaced following the murder of Guatemalan anthropologist Myrna Mack Chang, who was stabbed repeatedly on a Guatemala City street in broad daylight on September 11, 1990. Early newspaper accounts, cued by army intelligence sources, suggested she might have been killed by a jealous lover. Mack, who had studied and worked in the United States, was co-founder of the Association for the Advancement of Social Sciences (AVANCSO), the first independent institution of its kind in Guatemala for a number of years. At the time of her assassination she was collecting sensitive data on the lives of refugees and displaced Guatemalans. Her brutal murder and the cynical evasions by the authorities had the familiar, chilling effect of paralyzing all independent investigation in the social sciences, at least temporarily. The sinister elements who operate the country's death squads in the shadow of the army or police choose their victims with consummate care. From long experience, they assume that if they cannot kill a hundred birds with one stone, they can at least frighten them into silence. The tenacity of ongoing investigations into the abduction of Sister Dianna Ortiz and the assassinations of Myrna Mack Chang and U.S. citizen Michael DeVine—whose grisly murder in the Petén in June 1990 led to the first prosecution of army officers in Guatemala's history—are an indication that this may not be tolerated much longer, at least where foreign nationals or Guatemalans with U.S. connections are concerned.

3

The view that the contemporary Maya, in particular, is in some way subhuman is all too common among Guatemala's military officers, worthy successors to conquistador Pedro de Alvarado. Their training in the Politécnica, Guatemala's military academy, includes an insidious conditioning that breeds contempt for everything Indian, as well as a visceral disdain for all intellectuals and most politicians.

As troubling as President Arana Osorio's demeaning descriptions of Mayas as "robots and kamikazes" who are a "deadweight on Guatemalan society" is the leftist rhetoric that portrays the Maya as a "proletariat comrade" who would march under the Marxist-Leninist banner against the "capitalist imperialist oppressor." In the sixties, FAR's tendency to view the campesino as a pawn in an ideological chess game alienated many potential recruits to their cause.

With rare exceptions, the military's purported shifts in attitude toward the Mayan communities have been cosmetic—public relations strategies intended for foreign consumption. In the southeast provinces of the Oriente, a short distance from the Salvadoran border, special army indoctrination centers still condition Mayan conscripts to despise their origins. After their reeducation, many are sent back to the highlands to prey on their own people. Most of the massacres there have been carried out by Mayas whose communal and blood bonds have been broken or warped by the army. And all too often the officers in charge of the indoctrination, and those who give the orders for the massacres, are themselves of Maya or mestizo descent. Romeo Lucas García, the most Indian-blooded of recent presidents, justified the killing and torture of thousands of Mayan peasants as a purging of the fatherland of subversives and of the gullible dupes— i.e., the Indians—they had managed to enthrall. During his years as a parish priest, Archbishop Penados del Barrio heard countless macabre confessions from brutalized former soldiers of Maya or mestizo origin. He spoke in anguished terms of "a generation of mad soldiers" who cannot be reintegrated into their communities and who are set loose in society as recidivist killers, rapists, and torturers.

In trying to gain perspective on Guatemala's violencia, I groped for historical parallels: Mexico in the twenties, Algeria prior to independence, Peru and its Maoist Shining Path guerrillas. None of them measure up. Even the 15,000 who disappeared during Argen-

Marta Verónica, "La Flaca," beside her *champa* in the Guatemala City municipal dump.

Scavengers scrabbling for discarded food and recyclable scrap materials in the municipal dump.

Young scavenger with medallion, municipal dump.

Four *basurero* rats, municipal dump.

"Doña Micaela" (in center with small child in arms) with extended family in
New Dawn, a barrio on the edge of the municipal dump.

A family scavenging on Avenida del Ferrocarril (Railroad Avenue), a slum neighborhood in Guatemala City.

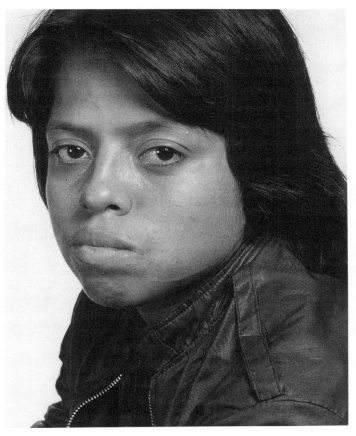

Chepa, a fourteen-year-old prostitute in Guatemala City.

A barrio in Zone 5, Guatemala City.

tina's seven-year "dirty war" are only a fraction of Guatemala's 40,000, which in 1989 made up—according to Americas Watch—45 percent of Latin America's total of disappeared and unaccounted for.

Christian Democrat René de León Schlotter sees a dark parallel in Guatemala with an episode from the Spanish Civil War, when a Franco general broke into Salamanca University and assailed its distinguished rector, Miguel de Unamuno, with the shouted slogans: "Down with intelligence! Long live death!" De León Schlotter cites as evidence the army's raids on San Carlos University—the most recent one in September 1985—under the pretext of searching for hidden caches of arms, which did not exist. Despite laws and a long tradition that protect San Carlos University's immunity from governmental intervention, the army invaded the campus to confiscate student files for the death lists.

Guatemalan ladino culture has suffered in the climate of violence. Art galleries often close for lack of business, and the conservatory of music long ago fell into disrepair. A recent study found Guatemala's sixty public libraries are allocated an average of $6 a month for acquisition of new books. The opulent Teatro Nacional, the gem of Guatemala's cultural revival, has been used only sporadically for artistic performances; in its first years it more often served as a forum for political rallies and evangelical revivals. Guatemala's movie houses deal almost exclusively in North American and other foreign imports that glorify the "culture of violence." And in the crowded videotape shacks that are proliferating throughout the Mayan highlands, Rambo, Robocop, and Conan the Barbarian have become improbable cult figures for their quick, efficient dispatch of hated "ladinos."

Too many of the country's surviving writers and intellectuals are in jail or involuntary exile. Miguel Angel Asturias, whose books were available in Guatemala chiefly in translation before he won the Nobel Prize in 1967, lived in Paris for many years, and resigned as ambassador to France before he died to protest President Arana Osorio's Pacification Campaign. His son Rodrigo, known in the underground as Gaspar Ilom, is the maximum leader and one of the founders of the Revolutionary Organization of People in Arms (ORPA). Although his guerrilla activities embittered his father's final years, they were reconciled before Miguel Angel's death. Rodrigo Asturias is one of the guerrilla commanders engaged in ongoing talks with Guatemalan military and civilian representatives, as required by the Esquipulas Peace Accords signed by the five Central American presidents in 1988. The military delegates later bragged their only reason for taking part in the talks—which have proved fruitless—was to "take measure" of their opponents. In exchange, the business-suited, middle-aged guerrilla representatives may have gained a certain measure of respectability from the exposure. (The most startling result of the 1990 talks in Madrid were newspaper photographs of a mellowed, disconcertingly teary-eyed Sandoval Alarcón exchanging mementos with guerrilla commanders in a very short-lived spirit of reconciliation.)

During the last days of my visit to Guatemala I began to experience the numbness and odd detachment I had discerned in my relatives and friends. When the cousin I stayed with had his car seized at gunpoint by masked men who could have been guerrillas, off-duty secret service agents, or common delinquents, his children were so traumatized they would not allow both parents to leave the house at once. A month later his car was stolen again and was found a burnt-out shell days later in a remote suburb. His daughters would not allow either parent out of the house without an escort.

When a shopping bag full of crockery was delivered to my cousin's house by a smiling servant girl, I tipped her calmly, then ran with my heart in my teeth to the kitchen sink, where I shook each plastic teacup and soup plate for the ticking bomb I was certain had been planted inside. In the evening I slipped easily into my cousin's offhand machismo as we laughed off the incident. It was a small thing, but I recognized it as an early sign of the brutalization I had been warned about. In a few more weeks my eight years of liberal education in two U.S. universities, along with what I learned on my travels in Europe and the Far East, would begin to peel away, layer by layer; it had happened to so many of my relatives and former schoolmates after they returned from abroad. Perhaps I would even come to accept the machine-gunning of a semi-paralyzed law professor with a stoical shrug and the catchall "mala saña." The only alternatives seemed to be a quick martyrdom or armed subversion.

I learned from La Violencia in Guatemala how quickly one can sink beneath the anger and outrage that is translatable into purposeful energy, the will to act. I learned also that such stock phrases as "police state," "totalitarian repression," and "systematic genocide" can be blunted by premature or inappropriate use, so that when the real thing looms in the doorway, all their energy is spent and there are no words left. There is only exhaustion, deadness of spirit, and paralyzed acquiescence.

One comes back always to the violence. It is as if, to try another analogy, the C.I.A. and the F.B.I., in response to accelerated terrorist activity by black nationalists and a revived Weatherman underground, were secretly to enlist and equip the white supremacist and Nazi factions as well as the Ku Klux Klan. They would fill out their ranks with Green Berets and mercenaries recruited by *Soldier of Fortune* magazine and set them loose, leaving 41,000 dead in six weeks. Among the casualties from both sides over a year-long period would be George Meany and César Chavez, Robert Gates and James Baker, Max Frankel, Anthony Lewis, William Safire, Benjamin Bradlee and Rupert Murdoch, Ralph Nader, John Kenneth Galbraith and Noam Chomsky, Mario Cuomo, Paul Nitze, Pat Buchanan, Oliver North, Dick Cheney and a dozen big-city mayors, including David Dinkins, Richard Daley, Frank Jordan, and Tom Bradley; among the victims of contract killings would be Jesse Jackson, Ramsey Clark, former Congressmen Stephen Solarz and Jim Wright, as well as Jack Kemp and Newt Gingrich, Senators Mark Hatfield, Barbara Boxer, Jesse Helms, and Edward Kennedy, along with Jane Fonda and Ted Turner and 3,000 to 4,000 other prominent citizens from the whole spectrum of U.S. public life. Also among the victims would be 10,000 students from Harvard, Berkeley, and a dozen other prestigious universities. Among the hundreds kidnapped by both sides and held for ransom or exchange or simply to embarrass the government would be Chief Justice Rehnquist, Vice President Al Gore, Archbishop O'Connor, Donald Trump, Frank Carlucci, Edwin Meese, and Ron Reagan, Jr.; David Rockefeller, Jack Valenti, Paul Laxalt, and Paul Getty, Jr.; James Brady and the British, French, and German ambassadors. Stretch the analogy back to 1979, and the equivalent would be half a million U.S. citizens murdered, another half million "disappeared," and no less than 15 million forced into exile or held in secret detention centers where they would be subjected to systematic torture and mutilation. This is a rough idea of the scale of the war that has raged for over a quarter century in this picturesque, Tennessee-sized republic of 9 million.

3

[logo]

The New Conquerors

"The enemy is not destroyed in battle. You win over him by
destroying his mind, his intelligence, and his will."

Military poster, Petén

On a cool, sunny afternoon in August 1987, Guatemala's top military
brass gathered in the capital's luxurious Camino Real Hotel to take
part in a public symposium sponsored by the Chambers of Commerce,
Industry, and Finances (CACIF). The event, which packed the hotel's
largest conference hall, was attended by the country's leading politicians from the right, as well as by captains of industry and commerce
and members of the traditionally conservative landowning elite.

One of the army's chief objectives in accepting CACIF's invitation
was to divulge for the first time the military strategy that had enabled
it to defeat a twenty-seven-year-long insurgency inspired by Cuba's
revolution and fanned by the Sandinistas' triumph in Nicaragua. A
second and equally important objective was to take official credit for
having shepherded Guatemala to a civilian democracy under President
Vinicio Cerezo Arévalo.

The military historians expounding on each phase of the counterinsurgency strategy spoke in the expected tone of patronizing self-
congratulation; but they did make some token attempts at objectivity.
A field colonel in full military regalia conceded that the two disaffected army officers who founded Guatemala's first modern guerrilla
organizations in the early sixties had been moved by "repugnance
against conditions of social injustice."

Another officer credited leaders of the Guerrilla Army of the Poor
(EGP), which arose in the early seventies, with mastering indigenous

languages in order to address the grievances of the Mayan communities. Despite his insistence that the army's campaigns had reduced the guerrilla threat to a mere nuisance, the officer conceded that in the early eighties the guerrillas had recruited three hundred thousand campesinos and controlled a sizable portion of the western and central highlands. Had they armed and mobilized their following, the officer added, the two chief guerrilla groups, EGP and ORPA, would have posed a direct threat to the established order. The remainder of the army's presentation extolled the military's genius in devising strategies—such as the so-called model villages and the civil defense patrols—that effectively neutralized the guerrillas' gains among the peasant population and ultimately defeated them.

In his own peroration, the minister of defense, Héctor Gramajo, voiced his unconditional support for Cerezo's government and its economic policies. These policies included a tax restructuring initiative that had aroused the wrath of the private sector, despite the fact that Guatemala's businessmen, industrialists, and large plantation owners pay the lowest income taxes in the Western Hemisphere. Gramajo invited the private sector to contribute its share to maintain a strong military shield, as well as to support Cerezo's popularly elected democratic government. Then came a historic moment.

An ultrarightist landowner arose and asked Gramajo when he was going to put on his trousers and go back to ridding the country of labor leaders, agitators, and other Marxist subversives. Gramajo replied in a hard-edged voice that the time was long past when the army would serve as the ruling classes' strike-breakers and private policemen. "You people have been asking us to kill your Marxists for you for the past four hundred years." The message was clear. From now on the army would enter into any new alliance with the landowners and businessmen as an equal partner. In private, an officer told an influential landowner, "We are not your lackeys any more."

The Guatemalan military's rise to a social class rivaling the landowners, the businessmen, and industrialists they have traditionally served results directly from fighting leftist guerrillas, whose numbers have never exceeded 7,500 hard-core militants. Since the C.I.A.-assisted overthrow of socialist president Jacobo Arbenz in 1954, nine progressively more brutal military dictatorships held power until Cerezo's election.

Today, the army owns its own bank and administers the telephone and airline companies; its top officers award themselves princely salaries, and they have taken over vast stretches of mineral-rich land in the transversal strip below El Petén, which has come to be known as the "Zone of the Generals." The generals have been the ones to dictate how and when the country would pass into an electoral democracy to be led by a tightly reined civilian president. And after the unraveling of democracy under Cerezo, it is the army generals that the United States is turning to once again to guarantee stability. (More recently, the U.S. Drug Enforcement Agency has collaborated with the military in an attempt to stem the flow of Colombian cocaine through Guatemala.)

The military officers who staged the symposium at the Camino Real Hotel had much to crow about, though neither their victory over the guerrillas nor their domination of Guatemala's ladino and Mayan sectors is as conclusive as they would have everyone believe.

2

One of the victims of the army's counterinsurgency campaign who lived to tell his story is a poet and schoolmaster named Victor Montejo. His experience is not unlike that of hundreds of other highland Mayas, but his telling of it is transcendent. Montejo, a Jacaltecan Mayan educated in Antigua, was forced to leave Guatemala after witnessing a massacre by a special forces army unit in the small village high in the mountains of Huehuetenango, where he taught primary school.

I met Victor Montejo in the summer of 1983, when he knocked on my hotel door in San Cristóbal de las Casas in Chiapas, Mexico. Montejo had recently returned from a visit to the United States on the invitation of Wallace Kaufman, an American writer who had translated his poetry. After touring the Northeast giving readings from his newly published work, Montejo learned that his name had appeared on a death list in his home town and that his parents had fled to Mexico. He returned as a refugee and lived for several months with his parents near the Mexican/Guatemalan border. He had come to San Cristóbal to look for work, and a refugee aid agency had given him my name.

On that summer day, Montejo told me he had written an account of his experience, and I expressed interest in reading and possibly translating it. The following is a brief summary of his testimony.

Victor Montejo was teaching classes on the morning of September 9, 1982, when an army special forces—*kaibiles*—wearing green camouflage fatigues marched unannounced into the village. The members of the civil defense patrol, all Jacaltecan Mayas, mistook the soldiers for guerrillas disguised in army dress. Marching forward with clubs and stones, the civil defenders fired their only rifle—a muzzle-loading Mauser—and wounded one of the advancing soldiers. After scattering in panic, the soldiers regrouped and returned the fire with Galil automatic rifles, killing and wounding several members of the civil patrol. The villagers thereupon realized their mistake—only the army uses Galil automatics—and lowered their weapons in surrender.

The head of the kaibil patrol, an illiterate Indian lieutenant, accused the civil defenders of harboring subversives and lined them up in the village plaza for interrogation. The lieutenant produced a list containing the names of ten villagers who were singled out for execution. "The army officers know," Montejo writes with understated irony, "that they will rise in rank in accordance with the number of unfortunates they execute, and he must have anticipated at least a promotion for uncovering such a large cache of 'subversives' at one blow."

When Montejo stepped forward to inquire into the charges against the villagers and to explain that the shooting had been the result of mistaken identity, the lieutenant responded by shoving him in with the suspects even though his name did not appear on the list. Cursing and shouting profanities in the broken Spanish commonly spoken by unschooled soldiers, the officer ordered that a youth be tortured inside the schoolhouse to obtain more names for his list.

Montejo writes that two weeks earlier another army patrol had ordered the four hundred civil defenders to execute two young villagers they had themselves turned in for "suspicious activities." He describes in excruciating detail how the elders had been forced on pain of death to lift their clubs with the others and strike at the two men, who bled slowly and agonizingly to death while pleading in vain for mercy. The main charge against them was that they had left the village without explanation. After the execution a ghastly silence descended among the villagers, as the soldiers went about sacking their houses of radios, jewelry, and other valuables, which they stuffed into large canvas bags.

"It was," Montejo writes, "as if a light had gone out of the faces of each of the men, the murdered as well as the survivors, the accused along with the executioners. . . . But the seeds of our degradation had been sown long before. The military indoctrination was the last step in a process that had gradually undermined the foundations of indigenous culture, causing the Indian to act against his own will and best interests and destroying what is most sacred in his ancient Mayan legacy: love and respect for one's neighbors."

When the tortured youth would not divulge any names of villagers—although he indirectly implicated Montejo as an "outsider"—the enraged lieutenant ordered his soldiers to tie the youth and four other suspects to the posts of the municipality. The five were executed by firing squad, as their families looked on in helpless horror. Montejo was spared because he had information that was potentially useful to army intelligence. When a helicopter failed to pick him up he was marched in the dead of night to the army base in the municipal capital, which was Montejo's home; and that is where his personal ordeal took place.

Inside the barracks he was tied to a pillar and tortured in an almost random way by a succession of sadistic officers and soldiers. In the morning, more dead than alive, Montejo's spirits rallied when a humane soldier brought him coffee and tortillas sent by his wife. She had learned of his captivity and was standing vigil outside the barracks.

Finally the commanding officer, a fair-skinned colonel with light-brown hair—the first non-Indian Montejo had confronted—subjected him to a lengthy interrogation. The officer intended to browbeat him into reporting townspeople suspected of guerrilla connections. When he refused, Montejo was dismissed and ordered to show up at the barracks every day, morning and evening, until he had handed in a list of "communists" and their accomplices.

With his wounds still festering, but immensely grateful that his life was spared, Montejo appeared at the barracks four days in a row, each time with some pretext for not turning in any names. After five days he had recovered his strength. He gathered a few belongings and stole out of town after nightfall. In the capital he picked up his passport and used the ticket Kaufman had mailed him to fly to the United States.

Montejo returned to the United States shortly after our meeting in San Cristóbal and was joined six months later by his wife and three children.

Victor Montejo's story is unusual only in the lucid, poetic voice in which it is recorded by a gifted writer. He describes in vivid detail his weekly hikes to the village, and the beauty of the Jacaltecan countryside. As he is led away with a noose around his neck, he raises his voice in praise of the verdant valley where he taught school. His testimony abounds with patriotic allusions, and he manifests indignation whenever his interrogators impugn his loyalty to his homeland. That Montejo escaped his torturers with his dignity sullied but unbroken is one testament, among hundreds of others, to the remarkable resilience of Guatemala's indigenous peoples. But the price of survival has been fearful.

A number of other testimonies by Mayan survivors relating experiences far worse than those described by Victor Montejo have appeared in print. The best known is the autobiographical memoir of Rigoberta Menchú, a thirty-four-year-old militant and human rights observer from Uspantán, in northern Quiché. During a three-year period four members of Rigoberta's immediate family—including her father and mother—were killed by the army with a calculated brutality that taxes the limits of human comprehension. Her memoir, *I, Rigoberta Menchú,* written in collaboration with the French-Venezuelan journalist Elisabeth Burgos, has become a worldwide best-seller and has made Menchú's name better known than that of any living Guatemalan. The Nobel Prize Committee recognized her work of "peace and reconciliation" across ethnic, cultural, and social dividing lines by awarding her the 1992 Peace Prize.

In April 1988, when Rigoberta and three other members of a political resistance group decided to test Guatemala's tolerance for dissent by traveling there on a brief visit, she and one of her colleagues were arrested at the airport and detained on charges of inciting violence. But the flood of telegrams and telephone calls from European government heads and world figures caused the government to reconsider; seven hours after her arrival she and her colleague appeared before a Supreme Court judge who dismissed the charges against them.

After her release, Menchú immediately held a press conference. Dressed in her bright native Quiché *traje* of woven blouse and ankle-length skirt, Menchú faced the TV cameras, while outside the El Dorado Hotel 1,500 university students, together with union workers and GAM members, chanted slogans in solidarity.

In her measured, unerring replies to reporters, Menchú pointedly alluded to the army's torturing and killing of her brother and mother. She also referred to the 1980 Spanish Embassy break-in by the National Police, who had burned alive her father, peasant-militant Vicente Menchú, and thirty-eight other demonstrators and sympathizers. When she'd finished her presentation, a respectful silence descended over the assemblage. Nothing like this had ever happened in Guatemala before, and nothing would be the same after it.

Two weeks after Rigoberta's visit two army officers from remote outposts in the eastern provinces, who came to be known as the "officers from the mountain," joined forces with ultraright landowners and politicians to try to put an end to Vinicio Cerezo's government. The coup attempt did not succeed in overthrowing Cerezo, who was backed by Minister of Defense Héctor Gramajo; but it did set back the two-year-old democratic "opening" and forced Cerezo to roll back his social and economic reforms. As one of the reasons for their revolt the officers gave the government's decision to release Rigoberta Menchú. If a former leader of the outlawed Committee for Peasant Unity—an Indian woman at that—was allowed to thumb her nose at the authorities and leave the country intact, it meant to them that the military had lost its grip on the country. And anything had become possible.

PART II

The Ixil Triangle

4

Nebaj

"We believe the war against subversion is total, permanent, and universal; we must defeat the communists not only in their mountain hideouts but in every city, town, village, and hamlet."

Military comandante of Nebaj

"The army does not kill Indians, it kills devils; because the Indians are bedeviled, they are communists."

Pastor with Church of the Word

The army garrison of Sacapulas guards the gateway to the "Zones of Conflict" in northern Quiché—including the Ixil Triangle—and in Huehuetenango to the west. The Ixil Triangle, a term given currency by anthropologists and military strategists in the past decade, describes an area of 2,300 square kilometers (about 888 square miles) in the northern half of the Department of Quiché. The three towns (and numerous satellite villages) that form this triangle, Santa María Nebaj, San Juan Cotzal, and San Gaspar Chajul, have their own language, Ixil, their own distinct customs and regional dress, and a proud history of independence that predates the arrival of the Spanish conquistadores in the sixteenth century. The many pyramids, painted stelae, and other monuments unearthed in the Ixil area suggest continuous habitation by a stable culture at least since the end of the classical Maya era, between the sixth and ninth centuries A.D. In the fifteenth century the Ixils were conquered by the Quiché king, Quicab the Great, whose dominions spread north to the Ixcán and the borders of Petén. The Ixil region and Ixcán have remained part of Quiché ever since.

The Sacapulas barracks sit prominently in the town's central plaza, next to the school and the colonial church. The basketball court adjacent to the church is usually crowded with youngsters. Above the high-walled barracks, plainly visible to the schoolchildren and to

motorists passing through town is a bold-lettered poster, guarded by
a sentry with a Galil automatic rifle:

> SOLO EL QUE LUCHA TIENE DERECHO A VENCER
>
> SOLO EL QUE VENCE TIENE DERECHO A VIVIR
>
> (Only he who fights has the right to win
>
> Only he who wins has the right to live)

Only gradually does an outsider learn the extent to which this
slogan reflects the military's view of its opponents and of the civilian
populations living under its domination.

In July 1986, I made the first of several visits to the Ixil Triangle
in search of evidence that army operations in that corner of Guatemala's western highlands, carried out between 1978 and 1983, had
killed or displaced upwards of 25,000 Ixil residents of Mayan descent.
Population estimates for that region in 1978 were no higher than
85,000. If the claims by church groups and human rights organizations
are accurate, it means that roughly one of every three Ixil Mayan
residents was killed or driven out by the Guatemalan army during a
five-year campaign. Figures like these inevitably raise the ugly specter
of genocide. And indeed, Americas Watch, Amnesty International, a
Guatemalan bishops' pastoral letter, and the British parliamentary
report "Bitter and Cruel" have all charged the Guatemalan military
with carrying out a planned program of ethnic extermination against
Mayan communities suspected of collaborating with leftist guerrillas.

"*Operación Ixil*," as the campaign was described in military publications, was the cornerstone of a much larger plan of counterinsurgency whose objective was to wipe out the peasant support bases
of the two leftist guerrilla organizations most active in the highlands
and to bring the 4 million Mayas living there (out of a total Guatemalan population of about 7.5 million in 1981) under direct military
control.

When Pedro de Alvarado led his expedition from Mexico into the
Guatemalan highlands in 1523, he found a fractious region riven with
internecine dissension and rivalries. In spite of these fissures, the Mayas
proved more resistant to conquest than their Mexican counterparts,

whose fighting spirit had been undermined by Montezuma's belief in the prophecy of invincible pale gods arriving from the east. After the Spaniards seized and set fire to the Quiché citadel at Utatlán, they met stiff resistance from the isolated Ixil fortress towns of Nebaj and Chajul, before the Spaniards prevailed. Subsequently they were soundly defeated by the Ixils' neighbors and allies, the Uspantecs. Two thousand warriors ambushed the Spanish infantry from the rear, and inflicted heavy losses on their Indian auxiliaries.

The Ixils and their Quiché-speaking Uspantec allies had one full year to savor their victory. One may picture the fires burning around the sacrificial altars of Uspantán, as the hearts of a handful of Spanish captives and hundreds of their Cakchiquel and Mexican auxiliaries were offered in tribute to the Uspantec god, Exbalamquen.

In 1530, a second expedition set out from Guatemala's colonial capital to put down the Ixils and Uspantecs. After a tortuous ascent of the western Cuchumatán range, this larger and better led *entrada* subdued Nebaj and Chajul a second time. Uspantán sent 10,000 warriors to meet the Spaniards, but this time their superior firearms and their tactical deployment of cavalry confounded the Mayas, and Uspantán was overwhelmed. Many of the warriors not killed outright were branded and sold into slavery. In the end, the horses spelled the difference; the horses, European diseases, and the iron Spanish will. When the Spaniards vanquished the Quichés and the Ixils with the aid of secessionist Cakchiquels, they took over a structure of subjugation and tribute already laid out by the Quichés and the Toltecs before them. The recurring cycles of Guatemala's history reveal a remarkable symmetry, across the centuries.

Once the Spanish friars secured the souls of the Ixils for Christianity, just as their precursors had secured their scant gold and treasures for Isabella and Ferdinand, the area fell into long neglect. The inhospitable western Cuchumatanes held few attractions for the conquering Spaniards, who established their vast cattle ranches, and later on their cacao and indigo estates, in the lower highlands and coastal regions. Nevertheless, the Spanish incursions were to cost the Ixils dearly, as epidemics of typhus and smallpox spread throughout the altiplano.

The Ixil population did not recover until well into the nineteenth century, when Dominican friars returned to evangelize the isolated mountain communities. In the mid-nineteenth century, a visiting Spanish priest wrote of the Ixils: "After 300 years of being evangelized, they are seen today to be in a worse state than in the first century [i.e., the sixteenth], marching backward toward their ancient barbarities, mixed with vices and irreligion of other castes."

When the first coffee plantations arose in the 1880s on the Pacific littoral, landowners turned to northern Quiché for a ready source of cheap migrant labor. President Justo Rufino Barrios, the Liberal dictator and "Father of Reform," laid the legislative foundation for the enslavement of the Ixil migrant labor force that persists, virtually unchanged, to this day.

The first ladinos to settle in the Ixil area were contractors, or *contratistas*, hired by finca owners to recruit armies of peons for the annual coffee harvests. The contractors often doubled as loan sharks and liquor traders in order to hook campesinos into debt servitude for the remainder of their working lives. Travelers to Nebaj in the early part of the twentieth century reported stumbling over the bodies of drunken Indians that littered the streets. Most of these Ixils were forced to spend their sober hours picking coffee on coastal fincas under the sweltering sun in order to pay off their liquor debts.

By the mid-twentieth century, a handful of patriarchal European families—the Brols, the Arenases, the Samayoas—owned vast coffee, cacao, cattle, and sugar estates in the lower elevations of the Ixil and neighboring regions. Working conditions for the indigenous laborers on these fincas have mirrored the worst abuses by sixteenth-century Spanish *hacendados*, who routinely seized Indian women as their private chattel and hung their protesting husbands from trees, after skinning them alive. These same landowning families—above all the Brol brothers and Luis Arenas—were the leading characters in a cruel frontier drama that has become a part of Quiché folklore. The closing chapters have been no gentle autumnal decline, as the patriarchs' scripts may have called for. They culminated instead with spectacular *ajusticiamientos*, or retributive executions, by a guerrilla organization whose rank and file had been victims of the landowners and their contractors.

Most notorious of all was the Brol family, whose patriarch had immigrated from Italy near the turn of the century and who began as a *contratista* for coastal planters. By the mid 1930s, four Brol sons owned vast ranch lands and coffee fincas covering thousands of acres as far south as Uspantán. During the harvests as many as four thousand resident and seasonal peons, the majority of them Ixils, worked in San Francisco finca, in the northern lowland region of Cotzal municipality.

The Ixils have a history of rebellion against abusive employers and their government allies. Only four years after the Spanish victory of 1530, the communities of Ilom and Salquil together with Uspantán revolted and killed a dozen Spanish officers and *encomenderos*. Chronicles record a significant Ixil uprising against colonial authorities again in 1799. In June 1936, after dictator Jorge Ubico replaced the debt peonage statutes with vagrancy laws that compelled landless Mayas to work fifty hours a month on the coastal fincas, two hundred Nebaj residents marched on the court house to register a formal complaint. At the head of the marchers were Ixil principales like Diego Brito and Miguel Ceto with proof that the landowners kept hundreds of peons under illegal debt bondage by neglecting to register their working hours on the small ledgers they were obliged to carry. Accompanying the protesters was an official investigator dispatched by Ubico.

Noé Palacios, a schoolmaster who witnessed the event as a young man, recalls the columns of marchers in their traditional bright red jackets. The first to see the protesters was Pedro Brol, the elder son and namesake of the Italian patriarch, who owned a finca and a general store in Nebaj. Brol alerted the garrison comandante that a mass Indian uprising—the ladinos' worst nightmare—was headed toward the court house. The burly officer and his seven soldiers intercepted the marchers and ordered them to turn back. When the leaders attempted to explain their purpose, the shaken comandante cursed aloud and fired his pistol in the air. Before he could aim it at the marchers, a baton knocked the gun from his hand. The protesters then disarmed the soldiers and cast their weapons on the ground. Frustrated in their intention to meet with the mayor, the marchers dispersed to their homes.

The following evening a company of infantry, led by General Daniel Corado on an imposing brown stallion, arrived from Santa Cruz del Quiché. By the following morning one hundred fifty of the marchers, among them most of Nebaj's Ixil principales, had been rounded up and placed in the town's four jails. General Corado, a draconian disciplinarian and an intimate of Ubico, vowed to set a precedent that would resonate in the community's memory. Eight men were removed from the town jails and placed before a firing squad in back of the church. (One of them, Sebastián Brito, vaulted an irrigation ditch seconds before the general gave the order to shoot and made good his escape.) The seven men executed by General Corado were Nebajeños imprisoned for minor crimes who had taken no part in the protest.

That night, the landowners' contractors and one or two leading ladinos interceded with the mayor, who agreed to release the protesters in their custody. The relieved protesters failed to realize at the time that they had succeeded only in incurring a more enduring debt toward the landowners who duped and exploited them. Nearly all the Ixil principales in positions of responsibility in Nebaj today, and others who defected to the guerrillas, are descendants of participants in the 1936 uprising.

The seven executed by General Corado's firing squad were buried in a common grave in the town cemetery. Their gravestone has become a pilgrimage site for two generations of Nebajeños who have not forgotten General Corado's summary executions of their neighbors or Pedro Brol's collusion in their deaths.

The Ixils' close communal bond was one of the factors that drew guerrillas to the region, seeking to create a base of popular support. Another attraction for the EGP strategists was the well organized church organizations in northern Quiché, and most particularly the catechists associated with Acción Católica, or Catholic Action. In 1955 Sacred Heart priests arrived in northern Quiché from Spain, infused with a mystical anticommunism inherited from the Spanish Civil War. In the course of two decades, many of the Sacred Heart pastors would become converts to Liberation Theology. Fathers Xavier and Luis Gurriarán head the list of foreign priests radicalized by the implacable exploitation of their parishioners by ladino landowners.

In the Ixil area, Father Xavier Gurriarán and other activist clerics helped establish agricultural and craft cooperatives with indigenous leaders drawn from Acción Católica. Starting in 1975 the army came after these leaders, whom they identified with Marxist subversion. The campaign against radical priests and indigenous community leaders intensified after General Romeo Lucas García took over the presidency in 1978. By 1979 the Guatemalan Church-in-Exile, based in Nicaragua, estimated that three hundred fifty cooperative leaders, schoolteachers, Acción Católica catechists, and three Sacred Heart pastors had been killed by the army in the three municipalities of the Ixil Triangle. Father Gurriarán fled to the mountains in 1979 and later crossed the border into Mexico. No longer active in the insurgency, Father Xavier and his brother Luis remain eloquent witnesses to the army massacres in the Quiché. In Nebaj I spoke with numerous Ixils who are convinced Father Xavier is still fighting with the guerrillas. I also met with active and former militants who reproached the Gurriarán brothers for having abandoned them when they were most needed.

But the army was unable to prevent the emergence of a peasant labor movement in the towns and numerous *aldeas,* or villages, of the Ixil Triangle and Uspantán. Propelling this movement was a strain of reform Catholicism that grew out of the Second Vatican Council and the Latin American Bishops' Conference held in Medellín, Colombia, in 1968. In Nebaj in particular, militant Acción Católica catechists, encouraged by their Spanish pastors, often initiated contacts with the guerrillas and invited them to attend their consciousness-raising sessions.

The largest and most important organization to emerge from this movement was the Committee of Peasant Unity (CUC), which arose in response to the horrendous abuses of Mayan workers in highland coffee fincas and to the equally deplorable conditions of servitude to which ladino and indigenous peons were subjected on the Pacific coast's sugar, coffee, and cotton plantations. Today, nearly three-quarters of the highland's work force of 300,000 still migrates to the coast every year to save a few centavos for the barest necessities. Their meager crops of corn and beans are grown on plots of land that have shrunk to less than two acres per person.

The vital statistics for the Ixil area are, if anything, worse than they are for the rest of the western highlands, where life expectancy at birth is less than forty-five. In 1989, 90 percent of Ixils who spoke Spanish could neither read nor write.

Rigoberta Menchú, whose father, Vicente, was one of the founders of the peasant labor movement, has vividly described the miserable living and working conditions in the coastal plantations that led to the formation of CUC. In the late seventies, cotton planters out for quick profits regularly sprayed three and four times the presumed "safe" limit of DDT; as a result, hundreds of field-workers died each year of liver and lung ailments, and the milk of indigenous mothers had the highest concentration of DDT in the Western Hemisphere. (DDT has since been replaced by subtler pesticides whose effects on humans—and the environment—are more difficult to trace.) In 1980, after a series of paralyzing strikes in the cotton, sugar, and coffee fincas by over 100,000 indigenous and ladino workers, Lucas García's government grudgingly legislated a $3.20 minimum daily wage, the first of its kind in the country's history. But this victory for CUC proved to be short-lived, as most landowners devised ruses for not paying even this basic wage. Between 1986 and 1991, as the Guatemalan quetzal lost two-thirds of its purchasing power against the dollar, most coffee and cotton workers earned the equivalent of 80 cents to $1.00 a day.

During Lucas García's presidency, CUC had organized large numbers of highland Mayas. Although CUC did not recruit actively in the Ixil Triangle, several hundred campesinos defected to the guerrillas. After the army began targeting peasant labor organizers, CUC was forced underground. These early successes of an aroused peasant movement convinced the landowners that the very foundation of their livelihood was in danger of collapse. Just as they had many times in the past, the landowners united behind the army to put down an indigenous insurrection and lent their support to *Operación Ixil*. By 1980 the army's strength had expanded from 27,000 to 40,000, which made it the largest standing military force in Central America at that time. And General Lucas García unleashed the most ruthless repression against the Mayas in Guatemala's long history of repressive military dictatorships.

Beginning in the mid 1970s, the Guerrilla Army of the Poor (EGP), which included elements from the two earlier rebel groups defeated by General Arana Osorio's Pacification Campaigns, sought to establish links with rural peasant communities in the Ixcán, north of the Ixil area. Mario Payeras, a founder and leader of the EGP, has written a memoir describing the organization's first awkward attempts to win over the proud Ixils and their northern neighbors. He tells about EGP's execution of the powerful coffee planter Luis Arenas, known as "The Tiger of Ixcán" by the hundreds of Mayan laborers he kept under inhuman conditions of debt bondage. In 1975 the guerrillas killed Arenas in his own finca after they failed to convince campesinos to execute him. The guerrillas shot him "like a bird of prey" as he was counting the payroll for his workers.

"From that moment on," writes Payeras, "the word spread throughout the region that the guerrillas were not foreigners, since they spoke the local dialect . . . and that they surely had come to do justice, since they had punished a man who had grown rich from the blood and sweat of the poor." Payeras does not mention what happened to local farmers whom the EGP persuaded to execute a ladino squatter who had confiscated their lands. Weeks after the killing the army rounded up several dozen participants in the plot. At least thirty of them, according to Amnesty International, were never heard from again. Hundreds more innocent peasants were to pay with their lives after the EGP killed Arenas. From the very beginning of their activities in northern Quiché, the EGP's ability to enlist thousands of campesinos to their cause was not matched by a logistical capacity to arm or supply the vast majority of them. In a sense, the EGP and the masses of campesinos who would form their popular base were to become victims of a premature success.

In January 1979 an EGP contingent composed of two hundred conscripts—most of them Ixils—occupied the town of Nebaj to hold a recruitment rally. Noé Palacios recognized many of his students among the young Ixil recruits dressed in olive fatigues and armed with assorted weapons. Palacios estimates that two to three thousand residents attended the meeting in the town square. The guerrillas had lined up the town's municipal officers, the firemen, and local police. One after the other, male and female Ixil guerrillas testified to the injustices that had driven them to join the EGP: the subhuman pay scale on the fincas, the rape of workers' wives by landowners, the extortions by contratistas who created a vicious cycle of indebted labor through a variety of devious schemes and entrapments. Each of these grievances drew a response from the gathered Ixils, who clapped and shouted in assent. The guerrilla spokesmen reminded the townspeople they were a part of the struggle. "The army tells you we are in the mountains. Don't believe it. We are among you." The rally ended with the guerrillas shouting slogans: "Long live the EGP! Long live the people of Nebaj!" They then helped themselves to boots, machetes, and provisions from a local ladino-owned store. Hundreds of townspeople, convinced they had met the army of liberation, plied the guerrillas with food, money, and other gifts before they left to disappear into the mountains.

Earlier that same day, a guerrilla patrol shot another notorious landowner, Enrique Brol, younger brother of Pedro, whom they had intended to apprehend and place on public trial. Finca San Francisco, east of Cotzal, was infamous for the Brols' wretched pay and for treating their workers like indentured slaves. When harvest season approached, the Brols' contractors would advance small sums to Mayan heads of families desperately in need of a few centavos to pay their debts or to buy seedcorn for their milpas. Enrique Brol's miserly wages and underhanded extortions assured that the peons would remain indebted through the end of the harvest and beyond. Brol's sons were reputed bullies who seized any women they wanted as slaves and concubines. (In the highlands a Mayan worker's wife or daughter may be taken as loan collateral.) A young married woman who rejected the advances of the elder son of Enrique Brol was found dead the next day, hacked to pieces by one of the Brols' bodyguards. What is unusual about this otherwise unexceptional event is that the bodyguard was given fifteen days in jail to cool down.

A woman in olive fatigues who had been abused as a servant in the Brol household was the first to approach Enrique after her companions disarmed his son and bodyguard, Fita Brol. Confronted by a former servant clasping a submachine gun, Enrique cursed and reached for his holster. She shot him through the jaw and he fell to the ground. (A popular Ixil version tells of howling German shepherds rushing to their master's defense, only to be shot down by the guerrillas.) The executioner and her companions then led Fita to the square and placed him on public exhibition together with their other captives.

Enrique Brol was the only victim of the EGP's daring occupation of Nebaj and Finca San Francisco in 1979. But the shock waves from the event went far beyond the triangle to alter the power balance in the western highlands. The first to arrive in the area were Brol family members, who flew in from the capital in a helicopter and immediately began funeral preparations for the paterfamilias. (Among the dozens of relatives, government dignitaries, and finca workers attending the funeral were the Mayan and ladino mothers of Enrique Brol's numerous illegitimate progeny. With rare exceptions, however, it was the ladino *queridas* (mistresses) and offspring who reaped the benefits several years later when Brol's sons parceled out large tracts of land.)

Jorge Brol, Enrique's younger brother, had also suffered a violent death. He was murdered in 1969 while driving to the finca to deliver the monthly payroll. Although robbery was probably the chief motive, the assassination inevitably took on political overtones, as it was the first carried out against a plantation owner in Ixil country. The suspected culprit, a local labor contractor, was reportedly caught by the Brols' spies and baked alive in the finca's coffee-drying furnace.

The political execution of the two widely hated ladino landowners—Luis Arenas and Enrique Brol—won the EGP hundreds of Mayan recruits. More important, it created an infrastructure of thousands of residents of the Ixil Triangle who were willing to risk their lives to provide food, shelter, and military intelligence to the four or five hundred guerrillas entrenched in the neighboring mountains.

The army was determined to stamp out the grassroots support for the guerrillas. A company of one hundred soldiers from Santa Cruz del Quiché moved into Nebaj the next day and installed a detachment of military police. Within days, leading citizens of the town began to disappear. Later their bodies were found mutilated and strung up on posts in the town square. Hundreds of other corpses appeared in clandestine cemeteries as far away as Cotzal. In June 1979, the army set up its barracks in the center of Nebaj and moved in more or less permanently. To this day, the Ixil communities continue to pay a steep price for the guerrillas' execution of their oppressors.

Noé Palacios, whose own uncle had been one of Nebaj's notorious landowners, was a correspondent and columnist for the Guatemalan newspaper *El Independiente*. In the following months, he reported on the massacres and mass executions of hundreds of Ixils suspected of collaborating with the guerrillas. Palacios heard Colonel Francisco "Pancho" Carranza threaten to wipe out half the population of the triangle in order to "pacify" it. And he was nearly as good as his word. Palacios's eyes smolder when he speaks of the ninety-six laborers butchered in the Finca Estrella Polar; the razing of entire villages such as Cocop, where ninety-eight residents were killed; the twenty-four teenagers who were bound up and shot in the plaza of Acul. He remembers dogs fighting over the remains of twenty youths who had been tortured and then shot by the small reservoir outside Nebaj. When the military killed his son and threatened his own life, Palacios had to "swallow" his tongue and stop dispatching eyewitness reports.

Three years after he retired as a government-salaried schoolteacher and nearly a decade since he stopped reporting, seventy-year-old Noé Palacios's blood still boiled at the memory of his interview with the comandante. "I told the colonel, the only peace the army achieved was that of the grave, and instead of stamping out the insurrection, they created a generation of Ixil warriors determined to avenge their dead." (In 1989 Palacios came out of retirement to teach in a remote village reclaimed from guerrilla control.)

At the same time that Lucas's army was carrying out its massacres and executions, they also sent civic action delegations to distribute food supplies, medicines, and free medical care, as loudspeakers proclaimed the military's identification with the people's welfare. This was the first crude instance of the stick-and-carrot formula that would form the core of military counterinsurgency in the highlands.

With the assassination of Enrique Brol and Luis Arenas the ladino landowning families lost their feudal domination of the Ixil labor force. Approximately three-quarters of the Brol properties have been sold or parceled out since the guerrillas executed Enrique. The surviving grandsons of the patriarch Pedro Brol have moved to Guatemala City or to the coast, where they have invested their coffee revenues in cattle ranches. Finca San Francisco is run by an *administrador*, with regular helicopter inspection tours by one of Enrique's sons. The heirs of Guillermo Samayoa, another large landholder in Ixil country, have also put up for sale most of their extensive holdings. Ironically, as David Stoll points out in his doctoral dissertation, the thousands of hectares of fallow land released by the Brols, the Samayoas, and other latifundistas will not begin to ease the land hunger of an exploding Ixil population, which is expected to double by the year 1995.

Less than a decade after the EGP executed Luis Arenas and won thousands of Ixil recruits to their cause, Arenas's sons Ricardo and Enrique became born-again Christians. In the mid-eighties they opened La Perla, their father's vast and near-bankrupt estate, to a proselytizing experiment of the Full Gospel Businessmen's Fellowship International, a right-wing evangelical/charismatic organization based in California. Enrique Arenas, who still pays his workers less than $1 a day and whose plantation is guarded by army outposts that control all entering and exiting traffic, is also the Guatemalan representative of Americans for Freedom in Central America. After turning La Perla "over to the Lord," Arenas invited gringo evangelicals to invest their souls and money in the explosive Ixcán region, where the EGP maintains its largest presence. The opportunity to do battle for the Lord against the godless hosts of communism proved irresistible. Among the groups that accepted the invitation to save souls in La Perla was the Florida-based Facts of Faith, a slickly run operation that provided medical aid and provisions to undernourished coffee pickers. The army generously contributed its Civil Affairs vehicles and personnel to distribute supplies in the common effort to colonize the region with evangelized collaborators.

Another experiment in free enterprise that has the backing of fervently anticommunist evangelicals is the *Plan Solidarista,* a stock-sharing venture between management and employees that soon spread to 1,500 Central American companies, most of them in Costa Rica. In Guatemala the leading Solidarista participant is the La Perla Project, with Enrique and Ricardo Arenas at the helm. The Solidarity Plan started off modestly with a voluntary savings program for hired help at the finca that would match a 3 to 10 percent salary savings with company funds. The Arenas went on to announce the sale of 40 percent of their finca's stock to their five hundred *colonos,* or permanent workers. La Perla was so heavily indebted that as of 1990 none of the colonos had received any earnings on their investment.

The Solidarity incentives look much better on paper than the way they work out in actuality. In many of the Costa Rican participating companies, a loss of up to 10 percent in employee salaries has been reported, owing to inefficiency or poor management of the plan. Still, the Solidaristas had the staunch backing of the ideologues in the Reagan White House, including the president himself, who on May 8, 1986, wrote Ricardo Arenas, author of a pamphlet on the Solidarity Movement:

> I was so pleased to receive, just before Nancy and I departed for the Far East, the copy of your book on Solidarity which you kindly inscribed for me. It's truly heartening to know that the Solidarista movement is spreading throughout Guatemala and other Central American countries. Thank you for sharing your new work with me and for your dedicated efforts toward providing workers with a stake in the free enterprise system. With my deep appreciation, and with my best wishes to you and your colleagues for continued success in your vital work,
>
> Sincerely,
Ronald Reagan

In June 1989, the publisher of the centrist newspaper *La Hora* accused Enrique Arenas of having laundered a fraudulent loan from the Workers' Bank (*El Banco de los Trabajadores*), of which there was no record in La Perla's ledgers. In a long letter to *La Hora*, Enrique Arenas vehemently denied the charges and emphasized the benefits of the Solidarista project to his two thousand workers. (In fact, the five hundred or so seasonal workers who live in the region were not even included in the Solidarity plan.) A year later, Guatemala's labor unions launched a campaign against the Solidarista movement, which they accused of defrauding its members and of subverting the labor union movement.

2

In a four-wheel drive vehicle, the climb up the Cuchumatanes from Sacapulas is steep but relatively rapid. Our rented red jeep is driven by my traveling companion, George Lovell, a Scottish historical geographer teaching in Canada who has written a book about the Cuchumatán Mayan communities at the time of the Conquest. After passing the side road to Cunén, the northern range of the Cuchumatanes opens suddenly to our left on one of the most breathtaking panoramas in the Mesoamerican isthmus. The fires of small villages in Huehuetenango can be seen across the Río Negro valley. Visible on the horizon far to the south are the tops of fifteen volcanoes from a chain of thirty-three whose names—Agua, Fuego, Tolimán, Atitlán, Santa María, Tajumulco—evoke an unbroken history of natural disasters in one of the world's most convulsive geological regions.

We drive through Chiul, a village dominated by its civilian militia, or civil defense patrol, a dozen of whose members sit in front of the churchyard clutching vintage M-1 rifles. In February and March 1982, shortly before Ríos Montt took over the presidency, as many as five hundred residents of outlying *aldeas* of Chiul and neighboring Parraxtut—most of them unarmed men, women, and children—were brutally murdered by civil defenders from Chiul. The military commander who bullied the Chiul patrollers into committing the atrocities was evidently convinced he was dealing the guerrillas a mortal blow. Other human rights abuses occurred in Parraxtut as reported by Americas Watch and Guatemala's Attorney for Human Rights. In May 1990 two *comisionados,* or civilian commissioners appointed by the army, in that town killed a woman named María Mejía and left her companion Pedro Castro Tojín for dead after shooting him twice. But Castro Tojín survived and gave his eyewitness account to the Human Rights Attorney and the police. The couple had been active in CERJ (Runujel Junam Council of Ethnic Communities), a human rights organization that supports campesinos' constitutional right to refuse to serve in the civil defense patrols, which are ostensibly voluntary. As the protests against the murder of María Mejía mounted, the army took the highly unusual step of arresting two of its own civilian commissioners. Although the army's apparent sensitivity to international pressures was encouraging, hardly anyone expected the two men to stand trial, much less receive long prison sentences. Two weeks after their arrest, the two comisionados were released "for lack of evidence." Castro Tojín has since returned to his family in a neighboring aldea of Parraxtut, where he remains a marked man. Today, Chiul and Parraxtut are so dominated by their civil defense patrols they are two of the most militarized communities in all of Guatemala. In 1990 and 1991, hundreds of patrollers and villagers in both Chiul and Parraxtut roughed up and threatened human rights attorneys, whom they called "communists," after they were summoned by terrified residents to investigate the patrols' alleged abuses of their authority.

After an hour's climb the fog closes in. We descend a ridge, slowly, as the poorly banked road is rough and muddy from many days of sopping rains. Although we are above 8,000 feet, the hot lowland rain forests of the Ixcán and Petén are less than 100 kilometers to the north. During the classical period the Ixils carried on a lively commerce of highland salt, obsidian, and pyrite with the Mayas of Petén and Chiapas's Lacandón forest. In exchange they received rubber, animal pelts, and bird feathers. After the collapse of the Classical Mayas, the trade routes dried up. The isolated Ixils' only contact was with the wild Lacandón Mayas, who carried out raids for goods and women on the Ixil communities that lasted until the eighteenth century.

Suddenly the clouds part and the town of Santa María Nebaj, the largest in the triangle, is spread out below us. Cupped in a valley enclosed by high mountains, Nebaj's rows of whitewashed adobe and ochre-tiled houses radiate outward from the colonial church. This is my first visit to Ixil country, but I experience an immediate familiarity, as well as a sense of foreboding.

Nebaj has always been spoken of as a remote and mysterious Mayan outpost. Its inhabitants are fiercely independent; its women are fair and wear the most spectacular regional dress, or *traje*. Their language, Ixil, whose phrases abound with subtle idiosyncracies and a native gallows wit, is an offshoot of Mam that has evolved into a language so distinct it cannot be understood by any of the Ixils' neighbors. Of the twenty-two languages spoken in Guatemala by the five dominant Mayan groups, Ixil is one of the best conserved and to this day retains its community's folktales and creation myths.

On entering the town we are delighted to find all the women wearing the stunning *huipil*, or cotton blouse, interwoven with animal and floral patterns and the equally vivid red *corte*, or wraparound skirt. A distinctive feature of Nebaj dress is the long woven cloth the women coil artfully into their hair, with four to seven bouncing tassels. Although it retains traditional elements, the present-day traje has evolved from the regional dress introduced by Spanish authorities to facilitate identification and control. On seeing the two foreigners in their bright red jeep, some of the women smile openly, while others beckon us to their homes to show us their handicrafts. We soon discover that Nebaj women are willing to sell, at bargain prices, not only their precious weavings but also their oldest family treasures, or so we surmise from the array of well-worn cloth garments and wooden carvings that are laid out before us. To the outsider with money, nearly everything in Nebaj—save for their millennial pride—can be bought for a price.

As we turn the corner toward the *Pensión de las Tres Hermanas*—the three sisters—we encounter a company of soldiers in green fatigues entering the plaza from the opposite direction. They march in parade formation to the beat of a drum.

In the corridor of the pensión—a favorite with travelers—we find a group of children surrounding a foreigner who tells us he is "awaiting the colonel." He turns out to be a U.S. journalist, Edward Sheehan, who is writing a book on Central America. The colonel, he suggests, might be better disposed to join us for dinner if we added our invitation to his, which we agree to do.

The three sisters who manage the pensión are spinster daughters of ladino parents who exude an odd blend of provincial innocence and worldliness—although we soon learn that they seldom travel outside Nebaj. Their conversation, sprinkled liberally with Christian imagery and local folklore, might have leapt out of the pages of Gabriel García Márquez or Federico García Lorca, save for the jarring shift in contexts. We would hear residents of Nebaj describe the sisters as witches who practice *brujería* on their enemies after dark. But to outsiders such as ourselves, they are the soul of hospitality.

Before dinner we drop by the court house to pay a visit on Virgilio Gerónimo Guzmán, the elected mayor of Nebaj and one of the very few Ixils to hold municipal office since the ladinos arrived at the turn of the century. A Christian Democrat loyal to President Cerezo, Mayor Guzmán, who is thirty, admits to being an evangelical convert who nonetheless likes to drink and smoke. Guzmán belongs to one of Nebaj's most influential—and controversial—families, whose members include the area's first Ixil contractors for the coastal coffee plantations.

When I ask if his election has strained relations with the powerful ladino families in town, Mayor Guzmán nods affirmatively and then shakes his head. "Many ladino families have left the area since the violence broke out—but those which remain are accustomed to exercising control over our civic affairs. Lamentably, I don't expect relations between Mayas and ladinos to improve materially before the year 2000."

The close of the millennium appeared to hold a symbolic import for Mayor Guzmán, as he alluded to it repeatedly during our brief interview. When I asked for his estimate of the number of victims of the violence in Nebaj, Mayor Guzmán replied, "Lamentably, exact figures are impossible to obtain, but I would estimate that one-fourth to one-third of the population in our municipality has been killed or has fled the area since 1979."

Mayor Guzmán would not speculate on what percentage of the victims had been killed or displaced by the army, but he blamed the guerrillas for provoking most of the killings. He then came up with the startling estimate that at least 25 percent of the Nebaj municipality's six hundred square kilometers were still under guerrilla control. The mayor's estimate flatly contradicted the military's claim to have the entire Ixil territory under their domination.

"Nine villages have been liberated by the army and turned into 'model villages,'" the mayor said, "but seven others are still on the guerrilla side of the line."

"I am not a friend of the guerrillas," Mayor Guzmán concluded, "and I believe they have to shoulder most of the blame for the violence that has been unleashed on our community. But until they showed up, our people were mired in official neglect. At least now the government in the capital is beginning to pay some attention to our needs."

The Catholic Sisters of Charity were about to open a new orphanage next to the town church. A census of the orphans of the violence carried out in 1984 by a commission for Guatemala's Supreme Court found 120,000 children in the highlands who had lost one or both parents. The new orphanage was to care for several dozen orphans and nearly three hundred undernourished children from Nebaj alone; and I was later to visit with evangelical pastors who were looking after two hundred other undernourished children and orphans.

Father Juan Vásquez, the young parish priest of Nebaj, arrived in 1982 from Guatemala City as church deacon. He is tall and slender for a Guatemalan and looks younger than his thirty years. When we spoke in the parish center, he admitted feeling apprehensive about serving in the Ixil parish. His mother, convinced that he would disappear, had wept for days when he received the cardinal's letter. She had good cause for concern. Father José María Gran Cirera, a Spanish clergyman and former diocesan priest of Chajul, had been murdered by the army soon after he witnessed the shooting by nervous soldiers of eighteen women who had marched to the Nebaj barracks to inquire after their men. As a result of this and two other murders of Sacred Heart priests and of dozens of lay catechists, the bishop of Quiché, who was also forced to flee, had withdrawn all clergy from the diocese in 1980.

Father Vásquez was among the first priests to return to Quiché. He described his task as one of reconciliation with his parishioners, who had felt abandoned and exposed to army recriminations after the clergy withdrew. I asked him how he viewed the challenge to the church posed by the growing evangelical influence.

"We maintain correct but distant relations with the evangelicals, some of whose pastoral aims coincide with our own. They have had success in winning over some of our parishioners who feel they will have protection from the army after they convert, but that is not always the case. This parish used to be 90 percent Catholic and 10 percent animist; now the evangelicals represent about 30 percent. But I believe that their influence has peaked, and many are returning to the fold."

3

On our return to the pensión we are joined in the dining room by Edward Sheehan and an American couple who work for UNICEF. At about 8 P.M., just as we are finishing our dinner, a stocky ladino in a straw rancher's hat and boots swaggers into the dining room, with a plainclothes bodyguard at each shoulder.

"Comandante! How good that you've come!" Sheehan calls out in Spanish.

"Forgive my lateness," the comandante says, with no trace of apology. "We have been to a neighboring barracks to win at volleyball." (He uses the military term *vencer* rather than the sporting *ganar*.)

Though known as the colonel, the comandante is, in fact, only an infantry captain. He sits down at the table with his two bodyguards behind him and immediately sets the rules for our tête-à-tête.

"No English spoken here," he announces, as his dark eyes dart to either end of the table, taking us in. I surmise that he has been drawn here by curiosity and by a jousting impulse. He has come to take our measure.

"We have been talking about ideas," Sheehan cues him, "and their place in history."

The comandante smiles confidently. He is on familiar ground. He is about thirty-five, and no more than 5'7", but he has a commanding presence. He is endowed with a thick chest and neck, marred by a hint of a double chin. In another ten years he will require oversize custom-made uniforms, like most of Guatemala's top brass. His black eyes are bright, challenging. A European woman staying at the pensión remarks later, "The comandante is not unattractive, but he has a cruel mouth." Like most officers of the Guatemalan army, the captain is a native of the ladino eastern provinces near the Salvadoran border, but he claims to speak several Mayan languages and quotes liberally from the *Popol Vuh.*

"Outside of history, ideas are mere abstractions," the comandante says. "They must be tested by events. Ideas are empty vessels until they have become . . ."

"Materialized?" suggests one of the UNICEF representatives.

"Yes, exactly. Ideas in history are meaningless until they become manifest in concrete events."

"You know, comandante," puts in George Lovell, "forgive my saying so, but that happens to be a fundamental Marxist concept."

The comandante blanches, but his composure falters only an instant. "Then it is a contradiction," he parries. "Obviously, by training and by vocation I am anti-Marxist. But I have studied *Das Kapital* and others of their writings, and dammit—," he slaps his hand on the table, "those Marxists have stolen our language!"

Firmly in command, the captain turns homilitic. "In the military we believe that when we come to know someone, we value that person. When we value that person, we defend him. That is true of all those who enlist voluntarily in the army or are recruited by the army. Once we come to know them, we value them and we defend

A sergeant in the paratroops of the Guatemalan army.

Margarita, an Ixil woman who fled a guerrilla-controlled village north of Nebaj.

Margarita and her acutely undernourished son in Las Violetas, an internationally funded refugee camp in Nebaj.

A patriotism session in Xemamatzé, the U.N.-administered repatriation camp in Nebaj, controlled by the Guatemalan army.

Juana, an invalid who served as translator for refugee and captured Ixils in Xemamatzé.

The "Three Sisters," proprietors of Nebaj's popular pensión, Las Tres Hermanas.

them." He pauses as his restless eyes range over ours, testing our response.

"In the case of soldiers who come from broken families, we take the place of that family. We become both father and mother. We help to uphold that person's moral and religious principles.

"Now, this is also the case with those who seek our protection. Villagers whose homes have been sacked and burned by subversives; villagers who have fled to the mountains—and yes, even those who have lived with the guerrillas . . . If they accept our offer of amnesty and return in good faith to their villages—just as a family of eleven did this past week, who came down from the mountains, starving, their clothes all in tatters because the guerrillas neither fed them nor protected them—when they return in good faith to seek our protection, we come to know them, we learn to value them, and we defend them."

After a tense silence, Sheehan mentioned the mayor of Cotzal, whom he had interviewed the day before. Mayor Sánchez had given a very different account of the villagers and townspeople who returned from the mountains and who had to undergo a rigorous "reeducation" before being placed in so-called model villages.

The comandante bristled. "What mayor did you speak to?"

"The only mayor, so far as I know," Sheehan said. "Nicolás Sánchez."

"Well, you did not speak to the mayor of Cotzal," the captain said, his eyes flashing. "The mayor of Cotzal is an Indian who does not speak Spanish."

"Yes, Mayor Sánchez is an Ixil Maya, and his Spanish is somewhat halting; but he expressed himself quite clearly on the subject of the reeducation of—"

The comandante threw up his hands, signaling an end to discussion on this topic. "The mayor may speak Spanish," he said, "but he does not understand it."

Since we intended to visit Cotzal, we chose not to challenge the comandante's extraordinary statement; and Sheehan evidently decided that he had pushed him far enough.

"Ask your so-called mayor," the captain went on, "who built the road from Nebaj to Cotzal that allows him to travel freely in the area? Who erected the medical clinic that looks after the health of his constituents; who built the school that educates his children? The so-called mayor of Cotzal is an evangelical. Ask him if he reads his Bible: Saint Paul's Epistle to the Romans 13, where it says, 'Everyone has to obey authority, for it was placed there by God.' Ask this little mayor of yours, who set up the model villages that provide shelter, running water, electricity, and free provisions to his neighbors who have fled persecution by the guerrillas? If you had spoken to the duly elected mayor of Cotzal, instead of to an obvious impostor, he would have given you the correct answers to all of these questions—the only possible answers." Again he slapped his hand on the table, which caused his two bodyguards, who sat in stony silence, to smile with the faintest suggestion of menace.

"The fact is that the army is the only bulwark against a guerrilla organization armed with sophisticated weaponry supplied by Cuba, the USSR, and Nicaragua. We believe the war against subversion is total, permanent, and universal—and we must defeat the communists not only in their mountain hideouts but in every city, town, village, and hamlet. In the words of Mao Zedong, with whom I'm certain all of you here are familiar, our aim is to drain the ocean to flush out the fish."

The captain's outburst subsided as suddenly as it flared up. "As you can see," he said smiling, "I have been well trained by your compatriots." The comandante had received part of his military training at a U.S. army base in the Panama Canal Zone.

But he had little else good to say about the United States, which he referred to several times as a modern "Roman Empire" that had entered a spiritual and moral decline. He reserved most of his praise for Israel, which had sent arms and advisers to Guatemala after 1977, when President Carter threatened to suspend military credits because of the army's abysmal record of human rights abuses—the worst in the Western Hemisphere. "Israel today is stronger and more united than your country. They are a nation of soldiers who know how to work their lands and uphold moral principles. They are surrounded by enemies, but no one dares to tread on Israel. That is a model worth emulating!"

Not only Israel but Taiwan, South Africa, Argentina, and Somoza's National Guard have served as models for the Guatemalan army, and most of these countries have provided arms and technical training as well. One of the captain's predecessors as commander of Nebaj was Colonel Mario Aquino Flores, who had trained at Fort Bragg, North Carolina, and whose proficient English made him a persuasive lobbyist for more military aid whenever U.S. congressmen flew into the country. Colonel Flores fought with South African troops against Namibian guerrillas, and taught military intelligence courses in El Salvador, aimed at winning hearts and minds in the civilian population.

The comandante surprised us by shifting to literary terrain and laying siege to it as determinedly as he had to all other subjects under discussion. He expressed some admiration for Latin America's Nobel Prize winners in literature—Miguel Angel Asturias, Gabriel García Márquez, Pablo Neruda—but he then accused them of writing negatively about their countries. "Name me one work by a Latin American Nobel Prize winner that is not critical of his country," he challenged.

After some reflection, I brought up Chilean Gabriela Mistral's poems to motherhood and Asturias's *Men of Maize*.

"Those are exceptions that prove nothing," the comandante said. "All of Asturias's other works are stains on Guatemala's honor, and *El Señor Presidente* is a direct incitement to commit violence against the state. And the same can be said of García Márquez and Neruda. When they traveled abroad or took up diplomatic posts, they said terrible things about their governments."

In another abrupt shift, the comandante asked which of us thought that General Augusto Pinochet would not last as president of Chile until 1989.

Hesitantly, I raised my hand and put forward the opinion that General Pinochet would be out of office in less than a year.

The comandante smiled. "My friend," he said, "you know nothing about military solidarity. The only one who can overthrow General Pinochet is Uncle Sam, and I rather doubt he has the will or the desire to do so."

When he brought up patriotism once again and claimed the military sets a moral and spiritual example for the entire nation, I took a calculated risk. Citing Plato, which I knew would impress the comandante, I spoke of the perils posed to a democratic republic when any of its institutions—the army, for example—oversteps its assigned functions and becomes the sole moral arbiter. The captain's eyes narrowed as all the humor went out of them. He had guessed my drift at once, and I desisted from pressing my argument when he flung up his arms and burst out, "*Yo no sé quién es Usted!*" (I don't know who you are.)

My next encounter with the comandante was in December, at a reception for the papal nuncio in Nebaj. The captain was ending his tour of duty in the Ixil Triangle and seemed relaxed and jovial. He recognized me at once, and pointed to his digital watch as he approached me.

"I am winning, you know," he said, smiling. "General Pinochet has lasted four more months in office."

I conceded to the comandante that he would most likely win his bet.

The morning after our dinner with the comandante we paid a visit to Brother Andrés Velasco Brito, an evangelical preacher who had been converted by an American Methodist missionary, Donald Lawrence, fifteen years earlier.

Brother Andrés, who is thirty-five and fair-complexioned enough to pass for a ladino, is heir to the most powerful of Nebaj's principal Ixil families. His great grandfather had been a *b'alb'axtix,* or Ixil shaman. Andrés's grandmother once saw him escape from an unjust imprisonment "as if by magic." His grand uncle, Diego Brito, one of the first Nebaj Mayas to attend secondary school, had married a ladina and amassed a modest fortune as a labor contractor for coastal planters. Nevertheless, Diego had been a leader of the 1936 march on the court house. Andrés's younger brother, also named Diego, was the Christian Democrat congressional deputy for northern Quiché.

Brother Andrés is proud of his brother's winning elective office but fears that his sojourn in the capital might turn his head and make him forget his origins. "When my brother Diego comes to town, the first thing we look for is the way he dresses. If he puts on airs and wears a tie and jacket, we'll know he has become a ladino and is no longer one of us."

He expressed similar misgivings about Mayor Guzmán, a member of a rival principal Ixil family, which has also converted to Protestantism. "My brother Diego helped to put Gerónimo Guzmán in office. But now Guzmán is starting to drink too much, which violates our religious precepts. And although he has become friendly with powerful ladinos in the capital and is building himself a new home, Guzmán has not brought any material benefits to our municipality, which is flat broke."

Brother Andrés, an eloquent and forthright pastor, was the first member of his family to renounce Catholicism, for which he was shunned and even beaten by his uncles and older brothers; eventually, however, the rest of the family also converted. Brother Andrés was in charge of an orphan-support program in the evangelical community. He calculated that there were at least a thousand orphans in Nebaj's outlying villages and hamlets and hundreds more in town. "Our work is only a drop in the ocean," he said, "but it is a beginning."

Like other members of his community, Andrés walks a tightrope between the Mayan and ladino communities and between the guerrillas and the military. Far from its being an asset to him and his wife, who has fair skin and light brown hair as he does, their Caucasian appearance seems to intensify the ladinos' disdain.

Brother Andrés's father, Juan Velasco, was killed by the army after the EGP laid an ambush near his house that killed several soldiers. "My father was sympathetic to the guerrillas," Andrés said, "as we all were. But he refused to become a part of them. They would come into town and say to us, 'Look how the ladinos treat us—worse than dogs. Their landowners' dogs eat better than we do. They have cars, while we have to walk. They have lights in their homes—where is your light? Let's fight for our rights.' And we knew in our hearts that they were right. Many of us committed ourselves and joined them in the mountains, but my father knew that disaster would follow, and he would not commit himself. When the guerrillas planned the ambush near our house, my father heard of it and went up into the villages where some of them lived and begged them not to endanger his family. And so they did not lay the ambush. But three months later they came down to lay an ambush about one hundred meters from the house and killed some soldiers. The next day the army came to kill my father. They did not torture him first because they knew he was not a guerrilla; but they burned down our house and killed our livestock. Some months later I met one of the villagers who had laid the ambush on a mountain trail. I accused him of having caused my father's death, but he denied it. And then he said, 'If you denounce me, I will be killed first—and you will be second.'

"The guerrillas made too many promises," Andrés concluded. "They told us they would defeat the army in three months if all of us participated. But they were like the boy who cried wolf. When the real wolf came, he was much bigger and more powerful than any of them ever imagined."

Brother Andrés calculated that at least half the population of the Ixil Triangle had given the guerrillas material or logistical aid between 1979 and 1986, and another 30 percent "supported them in [their] hearts. Today, I would be surprised if more than 5 percent actively help the guerrillas." Andrés estimated that as many as ten thousand residents of Nebaj had been killed "between two fires," and he assured us thousands more were still hiding in the mountains.

Like most evangelicals, Brother Andrés had supported José Efraín Ríos Montt, the evangelical general who became president as a result of an army coup shortly before Lucas García's term ended. He said Ríos Montt was not the wild-eyed fanatic and butcher of Indians the foreign press made him out to be. He had tried to follow a coherent program of civic reforms and economic development, but he had been undermined by local commanders who disliked Indians and took matters into their own hands. In the end, power lust undid Ríos Montt's best intentions, according to Andrés. "He lost his humility and favored his own followers over everyone else. That's when the army turned against him."

The evangelical sects, while hardly immune from army persecution, tend to maintain far better public relations with the military than the Catholic church. Since 1976, the church has shed its monolithic conservatism of centuries past and spawned "progressive" Christian base communities and Acción Católica, which the military regards as hotbeds of insurgency. Thousands of practicing Catholics in the Ixil Triangle converted in the hope of gaining a measure of protection; thousands of others who lived through the earthquake of February 1976 found the evangelicals' apocalyptic prophecies in tune with their experience. Ríos Montt, who claims—rightly—that he was defrauded of an electoral victory when he ran for president as a Christian Democrat in 1974, subsequently became a convert to the Church of the Word, an offshoot of the California-based Gospel Outreach fundamentalist movement.

The head of Gospel Outreach, a real estate broker and reformed alcoholic named Jim Durkin, became Ríos Montt's personal counselor after he seized the presidency with the help of rebellious junior officers in March 1982. To Durkin and his followers, the ascendancy of Ríos Montt provided a golden opportunity to propagate their teachings throughout Guatemala, which they hoped to convert into the first Latin American country with a Protestant majority by the early 1990s. Ríos Montt's born-again zeal seemed to fit the bill perfectly. In his free-wheeling television addresses to the nation he reiterated that he had become president "not by bullets, boots, or votes, but by the hand of God."

The seventeen months of Ríos Montt's Plan Victory—and of his short-lived presidency—coincided with a period of relative calm in Guatemala's cities and larger towns, where the notorious paramilitary death squadrons suspended operations. Hundreds of common criminals as well as avowed Marxist rebels were tried in ad hoc military tribunals. Of the fifteen that were sentenced to death, nine were executed before the tribunals were suspended, partly in response to the protests of the visiting Pope John Paul II. In the Ixil Triangle and other parts of the western and central highlands, the most intensive phase of military counterinsurgency began. Ríos Montt's scorched-earth policy destroyed a total of 440 villages and killed at least 10,000 Guatemalans, most of them descendants of the Mayas.

Gospel Outreach regards the Guatemalan highlands as one of the battlegrounds for the inevitable showdown between heralds of Christ's Second Coming and purveyors of the satanic tenets of Liberation Theology. David Stoll's study of the church in *Harvest of Violence* (Carmack, 1988) uncovered baser material motives. He quotes a Church of the Word elder's prediction that the fundamentalist gospel would transform Guatemala into a "spiritual stronghold" to prevent rich oil and titanium reserves from falling into Marxist hands. The elder envisioned an evangelized Guatemala as a buffer between the United States and the communist advance and warned ominously, "After Guatemala, only Mexico remains!" In one of several bizarre twists connected with this chapter in Guatemalan history, the "Israel of the New World" under evangelist Ríos Montt was armed and trained by unevangelized Old World Israelis.

Other evangelicals chose the paths of philanthropy and enlightened self-help. Helen and Ray Elliott of the Summer Institute of Linguistics and Wycliffe Bible Translators (SIL/WBT), who arrived in Nebaj in 1953, assisted in the implementation of Ríos Montt's "beans and rifles" program. They trucked large supplies of medicines, housing materials, and food provisions into the Ixil area. They also attempted to raise the local military commander's appreciation of Indian values and recommended the army improve its image in the community by paying Mayan laborers for obligatory services and supplying better weapons to the civil patrols. In August 1982, an Ixil evangelical converted by Ray Elliott led the midnight exodus of 287 evangelicals from the village of Salquil Grande, which was then under guerrilla control. The battle to wrest the souls of Guatemala's new converts from the clutches of godless guerrillas was rapidly gaining ground.

The Elliotts' efforts to "turn the Ixil area around" seemed even nearer fruition when Ríos Montt announced that his Church of the Word had selected Love Lift International, the relief arm of Gospel Outreach, to "coordinate the involvement of Christian ministries and churches . . . in relief and development projects" for the displaced persons of Guatemala. The Love Lift plan called for an immediate delivery of food and housing supplies to the Ixil area, which was to be accomplished through consciousness-raising and fund-raising among North American fundamentalists. Representative Jack Kemp, Reverend Pat Robertson, and others would raise $1 billion to send a ship loaded with relief and building supplies to Guatemala by January 1983.

The grandiose Love Lift scheme collapsed even before Ríos Montt was ousted from office by General Mejía Víctores in another palace coup in August 1983. The Church of the Word's messianic anticommunism, combined with Gospel Outreach's extravagant philanthropy to save Indian souls, apparently proved too rich a mixture for Guatemala's hard-nosed generals, most of whom remained nominally Catholic and who felt they were not getting their slice of the pie.

When I met with Ray Elliott at the SIL/WBT mission in Guatemala City, he spoke warmly of Ríos Montt but regretted that Jim Durkin's obsession with Armageddon had impaired Ríos Montt's ability to maintain support from fellow officers. Elliott was harshly critical of the army's activities in the Ixil area and said he feared a total military victory as much as a guerrilla takeover.

"One way or another," he said, "the Indian always gets it in the neck."

Despite the overthrow of Ríos Montt, the evangelical tide in the Ixil Triangle was not easily reversed. Although SIL/WBT's contract has been terminated by Vinicio Cerezo, the Elliotts and other missionaries hang on stubbornly to their spheres of influence in the Mayan highlands and with key ladino officials and congressmen. SIL/WBT plans to be in Guatemala at the dawn of the new millennium, after the last "unreached peoples" have been converted and Christ's Second Kingdom is assured.

Approximately one-third of Guatemala's population has converted to one of dozens of Pentecostal and fundamentalist sects, and in spite of Father Vásquez's disclaimer, their numbers appear to be growing. (Notwithstanding the intense recruitment, however, Nebaj's evangelical churches began reporting a rise in drop-outs and absentees, starting in 1989.) Since his ouster, Ríos Montt has returned to the evangelical circuit in the United States and Guatemala, where he remains a magnetic and popular, if less than messianic, preacher.

On his return to Guatemala to launch his presidential campaign in 1991, Ríos Montt was immediately proclaimed the frontrunner in all the early polls. In the highlands, thousands of supporters promoted his candidacy, despite a constitutional ban against his seeking reelection. "The Guatemalan people know who I am, and what I stand for," he told his masses of cheering supporters. "I stand with the law, but if we are denied our rightful victory, we will take to the streets." The divine light of madness in Ríos Montt's eyes shone brighter than ever.

5

⬚

Cotzal

"The army killed us like dogs."

Nicolás Sánchez, former mayor of Cotzal

The town of San Juan Cotzal, where we expected to meet Mayor Nicolás Sánchez, looked half-deserted. The scars of army occupation were visible everywhere. Emaciated dogs, ducks, and chickens roamed freely in the empty plaza. Few of the women in the streets, weaving rope from long strands of maguey, wore the regional dress. As we drove in, two soldiers stood at the entrance to the church with Galil rifles at the ready. The comandante of Nebaj had assured us that all Ixil residents had complete freedom of movement. "If you see soldiers in any of the towns," he said, "they are most likely on an errand." On spying us, the two soldiers lowered their weapons and took off down the street as if they were, in effect, running an errand. At the opposite end of the church sat a dozen members of the civil defense patrol, who serve in rotating twenty-four-hour shifts at least once a week. Most of them were armed with World War II vintage M-1 rifles. They looked dour and dejected. In other highland towns, the civil patrols have been voted out since Cerezo took office; in the three Ixil municipalities and in the model villages, the civil patrols remain vigorously in place.

We stepped inside the church and were shocked to find a vast empty nave. Well up toward the front of the basilica, seated on a dozen benches were about twenty women on the right and three men on the left. In stark contrast to the churches of Nebaj and Chajul, the walls looked barren, and there was no evidence of a priest in at-

90

tendance. At the height of the violence the icons and reliquaries had been removed and placed in storage. Two wooden saints now stood against the western wall: a blue-robed Christ whose hands were tied with rope, his blood-stained face hidden behind a broken pane of glass. Next to him stood a mater dolorosa with the left eye socket empty.

Of the three Ixil municipalities, Cotzal has been the most heavily exploited by landowners. While wages in the rest of the highlands and on the coastal plantations average about two quetzales for a day's work picking coffee or cotton, the Brol family and other local planters paid seasonal workers one quetzal (around 30 U.S. cents) a day.

Paul Townsend, a Summer Institute of Linguistics colleague of Ray and Helen Elliott's, raised literacy levels in Cotzal by starting a bilingual school program in the outlying villages. Although it is tuition free, the mission school exacts a cultural price. Linguists with the Academy of Mayan Languages accuse the SIL/WBT of using bilingual texts to wean the Mayan children away from their native tongues. Like the Elliotts, Townsend actively supported Ríos Montt's declared intention of "humanizing" the army's activities in the highlands.

In January 1982 an Ixil Pentecostal pastor from Cotzal who worked with Townsend—Nicolás Toma—assisted in the formation of the first civilian militia in the altiplano. When Ríos Montt seized office two months later, he turned these civilian militias into the Civil Self-Defense Patrol (PAC) and eventually instituted them throughout the highlands. The organization of the first civil patrols in Cotzal laid the groundwork for the EGP's early defeats in the triangle. After a brother of Pastor Nicolás's was killed with sixty-three other Cotzaleños in an army reprisal, the embittered church-man blamed the guerrillas for provoking the army. Pastor Nicolás used his contacts to help the army expose the EGP infrastructure linking Cotzal to its outlying villages. The local army comandante at the time evidently believed all Cotzal residents to be EGP collaborators and warned the pastor that anyone who did not move into town and march with the patrols would be shot on sight. The impact of this directive on the Mayan communities was devastating. Several months later, when a government official visited Cotzal, he discovered that of the twenty-nine villages and hamlets on his list, only three remained standing. The rest had been torched after their residents were killed or driven out by the army and the civil patrols.

From a few hundred patrollers in Cotzal, Chajul, and Nebaj early in 1982, the civil defense patrols had grown by 1986 to nearly a million; that is, close to 90 percent of all Mayan highland males between the ages of fourteen and sixty became unpaid servants of the army. By mobilizing campesinos in every town and village infiltrated by guerrilla ideology and training them to ferret out guerrilla sympathizers, the army hit on a tactic to co-opt peasant militancy without having to pay them a soldier's wages. No other program reflected more insidiously the military's plans for "pacifying" the countryside. In 1984 a British parliamentary report denounced the civil defense patrols as a "form of involuntary slavery" that forced peasants to participate in the kidnapping, torture, and murder of their own neighbors or risk suffering a similar fate themselves.

In 1992, at around 500,000, the civil defense patrols continued to be the largest civilian militia in Latin America and one of the largest in the world. There is no more humiliating spectacle in the highlands than the sight of schoolboys and gray-haired elders reduced to a common degradation as they shuffle along a country road, cowed and glassy-eyed, carrying wooden rifles—or old M-1's—and a Guatemalan flag. Catholic prelates have denounced the patrols with particular vehemence, in part because they compete with church attendance and religious observance. In a pastoral letter of May 1983, Guatemala's bishops called them "an imposed service of obligatory nature, which weighs upon the weakest and neediest of the country." Guatemala's former Supreme Court President Edmundo Vásquez Martínez told Americas Watch the civil patrol system is "unconstitutional, illegal, and despicable."

The roots of the civil patrol system can be found in the Indian militias raised by colonial Spanish *hacendados* as private armies. The head of these militias was usually an Indian *principal*, who was also in charge of collecting tribute so that, in effect, these early "slave patrols" had to pay for the privilege of protecting their masters.

In Santa Cruz del Quiché in July 1988 the Runujel Junam Council of Ethnic Communities (CERJ) began the first organized efforts to resist induction into the patrols. In Quiché, the organization's name means "We are all equal." Its founder, the forty-year-old ladino schoolteacher Amílcar Méndez Urízar, has received numerous threats to his life, amid accusations that he works hand in glove with the guerrillas. Since CERJ was founded, twenty-five Mayan members who exercized their constitutional rights by refusing to march in civil defense patrols have been killed or disappeared by soldiers and death squadrons.

2

Walking from the Cotzal church, past some of the most ruinous dirt and cobble streets we had seen, with rows of gutted houses and new construction, we came to Mayor Sánchez's house. Apparently it was undergoing renovation, as there was not a single stick of furniture in sight, except for the chair on which the mayor sat. The anteroom of his house served as his private office and also as a storefront where he sold soap and other staples. Eight men sat on the floor with their backs to the wall.

Mayor Sánchez is a sturdy man in his early forties, with the burnished complexion and high cheekbones typical of the highland Maya. He was dressed in cotton pants and a shirt open at the neck, as were his deputies and municipal officers, all of whom were also members of the town's civil defense patrol.

We accommodated ourselves on a plank, and I asked Nicolás Sánchez how he came to be mayor of Cotzal. He spoke in a clipped, heavily accented but perfectly comprehensible Spanish. "I was elected mayor by the small number of residents of this municipality who voted," Mayor Sánchez said. "Most of them were too frightened to cast a ballot."

"But I understand that voting was obligatory, and the government levied a five-quetzal penalty on those who failed to vote."

"Well, yes, but that is not easy to enforce. So many of our people have fled their villages and hamlets, only those in town could be fined for not voting. So it was mostly they who elected me mayor, by the grace of God."

"Are you a Christian Democrat, like Cerezo?"

"Yes and no. The people of Cotzal no longer belong to political parties. It's too risky. But I would say most of them sympathize with the president, although they have never seen him, and very few know what he stands for."

"What do you think he represents?"

"An end to the violence." He passed a hand through his thick black hair. "Also, economic improvement for the poor. The opportunity to find work."

"And have any of these things come about?"

The mayor smiled thinly, with inexpressibly sad eyes. "Only a little, to the extent the army lets them. Well, it is quieter now than before, by the grace of God. But I am not certain it is due to Cerezo. We have no relief economically. There is no work in Cotzal. We have nothing to eat. We have no beans, no meat or eggs, as we did in times past—only a few kernels of corn we scratch out of the hillsides." He shrugged. "But at least it is quieter now than some years ago."

"What is the population of Cotzal municipality?"

"It is very difficult to say. Many people are only now beginning to come back, particularly to the villages. Altogether, perhaps five to six thousand. There were many more before the turbulence."

"And how large was the population of Cotzal before 'the turbulence,' as you call it? Let's say, eight or nine years ago?"

The mayor consulted his deputies. The figure they agreed on was "approximately twenty thousand" for the entire municipality, or about five thousand above the last official census, taken in 1977.

"Twenty thousand? You mean three-quarters of your population is gone?"

"That is one way to put it," said Mayor Sánchez. "We know many of our people went down to the coast, to Santa Lucía Cotzumalguapa and other towns, where they look for work. Perhaps five to six thousand are still there."

I pointed out that this still did not account for nearly half the population of eight years ago. "What happened to the remaining nine or ten thousand?"

"Many of them have been killed," Mayor Sánchez said. He consulted his officers once more. "Perhaps five to six thousand are not accounted for. We cannot be certain because the outlying villages and hamlets are inaccessible, and some residents are still hiding out in the mountains. Here in town there may be three thousand."

"Mayor Sánchez," I said, taking a deep breath, "who killed these thousands of people?"

"The army," he said, without a moment's hesitation. "The army killed most of them. A few were killed by the guerrillas after Ríos Montt declared an amnesty in 1982. Some of our people who had fled to the mountains believed in the amnesty and tried to return, and that is when the guerrillas killed some of them. But not many. The army killed most of our people who are missing."

"How were they killed, Mayor Sánchez?"

"The army killed us like *chuchos* [dogs]. I myself saw many killed with my own eyes—old men, women, and children. After the guerrillas came in 1979 to recruit people—and particularly after they killed Don Enrique Brol—the army occupied the town. First they killed the civic leaders and all those they suspected of collaborating with the guerrillas. They drew up lists and took advantage of personal antagonisms among ourselves to denounce people whether they helped the guerrillas or not. Most of the heads of the religious brotherhoods—*cofradías*—and those involved with Acción Católica were killed. We would find them in the morning, mutilated, with missing limbs and eyes. This way they killed nearly all our leading townspeople. That is when our people started to leave town. In the villages the soldiers killed people more openly, because they had no fear of outside witnesses. First they massacred the people, and then they burned the villages down. We know of twenty-four villages and hamlets that have been destroyed.

"By 1980, many hundreds had left. There was no food. Our cattle and poultry were killed. Our fields were scorched. Our houses were burned. We can no longer keep our *costumbres,* because we have no animals to offer for our feast days and our weddings. We have no money for yarn to weave our native dress, our huipiles, so our women wear towels instead. Toward the end of 1981 there were only forty or forty-five people left here in town, and that is when they came to bomb our houses with incendiary bombs, and their helicopters strafed our roofs with bullets. I was here. I lived through it all."

"Mayor Sánchez, are you not concerned about the consequences of telling us all this?"

He sat up straight. "I am an evangelical. I owe no one—neither the guerrillas nor the army—and therefore I fear no one except for

God, because of whose grace my life has been spared. Everyone here can tell you what the army has done to us and to our town, how they have killed us and robbed us of our dignity. We are humans, not dogs, to be treated in this way."

One of the municipal officers who had become increasingly agitated spoke up. "They force us to march in the civil patrols, to do their dirty work for them, and they pay us nothing for it."

"What kind of work?"

"We are forced to march and seek out subversives. If we do not find them, we are accused of hiding them or of being subversives ourselves. They force us to search the houses of our neighbors as if they were criminals. They tell us again and again: 'You must turn in anyone who is a subversive, even if it is your own mother or father.' They force us to march in twenty-four-hour shifts that take us away from our fields and our families, and when we return we are too exhausted to work. And all of this we have to do without pay."

"Can't you refuse to march?"

Several men spoke at once.

"If we refuse," one of the officers said, "they call us subversives and throw us in jail—or they kill us. Only those who have money can buy their way out of patrolling, but who has money anymore? No one."

"I used to have cattle," said another municipal officer. "I had my own ranch and twenty head of cattle. Eleven of them have been stolen or killed. The army says the guerrillas did it—but I know better."

Mayor Sánchez said, "The army divides us by turning neighbor against neighbor. They exploit the tensions between Catholics and evangelicals, they prey on old animosities between families. We used to be a united community that was able to resolve our differences in a peaceful way. But not anymore. Everyone is afraid of everyone else because they know almost anyone could be an *oreja* [ear, or informer]."

The officer who had spoken first stood up to speak again, gesturing with open palms. "Two years ago, they even forced us to kill our own people. The army would lead the patrols in sweeps of the town, to places where guerrilla sympathizers were thought to be hiding. They would take them out and force us to kill them, so that our hands would be stained with blood, and they could claim that they were blameless, that this was a matter among ourselves. That is why so many of us fled to the mountains or refused to patrol and would rather accept the army's punishment."

The municipal officer who owned cattle burst in again. "And in the villages it is much worse. I went with a patrol into the mountains, where my wife's family lived. The patrollers went ahead, then a platoon of soldiers; the officers were in back and took no part in the operation. We were told that anyone we encountered was a guerrilla, even if it was a friend or our own relative, because only guerrillas lived in those mountains. They forced us to stop and kill anyone they pleased—even women and children; they made us cut them up with machetes, even as they knelt before us and begged for mercy. Now we are not able to look our neighbors in the eyes."

I had spoken with hundreds of Guatemalans in Mexican refugee camps, where they felt free to speak their minds. None of them had been more forthcoming about the horrors they had lived through than Mayor Sánchez and his municipal officers.

Collecting myself, I said to Mayor Sánchez, "Last week we spoke with the comandante in Nebaj, and he denied that you are the mayor of Cotzal. He said the mayor of Cotzal is an Indian who does not speak Spanish, and if he does speak Spanish, he does not understand it."

Mayor Sánchez reflected a moment.

"What comandante are you speaking of? I don't know any comandante. I know only his soldiers, his bullets, and his bombs."

When I revisited Cotzal four months later, Mayor Sánchez was overseeing the paving of the street that went past his house. He told me that the government was providing a hundred thousand quetzales for street repair and new road construction and that this had already eased the unemployment in town. This time he proposed we meet in his office atop the municipal building, which was guarded by three soldiers with the short-cropped hair and ramrod postures of *kaibiles*.

Mayor Sánchez wore a hat and appeared decidedly more bullish about his job than the last time we spoke. When one of his deputies joined us, I asked if they had come up with a firmer figure for Cotzal's dead and missing. He said, "Our current estimate is that 7,500 died in Cotzal municipality." But he then astonished me by putting all the blame squarely on the guerrillas.

"They are the ones," he said, "who abused our good will for their own selfish aims."

When I asked about the situation in the countryside, he assured me that things were much calmer now and that the guerrillas controlled "only two or three villages."

"The civil patrols are now entirely voluntary," he said, "and anyone can go work on the coast any time they wish. Right now, many of our men are cutting sugarcane in Santa Rosa, which is why the town may look empty to you. There is *pisto* [money] now in the town, and our costumbres are coming back." And it was true that several women were weaving the colorful regional huipiles on backstrap looms in their courtyards.

"And all of this because of the money the government gave you for the roads?"

The Mayor nodded and then grinned.

"But what happens when the roads are finished?"

"You don't understand." Mayor Sánchez shook his head, with the fixed grin on his face. "There will be many roads. More money is being contracted by the Army Corps of Engineers for a road to Cunén that will connect Cotzal directly with Uspantán and the central highlands. We are coming into our own."

Mayor Sánchez devoted the remainder of our interview to an evangelical homily denouncing the "pernicious" guerrillas who lived on the sweat of the poor and advanced their purposes by exploiting the poverty and *envidia* endemic in Mayan communities. He made a passing allusion to Romans 13, and Saint Paul's injunction to obey temporal authority. His final denunciation was in the form of a direct quote from "my good friend Pedro Brol," the "more reasonable" older brother of Enrique.

Evidently, Mayor Sánchez had learned the comandante's language.

Eleven months after my second interview with Mayor Sánchez, I met in Guatemala City with congressional deputy Diego Velasco Brito, the thirty-year-old younger brother of the Protestant pastor Andrés. Although Diego is nearly as light-complexioned as his brother, the congressman's suit and tie did not entirely disguise the aquiline Mayan nose and high cheeks. He assured me that he and eight other elected indigenous delegates were drafting legislation to protect the Mayan communities' land titles, civil rights, regional languages, and costumbres. And he said they were also working to make the civil patrols strictly voluntary, in accordance with the Constitution. (Despite Mayor Sánchez's assertion, patrol duty in Cotzal was still in fact compulsory.) He also said that he had embarked on a campaign to buy large tracts of land from the Samayoa family, which would be parceled out to landless peasants.

Turning somber, Congressman Velasco Brito confided that Mayor Sánchez was under juridical investigation over the purchase of a house and several lots that were far beyond his means on a mayoral salary. He added that the Ixil mayor of Chajul was in jail on charges of embezzlement, and Nebaj's Mayor Guzmán was driven to alcoholism by his frustrations in office. (In 1988 a posse of Nebajeños denounced Mayor Guzmán for numerous acts of corruption in office and rode him out of town. It required the personal intervention of the local governor to reinstate Mayor Guzmán so that he could complete his term. His successor, Diego Rivera Santiago, another Ixil Protestant and Christian Democrat, nearly suffered the same fate. In 1991 Nebajeños voted in a ladino mayor, Obdulio Herrera Cano.)

Hinting that he'd had personal problems of his own, Congressman Velasco Brito credited his evangelical faith with helping him maintain his balance. "Our people are not aware of the pressures that come down on us when we win elective office," he said. "In their attempt to corrupt us and bend us to their will, the ladino power brokers extend to us special little privileges that they deny our constituents. And when we cannot meet the unrealistic expectations of the communities that elected us, they accuse us of becoming ladinos and they turn against us. In order to keep our balance, we have to become like tightrope walkers in a circus and perform without a net."

The accuracy of Congressman Velasco Brito's characterization was borne out in the spring of 1990, when he led the congressional lobby against ratifying the Academy of Mayan Languages, whose membership is predominantly indigenous. In the halls of Congress some days later I queried him about his puzzling stand. Congressman Velasco Brito admitted that he was under pressure from senior officials of the Summer Institute of Linguistics, who had underwritten his education

and coached his political career. Two months earlier, Velasco Brito
had left the Christian Democratic party that had gained him elected
office and hitched his fortunes to the resurgent star of Ríos Montt.
As one of the congressional leaders of Ríos Montt's presidential campaign, Diego Velasco Brito captained the strategy to unleash thousands of his supporters into the streets to overturn the constitutional
ban.

3

In spring of 1990 I returned to Cotzal. It still looked like a town
devastated by some nameless catastrophe. A report at that time by
the Washington Office on Latin America calculated that 40 to 50
percent of Cotzal's population had died from violence or disease.
With thousands of survivors still scattered along the coast or scratch-
ing out a meager existence in Mexico, Cotzal is one of the three or
four Guatemalan towns whose fate can be compared to the devastation of Cambodia by Pol Pot and his Khmer Rouge.

As photographer Daniel Chauche and I drive into town, we are
stopped by a tall ladino in cowboy hat, boots, and light-deflecting
Polaroid glasses. He introduces himself as Marciano Monroy Vides,
the schoolmaster from the aldea of Chichel.

"Marshall," as he prefers to be called, confesses to having had a
few drinks—a redundant admission, as the alcohol fumes reached us
well in advance. He says that Chichel had just been visited by gringo
volunteers who planned to build a water-filtering plant in the community, the first of its kind in the Cotzal municipality. "To the villagers, the gringo do-gooders have fallen from the skies like gods,
but I have my suspicions. Tell me, are they to be trusted?"

We assure him of the good intentions of the gringos, whose organization we were acquainted with, and Marshall relaxes his guard.

"I come from Chiquimula, in the Oriente, where we have a tradition
of distrusting foreigners." Marshall speaks with an accentuated tic in
the left side of an otherwise immobile face, as if he were wearing an
ill-fitting mask. "Hostility to outsiders is in our nature. That is why
people from the Oriente make the best bodyguards and professional
matones [killers] and fill the ranks of the kaibiles. I am a humble
schoolteacher who has been stranded here by a horrendous miscar-

riage of the government's good intentions. I have been an educator for nineteen years and have accumulated excellent credentials, so they sent me to Chichel to educate the rustic children of this forsaken region. The trouble is, I speak not a word of Ixil, and the children of Chichel speak no Spanish. The statutes of literacy education in the Constitution stipulate clearly that indigenous communities are to be taught in their native languages. This is not the United States of America, where the Sioux and the Apaches are put away in reservations to fend for themselves. . . . So what do I do? I sit by the waterfall of Chichel and watch the leafy green vistas, like King Kong playing yoyo with the little monkeys of the forest."

Emboldened by our amused response, Marshall asks us the purpose of our visit. When I tell him we intend to drop in on the outgoing mayor, Nicolás Sánchez, and pay a visit to his newly elected replacement, he volunteers to escort us personally to both these excellent gentlemen, who are his intimate friends.

With Marshall as our intermediary, the visit to the municipality turned into a near disaster, as anyone versed in the dynamics of Oriente/Occidente confrontations might have predicted.

Marshall marched into the mayor's office and dominated the proceedings from entry to exit, except for a ten-minute interval when he stepped outside for "refreshment." The new mayor, an Ixil named Domingo de la Cruz, and his fair-skinned secretary, Hugo Girón, sat in captive silence as Marshall lectured them on the duties of municipal office. By turns cajoling and threatening, he admonished them to observe the letter of the law, even if it meant jailing him and his drinking buddy, the former mayor, for unruly conduct. Continually drawing on a nonexistent revolver at his hip he invoked his affection for the indigenous communities but insisted he stood every chance of returning to his hometown in a coffin, because of the enmity of unnamed "sinister elements" in Cotzal. He raised chuckles from the two rows of municipal *concejales* (councilmen) seated against the wall when he exhorted them to keep a close eye on the secretary, whose fair complexion and light hair were suspect; and he likewise advised the mayor to keep a close watch on the ledgers, even if it meant hiring a literate person to read them for him.

The mixture of abuse and cajolery was familiar to everyone in the municipality who had been forced to endure abuses by ladino authorities most of their lives; but the mayor's patience with a mere schoolmaster—and an inebriated one at that—was remarkable. (The head concejal assured me afterward that Marshall had staged similar performances while cold sober.) When his outlandish preamble was finally over, Marshall introduced me to the mayor as a "so-called journalist" whose motives should be carefully scrutinized, although he assumed I was an honest man. In another abrupt about-face he chastised the mayor and his officers for their obdurate insularity, urging them to seize the initiative in lifting their community out of the mire of wretched poverty.

During the ten minutes Marshall excused himself, I learned that the new mayor was as ill-informed as his predecessor had been about the current population of Cotzal or its aldeas and had no idea how many still remained under guerrilla control. He consulted his secretary about the most urgent requirements of the community, a list headed by potable water, health services, and a school. Mayor Domingo de la Cruz appeared overwhelmed by the inherited burdens of his office and protested feebly that he had only begun to assess the situation. But he mustered a measure of eloquence when he appealed to us to communicate to the world "the woeful state of abandon in which Cotzal finds itself."

As we rose to leave, Marshall stumbled in with eyes glazed and cheeks ruddy. The head councilman glanced at me and tugged once at his earlobe. His gesture confirmed my growing suspicion: Marshall was an *oreja*. The Oriente's notoriety as a breeding ground for bodyguards, paid killers, kaibiles, and hard-nosed military officers extends to army informers as well.

We found ex-mayor Nicolás Sánchez in his shabby dry-goods store, which looked as if it had profited little from his two and a half years in office. When I questioned him regarding Deputy Diego Velasco Brito's claim that he was under investigation for some questionable real estate transactions, Nicolás Sánchez responded as straightforwardly as he had the first time we met.

"The truth of the matter is that the government could care less about the people of Cotzal municipality. We received some funds to pave our streets, and the National Reconstruction Committee gave us corrugated tin sheets, which provided roofs for a few homes in the aldeas. Our people are still sunk in misery; we have seven hundred widows of the violence without work, and two thousand residents who recently returned are without homes or provisions. Cotzaleños still have the lowest rate of land-ownership in the region, which continues to be dominated by ladinos. All our applications for outside help have fallen on deaf ears. Even the justice of the peace they sent us departed after a few weeks. The benefits I was able to work for my people were minimal, but personally"—the former mayor grinned—"*Hice mis pequeños negocitos* [I struck some modest deals for myself]. In this world, one has to strive to improve one's own situation, or he will be left in the gutter, like a dog."

6

⟨≡⊙≡⟩

The War Goes On

"The war between the two superpowers has ended; but in
the minds of Guatemala's military, the cold war has found
a permanent abode."

Archbishop Próspero Penados del Barrio

Early in 1979, after the Guerrilla Army of the Poor held its first rally
in Nebaj and executed Enrique Brol, hundreds of residents of Chajul—
the third and largest municipality of the Ixil Triangle—joined the
insurgency and reappeared months later to lead recruitment rallies in
outlying villages. In July several hundred peasants attended rallies in
the aldea of Xix and burned down the local prison. In response to
this and other acts of defiance, the army selected the church plaza
of Chajul to teach residents of the triangle a lesson they would not
soon forget.

Toward the end of 1979, several hundred Mayas gathered in the plaza
of Chajul. The local comandante exhorted the campesinos to be content with their lot and reject the satanic slogans of communist subversives. Then three trucks drove into the plaza, the middle one of which
contained seven captives of the army, dressed in army fatigues. Eyewitnesses estimate that as many as five hundred heavily armed soldiers
surrounded the town. Throughout the ensuing Dantesque drama, described in her autobiography by Rigoberta Menchú, army helicopters
hovered overhead to discourage a guerrilla raid.

The seven prisoners, among them Rigoberta's younger brother,
were in their teens and early twenties, and came from the Ixil area
and northern Quiché. They were accused of collaborating with the
communists as labor organizers and subversives. According to Menchú, all the captives bore signs of hideous torture. She describes in

excruciating detail their distended bellies, lacerated breasts, and bloated faces. A number of them had been partially scalped and had had one or both eyes gouged out. Others were missing ears or fingernails, and their tongues had been cleft in two. Most of them were unrecognizable to their own relatives, who wept openly as the captain calmly described their methods of torture, such as the application of electric wires to vital organs, perforation of the skin with needles, castration. A young woman's breast had been entirely cut off, and the nipple of her other breast was lacerated. Her ears and tongue were also missing, and the soles of her feet had been cut off. The weeping and mourning spread to the entire plaza, but no one dared approach a relative for fear of being grabbed as an accomplice.

The commander announced, "We have one more little punishment for these subversives." He then delivered the prisoners to members of the kaibiles, who proceeded to douse the youths with gasoline. Mutilated and half-conscious as most of them were, they fell to their knees to plead for mercy. Cries of outrage now arose from the onlookers, as they realized what was about to happen. Farmers who had come directly from their fields drew machetes, and others began to pick up stones. The mourning was turning into open rebellion. As the kaibiles set fire to the prisoners, the soldiers encircled them, their weapons aimed at the advancing villagers. Then came the most grotesque moment of all, as the commander and the soldiers began to laugh aloud and shout slogans: "Long live the fatherland! Long live the army! Long live President Lucas!"

Public burnings of Mayan captives by their white conquerors are deeply embedded in the collective memory of Guatemala's Quiché and Cakchiquel communities. In 1524, more than half a century after the Spanish Inquisition began burning relapsed Jewish converts alive in the infamous autos-da-fé, Pedro de Alvarado wrote Emperor Charles V from the gutted Quiché citadel of Utatlán:

> There are many ravines in this land, some as deep as 200 estados, and because of these we cannot make war on the people, nor punish them as they deserve; but seeing that if I could overrun the land and burn it I could bend the people to His Majesty's service, I decided to begin by burning the lords.

As the pyres were lighted, the Quiché lords, in a desperate attempt to save themselves, confessed their plan to kill the Spaniards by luring them into their citadel and setting it on fire. Their appeals fell on deaf ears, and the Quiché lords were burned alive.

Investigator David Stoll, who carried out extensive interviews in Chajul, gathered eyewitness testimony of the massacre that diverged in some important details from that of Rigoberta Menchú. According to these reports, the seven "guerrillas" dressed in camouflage fatigues were brought into the village plaza after being flown to Chajul's army base in a helicopter. The prisoners, including Rigoberta's younger brother, Petrocinio Menchú Tum, showed few outward signs of torture. The soldiers shot the seven in the plaza with automatic weapons, and then dragged one of the bodies in front of the church, where they set it on fire. They then buried the seven bodies in a common grave. Although Vicente Menchú was reported present at the scene, none of the eyewitnesses interviewed by David Stoll recalled seeing his daughter Rigoberta. Mario Payeras, the former EGP militant, bears out David Stoll's version of the Chajul massacre in his memoir, "Trueno en la ciudad," published in 1987. (According to Payeras, the seven prisoners were executed on December 6, not September 24, as Rigoberta claims.) These discrepancies are all the more disconcerting given Rigoberta's painstaking descriptions of the torture to which the victims had been subjected and her persuasive account of her father's, her mother's, and her own horrified reactions. Menchú's original testimony, which she first presented to her own and other Mayan communities, was rooted in an oral tradition that favors collective experience and impassioned subjectivity over documentary accuracy. Thus, for instance, Rigoberta does not specify the number of prisoners that were brought into the plaza but suggests there were at least twenty. And while Payeras and other witnesses assert the army took the bodies away to bury them in a mass grave, Rigoberta describes in some detail how the bodies remained in the plaza until the townspeople themselves buried them in individual coffins.

Although these divergences are not readily accounted for, Rigoberta Menchú's testimony is entirely consistent with other eyewitness accounts of torture, burnings, and mass executions that I have gathered myself, including those given by "Marina" and Victor Montejo.

To the military's chagrin, the show trial and executions in Chajul had the opposite effect of what they intended. Hundreds of Ixils continued to join the Guerrilla Army of the Poor; and thousands provided the EGP with food, shelter, and information about the army's movements. By the following year, the army itself estimated that roughly half the population of the triangle had become active or potential collaborators with the insurgents.

Shortly after the public execution at Chajul, in January 1980, a delegation of five peasant leaders headed by Rigoberta's father, Vicente Menchú, and twenty-two supporters took over the Spanish Embassy in Guatemala City to protest the killings. They were greeted sympathetically by embassy personnel, and despite repeated assurances by the Spanish ambassador that the occupation was a peaceful one, agents of the National Police acting on Lucas García's orders violated diplomatic sanctuary and broke into the building. An incendiary device set fire to the embassy, and thirty-nine occupants were incinerated in the blaze, including twenty-six of the twenty-seven demonstrators, the former Guatemalan vice-president, a foreign minister, and the entire staff, except for the ambassador, who barely escaped with his life. The following day he denounced the police's attack on a peaceful demonstration, and Spain broke off diplomatic relations with the Guatemalan government. (Relations were renewed shortly before Cerezo took office in January 1986.) The only peasant survivor was taken to a hospital. That night he was kidnapped by plainclothes abductors, and his bullet-riddled body was later found in the streets. Lucas García shrugged off the police assault on the embassy as "communist-inspired" and claimed that one of the demonstrators had set off the fire with a Molotov cocktail.

The public executions at Chajul and the Spanish embassy massacre marked a watershed in Romeo Lucas García's iron-fisted policy in the highlands. Soon after he took office, Ríos Montt openly jeered Lucas's crude and unproductive methods of counterinsurgency. Ríos Montt's "Plan Victory '82" and Mejía Víctores's "Plan Stabilization '84" would introduce far more sophisticated strategies that included civic action programs, psychological indoctrination, the institutionalizing of the civil defense patrols, and the establishment of model villages. The army discovered a more effective form of *vencer* by combining the whip, the electric prod, and the gun with a public show of concern for the Mayan communities' welfare.

By the end of 1982 the Guatemalan army had become the deadliest and most efficient instrument of counterinsurgency in Central America. It also gained a reputation as the most contemptuous of elementary human rights. Americas Watch estimated that, based on a Guatemalan Supreme Court census of 200,000 children who had lost one or both parents, 45,000 to 60,000 adult Guatemalans were killed between 1980 and 1985. The Ixil Triangle may account for as much as half of those losses.

Altogether, approximately one and a half million Mayas in the highlands fled their villages and became internal refugees. Guatemala's cultural and ethnic landscape has been more disfigured in the six years prior to Cerezo's election—again according to Americas Watch—than it was in the previous century.

2

In October 1987, the army launched an end-of-the-year offensive against EGP outposts in Nebaj municipality, north of the model village of Salquil Grande. After years of sporadic search and destroy missions in the area, the army sent in 4,500 kaibil units of the newly formed Kaibil Balam regiment, reinforced by 2,300 regular infantry, and the armed civil defense patrols. At the same time, the army more than doubled its garrisons in the triangle, from six to thirteen. The military claimed to have liberated over a dozen villages from the guerrillas and freed nearly 4,000 civilians, who were granted amnesty and sent to special camps for "psychological reeducation." For the first time, the army admitted that as many as 6,000 Ixils remained in over a dozen EGP-controlled villages and confidently predicted they would be liberated before the end of the new year. But they did not officially acknowledge that as many as five hundred army officers and soldiers had been killed in the offensive, as was later reported by the *Christian Science Monitor.*

The week before President Cerezo was to visit the White House, in May 1987, he violated his own policy of "active neutrality" to request the aid of three U.S. Chinook CH-147 helicopters and their crews, which were based in Honduras. The helicopters were used to airlift three hundred Guatemalan troops to Playa Grande, in the Ixcán, in preparation for the army's end-of-the-year offensive. This joint operation turned out to be an early sign of a renewed U.S. military involvement in Guatemala's internal war. Although the dollar amount of U.S. aid to Guatemala's military remains modest relative to aid to El Salvador and Honduras—only $30 million of credit was awarded during the Reagan presidency—the Bush administration increased its participation in Guatemala. U.S. Army Engineers began blasting a road of strategic military importance around the periphery of Lake Atitlán; U.S. air force pilots held training exercises in Guatemala's A-37 attack planes; and U.S. mechanics serviced Guatemala's aging C-47 transports. In 1989 Green Berets took part in jungle-survival training in the Petén's kaibil base. In the teeth of congressional denunciations of Guatemala's persisting human rights violations, the U.S. army delivered 20,000 M-16 rifles worth $13.8 million—the largest U.S. arms sale to Guatemala since President Carter suspended military credits in 1977. In the Ixil Triangle, the new M-16's replaced the heavier and less accurate Israeli Galils, whose name had come to evoke a dark iconic resonance to thousands of highland Mayas.

In August 1988, President Cerezo himself boasted to the press that the guerrillas—who were now referred to as "delinquent terrorists"— had been reduced to seven hundred. He claimed that 4,500 of the URNG's combatants and supporters had accepted the government's amnesty, in keeping with the terms of the Esquipulas Peace Accords. Thousands of refugees, many of whom left relatives in the mountains, were provided food, medicine, and temporary housing by the United Nations Special Commission for Aid to Refugees and the Displaced (CEARD). The army called for further aid from the private sector to feed the acutely undernourished civilians, but the response was meager. The bulk of the guerrilla-controlled area lay between the northern reaches of Chajul, bordering on the Ixcán, and the evangelized finca of La Perla.

In the summer of 1989 I returned to the Ixil Triangle with photographer Daniel Chauche to meet with some of the 4,000 refugees the army claimed had voluntarily fled from guerrilla control and to investigate conditions inside the army's model villages in Nebaj and Chajul.

The Tres Hermanas Pensión was overbooked with U.S. and European journalists, secular and evangelical relief volunteers, as well as long-haired travelers from Lake Atitlán attracted by the convivial atmosphere and dirt-cheap rentals of Nebaj. The youngest of the sisters complained good-humoredly that their predilection for gringo clients had peaked, and she wished most of them would go back to Lake Atitlán, where they belonged. (She died of a heart attack later that year, and the surviving sisters enlisted a niece to take her place. The younger sister's demise had no effect on the abundant good food, cheap prices and nurturing affection the pension has become famous for.)

The evening of our arrival marked the start of Nebaj's fiesta patronal. I bypassed the dance parlors attended by evangelicals, soldiers, and model villagers and attended the festive observances of the traditional Catholic/Mayan cofradías, or religious sodalities, which had suffered heavy casualties in the war. Against a background of marimba and saxophone *rancheras*, a ritual mass exorcism appeared to be taking place. Brightly attired widows of the violence with grief-contorted faces danced erratically under a palm-thatched canopy, alone or with poker-faced members of their cofradías. The women swilled cheap rum proffered by sympathetic relatives and continued to spin and lurch about until they lost their footing and fell to the ground, keening, cursing aloud, and flailing their limbs before they finally passed out. It is a scene that leaps to mind every time a ladino brings up the centuries-old stereotype of the Mayas as callous *inditos* who bear their suffering in sullen silence.

After requesting permission at the army base to visit the Xemamatzé internment camp the next day, we headed for Salquil Grande, the model village near the northernmost edges of the newly liberated territory. It is a staging area for most of the returning or captured refugees. En route we made brief stops in Acul and Tzalbal, two of the twenty-eight model villages that made up the Ixil Triangle's so-called Poles of Development. Acul, an unsightly but orderly aggregation of tin-roofed huts on the edge of a lovely alpine valley, looked as if it had been dropped on the landscape from some remote army outpost. Like the other model villages, Acul was designed in a characteristic grid pattern of adobe or board-paneled dwellings, with graveled streets and incongruously broad avenues bearing the names of military heroes.

In 1984, when President Mejía Víctores inaugurated Acul as a showcase village, the first in the triangle, a gaudy Señorita Acul greeted foreign dignitaries and led them on a tour of the new electrical plant, the weaving looms, the gaily decorated washing fountain. On the feast day of Nebaj's patron saint two years later, the young women of Acul marched behind baton-twirling drum majorettes wearing bright Indian huipiles atop ladino short skirts. In the evening, the miniskirted drum majorettes danced with soldiers who had Galil rifles slung over one shoulder and hand grenades dangling from their belts.

Behind a grotesque public relations facade, model villages remain, with the civil defense patrols, the hammer and tong of the army's counterinsurgency in the Mayan highlands. The residents of Acul were nearly all Nebaj Ixils who had been gathered together from the surrounding hamlets and provided with basic necessities, including an electric mill for their corn. In exchange for these conveniences, the residents had been forced to give up their costumbres, their livestock, and their communal bonds. Several villagers told us they had to travel miles to work their old cornfields, because all the cultivable lands in the vicinity were already taken up. Until 1988, all residents needed army permits to travel outside the village, even as far as their own milpas, and they had to pay someone to replace them in the civil defense patrols when they traveled to the coast in search of work.

Like Acul, most model villages are erected on the ruins of villages destroyed by the army. For all their frequently touted resemblance to the Vietnam War's notorious "strategic hamlets," the model villages more accurately reflect the colonial Spaniards' reduction of rebellious Indian communities into nucleated settlements for the convenience of landowners and the missionary priests. More and more features from the sixteenth and seventeenth centuries have been adopted by the army, in what their own strategists have called the climactic phase of the conquest and transformation of Guatemala's indigenous population.

By 1987 the army had conceded that the model village program as originally designed had outlived its usefulness. The cost of provisioning the closed villages had proved beyond the army's means after international agencies cut down on aid. Furthermore, coastal finca owners complained of a lack of migrant workers for their harvests. Only twenty-eight of the projected forty-four model villages had been

completed, and by early 1988 all but a handful of these had been
taken off the government dole. In villages north of Nebaj newly
reclaimed from the guerrillas, government and international agencies
had taken over from the army with work-incentive projects; residents
were encouraged to form craft cooperatives, grow cash crops, and
travel to the coast as migrant workers. But the switch from army to
civilian patronage still left most residents with little or no land to
cultivate, nor did it alleviate the endemic scarcity of health and sanitary services. In the older model villages like Acul, conditions had
likewise deteriorated, as the army and civilian bureaucrats traded
charges of incompetence and did nothing.

   In 1989 Salquil Grande and the dozen or so reclaimed villages to
the north and east, among them Quejchip, Palop, Cotzol, and Bicalamá, were receiving a disproportionate share of government assistance, as conspicuous inducements to the thousands of Ixils still
living across the line in guerrilla-controlled villages. Convinced that
they had essentially won the military conflict with the guerrillas, the
army was more concerned with winning hearts and minds. Electric
posts had gone up in Salquil, and a new school and a cinder-block
municipality were under construction. None of these civic improvements lightened the countenances of the villagers, who were uni-
formly dour and incommunicative. A year later Salquileños would
greet all glad-handing government officials and foreign relief volunteers as if they were the bearers of a nameless plague.

   In the newly resettled aldea of Quejchip, a Ministry of Development delegation that brought latrines and tin roofs encouraged returning residents to start their own bakery and a weaving cooperative.
The army is extending its network of new roads beyond Bicalamá to
connect the reclaimed areas of the Ixil Triangle with those of the
Ixcán. Altogether, the old and new model villages accounted for a
total of 26,000 residents, or roughly a third of the population of the
Ixil Triangle.

   The 4.5-kilometer ridge road from Salquil Grande to Quejchip
looks out on one of the most majestic prospects in northern Quiché.
It was the second day of the *canícula*, or dry interlude of mid-July,
when the rain-washed skies are at their bluest, and the green carpet
covering the hillsides is strewn with wildflowers. Across the river gorge

lacy waterfalls hung from cupped meadows. A year ago only an occasional hut or two had been visible there; now, the lone huts and isolated milpas were blooming into "reborn" *caseríos* and model villages with names like Xoloché and Parramos Grande. It strained credulity almost beyond endurance to recall that less than a decade earlier each of those pastoral hamlets had been razed by the army, which butchered as much as half of their populations and condemned the remainder to a fugitive existence in the mountains.

On the way to Salquil we had stopped to visit Don José Azzari, a ninety-seven-year-old immigrant from Locarno, Italy, who started a dairy in the verdant valley beside Acul over half a century ago. In 1980 Don José, the last survivor among the European immigrants who settled in Ixil country after the turn of the century, had ignored the army's friendly advice to leave his cows and dairy behind and evacuate the area, which they claimed had become infested with subversives.

"I had no enemies, so why should I leave?" recalled the bright-eyed, white-bearded dairyman. "Unlike my good friend Enrique Brol, I paid my workers well, and the guerrillas left me alone. One day I heard a shot, and later found the bullet hole on the wall, inches above where my head had been. Two weeks later, they burned down my dairy and home and killed my cows, and I had to go into hiding in southern Quiché." In his nineties, Don José had come back to rebuild his dairy after the "turbulence" blew over. He now lives with two of his grown sons, drawing comfort from the hills and wildflowers that evoke his birthplace in the Italian Alps. Grazing outside his bedroom window are his beloved guernsey cows, whose milk yields the most coveted cream cheese in the altiplano. A third son, Agustín, is married to a daughter of Enrique Brol, and lives in Guatemala City.

"I used to be potent, before all this happened," Don José says, rolling his consonants with an Old World finesse. "I've had many sons and grandchildren. But now, I am in my final days, and my heart is filled with sadness." What Don José will no longer admit, not even to himself, is that the "they" who burned down his house and dairy were not the guerrillas—as he insistently informs visitors—but the soldiers whose amicable warnings he ignored. The army wanted no witnesses present when they razed Acul.

South of Salquil we hiked an hour uphill to Xoloché, one of the recently rehabilitated model villages. The West German embassy and a private aid agency were investing in a potable water system for the village, a corn mill, and a washing fountain. The first to greet us, by the water spring just south of Xoloché, was a weathered-looking gringo of about twenty-five with the Shawcross Project who was laying in the pipes and electric pump for the water system.

"Welcome to the latest show village," he joked, a reminder that it took less than a year for a new model village to fade into relative oblivion. Although strapped for funds, the Shawcross volunteers are among the increasingly scarce relief workers who follow through on projects they undertake.

From the village center, the view of Salquil Grande and the ranges beyond was as dramatic as the prospect we had enjoyed from Quejchip. Billowing white clouds spilled over the mountain passes as the soft afternoon light cast lengthening shadows over the valley. On our arrival, a dozen armed men between fifteen and fifty were about to set out on a night-long patrol. They told us they had to march round the clock every four days, whether they wanted to or not, for fear of angering the comandante. The newly planted corn crops covered much of the valley and climbed, terrace upon terrace, until they reached mountain inclines too steep for cultivation.

One of the Xoloché elders who greeted us claimed the soil was so rich that apples and other fruit trees had grown practically unattended in their backyards and that many had raised cattle, sheep, and horses. But all that was in the past. Of the six hundred families in Xoloché before the army burned the village down in 1981, there were only 125 families left, including thirty-three widows and as many orphans; survivors feared more than three hundred families had died, either directly from the violence or from hunger and disease in the mountains.

We were introduced to the schoolmaster, a Nebajeño of twenty-six who spoke fluent Ixil. He pointed out the tile floor of the old school—all that remained—on which six spirited girls in bright red cortes were dancing an Ixil version of ring around the rosie. The new school, in which fifty children were taught to read and write in Spanish, was a humble log cabin with a thatched roof. Only the oldest children remembered Xoloché as it had once been.

I asked the elder who led us around how a village like Xoloché was "reborn," in the army's specious euphemism. "After three months of army indoctrination in Xemamatzé, those of us who were healthy enough traveled to the coast to make money for our seed corn, our hoe, and machete. Then we planted our milpa. With the money left over we had to buy the tin roof for our homes, or we made one of wattle. The women used the few centavos they saved to buy a *metate* [mortar], on which they grind the corn and chilis. Next, they will save up to buy yarn, so they can make themselves a new huipil. When we came down from the mountains, many of us still wore the clothes we had on our backs when we fled. We had no yarn and no loom to make new ones. Only after we harvest our first crops will we have enough money for medicines, a few pots and utensils, a stick of furniture. We still don't have enough to build latrines and a washing fountain or to buy a corn mill. Without the help from abroad, we would be reduced to living in the same way we lived in the mountains."

"What about costumbre?" I ask the headman.

"The b'alb'axtix and calendar keepers, the healers are with us. But we have no money for herbs or candles or to offer chickens in sacrifice. If we get sick, we must fend for ourselves, unless the healers extend us credit."

It would be another year before any of them could afford a small animal or two and some fruit trees. But several men were already knitting the traditional Ixil shoulder bags, and on our way out of the village we met a young widow who had just begun to weave, on a backstrap loom her mother had jealously guarded during their prolonged exile, a rainbow-colored huipil.

3

It was a wholly different story in the internment camp of Xemamatzé, one mile south of Nebaj. Although the camp is funded by the United Nations through CEARD, the special commission for aid to refugees and the displaced, its day-to-day activities are overseen by specialists of the army's Civilian Affairs Unit, or S-5. The camp was packed with two hundred displaced and recaptured campesinos who had lived for as long as eight years under the guerrillas and who were being put through a harsh ninety-day "repatriation" before they would be permitted to resettle in liberated villages. The refugees had first been kept for some days in the army barracks, where their names were checked against lists of "subversives." The comandante did not mention what they did with those whose names appeared on the lists and who were legally protected by the amnesty provisions of the Esquipulas Peace Accords.

In late afternoon, about one hundred fifty men, women, and children were lined up outside their barracks to salute the lowering of the flag. The remainder of the internees were lying on their cots, too sick to answer roll call. The camp, which had opened fifteen months earlier, consisted of three large *galeras*, or barracks, where the internees slept and ate. The camp's yard was slightly larger than a football field; rows of pine saplings planted in front of the drab barracks were browned with dust and would not thrive.

"Buenas noches, Guatemala," the residents shouted in unison, raising their fists in patriotic salute. The civilian affairs officer, who spoke fluent Ixil, lectured them about a missing huipil and warned that theft would not be tolerated in the camp. If the huipil did not appear by morning, the entire barracks would be disciplined. He followed this with a daily lecture on the danger of allowing "subversives" to reenter their villages. "You see now the price you have paid for collaborating with the subversives," the officer said. "You, as patriotic Guatemalans living under the army's protection, must never again be taken in by the lies and deceptions of delinquent terrorists, who masquerade as protectors of the campesinos."

Inside the barracks, we were met by the hollow-eyed faces, reddish hair, and distended bellies of acute malnutrition. Approximately half of the residents were afflicted with bronchial pneumonia. A couple near the entrance sat in glazed silence, mourning a seven-month-old child, their first, who had died of dehydration the previous evening. The coffin was yet to arrive.

The couple came from Sumalito, a village captured by the army during the end-of-the-year offensive. The father remarked that the guerrillas also made them line up for roll call every morning and evening and put them through similar "consciousness-raising" drills.

"*Ni estos ni aquellos,*" he said. "Neither these nor the others. When the guerrillas came to Sumalito several years ago, we grew two crops of corn a year, and we ate well. By the time the soldiers came, salt was so scarce it cost 16 quetzales [about $5] a pound, which none of us could afford. We had no salt, or meat, or milk for our children. Instead of fleeing once again with the guerrillas, we stayed in Sumalito and let ourselves be captured. And now we have lost our only child."

A CEARD doctor arrived in the camp during our visit. He said most of the sick people had contracted pneumonia and other infectious diseases after they arrived in the camp, because of the crowded living conditions. He told me of a woman whose child died in partum the night before, when she went outside to muffle her moans because she feared exposing herself to ridicule. The mother, who had refused to reveal her name, was gravely ill; she had been taken to the General Hospital in Nebaj, a notorious white elephant that had only thirty beds and no medicines and admitted only those on the verge of death.

On my first visit there, Xemamatzé was the closest thing to a living hell that I had ever witnessed in Guatemala or anywhere else. In physical appearance and the conditions of existence, it was more like a concentration camp than any of the refugee settlements I had visited in Guatemala and Mexico. (In 1991 CEARD claimed that 8,000 to 11,000 refugees had passed through Xemamatzé.) And yet even here I found evidence of the Mayan communities' remarkable resilience. In two of the barracks, the women had set up makeshift looms to weave their brilliant red huipiles, and a number of men crocheted shoulder bags. The healthier women who were assigned to cook for the camp stretched the meager rations as far as was humanly possible. On the gray and peeling plyboard walls of the barracks, the Ixil children had drawn helicopters. All the walls of Xemamatzé, inside and out, were covered with drawings of helicopters. Later helicopters began appearing as well on the shoulder bags crocheted by the younger men.

Elba Méndez Girón, a psychologist from San Carlos University assigned to the camp by CEARD, reported that helicopters were the first mechanical craft many refugee children had ever seen. When their villages were recaptured, the soldiers would scatter leaflets from the aircraft or address them through loudspeakers, assuring them of the "new" army's beneficence and offering guarantees for their safety if they accepted amnesty. Most of the refugees from remote liberated villages like Ama'chel and Caba were flown to Nebaj on the same "choppers," as the kids called them.

"Children who never saw a bicycle were confronted by these enormous flying machines that spoke to them in their own language; they were frightened but also fascinated. In terms of capturing a child's attention, the guerrillas had nothing to compare with that." Elba Méndez said she had found surprisingly scant evidence of psychopathology among the children—even among those who had lost both parents—so long as they had a brother or sister to look after them. Many exhibited symptoms of repressed aggression, which they acted out in their games and their daily interactions with their families. And undernourished Ixil children, she pointed out, appeared to tolerate extremely low hemoglobin levels without suffering permanent ill effects. "Unlike Western children and ladinos, Ixils are in constant physical contact with one another, even when they are not particularly demonstrative of their feelings. Apparently, this physical closeness cushions them against the traumatic effects of their experiences in the mountains and in the repatriation camps." Méndez, a middle-class ladina, admitted that her diagnosis was hampered by her unfamiliarity with the Ixil language and customs. At times, she said, she sensed the children were telling her what they thought she wanted to hear.

The former refugee center of Las Violetas, which I had visited on previous occasions, has been turned into a squatters' camp for rehabilitated refugees after they are released from Xemamatzé. A European-based relief agency, Refugee Children of the World, has erected a school, an orphanage, even a carpentry workshop. Foreign doctors visit occasionally with desperately needed medical supplies.

On the slope above us, around twenty widows in brilliant Nebaj traje and tasseled headdresses were working on a newly planted field of cabbage, broccoli, potatoes, and cauliflower, the seeds for which had been donated by the Europeans. Most of the other residents were planting their milpas or foraging for work in town. During our tour of the facilities I was approached by an Ixil woman who mistook me for a doctor and pushed her carrot-haired, acutely undernourished small son in my way. When I assured her I was no doctor but a journalist, she pleaded with me to take the boy with me, because she could no longer feed him.

Margarita, as I will call her, had recently been given a small plot of land and a tin roof by the Sisters of Charity, and she invited me to visit her home. Although she appeared pale and frail from long illness, her burning black eyes were clear and aristocratic. She looked, in fact, like a noblewoman from a Roman mosaic. As we climbed the steep slope toward her home, Margarita told me her story. Her intense dark eyes seldom wandered from mine, and her voice was soft but firm.

She said she was the wife of a municipal officer in the aldea of Xeucalvitz, nine hours' walk to the north of Nebaj, which had been seized by the EGP in 1981. During the first four years of guerrilla occupation, life continued more or less as usual. She and her husband had sixty *cuerdas* (two acres) of coffee and ten of sugarcane, which they worked and harvested. On occasion, an EGP comandante would visit their home and request provisions, for which the guerrillas paid promptly and at a fair price. The guerrillas then began asking the women of the aldea to prepare food on a regular basis. They gave several days' advance notice and paid cash on delivery.

After the EGP's military setbacks in the area, beginning in 1985, the morale in the ranks declined, and relations with many of the campesinos under their protection degenerated rapidly. In a matter of months, the lives of Margarita, her husband, and their five children turned into a nightmare. They would be wakened in the middle of the night and forced to travel to a village in the Ixcán. There, the men were made to carry provisions like beasts of burden, and the women were forced to cook for the guerrilla rank and file. The scale of payment dropped until it was practically nonexistent. Margarita and her husband could no longer afford to buy salt or basic provisions for their growing children.

When several families of Xeucalvitz decided to confront the guerrillas and refused to work for them for little or no pay, they were warned not to attempt to flee the village, on pain of death. "They told us that the army would kill us if we crossed the line. They said that Nebaj had been destroyed, which we knew was not true. They told us that if we returned there, they would kill our men, rape our women, and sell the children abroad for their organs. Before, they had been straightforward; now they lied to us."

One night, a guerrilla patrol broke into their corral and seized their mule. Two days later they found the burned entrails and skeleton nearby. The next day, Margarita's husband stole out of the village before daybreak with their only cow, which he managed to sell in a neighboring aldea. After several more months of being awakened at midnight and taken to lowland villages to work for a pittance, Margarita and her family made the bold decision to escape. They packed their most precious belongings and set out in the dead of night on the long trek to Nebaj. After they arrived, they and four other families from Xeucalvitz were handed over to the army by Nebaj's civil defense patrol. They underwent interrogation in the barracks and then were taken to Xemamatzé, where Margarita, pregnant with her sixth child, fell ill with peritonitis. She lost her child and convalesced for three months, but she was still frail. All but one of her children remain severely undernourished.

She said, "When the army freed us, we went to some relatives of my husband's here in Nebaj. But there were six families living in a small house, and they had no room for us. That's when we came here, and the sisters arranged for a plot of land to build our home. But we have no money to buy the wooden sidings for the house or to obtain provisions."

Despite their bitter experience, the news of their successful escape had filtered back to Xeucalvitz, where it sparked the flight of several more families. One of these families now lived close by in the settlement. The new neighbors informed Margarita and her husband that since their departure the guerrillas had "commandeered" their coffee and sugar crops and distributed them among their rank and file.

Before the end of her story we reached Margarita's plot, which turned out to be the farthest one from the school and medical facility. There was no electricity in camp, and there was no certainty that the water installation under construction would reach Margarita's home, which consisted of three sidings of board and plastic, the tin roof, and an empty hearth. There were over twenty national and international relief agencies active in the Nebaj area, but this meant very little to Margarita and her family who, like hundreds of others, seemed to have drifted into a backwater outside the flow of refugee relief.

On my return to Nebaj in May 1990, I learned that Margarita and her family had gone back to Xeucalvitz, rebuilt their home, and planted new crops of coffee and sugarcane. Xeucalvitz was among the newly rehabilitated model villages, with an active crafts cooperative and other self-help projects. I spoke with residents of Xeucalvitz who questioned portions of Margarita's account. Although living conditions have improved since the army reclaimed the village, they insisted that relations with the guerrillas had remained cordial to the end and that they had continued to pay for the produce and services they required. One resident suggested Margarita's case may have involved a personal conflict or that her traumatic experiences may have in some way affected her memory. At the time of my visit, guerrillas continued to be active in the vicinity, so the wary residents I spoke with may have been protecting their flanks. In the Ixil Triangle, as elsewhere in Guatemala, the most credible testimony may be distorted by the imperatives of survival.

4

Before going on to Chajul we met briefly with Nebaj's new parish priest, Tomás Ventura Lux, a Quiché native from Chichicastenango who had replaced Father Juan Vásquez. Since my first visit to the triangle in 1986, the evangelicals had grown ever more aggressive, proselytizing vigorously in the new model villages and accusing Catholic prelates of being in league with the devil. The church responded by assigning to Nebaj an indigenous pastor who spoke Ixil and addressed the community's needs on its own terms.

Father Tomás makes a point of including Ixil sorcerers in his services. Although he is not as outspoken as his namesake and fellow seminary graduate, Father Ventura Lux, who was driven out of Chichicastenango for celebrating Quiché-language masses in which parishioners openly denounced the army and civil patrols, Father Tomás has repeatedly stood up to the army and refuses to celebrate mass in the barracks. "People lose confidence in you if you are seen working closely with the army," he says. "Like Father Vásquez before me, I have three separate parishes to cover, including the one I served for five years in Cunén. When the comandante asks me to deliver mass in the barracks or in Xemamatzé, I tell him I am simply too busy."

"Is there a price to be paid for this refusal?" I ask him.

"Of course. And since I am an indigenous pastor, my loyalty to

the army is intensely questioned. But so far there have been no repercussions. I find far more worrisome the increased militarization of
the civil defense patrols. The patrols in Nebaj used to be organized
into platoons of twenty to twenty-five participants. Now they are
organized by *cantones,* or neighborhoods. If there are sixty men in
a cantón, thirty of them have to march on a given twenty-four-hour
shift. If there are only thirty, then all of them have to patrol. In a
confrontation with the guerrillas, the males of an entire cantón could
be wiped out. The army is now so certain of its domination over the
population of Nebaj that they are pulling out of their barracks and
leaving the civil patrols in their place."

I ask Father Tomás if there is any sign of resistance to the patrols,
as there is in southern Quiché. He sighs and nods his head. "Groups
like CERJ have not yet made an impact in the triangle, although they
are becoming active in aldeas to the south of here. But even here,
the patrollers rebel against taking risks when their immediate security
is not involved. The villagers of Baxchocolá, who live along the unfinished road to Xeucalvitz and Sumalito, are protesting orders to stand
watch over the bulldozer. The comandante ordered twenty patrollers
to guard the bulldozer on twenty-four-hour shifts. At the last meeting,
several patrollers insisted on receiving payment for guarding the bulldozer, saying they would not shed blood gratuitously over a piece of
machinery. Others suggested ladinos, teachers, and public officials
should also stand watch and march in the patrols. Needless to say,
the comandante was not pleased with that meeting. He became angry
and put his fist down, ordering the patrollers to stand guard over the
bulldozer. Of course, they had no real choice but to comply. The
army knows how to squeeze the lifeblood out of the people here."

"Have you made any reference to these abuses in your sermons or
reported any of them to the Human Rights Attorney?"

Father Tomás, who has learned to veil his emotions, turned to me
with a look of profound sadness. "If I make direct denunciations, I
will be endangering my parishioners as well as myself. And for the
same reason, I hardly ever leave my parish. Guatemala City and the
Human Rights Attorney might as well be on another planet."

5

Compared with Nebaj, Chajul seems an overgrown village, with a
river cascading across its center and the church plaza rising at its far

end. On every other rock, townswomen washed their bright red cortes and red or white huipiles embroidered with fanciful animal figures taken from Ixil folklore. Of a more recent vintage is the elegant red jacket with black braid still worn by Chajul and Nebaj elders, which was modeled on the Spanish officers' regimental uniform. The church's bell tower looks out on open sky, like an operatic prop. The dark-complexioned Christ in the back of the church—said to be the brother of the famous Black Christ of Esquipulas—is especially revered by residents of Chajul and by religious pilgrims. Two sculpted figures resembling Pretorian guards stand at either side of the glass case housing the Christ. Some years ago the local comandante mockingly ordered the figures to be dressed in army fatigues, so the black Savior would have the army's protection.

Although Chajul has begun to receive some aid from the agencies active in Nebaj, on revisiting the town plaza after a year's absence, I was engulfed by women of all ages who were eager to sell me not only the bright red or blue woven huipiles on their backs, but jade utensils, obsidian cores, and other Mayan artifacts they had found in their cornfields or dug up from an ancestor's tomb. The elegant four-foot-long wooden blowguns that form part of Chajul's folklore sold for an absurdly low price of four dollars. Like Nebaj, Chajul seemed to have recovered some of its communal way of life. The bright colors and warm sunshine gave an impression of vibrancy and purposeful activity; but the wounds lie close to the surface. We approached a young woman who spoke Spanish, and she told us that most of her companions who had offered us their handicrafts had lost relatives during the height of the violence in 1982. She also said that guerrillas still entered the town periodically and were active once more in the villages nearby. The previous week, several soldiers had been wounded in an armed clash outside a model village. "*Mucha matanza*," she said soberly. "Too much killing."

The municipality of Chajul, including a dozen surrounding villages and numerous small hamlets, had about 18,000 residents in 1978, when General Lucas García became president. Today, the town of Chajul has about 3,000 residents; another 5,000 to 6,000 live in guerrilla-controlled areas or in model villages. As many as 3,000 to 4,000 may still be hiding out in the mountains, and no one knows how many have fled to the coast or across the border into Mexico. The former mayor of Chajul estimates that 5,000 Chajuleños, or

close to a third of the original population, lost their lives in the past
decade.

In *Between Two Fires: Dual Violence and the Reassertion of Civil
Society in Nebaj, Guatemala,* David Stoll assembled estimated population figures for the Ixil Triangle, from 1893 to 1989. The projec-
tions by the United Nations and Guatemala's General Department of
Statistics show a remarkable population recovery in each of the three
municipalities beginning in 1989. Although all population censuses
in Guatemala's highlands are notoriously unreliable, the figures gathered by Stoll suggest that Nebaj, Chajul, and Cotzal may already have
recovered their pre-1981 combined population of around 85,000. As
another indication of this population explosion, Stoll points to a new
wave of mass emigrations from the Ixil region to the coastal areas
and across the northern borders into Mexico and the United States.
As is the case with other departments of the altiplano that were spared
the brunt of the violence, this new diaspora is being sparked by a
desperate search for cultivable lands.

6

In the parish office next to the old convent, I met with Father Rosolino
Biancetti, who had been the parish priest of Chajul for a year and a
half. A Catholic missionary from Milan, Italy, with charismatic lean-
ings, Father Rosolino has large, Byzantine eyes shadowed by over-
work. The previous evening he had driven the four miles on the newly
opened road to Cotzal to visit an ailing widow and had not gotten
back until midnight. Both the EGP and the army were known to
patrol that area after dark, but Father Rosolino seemed to take the
risks in stride.

While waiting for Father Rosolino to rise from his nap, I spoke
with two of five Carmelite nuns newly assigned to the parish. Although
they were Guatemalan, both sisters had served in El Salvador for a
number of years, and one—Sister Olga—had worked with Archbishop
Oscar Arnulfo Romero prior to his assassination. When I asked if
they planned to help reorganize Acción Católica committees in the
parish, the sisters visibly blanched.

"That will not be appropriate for Chajul," said Sister Olga, who
had just alluded to the memorial stone laid in the church for Father

Gran Cirera, murdered by the army in part because of his work with Acción Católica. "Ninety percent of our parishioners are charismatics, and they are not interested in militancy or religious reform. Their faith is founded firmly on Holy Scripture." The charismatic renovation, one of the fastest growing religious movements in the highlands, was another Catholic response to the evangelicals, one that threatened to get out of control. The new mayor of Chajul, a former Acción Católica catechist, had formed part of a charismatic splinter group that briefly joined the Church of the Word and later founded their own evangelical movement, "Jesus Heals and Saves."

Father Rosolino, a tall, spectrally thin cleric of about forty-five, backed Sister Olga's assessment. "Our charismatics are not interested in abstractions or icons, real or theoretical," he intoned, picking up a gold-plated New Testament. "*This* is what engrosses them. The *naturales,* in contrast to ladinos, begin with God and descend from there to humans, to nature, to their economic needs. To the charismatics, Acción Católica has become synonymous with death. They are not interested in Liberation Theology or abstract social justice. They began with an oral Christo-pagan tradition, went from there to burning candles to their saints, and that has led them back to the Holy Word itself."

I asked Father Rosolino if the more pragmatic charismatics in his parish supported the army, as did many evangelicals. "Not at all," he said, momentarily flustered. "Their pragmatism takes other forms. In the past years, most Chajuleños have been concerned mainly with physical survival. Now they want more, a small breathing space. Two years ago, it appeared that the guerrilla issue had been resolved. But now they are staging a comeback, and my parishioners are inclined to suspend judgment."

I pointed out that in other highland communities, such as San Pedro la Laguna, the charismatics have left the Catholic church and joined the neo-Pentecostals and other recently arrived sects. What is to prevent the same thing from happening in Chajul?

Father Rosolino's eyes open wide. Charismatic defection is a sensitive subject within the church. I had recently read a pamphlet from Guatemala's bishops warning about the "aberrant" directions charismatics could take without proper shepherding from their Catholic clergy. But he parries my question gracefully.

"Chajuleños are less aggressive than other highland groups. They are gentle and nonconfrontational even by comparison with their Ixil brothers in Cotzal, where evangelical sects became established a long time ago. The fact is, my parishioners are less interested in costumbre or theology than they are in a social integration that will reap them benefits from the larger ladino community as well as their own. They see no contradiction whatsoever between a heightened spirituality and enhanced material benefits."

On my return to Chajul in 1990, a combative Sister Olga conceded that the evangelicals had made inroads in their congregation by accusing the church of "devil worship" and of loyalty to a "satanic" Pope John Paul. She was equally concerned that the resumption of guerrilla activity had given the army all the excuse it needed to clamp down ruthlessly on the long-suffering Chajuleños.

"The army is subjecting the men to a harsher indoctrination than ever before. After mass on Sunday, all the males are forced to go directly to the barracks for an 8 A.M. 'military mass,' where they are made to denounce their own relatives and neighbors. At night, fifty to sixty patrollers are assigned to guard the barracks from a possible guerrilla assault. When two patrollers were killed in a confrontation, the army put their bodies on display in the square as if they were sides of beef put up for auction. Nearly all the soldiers here are ladinos from the Oriente who regard Indians as less than human. In Nebaj, the soldiers may be pulling out of their barracks, but here they remain as dominant a presence as ever before. There is a new civil war in the making with a heightened religious emphasis, a war of Maya against Maya, of Catholic against evangelical, and the heart of this war is once again right here in the Ixil Triangle."

In October 1990, a member of a Swiss human rights delegation visiting Guatemala, Marcel Bossenet, described the army's new "*Plan Victoria*," which targeted the Ixil communities in resistance in the mountains of northern Chajul. In early March, Bossenet reported, the army had torched forty-eight dwellings, two chapels, and three schools, signaling a return to the scorched-earth policies of Lucas García and Ríos Montt.

Toward the end of 1991, guerrilla activity in the triangle rose significantly. On December 16, a guerrilla patrol attacked an army outpost in Cotzal, north of Finca San Francisco, and destroyed a helicopter on the ground with a Chinese grenade launcher. On December 28 and again on January 16, 1992, guerrillas blew up the vehicles of a government agency responsible for, among other things, setting up peasant cooperatives. In another incident unreported by army spokesmen, four soldiers were killed by a claymore mine. As guerrilla activities intensified throughout the country prior to a new round of talks with the government, the EGP warned CEARD and other relief agencies to get out of the Ixil Triangle.

7

On my return to Nebaj, I stopped briefly in the barracks to interview Captain Marco Antonio Mendoza, the interim comandante of the Ixil Triangle. He is a portly officer of about forty, whose high forehead and rimless glasses make him look more studious than his predecessors. Like most army officers, he received postgraduate military training in the United States. Captain Mendoza, an evangelical, lets me know at once that he is from the new ranks of university-trained officers who have studied a non-military vocation.

"After graduating from the Politécnica Academy I entered Mariano Gálvez University to study economics. This is encouraged under our new command, in order to broaden our perspective on the world. We are learning to speak to Indian communities in their own languages. By educating them in civic responsibilities and democratic principles, we prevent their becoming victims of the communists' stratagems. Our opponent is disciplined and astute, and we must keep several moves ahead of him. Our newest weapons are psychological ones. We support constitutional democracy. In the past, when the army killed one hundred guerrillas in one place, five hundred rose up somewhere else. Now, we consider the psychological factors, we make socioeconomic studies of the areas they operate in, and we wage a propaganda campaign that is more effective and sophisticated than theirs."

"Does that mean the guerrillas still pose a real military threat here in the Ixil Triangle?"

"I am speaking of the international communist conspiracy, of which the guerrillas are a relatively insignificant part. After the defeats we have dealt them in the past three years, they have become little more than a nuisance—a band of delinquent terrorists bent on maintaining a presence in order to continue to obtain funds from their foreign backers."

I carefully point out to the comandante that since the advent of *perestroika* and the fall of the Berlin Wall, the international communist conspiracy is not what it once was, if indeed it ever was.

"It's true of course that Gorbachev is a very astute adversary," the comandante replies. "His public relations ploys have pulled the wool over the eyes of otherwise alert world leaders, among them George Bush. But we in the military remember very well what became of Krushchev. As an evangelical, I could speak to you of the significance of the mark on Gorbachev's forehead, which Holy Scripture associates with the Antichrist. But that is matter for another discussion. The point I want to emphasize is that the international communist conspiracy is more present among us than ever before. What has changed are the rules of engagement."

I ask the comandante if Defense Minister Héctor Gramajo's avowed respect for constitutional democracy is now included in their military curriculum in the Politécnica Academy.

This time the comandante stiffens and slowly exhales; evidently, I have touched a nerve. But his public relations smile remains firmly in place. "You are perhaps alluding to recent events—such as the May barracks revolt—that may suggest ideological cleavages within the army high command. It is an undeniable fact that our officer class is composed of individuals of diverse backgrounds: we have officers of landowning elite families, of middle-class families such as my own, and we have officers of indigenous background, such as the Lucas García brothers, Romeo and Benedicto. It is our training at the Politécnica that forges us into a homogenous officer corps. Our education inculcates in each of us the strict discipline and the hierarchical loyalties that have always characterized the Guatemalan army. Now, following our graduation, we are permitted a certain latitude in our political education. Many of us complete our military formation in the United States or in Israel. We attend university. In our heads we can hold private opinions of political leaders, although the Constitution prohibits us explicitly from taking part in partisan politics. However, in our training as combatants and mortal foes of the enemies of our homeland, we are indivisible."

With images of Xemamatzé fresh in my mind, I ask the comandante about the fate of the thousands of orphaned children who have become victims of the war. This time he answers without hesitation, as his eyes widen and become unnaturally bright. "You and I, who are educated, know about the lies and stratagems employed by the communists, who spread their ideology through the children. They reach children in the schools, in the churches, and in the city slums. In the countryside, the subversives use children as beasts of burden; children are made to distribute leaflets, to break into homes, and steal from innocent people in order to keep the subversives well provisioned. Lamentably, we are not in control of the Ministries of Education and Culture. Our influence in church organizations is obviously limited. We cannot let them know that they are helping to train delinquents and future subversive terrorists, whom we will have to deal with after they become adults. Here, in the countryside, at least we can help to inform the uneducated indigenous communities about the reality of the communist menace. The enemy is crafty and resourceful; taking their cue from their new Soviet leaders, they have become experts at public relations. In order to defeat them, we have to stay several moves ahead of them. We must know at all times what they are thinking and analyze exactly how they operate. If the army were not here, the communists would take over immediately."

8

Early in my investigation, a priest who had served a decade in the Ixil area had warned me, "You will never be able to get exact figures on how many people were killed by the army, how many by the guerrillas, and how many have fled to the mountains, to the capital, or to Mexico. But if you keep your eyes and ears open, you will see and hear enough to make statistics, in themselves, irrelevant."

And yet I had gone to the Ixil Triangle as a reporter, not a moral philosopher; in my determination to nail down credible statistics on the dead and disappeared that would help to establish degrees of culpability, I had lost sight of the dimension of the horror I was witnessing. So often during my four visits to the Ixil region I heard testimony that strained my capacity to comprehend to the breaking point.

After hearing a particularly harrowing account by an Ixil migrant worker whose wife had been cut to pieces by a coffee planter's bodyguard because she had refused the landowner's sexual advances, I reacted reflexively like a ladino; at first with incredulity, and then with self-righteous condescension. Surely, I thought, no *Westerner* would allow himself to be victimized in this way. After several months in the Guatemalan highlands I was falling prey to the numbness and paranoia that overtake the hardiest and best-intentioned Guatemalans.

The fact is that the Ixil communities of Nebaj, Chajul, and Cotzal, like most other Mayan communities, have for centuries resisted their Spanish and ladino oppressors with all the means at their disposal. But these have never been sufficient. Overwhelmed by superior force and a well-lubricated machinery of domination, most Mayas developed a stoical attitude of nonconfrontation with the white man. But behind their repeated defeats and humiliations lurks a stubborn will to endure.

"Aroused from the sloth of ages," wrote the North American traveler John Lloyd Stephens in 1850, referring to the uprising of Rafael Carrera and his masses of Mayan followers, "a spirit was awakened among the Indians to make a bloody offering to the spirits of their fathers, and recover their inheritance." This is the nightmare all ladinos live with, and more than a century later, it threatened once again to become reality.

As the priest had predicted, I was unable to assess what percentage of the Ixil community's missing 25,000 were killed by the army and by the guerrillas—or to estimate how many were suffering involuntary exile in Guatemala City and other towns or in Mexican refugee camps.

I did gather sufficient evidence to indict the Guatemalan army of heinous crimes against the indigenous communities of northern Quiché. The campaign of ethnic extermination in the Ixil Triangle by a military elite armed and advised by Israel, the United States, Taiwan—among others—far exceeds the means necessary to neutralize a guerrilla force that never numbered more than eight thousand armed militants. The guerrillas' success in recruiting hundreds of thousands of Mayan peasants to their cause can be attributed in large part to the army's monstrous overreaction to the provocation. Anthropologist Robert Carmack, a specialist on the Quiché who lived there many years, has calculated that one hundred Mayas were killed by the army for every one killed by the guerrillas.

Nevertheless, the Guerrilla Army of the Poor—and the other three rebel organizations that make up the Guatemalan National Revolutionary Union—must bear responsibility for jeopardizing the lives of thousands of native Guatemalans who believed their impossible promises of a swift victory over their oppressors and redress of their centuries-old grievances.

PART III

Huehuetenango

7

The Crosses of Todos Santos

"Catechists and evangelicals come and go! Even shamans pass
from the scene . . . but the guardians of the four sacred peaks
endure forever!"

Head of Todos Santos cofradía

The marvels of Todos Santos Cuchumatán were made known to the
outside world by Maud Oakes, the intrepid traveler and social scientist
who would befriend Henry Miller in Big Sur and visit the home of
C. G. Jung in Switzerland. In November 1945, Maud Oakes rode into
Todos Santos on horseback and stayed for nearly two years.

In the two books she wrote about her experiences there, *The Two
Crosses of Todos Santos* and the more personable *Beyond the Windy
Place*, Oakes rivetingly described a village of proud Mayan farmers
sitting on the edge of a remote mountain fastness that time seemed
to have forgotten. From the outset of her two singular chronicles,
Oakes faced up to the impossibility of remaining an objective observer
in the close-knit community of Todos Santos. When townspeople
flocked to her house to request cures for their ailments, both medical
and metaphysical, she overcame her misgivings and accepted the role
of healer. What she usually dispensed, along with samples from her
Western medicine chest, was a hefty dose of Yankee common sense.
And yet, by the end of her residence, Oakes learned to see the world
through the eyes of a *natural*, and she became at least part Todo-
santera. Her neighbors referred to her as *la chimancita* (little sha-
maness) and believed she was the "owner" of one of the four mountain peaks sacred to the Mam-speaking Mayas.

In the mid-forties the only access to Todos Santos was on foot,
mule, or horseback; you climbed a winding road from Huehuetenango
and crossed an enchanted plateau nearly 12,000 feet high, strewn with

hedgerows of the giant agave, or maguey, houses with thatch roofs like Chinese pagodas, and steep cultivated terraces set against craggy alpine peaks. In the evenings, clouds spill over the sides of the mountains and insulate the valley from the outside world. The daily lives of Todosanteros were ruled by Mayan calendar keepers and shamans who knew the world of appearances conceals an invisible universe of dark and beneficent spirits; by conjuring them with appropriate offerings, these spirits could be induced to work to one's advantage or to harm one's adversaries.

The first of the two crosses in Oakes's book stands for the Mayas' World Tree. It symbolizes the older rituals and beliefs associated with *costumbre*, enshrined in the town's single *cofradía*. The second cross, made of stone, represents ladino authority and the Catholic church. To these has been added a third wooden cross, planted in the old Mayan ruins above the town, which commemorates the Todosanteros killed in the violence of 1981 and 1982.

In 1982, when I made my way to Maud Oakes's home in Carmel, California, her conversation teemed with images of Todos Santos, its townspeople, its costumbres, and myriad other presences, corporeal and incorporeal. The first news had filtered out that the war in the altiplano had reached Todos Santos, but none of Maud Oakes's friends had as yet been affected.

Shortly after she completed her memoir of personal transformation, *The Stone Speaks*, which was published in the fall of 1987, Oakes suffered, quite suddenly, an almost total loss of memory. When I last visited her, she was under twenty-four-hour care by a nurse whose name she could not remember. Nonetheless, Maud Oakes, lean and spry at eighty-four and with her indomitable will intact, could still recall the colors of Todos Santos and two or three names: Petrona, Domingo, Basilia. And yet Maud Oakes gave signs of acknowledging the reality that had overtaken the place she called her spiritual home. Once she looked out into her sun-filled patio at the leaves falling from her Japanese maple and called out, "Are those bullets?"

I have made several trips to the high mountain valleys of Todos Santos Cuchumatán to seek out the enchantment Maud Oakes found there over forty years ago. Could one of Guatemala's proudest and most traditional Mayan communities survive the incursions of Marx-indoctrinated guerrillas burning with a sense of social injustice? More to the point, could it recover from the swift and massive army reprisals which, in the autumn and winter of 1981/82, led to the execution of as many as one hundred Todos Santos residents and the torching of over a hundred and fifty homes?

The main towns along the northern spine of the Cuchumatán cordillera suffered even greater losses in the war. I spoke with priests, private citizens, and public officials in an attempt to determine why this cold, isolated, and fiercely beautiful region of farmers and shepherds was the most severely punished—after the Ixil Triangle—by the military's counterinsurgency campaigns of the late seventies to mid-eighties. As so often happens in Guatemala, my journey generated a host of questions beyond the scope of those I sought answers for.

I set out from the bustling provincial capital of Huehuetenango—a largely ladino town—in the jeep of photographer Daniel Chauche, who was touring the area on business. The ascent to the plateau that overlooks the valley and the chain of volcanoes beyond, rivals in sheer drama the approach to Nebaj, which sits about fifty kilometers east on the western spine of the Cuchumatanes. The ripening wheat and corn fields that hopscotch up vertiginous slopes give way at around 9,000 feet to the spiky maguey plants with their ten-foot-tall arching stalk. At the viewpoint, small children with frost-pinked cheeks ran out to meet our vehicle. They were raised on potatoes and other mountain tubers and more closely resembled Bolivian or Tibetan youngsters than descendants of the lowland Maya.

Atop the 11,000-foot plateau of Paquix the sudden appearance of bare hills smoothed by long-vanished glaciers evokes Alaska or the high Andes. Lime kilns and herds of sheep dot the undulating plain, crosshatched with veins of black granite. Only an occasional civil patrol checkpoint or a stalled bus obstructs our progress. The first Todosanteros, dressed in gaily collared shirts and red striped trousers, appear soon after we turn left at the Barillas intersection. They are taller by nearly a head than most highland Mayas, broader at the chest and shoulders than the strapping Ixils, and they walk with a spring in their step that exudes self-confidence. These are not a conquered people.

Below the aldea of Chayval we come to La Ventosa (the Windy Place) and encounter the first of many teams of yoked oxen plowing the rich dark earth. So far, no tractors have penetrated this alpine country. We stop at a turnout for the first view of Todos Santos situated on a shallow river valley 3,500 feet below us. Immediately two shepherd boys with bright, ruddy faces approach us to sell us their woven bags. They have easily distinguished our white civilian jeep from the army's olive drab.

After answering their eager questions about our origins and destination, we ask Andrés and Martín if their families suffered during the troubles.

"Fortunately not," replies the quicker Andrés, about twelve years old. "We stayed in the mountains until it passed over." He frowns with sudden concern. "What about you? Did you suffer during the violence?"

The boys' spontaneous regard for our safety vaults the cultural abyss between natural and foreigner and brings tears to my eyes. It is an enormous relief to be in the presence of Mayas whose lives do not fill me with apprehension. I buy two of their woven purses without the customary haggling, and they repay us by posing for Daniel's camera with glowing smiles, surrounded by baaing sheep and plump goats.

2

As we drove into Todos Santos two women raised lovely red and blue embroidered huipiles for our inspection. There had been no visitors in over a week. We pulled the jeep into the pensión La Paz (Peace), whose owner, Don Victoriano, is the first native Todosantero to drive his own pick-up. All the wealthy ladino families fled town shortly before or immediately after the guerrilla occupation and the army reprisals. So far, the butcher, Don Ramón, and Don Mario, the barber, were among the handful of ladinos who felt safe enough to return.

The Todos Santos families I interviewed in Mexican refugee camps in 1983 led me to believe that the violence had driven away all costumbre; but nearly all the townspeople wore their trajes, or native dress, and the patron saint's feast day on November 1 was once again being celebrated with a breakneck horse race, traditional dances, and the usual abundance of *aguardiente*. Sadly, the last of the elder shamans Maud Oakes sparred with had recently died. Mayan calendar keepers, prayer makers who perform divination with *mixes* (beans), and most other practitioners of white and black magic had passed from the scene, except in outlying aldeas where tradition persists. "Before we had shamans and prayer makers," an older vendor confided to us at the marketplace. "Now we have cars and television."

Still, no one discards fallen teeth or tufts of hair, lest they fall into the wrong hands and provoke mischief. On a return visit we would meet in the town's cofradía with the nine surviving elders—all but one in their seventies and eighties—who showed us old leather-bound land titles and ritual objects from the smaller of two *cajas reales,* or royal coffers. The larger or "true" royal coffer, which cannot be opened in the presence of outsiders, is said to contain old curanderos' tools, Spanish documents, and an ancient parchment with colored figures.

Don Francisco Matías, a former head of the cofradía, harangued us in a loud, crackling voice about the loss of respect for the ancient laws, which had led to venality, theft, and rampant violence. Bellowing with his craggy face thrust six inches below my nose, Don Francisco scoffed at the contentiousness in the community between the new evangelicals and the militant Acción Católica catechists. Both factions had threatened to confiscate the caja real and toss it in a ravine. Don Francisco held passionately to his conviction that the true caja real contained the laws and teachings of his ancestors, which maintained order and balance in the universe; but to the doctrinaire catechists they were superstitious nonsense. He shouted the names of the four peaks held sacred by Todosanteros, where he insisted the *dueños,* or guardian spirits, still resided and kept alive the holiest days of the ancient Mayan calendar.

"Catechists and evangelicals come and go!" Don Francisco boomed. "Even shamans pass from the scene, whether they are true or fakes—but the guardians of the four sacred peaks endure forever!" After we'd listened respectfully to the octogenarian's unburdening homily, he and Don Pascual, the head of the cofradía, performed costumbre for us with tall candles, mortars, and votive rum. For an added contribution, he proposed to sacrifice a turkey in our honor, an offer we politely declined.

In the evening we visited Don Lázaro, one of the important town dignitaries, or principales, to whom we were delivering a complimentary photograph Daniel had taken of him on a previous visit. Daniel, the only ambulant gringo photographer in the altiplano, had compiled a documentary file on Todos Santos, and built a reputation by giving away free samples of his work. In Barillas, the final stop on our tour, he was doing a thriving business selling prints both to the ladinos and to the indigenous community.

Don Lázaro, a handsome elder of fifty-eight who sports a bright pink scarf under his woven hat, is old enough to have met Maud Oakes, but he pretended not to remember, perhaps because he had been aligned with one of the rival shamans who considered her an intruder. Before the violence, Don Lázaro had been a contractor for the large landowners, responsible for recruiting migrant laborers for the coffee and cotton harvests.

Don Lázaro was obviously pleased with his likeness and joked that he needed it as proof that he had survived a recent bout of bronchial pneumonia. He addressed us, teasingly, as *patroncitos*, little masters, and tested our knowledge about arcane subjects of interest to him. These included the Catholic religion and the high-tech war films he had seen on the TV set of his next-door neighbor Jacobo Ramírez, one of the first Todosanteros to emigrate to the States. Ramírez was also the first natural in town to own a TV *and* a VCR, which he had brought with him on a recent visit. After working for years on farms in Florida and Long Island, Ramírez had landed a scholarship to study English at Harvard in an extension program for native American community leaders.

Our first subject of conversation was the Catholic church. Like other Todosanteros, Don Lázaro spoke of the New Testament as if it were a religious tract freshly dropped on his doorstep. When he asked if I thought its contents were credible, I said it ranked with other sacred scriptures, such as the Old Testament and the Popol Vuh.

"You know, patroncitos, Jacobo tells me that everyone in your country owns a car and a television, but that they eat meat, fruits, and vegetables, just as we do. Is that right?"

We nod in assent.

"And they have houses like ours, one story, two stories high?"

"Oh yes," I assure Don Lázaro. "And in the cities we have houses that are five, ten, twenty, and even one hundred stories."

"Is that so?" Don Lázaro's eyes open wide, and he whistles softly. "Lying down or standing up?"

Before we can respond, Don Lázaro is off on another tack. "This big white fellow on the television who beats up the smaller fellows and never gets hurt—is that really happening? Why is it we never see any blood?"

We explain to Don Lázaro that the Arnold Schwarzenegger film he had seen on the VCR was just a very fast succession of thousands of photographs projected on a screen so that they gave the illusion of movement.

"Aha." Don Lázaro strokes his jaw. "And this gringo priest who comes to preach in our church, is he the same? If we cut him with our machete, he will not bleed either?"

Don Lázaro's wife and daughter burst into peals of laughter. After inviting us to test his earthen sweat bath, which he calls *chuj*, Don Lázaro again turns playful.

"Ah, patroncitos, to think that my father would run away from the sight of white folk like you, terrified that they would eat him— and here you are sitting in my house, drinking my coffee, and I don't feel any fear of you at all. We are all *tranquilo*. I like having you here, drinking my coffee, and bathing in my chuj. In fact, tomorrow I will tie up the two white patroncitos to the beam of my roof, so I can ask them all the questions that come into my head. I will feed them tortillas now and then, and when I drink too much and get nasty I will throw stones at them. What do you say to that, eh, patroncitos?"

Don Lázaro's neighbor Jacobo arrived from the States for a visit the following week, and we met him briefly on our return from Barillas. He was dressed in a jogging sweatsuit, Adidas, and a knit cap, and looked for all the world like a Latino prospect for a minor league baseball team. In his broken English, he told us about his months as an underpaid worker on a Long Island duck farm and joked casually about the frigid Boston winters, as his wife and children gazed adoringly on their Harvard scholar. Two of Jacobo's younger brothers were preparing to join him in the States within a year and boned up on gringo vernacular by sitting glued to the new VCR, on which they played *Rambo* and *Commando* over and over again.

Across town we met with Felipa, a weaver and unwed mother of three whose sister Santa had married an American social worker and moved to San Francisco. In a room adjacent to Felipa's house lived Barbara, a Peace Corps volunteer from California who was completing her second year of service. Felipa was teaching Barbara to weave on her backstrap loom. She was also giving her lessons in Mam and twitting her about the scrawny condition of the chickens provided by the Peace Corps' poultry-breeding program. Felipa's two younger brothers had already joined her sister in California and found work as day laborers in the vineyards north of San Francisco. But when I asked her if she planned to join them, Felipa emphatically shook her head. She said Santa had lost weight her first year in the States and longed so for her foods and the *alegría* (joy) of feast days, that it was a long time before she adjusted to living abroad. Now, she was at last earning an income selling Felipa's and her own woven goods out of her home.

"Here we have the violence," Felipa said, as she kneaded the corn for the evening tortillas. "But most of the time we are *tranquilo*. Santa writes that she is surrounded by commotion all the time, and time slips through her fingers. There are dollars there, and many conveniences, but everything is expensive, and the people are not calm; they are running all the time and never have time to sit and watch the sun set behind the mountains. If they send me money for the airplane, I will go visit them, but this is my home and this is where I plan to grow old and die and be buried."

"But Felipa," asks Barbara, a lanky, energetic twenty-four-year-old who has learned to sit still and watch sunsets, "what if the violence comes back? What will you do then?"

Felipa's face darkens momentarily. "In that case," she says, pausing to wipe her hands on her apron, "I will do as before and hide out in the mountains until it passes."

Late that evening we saw the butcher, Don Ramón, draw and quarter a whole cow, which he would sell at market the following

day. The slaughterhouse sits above the town cemetery, a rather hap-
hazard collection of carelessly whitewashed sepulchres, few of which
had even rudimentary epitaphs. Except for All Saints' Day, November
1, when relatives visit the gravestones of departed relatives to light
candles, it appears that in Todos Santos the emphasis is on the living.
Well after dark, bandy-legged Don Ramón was still trudging from the
slaughterhouse up to the butcher shop, carrying on his back the
bleeding entrails of the freshly killed cow.

We managed to sleep through the subfreezing night by wearing all
our clothes and piling on several blankets. Just after sunup we heard
the sound of melting ice dripping from the corrugated tin roofs.

By 7 A.M. the market was in full swing. An old man from the
neighboring village of San Juan Atitán had sold a fine pair of goats
to Don Mario, the ladino barber, who tied them up to his house post
and later sold them at a handsome profit. For most of the naturales
who had traveled miles on foot, bartering or selling their produce
provides an excuse for the social exchanges highland Mayas thrive
on. The latest gossip was being swapped at every stall, accompanied
by high bursts of laughter and broad, theatrical gestures. And more
than one couple living in separate aldeas carried on daylong courtships
outside the church.

In late morning I was introduced to Petrona Calmo, a woman of
about eighty-five who had been Maud Oakes's neighbor, as well as
her most trusted friend. She and her daughter were selling vegetables,
and she invited us to visit her that afternoon.

A leisurely climb took us to Cumanchúm, the small post-classic
Mayan ceremonial center whose partially uncovered ruins overlook
the town, and which are still the setting for animal sacrifices and
other costumbre. We passed several market-goers on their way to
their aldeas with poultry, small pigs, and one ghetto-blaster that would
most likely drive out the traditional drum and flute. The cluster of
unexcavated structures looked out on the 12,000-foot-high Chemal,
the tallest peak in the Cuchumatán range, and the highest point in
Central America excluding volcanic crests. Next to the ruins a young
member of the town's civil defense patrol guarded his lookout with
an old M-1 rifle cradled in one arm, while he crocheted a shoulder

bag with his free hands. He told us there had been no subversives in the area for many months but that a fellow patroller had nearly shot a gringo for taking pictures from the ruins after dark.

We assured him we had no intention of taking pictures at night, and he returned to his handiwork. To our left and beside the old Maya costumbre cross described in Maud Oakes's books, rose a new wooden cross with the date "April 15 1982." This was a few months after the Guerrilla Army of the Poor (EGP) occupied Todos Santos and hoisted their red and black standard above the municipality. (The flag, according to a schoolteacher, bore the image of Che Guevara.) The army, which saw the flag as outright provocation, marched on the town and carried out its selection, based on a list of over two hundred "subversives" collected by informers. Some were executed on the spot, several others were systematically tortured, and at least five women were raped by soldiers. The next day hundreds of survivors fled to the mountains across the river. They lived on roots and wild plants for several days until the army decamped. On their return, many found their homes and milpas burned to the ground.

After 1982, the cross of violence eclipsed the other two crosses in the Todosanteros' pantheon. The town's spiritual center moved from the caja real in the cofradía and the crucified Christ in the church to the new cross standing next to the old Mayan altar atop Cumanchúm. Only recently have the symbols of a gentler Mayan tradition and of Christian worship begun, slowly, to reclaim their accustomed place. Part of the void is being filled by opportunistic evangelicals who have opened two chapels in town and are still gaining converts. But fear of the nightmare's return lies close to the surface.

When Ríos Montt seized the presidency in March 1982, he sent a civic action delegation to Todos Santos with sheets of corrugated tin. At the same time, his comandante beefed up the civil patrol to include every able-bodied Todosantero between the ages of fifteen and fifty. The recruits were forced to march on round-the-clock patrols at least once a week, to root out "subversives." Today, most adult males still march on the patrols and are subjected to regular drills and patriotic lectures by army personnel.

Father James Flaherty, an American Maryknoll missionary, stayed on in Todos Santos until just before Ríos Montt's takeover, when he moved to a new parish at Malacatancito, south of Huehuetenango.

Maguey, the giant aloe native to the upper Cuchumatán mountain range.

Don Lázaro, a leading *principal* from Todos Santos Cuchumatán.

The ladino butcher of Todos Santos.

Don Pascual, chief prayermaker of Todos Santos's sole
cofradía.

Caja real and four *cofrades, cofradía* of Todos Santos.

Doña Petrona, friend and former neighbor of Maud Oakes, Todos Santos.

Author at a gathering at the mayor's house, Todos Santos.

Benito Ramírez Mendoza as school supervisor in an aldea of Todos Santos.

When we visited him there, he filled in the details. He informed us that most of the victims of the army occupation had lived in the neighboring village of El Rancho, where the guerrillas had been active. And it was there as well that nearly all the 160 or so homes had been torched by the army. A greater tragedy had befallen thousands of Todosanteros who had moved to the Ixcán, about two days' walk to the north. Father Flaherty calculated that one member of every other family in Todos Santos municipality, from a total population of about 20,000, had moved to the fertile Ixcán lowlands over the past two decades in search of cultivable land. In the late 1970s and early 1980s at least two hundred of them had been killed by the army to deny the guerrillas a popular support base in that region. After the army massacres there, most of the survivors fled to Mexico, where several thousand are still living in refugee camps.

Father Flaherty, a gentle, silverhaired grandfatherly figure, had served long enough in Todos Santos to have witnessed many important changes, including those related to the rise of the EGP. He told us, "When I first arrived, the few Todosanteros who attended school turned into ladinos, just like their teachers. Now there are a growing number of native teachers and five hundred students, many of whom will go on to secondary study without giving up their Mayan identity. The civil war has taken a terrible toll, but it has pulled this area out of a centuries-long isolation and forced the government to pay attention to their needs." As parish priest, Father Flaherty befriended Todosanteros who joined the guerrillas; and he knew as well those few who became army informers and were subsequently executed by the EGP. "In the spring of 1982, the army barricaded the road, and no one could get in or out. I remember seeing EGP supporters scattering large rocks and boulders in the church courtyard, so the army helicopters could not land there. But of course, they landed anyway."

In the morning we hiked through the countryside to visit a group of about thirty-five village women who had started their own agricultural cooperative on a hillside in El Rancho. They purchased seeds from a government agency and planted broccoli, lettuce, beets, and other nontraditional crops in a communal field. During a break, I interviewed several exhausted but cheerful women, many of whose homes had been burned by the army during the *bulla*, the trouble.

Surprisingly, none of them seemed to harbor any rancor toward the soldiers who had destroyed their crops and houses, because, as one of them said, "That is what the army does." The military's strategy of transferring culpability to those who provoke the army's reprisals had apparently succeeded; but I sensed in these women a deeper resentment against those who had secured their loyalty by addressing their just grievances and who then failed to redress them.

One of the wives had recently returned from Mexico with her husband, after having been driven out of the Ixcán by the army. Julia, as I will call her, was particularly bitter that their contacts with guerrillas had forced them to become refugees twice over. In the Ixcán, where the EGP presence remains strong, Julia and her husband had their crops burned by soldiers who assumed they were subversives by virtue of their presence there. "The guerrillas demanded our allegiance, but when the army came, they abandoned us to our fate. As far as I am concerned, the army and the guerrillas are the same. They are all bad. If any of them show their faces here again, I will boil water and throw it in their faces."

Petrona, whose sharp aquiline features and large moist eyes liken her to a good witch from fairy tales, awaits us in her home with one of her granddaughters. (In Antigua I had met her friend Basilia, who had been one of Maud Oakes's two maids. At age sixty, Basilia was a robust and handsome businesswoman who sold Todos Santos handicrafts in Antigua and Guatemala City. I asked Basilia about Simona, Oakes's other maid, with whom Basilia often drank and swapped ladino lovers. She told me that Simona, her Todosantero husband, and two of their children had been killed by men dressed in camouflage fatigues, whom she assumed to be guerrillas. Had Maud Oakes known of this, I wondered, before she lost her memory?)

I inform Petrona that her former neighbor Doña Matilda—as Maud Oakes was known in town—had suffered a severe memory loss, and she nods sadly. "I too am losing my memory," she says. "Since my man, Domingo, died two years ago, I am counting the days until I can join him. It is not the same in Todos Santos since the troubles began. How about Matilda's country? Are people more contented there?" I tell Petrona most Americans are better off than Todosanteros, but I did not think they were more contented.

"Here, it used to be good," she says. "People worked very hard, and the land gave us our necessities. But now we are distracted. Our children and grandchildren have left for their safety or to look for better living conditions elsewhere. And we who remain are still frightened. A man told us it would all happen again after seven years, like a plague, and it is almost that time." She turns to me, her alert amber eyes clouded with cataracts. "Do you think they will come again?"

Not certain whom she meant by "they," I suggest that her son who had moved to the Ixcán should stay clear of the areas controlled by the army or by the guerrillas. Petrona becomes agitated. "But how does one know? Margarito, my older son, who knew Matilda, they came here to kill him because they said he got mixed up with the wrong people. I saw it with my own eyes. They came and accused him and gave him no chance to defend himself. I reached out to stop them, but it was too late. They shot him right in this courtyard. They said, 'Grandmother, our quarrel is not with you. But your son must pay.' How can they say that? It would have been better if they had killed Domingo and me together with my son."

"Petrona," I asked in consternation, "did the men who killed your son wear army uniforms?"

She brushed her hand at me and wiped her eyes. "What difference does that make? Will the color of their uniform bring back my son?"

Petrona Calmo died a year after our last interview, in the spring of 1990. Two months later her friend Maud Oakes passed away in her Carmel home. Obituaries gave the cause of her death as Alzheimer's disease.

3

On our way out of Todos Santos we stopped outside the aldea of Chayval, near the edge of the Paquix plateau, so Daniel could take pictures of the maguey. At this elevation the fog had only begun to lift, and it was so cold the trees shed their cover of frost in showers of ice crystals that formed neat white circles on the ground. The sound of falling ice eerily resembled the hollow ring of the axes we would hear two days later in the fast-disappearing cloud forests of San Mateo Ixtatán. The fields of potatoes and oats seemed bleak and arid in the Arctic cold, and even the scarecrows were frozen stiff. As in the rest of the highlands, the native farmers invariably dressed their scarecrows in ladino hat, shirt, and trousers. Was it because the colorful Indian *traje* was not menacing enough, I wondered. Daniel suggested it was because factory-made ladino clothes were more expendable.

Daniel had a file of maguey photos taken at different seasons—in fruit, in flower, and during the few weeks a year when the bare stalks stand like Delphic phalluses against a cobalt sky. Daniel has become obsessed with the magueys. He manages to find clusters of the giant agaves whose stiff radiating leaves perform fantastic choreographies or individual blades on which a passerby has carved an esoteric glyph.

A civil patrolman came over to warn us against taking photos, since we were being watched through binoculars from an army post. He pointed to a barren ridge in the distance, where Daniel knew there were no barracks. The patrolman simply wanted us out of his turf. But he calmed down after Daniel let him peer through his lens and fiddle with the controls. When Daniel asked if the M-1 was loaded, the patrolman shot back, "Is your camera?"

He told us he was a farmer and shepherd with eighty sheep and several hectares of wheat, potatoes, and lima beans. He also grew oats to feed his flock. He said they extracted the fiber from the maguey leaves to make cord and used the residue for fertilizer. The sheep and goats fed on the flowers, but the maguey fruit was useless. The patrolman told us the villagers travel to the coast to sell lamb's wool and meat and bring back corn and black beans. The potato crop was sold below, in Huehuetenango.

I asked him if the army patrolled the area, and he said they did, mostly after dark. But there had been no incidents in Chayval, an aldea of sixty to seventy families, because the patrols kept it well guarded. It was clear where his loyalties lay, but he did not have much choice. On our way out we saw from a distance a huge gathering of civil patrollers near the glacial moraine. Once a week, army officers gathered the men to drill them on how to protect their homes from the communist subversives.

In some aldeas of Huehuetenango, civil defense patrols have replaced the army as a counterinsurgency force, just as they have in parts of the Ixil Triangle. In July 1990, civil defenders from villages near Colotenango told an Americas Watch observer they had given chase to armed guerrillas with nothing but their machetes for weapons. Five civil defenders with shrapnel wounds explained that they feared the army's punishment for slacking off on the job more than they feared the guerrillas' grenades and submachine guns. Given their training, it was a wonder civil defenders allowed us to stop at all or engage them in conversation.

"Why do you take pictures of our maguey?" the patrolman asked, as he escorted us to our vehicle.

"Because they're pretty," Daniel said.

The patrolman shook his head. "Then we should charge you one quetzal for each one you photograph. Do you know how hard we work to dig them up from the hills and replant them here? They protect our fields from the winter winds and provide sustenance. To you they are a pretty picture, to us they are our livelihood."

At the *comedor* near the crossroads to Barillas we stop for a beer and run into a schoolmaster I had interviewed the year before. Benito Ramírez Mendoza, one of the first native schoolteachers in Todos Santos, has been promoted to supervisor of schools. He was returning from a training course at San Carlos University, where he is subjected to frequent small humiliations because he insists on wearing his traje. Although he speaks Spanish perfectly, to his ladino colleagues, he tells us, he is still an Indian, and they cannot accept that he has attained the same rank as they have. Father Flaherty had mentioned Benito Ramírez as a prime example of those Todosanteros who have risen in the ladino world without giving up their ethnic identity. But he did not mention the price they had to pay.

Benito says he enjoys visiting the schools of the municipality, but the hours and conditions of work are punishing. "I have to cover five hundred square kilometers of territory and am responsible for supervising three thousand pupils and ninety teachers. I spend my days on buses, eating in restaurants, and my nights in terrible pensiones. I have four children, whom I get to see only once or twice a month. As it is, too much of my salary is spent on travel, and my family derives less benefit from my work than they did when I was a schoolteacher. I will stay at this job for a year. If conditions do not improve, I will resign and return to Todos Santos as a humble schoolteacher."

I was to run into Benito Ramírez again on a number of occasions. When I met him a few months later at Todos Santos's fiesta patronal, he mimed a knife cutting his throat. After the teachers' strike of July 1989, Ramírez had been dismissed as supervisor of schools, and he was back at his old teaching post. "This is where I belong," he said, in a wistful tone that sounded unconvincing. Despite his modest disclaimers, Benito Ramírez was playing for higher stakes, trying to outwit the ladinos without having to become one.

That fall Olivia Carrescia, an Italian-American filmmaker who has completed two excellent documentaries on Todos Santos, made good on a promise to escort Benito Ramírez to her home in New York City. I ran into Ramírez, resplendent in his Todosantero traje, at Columbia University, where Rigoberta Menchú was speaking on Guatemala's civil war. Afterward, Ramírez took me aside to tell me of his adventures on the East Coast. In the dead of winter, he had been staying in the homes of Olivia's friends, including a houseboat in Connecticut and a penthouse apartment in Manhattan. He had attempted without success to contact Guatemala's U.N. ambassador, to denounce the enforced civil patrols and other problems in the highlands. Ramírez had ridden the subways, and in Times Square he had stopped to offer his solidarity to one of the first blacks he had ever seen, a huge man who glared at his funny hat, floppy collar, and striped, bright red trousers and threatened to knock his block off.

What impressed Ramírez the most about New York was the diversity of people he had met—the Latin Americans had been particularly friendly—but it troubled him that he had hardly seen any birds other than his hostess's Thanksgiving turkey, which he found too bland for his palate. Other than turkey, he ate foods of different nationalities wherever he went: Italian, Mexican, Chinese, French, and Middle Eastern. Unlike Todos Santos, he discovered, no two people in New York ate the same thing or lived in the same way. There seemed to be no accepted way of doing things.

After working several days as a "wetback" in a Manhattan flower shop so he could buy gifts for his wife and children, Ramírez concluded, "We have many problems in Guatemala. The violence has turned neighbor against neighbor, and the army continues to control us through the civil defense patrols. Our costumbres are dying, and we are forgetting the wisdom of our ancestors. But after visiting New

York, I realize our Mayan communities have more culture than I had thought. In spite of the city's great wealth and high technology, I found poor and broken people everywhere, most of whom did not appear to have a home. North American evangelicals come to tell us what to believe in, but their own people do not know what to believe in. Their anthropologists come to study our customs but don't seem to pay any attention to the homeless people in their own cities. North Americans should work to save their own culture before they come down to Guatemala to pretend to save ours."

In July 1990 I again visited Todos Santos to bring Ramírez a copy he had requested of Olivia Carrescia's film *Todos Santos: The Survivors,* which dramatizes the hard lives led by Todosanteros who survived the violence. (Carrescia's award-winning first documentary on Todos Santos had focused on costumbre and feast-day traditions.) As one of the eyewitnesses interviewed in *The Survivors,* Ramírez reports on the rape, torture, and other atrocities carried out by the army during its brief occupation of Todos Santos.

One evening a reflective Benito Ramírez gathered together a dozen leading townspeople, among them the head of the civil defense patrol, for a private screening of Carrescia's film. During the discussion that followed, in which I was invited to take part, old wounds were reopened when Ramírez's younger brother accused him of making baseless accusations against the army and siding with the guerrillas. He and two civil defenders argued for burning the film because "it was made by a subversive" and would prove prejudicial to Todos Santos. A schoolmaster named Julián objected that townspeople were mature enough to judge the film on its flaws or merits and decide on its accuracy. After an hour's discussion, opinion in the room divided about equally for and against showing the film. Asked to comment, I limited myself to complimenting the group on their observance of democratic procedure.

After everyone else had spoken the civil defense commander, who turned out to be Benito Ramírez's uncle, took an unexpected stand in defense of the film, describing it as "la verdad," the truth. He spoke in a self-deprecating manner with studied gestures, portraying himself as a former guerrilla sympathizer who did not fear the army. In 1982, when he showed up at the base because his car had been seized by soldiers, he was dismissed with a pointed threat. But he returned again and again to ask for the return of his car, until an officer informed him that it had been blown up after serving in undercover operations by G-2 agents. His months of wheedling, cajoling, and entreaty had seemingly come to nothing, but he had learned how to curry favor with base commanders.

The head of the civil patrols clearly was not the most intelligent person in the room, and his Spanish was so poor I had difficulty following him, but he possessed a native guile and the practiced gestures of an expert mime. He held us spellbound with impersonations of brutish officers who "spat [on him] like a dog" and of the more educated ones who briskly congratulated his civic responsibility and then ignored him.

I had heard about how he and his nephew Benito had made a heroic gesture to save their fellow villagers. After the army's first executions in Todos Santos, he and Benito had shown up at the base to offer themselves in place of the two hundred Todosanteros who remained on army death lists. The base commander of the time, a disciple of pro-democracy Defense Minister Gramajo, had been so impressed by his courage he offered him the post of comandante of the civil patrols. Benito's uncle accepted the office, seeing in it another way to be of service to his community. And he still harbored hopes of finding a replacement for his lost car. He played along with his bosses by singing the army's praises and denouncing the guerrillas; behind their backs he advised his civil defenders to look the other way if they encountered non-belligerent guerrillas on their patrols. As a result, not a single armed confrontation was reported during his seven years as comandante.

At the end of two more hours of heated discussion, the comandante underwent a subtle transformation. The self-mocking tone gave way to sarcasm and pregnant glances directed at the others in the room, each of whom he had known from infancy. Everyone was on edge, because the week before unknown persons—presumably guerrillas—had knocked out the town's electric power lines. As the night wore on, the comandante divulged a vital piece of information about everyone present, myself included. (He hinted that the book I was writing could land me in hot water.) His revelations had been meant to remind us of the personal risks he had undertaken for the sake of the community and for which he felt insufficiently appreciated. Had he lived in an earlier, more peaceful time, he might have become apprenticed to a shaman, as would his nephew Benito.

After viewing the film a second time, the comandante reminded the others that the army still held him as guarantor for the two hundred Todosanteros on their list. "If any of you have dealings with the guerrillas, my head will be on the block." He turned on Benito and said, "And if the guerrillas find out the things you say about the army and the patrols, I am the one they'll come after, and my head will be on your conscience." In contrast with the civil defenders from Colotenango, the comandante appeared to fear reprisals from the guerrillas he had once supported more than he feared the army, whose ways he had come to know intimately and to whom, when all was said and done, he belonged.

Shortly before midnight, the twelve town leaders finally decided that the film was likely to cause problems in the community and should be placed under lock and key.

8

San Mateo Ixtatán

"I will rid this place even of its seed!"
Army commander, Huehuetenango

As we started our descent from Paquix toward San Juan Ixcoy we entered a pine forest that had been reduced to wasteland by the deadly pine borer, a beetle that kills its host by chewing through the pine's outer layers and disrupting the flow of sap. Some kilometers farther north, we encountered a man-made desolation, where the army had felled all the trees within a hundred feet of the road to discourage guerrilla ambushes. Only a half dozen stands of pine forest remained along the two-hundred-kilometer distance to Barillas, and each of those was under assault from poor settlers in search of firewood. Daniel assured me that only ten years before unbroken forest had covered the mountain slopes as far as the eye could see. Thousands of hectares of pine and hemlock have been leveled by a lumber concern named La Cuchumadera, whose stockholders include a number of army officers and a former mayor of Todos Santos. Within another few years, the violence done to their environment is likely to visit as great a misery on the Mayan communities as all the human rights violations of the past three decades.

The women of San Juan Ixcoy wear long white woven shawls and cover their faces in the presence of strangers. Ladinos have felt unwelcome here since the revolt of 1898, when the Liberal government's expropriation of untitled Mayan lands for coffee cultivation led to the lynching of a dozen labor contractors and other ladinos. Although the uprising was as brutally put down as the 1936 *tumulto* in Nebaj would be years later, hostility toward ladino landowners has kept the pot boiling in this remote municipality of several hundred Kanjobal-speaking Mayan families.

The queer sensation that I had wandered into a misplaced Druze or Moslem village was reinforced by the steely looks aimed at me when I raised my camera to photograph a group of women in the local equivalent of purdah. It was market day, and the square was as packed as a Moroccan Casbah. "If you take a picture," a shawled fruit vendor warned me in an uninflected voice, "you will be lynched."

Despite their hostility to outsiders, I learned from a laborer in the park that dozens of San Juaneros have left to find work in the States and are sending valuable foreign exchange to their families. More natives of Huehuetenango are living abroad than from any other region of Guatemala. The dollars, automobiles, TV's and other electronic gadgets Huehuetecos send home are rapidly transforming their relatives' cultural identity, even as their costumbre has been infiltrated by U.S.-based evangelical sects. These gringo values have begun to undermine the old Mayan/ladino polarities in unexpected ways. Although those who return to traditional ways after exposure to Western values are a small minority, U.S. dollars are subsidizing a surge in property and land purchases. The postal money orders mailed every month by relatives in California and Florida are permitting native Mayas to buy title to their lands and to gradually replace the ladinos who for generations have owned the towns' businesses and transport. In ways that no one could have predicted a decade ago, Mayan refugees and expatriates are helping to underwrite a renascent indigenous movement inside Guatemala. For many of the communities dislocated by the violence of the early eighties, the price of the new prosperity includes the breakup of the traditional Mayan nuclear family, evangelical conversion, the alienation of exile.

One sinister aspect of Westernization takes the form of persistent rumors about shadowy entrepreneurs who show up in remote aldeas of San Juan Ixcoy and other Huehuetenango villages. They reportedly offer fistfuls of dollars for small children whom they spirit away in their vehicles, never to be seen again. In the late eighties, horror stories appeared weekly in the Guatemalan press that implicated top government officials in the contraband traffic of children to the United States and Europe. The lucky ones were adopted by childless families.

The unlucky ones—according to these stories—were sent abroad for their organs, which were transplanted to monied invalids in the United States and Europe. Although no evidence has surfaced to substantiate these stories, they have taken root in the Guatemalan consciousness and refuse to die.

2

On a subsequent visit with Canadian geographer George Lovell we stopped in Yuval, a small Kanjobal aldea of corn farmers half an hour past San Juan Ixcoy on the road to Soloma. Even during the cold, dry "summer" season Yuval's terraced vegetable orchards were well irrigated and the peach trees were in full bloom. The stream that courses through the heart of Yuval looks clean and fast enough to support trout, except for the toxic detergent soap the village women now use for their wash.

Lovell had taken under his wing a twenty-year-old Yuval native, Genaro, who had left home six years earlier to seek his fortune. Genaro ended up in Kingston, Canada, leaving behind a skein of adventures and mishaps in Mexico and the United States that would enliven a sequel to the film *El Norte*. I had met Genaro in Kingston two years earlier and found him to be an intelligent, sensitive young man still chary of Western culture. After his arrival in Canada as an illegal immigrant he had changed his name several times to avoid discovery, and his closest friends were Vietnamese and Kampuchean refugees. Lovell, who invited Genaro into his home, rebuked him mildly for eccentricities like buying $50 shirts on his meager income and for inviting Seventh Day Adventist missionaries into the kitchen. At night, Genaro still jerks awake to nightmares in which he is seized and killed, sometimes by soldiers and sometimes by guerrillas.

Since Genaro's departure, nearly half the male residents of Yuval have followed in his tracks to find seasonal jobs or permanent residence in places like Indiantown, Florida, Tucson, and Los Angeles. Genaro's mother and sister have stayed behind, living in a small hut of adobe and sticks whose rustic design antedates the Conquest. Juana, the forty-year-old mother, speaks hardly a word of Spanish. Yuval's evangelical preacher, Luis Estéban, served as translator when Lovell presented her with $400 U.S., a cassette recording of Genaro's voice, and half a dozen photographs. The eight crisp $50 bills, a modest sum to those who had been abroad, were portentous enough that six principales were enlisted as witnesses when they changed hands.

Juana, who is half blind from a coronary condition, accepted the gifts gingerly. She then turned sharply to Lovell and asked why Genaro did not come home to look after her and his unmarried sister, Petrona. Her two older sons had been killed by the army in the early 1980s for suspected guerrilla activities. Juana's husband, a dealer in bootleg *kusha* who left her for another woman, had also been killed, either by guerrillas or the Treasury Police. No one seemed to know for certain or care much one way or the other.

Lovell explained patiently to Juana that Genaro worked as a taxi driver and waiter in Canada to pay for his college education. As soon as he had his engineering degree and his residence permit, he would return for a long visit. Unhappy Juana sighed, and posed patiently for Lovell's camera in her Sunday traje, apparently convinced she would never lay eyes on her son again. The last time Lovell had visited Yuval with news of Genaro, Juana had become so distraught she barricaded herself in his car and insisted on being taken to her son. After pleading with her in vain, Lovell required the assistance of two principales to extricate Juana from his jeep.

Only minutes after we parted, Juana ran downhill to ask the preacher to hold her fifty-dollar bills in safekeeping, because she feared the rats in her home would eat them. In any event, she confessed she did not know enough Spanish to be able to cash them in at the bank.

In the village center sat four late-model Toyota station wagons and VW vans that neighbors had driven back from the States. Since their owners lived in mountainside hamlets inaccessible by road, the vehicles sat in Yuval for months at a time. A resourceful resident had strung a clothesline between two of the vehicles and hung her wash. Our guide, Luis Mérida López, Yuval's schoolmaster, pointed to large tile-roofed houses on the hillside that had been paid for with U.S. dollars. Their owners had typically returned home after one or more seasons of working the tomato and citrus orchards in Florida and Georgia. He said every one of these spacious dwellings was a single-room home, like their former adobe huts, because the villagers were unaccustomed to privacy. Luis had fifty-six pupils in the hand-some new school. He said most of the kids showed no interest in local history and left for the States as soon as they learned the alphabet.

When I asked if the new wealth had spawned envidia in the com-munity, I was told the opposite was the case. "Now that everyone has the possibility of making dollars abroad, there is less reason for envying your neighbors." In the past years, all but five or six families have converted to Protestantism, and they pray together in the huge temple that sits on Yuval's highest hilltop. Brother Luis Estéban, who had sent his nephews to California, wore a black leather jacket with a day-glo Los Angeles Raiders insignia. He said his brother Cruz planned to start a Rotary Club in the village.

Yuval had been spared the worst of the violence, although EGP guerrillas had passed through town in the early 1980s, after success-fully recruiting in nearby Soloma and villages to the north. As else-where, every male in the village has to march regularly on the civil defense patrol, which has had no encounters with subversives in nearly a decade.

A somber mood had descended on the village since the outbreak of war in the Persian Gulf. Recently, several young men with green cards had returned because they feared being drafted into the U.S. Army. When asked what they thought of Saddam Hussein, a villager responded, "We have no television here, so we have not seen his face. But my cousin in Indiantown writes that he is stubborn like an ox and will not listen to reason—just like our neighbors in the next village down the road."

3

Santa Eulalia was socked in with fog, and the streets were churned into mud by a steady icy drizzle. The town church had burned down six months earlier, and no attempt was being made to rebuild it. The hollowed-out shell seemed appropriate somehow to the bleak, in-hospitable ambience. Most of the townspeople were gray and gaunt, and the children dull-eyed and undernourished. One small boy had tied a string to the lip of a plastic bag and was trying to fly it in the rain, in lieu of a kite. And yet Santa Eulalia is known in the altiplano for its gaily ornamented marimbas, the musical instrument of choice at most Guatemalan birthdays, weddings, saint-day celebrations, and wakes.

An American anthropologist, Shelton Davis, wrote his Ph.D. thesis on the Santa Eulalians' rituals of attachment to ancestral lands and the lasting trauma to the community when huge tracts had been turned over to unscrupulous ladino settlers after Justo Rufino Barrios's "Liberal Reform" measures of the 1880s.

On the shores of Lake Atitlán I had interviewed a retired German planter from the coast who remembered traveling on horseback as a young man to Santa Eulalia, to recruit laborers to harvest his coffee. He had advanced each of fifty *jornaleros* (seasonal workers) a nominal sum and then led them on foot all the way to the lowland province of Retalhuleu, a journey of over a week. The planter chuckled as he recalled that most of the men spent their meager allowance on drink in the finca canteen, and had to return the following year to work off the money he had advanced them. "That is how, in the old days, we assured ourselves a steady supply of peons for the harvest. And you know, you could always count on their keeping their word. You wrote their debt down on little books, and it was like sacred writ. Of course, other planters marked up their debts, and they wouldn't protest because they couldn't read. Those poor bastards had no land of their own to work anyhow. And the fact of the matter is, we paid them more, in real wages, than they get for the same work today."

4

After two hours of bumping along the rugged dirt road to Barillas the fog became so thick we could hardly see in front of the hood; but Daniel, who claimed to know these roads like the back of his hand, zipped right along, arguing that it was an easier ride if you flew over the potholes than if you merely rode over them. By the time we had climbed back up to the 8,300-foot elevation of San Mateo Ixtatán, a *norte* was blowing full blast, and I felt as frozen under my layers of sweaters and my down jacket as I ever had in any northern wilderness. We learned afterward that we had crossed the Cuchumatanes during the coldest January weather in eighteen years.

San Mateo, a Chuj-speaking community of two thousand whose

animus toward ladinos rivals that of San Juan Ixcoy's, had been the
hardest hit by the war of any town on our route. It is the market and
cultural center for a largely indigenous municipality of about 17,000
souls that has held on to its communal pride and continues to observe
its ancient traditions. Unlike Santa Eulalians, who regularly migrate
to the coast as laborers and who have resettled in remote areas, San
Mateans tend to stay put and work their lands. In addition to tending
sheep, they grow coffee, cardamom, wheat, oats, and other grains.

We entered the town church, one of Guatemala's oldest, which
like many of the altiplano's primitive churches had been erected on
the site of a Mayan temple. The church was awash in red and pink
pastel colors that glowed through the dripping gray fog. Townspeople
repaint the facade every year, always in bright colors that in no way
reflect their dour, inhospitable temperament. Daniel had been witness
some years earlier to townspeople roughing up a Florida newspaper
photographer who tried to photograph a funeral without permission.

In the rectory we met another North American Maryknoller, Fern
Goslin, a strapping French Canadian of forty-five who had been parish
priest of San Mateo for a little over two years. He invited us to warm
ourselves by the kitchen stove, where a resident nun was preparing
lasagna.

Father Goslin had served in Nicaragua before being assigned to
Guatemala eight years earlier; he informed us that the army had killed
eight hundred parishioners of San Mateo in 1981 and 1982, most of
them in outlying aldeas with names like Petenac, Bulej, Puente Alto.
Goslin had the information from his Maryknoll predecessor, Ron
Hennessey, who had remained in the area through the massacres,
crossing quarantine barriers, interrogating military officers, and stead-
fastly standing up for his parishioners. "Father Hennessey did not run
off to the States at the first sign of trouble," Fern Goslin said, "and
then write books about how grim it had all been. Some of the Maryknollers who served in this area and then denounced the army from
abroad made it hard for many of us, who had to answer not only to
the military but to our parishioners. The priests who stayed, like Ron
Hennessey and Stan Rother, those were the real heroes, in my
estimation."

On my return to the States I would learn that Ron Hennessey, a
conservative Iowan who had collaborated with the military when he

first arrived in Guatemala in the mid-sixties, had written a quietly eloquent, unsparing denunciation of the army's atrocities in San Mateo. In a deposition he had made before the U.S. Immigration and Naturalization Service in December 1985, he described in painstaking detail the climate of terror that had pervaded the province in the early eighties. He was the only outside witness to horrendous army massacres of over two hundred campesinos in each of two aldeas of his parish in early 1982. He had collected names and comforted survivors but did not report the killings right away, assuming that such horrors could not be concealed from the international press. When no word of the massacres appeared anywhere, he reported them, first to the U.S. Embassy, and three years later to the Immigration Service. And yet, the killings have remained largely unknown, except to U.S. lawyers working on the asylum petitions of hundreds of Kanjobal and Chuj survivors.

In questioning Fern Goslin, we learned that the eight hundred deaths he mentioned included another notorious army massacre in the neighboring municipality of Nentón, which is part of the San Mateo parish. Several reports have been written about the July 1982 slaughter of approximately three hundred fifty campesinos suspected of supplying cattle to the EGP. They all lived and worked in Finca San Francisco (unconnected to Cotzal's finca of the same name). Jesuit Ricardo Falla, an exiled Guatemalan anthropologist with the University of Mexico, wrote a detailed study of the event.

His account begins with the butchering and devouring of two bulls by a large patrol of kaibiles, who then turned on their owners. In cold systematic fashion, the soldiers shot and bludgeoned the women enclosed in the church, their infants and older children, and finally the men held inside the alcalde's office. Their intention was identical to that of the comandante who screamed at the villagers of Puente Alto, *"Voy a acabar hasta con la semilla aquí."* (I will rid this place even of its seed!)

The massacre at Finca San Francisco—the worst single atrocity on record in modern Guatemalan history—was accompanied by grisly individual barbarities; soldiers slowly sliced the throats of elders with rusty machetes as they laughed out loud, amused by the sheeplike sound produced by severed windpipes. Three survivors of the massacre rendered witness to macabre rapes of old women, ritual infanticide and cannibalism, in an atmosphere of saturnalia that beggars the imagination. Falla conjectures that the eyewitnesses were deliberately allowed to escape in order to sow panic among other residents who collaborated with the guerrillas. Within days of the massacre, nine thousand refugees fled across the Mexican border in the largest exodus of the war.

Father Goslin smiled when I brought up the Maryknollers' reputation for siding with rebels; he did not reject outright the charge made by a member of my family that Maryknollers train young catechists to join the guerrillas. "It's true that we try to educate people to the causes of their oppression and to help them make decisions with their eyes wide open. To that extent, your cousin is right." He then said that most San Mateans live in fear of the army, but that they also become agitated when EGP patrols pass near the area, as one had in the past week. The guerrillas' claymore mines had accidentally killed many innocent campesinos, and San Mateans who openly side with the army know they may become targets of EGP execution squads.

I asked Fern Goslin how he accounted for the San Mateo community's cohesion in the face of such onslaughts. He said, "One factor is the strength of their ancient Maya beliefs, which have proven a bulwark against the evangelical sects; you won't find here the incessant backbiting and the religious factionalism that are tearing apart so many communities in the altiplano, and which open the door both to the guerrillas and to the military's divisive tactics."

Father Goslin estimates that as many as 60 percent of San Mateans practice their ancient rituals and observe the Mayan calendar. Not much has changed in that respect since obdurate San Mateans killed the Franciscan and Mercedarian missionaries who tried to convert them nearly three hundred years ago. But even here, Father Goslin knew of at least a dozen San Mateans who had made their way to the States in search of work.

Father Ron Hennessey had been typical of Maryknollers who first arrived in Guatemala in the forties, imbued with an evangelizing, anticommunist vocation. In 1954, the Maryknolls sided with conservative Bishop Mariano Rossell and other prelates who had collaborated with the C.I.A. and hardline army officers to overthrow Presi-

dent Arbenz. Like the Gurriarán brothers and other Sacred Heart
priests, many Maryknollers embraced Liberation Theology after
years of serving in highland parishes. In Guatemala's holy war, Maryknoll and Sacred Heart missionaries stand out among militants of the
religious left, while the evangelical sects form the vanguard of the
religious right.

To date, the right clearly has the upper hand. The most embattled
of the Maryknollers, such as former missionaries Tom and Marjorie
Melville and Blase Bonpane, who openly sided with the guerrillas,
were forced to flee Guatemala after their names appeared on army
death lists. Most of the remaining Maryknoll missions in Guatemala
are to be phased out over the next few years. The official explanation
is that they have completed their pastoral assignments here, but their
hopes of leaving behind phalanxes of native priests to replace them
have not materialized. Of the hundreds of young Jacaltecans who
entered the seminary under Maryknoll patronage, only two have been
ordained. Still, the Maryknollers' political influence in Guatemala and
the United States has been substantial. When former congressional
majority leader Tip O'Neill framed the Democrats' opposition to the
Reagan Doctrine on Central America, his main source of information
on Guatemalan army abuses was his niece, a Maryknoll nun.

On our return to San Mateo several months later we were stranded
for several hours by an army convoy passing through town in response
to an incident earlier that morning. A guerrilla patrol had ambushed
and killed an army colonel and his escort about ten kilometers from
Barillas. He was the first rank officer killed by the guerrillas in a
number of years. Two hundred fifty grim-faced soldiers in thirty armored vehicles were on their way to the scene; this was the new
public-relations-conscious army under the command of Defense Minister Héctor Gramajo. Before leaving San Mateo the army had
rounded up about fifty men in the town plaza, as an officer looked
over a list handed to him by the head of the civil defense patrol. The
officer visibly blanched on seeing our approach, and the convoy
moved out about an hour later, followed by a helicopter that landed
beside the old Mayan temples and disgorged several officers. We considered ourselves fortunate to get out of town without a mishap. Had
it been 1981, Lucas García's army, notorious for its swift and massive

reprisals whenever an officer was killed, would hardly have been constrained by the presence of a couple of foreigners.

5

One hour past San Mateo we began the steep descent into Santa Cruz Barillas. At 4,500 feet, Barillas is only slightly lower than Antigua. From a ridge beneath the cloud cover we had an excellent view of the town, as well as of the cardamom and coffee cultivation in the surrounding hills. At the lower elevations, overlooking the Ixcán, Barillans grow sugarcane, bananas, and other lowland crops. Although Barillas sits close to the end of the road, it is a busy trading center that exports a large share of Guatemala's cardamom to the Middle East. Barillas was founded one hundred years ago by ladino settlers from the Oriente, whose descendants nearly all support the army. Daniel informed me that most people in Barillas are armed, and the guerrillas wisely keep their distance from the town.

That afternoon, the guerrillas had dynamited an electric tower below San Mateo, and Barillas was without light. But this did not prevent Daniel from making his rounds after dark. He delivered family portraits, ID photos, and enlargements of cherished snapshots to ladinos and well-off Mayas, who gazed lovingly on their candlelit likenesses, as if they had never looked into a mirror. This was to be Daniel's last tour as an ambulant photographer, and in Barillas I finally understood why he had gotten hooked on this line of work. I accompanied him as he delivered a photograph of a recently graduated kaibil, who stared menacingly into the distance. His mother received the photo stern-faced and paid Daniel without uttering a word. To a Mayan household he delivered the photo of a youth killed by soldiers, and we stood by as the grieving father unloosed an impassioned harangue against his son's military assassins. Daniel's photography provided an excuse to feel the pulse of rural Guatemala and to bear witness to the ravages of war.

After Daniel had delivered the pictures, we stopped in a street stall for a kerosene-lit dinner of tortillas with roast pork. Later we sat by the stove in the pensión kitchen with the ladino proprietress and a newly arrived justice of the peace, one of many assigned to rural outposts as part of Vinicio Cerezo's democratic reform. The respected lawyer and former Vice President Francisco Villagrán Kramer has written scathingly of the shameful state of the criminal justice system in rural Guatemala, where there is no court of appeals for cases involving water or land-title disputes and no judges qualified to rule specifically on Mayan affairs. The justices of the peace appointed by Cerezo were intended to compensate for these glaring deficiencies.

The justice, who dressed like a prosperous ladino, was the scion of a wealthy Quiché family from Quezaltenango. The burly man who sat next to him, shadowing his movements but rarely speaking, was the justice's bodyguard. After warming himself by the stove, the judge relaxed his official posture and entertained us with accounts of horrendous miscarriages of justice he had been obliged to pass judgment on. Nearly all involved policemen and petty officials who abused their authority in order to steal, maim, kill, or traffic in contraband. Perhaps the most striking feature of his peroration, apart from his sober judicial tone, was the justice's simple moral qualifiers; he invariably said "good" and "bad" policemen, eschewing legal terminology he probably assumed to be over our heads. Then, without missing a beat, he launched into a travelogue of the picturesque places in Guatemala that he knew intimately, and which he urged us to visit so we could become acquainted with the country's true grandeur.

He began by extolling the mist-enveloped beauty of the Fuentes Georginas, natural hot springs adorned with "magnificent" Hellenic statuary set on the upper slopes of Zunil volcano. He boasted of his repeated sightings in the Alta Verapaz cloud forests of the resplendent quetzal—Guatemala's symbol of freedom—which is on the verge of extinction after centuries of being hunted for its showy emerald tail. The justice explored the "incomparable" Mayan sites of Tikal, Uaxactún, and the isolated Piedras Negras, where Mayan lords perforated their penises with stingray spines to fecundate the earth and summon up visions. He scaled in memory the 13,000-foot peaks of majestic Fuego and Santa María volcanoes, whose periodic eruptions plagued both Mayan and colonial civilizations, even as their ashes replenished the soil. He dwelt briefly on the architectural glories of his native Quezaltenango, the "cradle of long-forgotten poets," and eulogized the former colonial capital of Antigua, thrice devastated by earthquakes, which he dubbed the crown jewel of Guatemala's national patrimony. With a climactic flourish that lifted him half off his chair, the justice trumpeted, "Tikal and Antigua are the brick and mortar of the Guatemalan national identity!"

In the riven soul of this Maya-born, ladinicized justice of the peace, the three crosses of Todos Santos had taken root; his efforts to reconcile them had birthed a private universe of manicheistic simplicity in which the horrors and the beauty of Guatemala cohabited naturally, without the least sense of contradiction.

PART IV

Santiago Atitlán

Sololá

San Andrés
Semetabaj

San Jorge
la Laguna

Santa Catarina
Palopó

San Antonio
Palopó

Panajachel

Santa Cruz
la Laguna

LAKE ATITLÁN

Cerro
de Oro

Pachitulul

San Lucas
Tolimán

San Marcos Tzununá
la Laguna

Tolimán△
Volcano

Santa María
Visitación San Pablo
la Laguna

Santiago
Atitlán

Santa Clara
la Laguna

San Juan
la Laguna

San Pedro
la Laguna

Finca Tzantziapá

Finca
Chacayá

San Pedro△
Volcano

△Atitlán Volcano

0 1 2 3 4 kms

9

[ΞΦΞ]

Father Stan Rother

"Shaking hands with an Indian has become a political act."
Father Stanley Rother, 1981

"He's a communist!"
President Romeo Lucas García on Stanley Rother

In the Oklahoma Catholic Mission of Santiago Atitlán, in Guatemala's central highlands, a simple chapel commemorates Stanley Rother, who served as pastor to Atitlán's Tz'utujil Mayan community for thirteen years. A Carmelite nun or Father Tom McSherry—Rother's successor—will show visitors the bullet hole in the tile floor and the blood stains on the wall from the night in July 1981 when three masked men broke into the mission in search of Father Rother.

A dozen years before leftist guerrillas made their first appearance in Atitlán, Stanley Francis Rother, a gentle six-foot-tall pastor from Okarchee, Oklahoma, heeded his bishop's summons to serve in Guatemala. He joined a group of six American churchmen and women who headed the Tulsa-based Catholic Mission. Prior to the arrival of the Americans, Santiago Atitlán had been without a full-time parish priest for nearly a century.

Stanley Rother did not impress the group of bright, pioneering missionaries who hoped to turn Atitlán into a healthy and prosperous Christian model for the highland Mayas. The soft-spoken elder son of a German immigrant farming family, Rother had not distinguished himself in academic studies. He flunked out of his first seminary in San Antonio, Texas, before moving on to Mt. Saint Mary's, in Maryland, where he was ordained in 1963. But his quiet demeanor and modest intellect masked a spiritual intensity that would dramatically transform the final year of his life. Rother's unswerving loyalty to his

Tz'utujil Maya parishioners, coupled with an ingrained repugnance
for social injustice, would earn him the enmity of Lucas García's
military government, which targeted Atitlán as a hotbed of supporters
for the Organization of People in Arms (ORPA). In July 1981, after
ignoring repeated warnings that his name appeared on the army's
death lists, Father Stan Rother was murdered. A movement to canonize him arose before his body was laid in its grave.

Santiago Atitlán is the largest of twelve Mayan towns that ring
spectacular Lake Atitlán. Aldous Huxley, when he visited the lake in
the 1930s, pronounced it more picturesque than Como. The pine-
and madrone-covered slopes of its three towering volcanoes, the play
of light and shadow on the emerald surface of the crater lake—which
reaches depths of more than one thousand feet—add credence to
Huxley's hyperbole. But the lake's natural beauty is tainted by still-
vivid memories of waters stained red with Maya blood. The Spaniards
overran the lakeside-dwelling Tz'utujil nation early in the sixteenth
century, routinely slaughtering hundreds of its warriors. According to
legend, the Tz'utujil king cast his gold crown in the lake before he
was captured; the crown still shimmers in the crystalline water, a vision
of past glory and instant wealth. When dazzled fishermen dive in after
it, it vanishes.

Ramiro (as I will call him), a respected craftsman and businessman
I have known for more than a dozen years, still becomes heated on
recalling the conquest of his people. He insists that the bravest warriors walled themselves up inside a cave on Chuitinamit, the hillside
citadel opposite Santiago that guarded the seat of the Tz'utujil kings.
So as not to cast dishonor on the spirits of their ancestors, the warriors
chose self-immolation rather than face the humiliation of captivity
and slavery.

When Pedro de Alvarado arrived with his Mexican and Cakchiquel
auxiliaries, the Tz'utujil lord Jo'ol No'j Quixcáp ruled over approximately fifty thousand cacao farmers, fishermen, and warriors who
engaged in unending territorial skirmishes with their neighboring Cakchiquels and Quichés. Colonial records indicate that Spanish missionaries persuaded Jo'ol No'j Quixcáp to convert, and they baptized
him Don José. He was permitted to stay on as cacique, or titular head
of his people, and his son and heir Don Juan was awarded his own

coat of arms. As in the other highland kingdoms they conquered, the Spaniards took over a system of tribute payment and servitude set up by the formerly dominant Quichés. The resulting encomienda not only provided hundreds of slaves to work the Spaniards' fields and gold mines, it supplied the labor for cottage industries that included the cultivation of cacao, honey, maguey, chili peppers, and the manufacture of various woven goods. The slavery introduced by the Spaniards and the huge tributes they exacted eventually broke the back of the Tz'utujil community. By 1585, smallpox epidemics and the graduated attrition inherent in the encomiendas had reduced the population of Santiago Atitlán to 1,005 tribute payers.

Today, the Tz'utujils of Atitlán gaze across the inlet at the ruined bastion of their former empire, which the Spaniards leveled to the ground. In recent years, gringo and ladino treasure hunters have begun carving up Chuitinamit into rustic rental properties and excavation sites, acquired from subsistence peasant farmers at bargain prices. The carving up and desecration of the hillside citadel reflects the fracturing of Atitlán's communal soul.

Since 1970, Santiago Atitlán has grown to over twenty thousand residents or nearly half of its original population, making it the third largest indigenous community in Guatemala. But unlike communities in northern Quiché and Huehuetenango, which have risen up against their Spanish and ladino oppressors over the centuries, the Tz'utujils by and large avoided confrontation with the dominant culture as the best hope for conserving their Maya *costumbres*. Only since the rise of the guerrilla organizations and the proliferation of evangelical sects, have the Tz'utujils roused themselves from a 450-year silence to give voice to their grievances. The awakening has proved costly. Well over one thousand Atitecos have died violent deaths since 1979, leaving behind five hundred widows and several thousand orphans. (In 1987, the municipality's records listed gunshot wounds as the third highest cause of death in Atitlán, behind infant diarrhea and respiratory diseases.)

Every day starting at about ten in the morning, boatloads of foreign visitors arrive from the tourist resort of Panajachel, an hour's ride across the lake. Few visitors wander outside the main street with its weaving displays, the market, and the colonial church. Although many snap photographs of supple Maya women with hitched-up skirts beating their laundry against the lakeshore rocks, they miss the undernourished, tubercular children playing listlessly inside the stone and thatch-roofed houses.

Only an occasional visitor will wander to the rear of the church, where a memorial stone marks the remains of Father Stanley Rother. (In 1989 the stone was moved nearer the front entrance.) And only the most determined will walk to the south end of town, where the army barracks sat until December 1990, half-concealed inside a coffee grove. Strings of bullets hung like unripe coffee berries from the straw canopies of the machine-gun emplacements. Nearly ten years after Father Rother's assassination, Santiago Atitlán remains one of the most embattled communities in the Guatemalan highlands, riven with political and religious feuds that pit family against family, ladino against *natural*, and Christians against one another. Atitlán's 240 ladinos control most of the town's businesses, and in the 1987 mayoral elections a ladino displaced the Tz'utujil mayor, Antonio Ixbalán Cuncz. No fewer than nineteen evangelical sects with thirty or so temples challenge the traditional dominance of the Catholic church; and the tenacious cult of Maximón, a raffish, libidinous deity with roots in Mayan prehistory, pits the conservative Christo-pagan cofradías against the politicized catechists of Acción Católica.

When I summered in Lake Atitlán as a boy of nine and ten, I was spellbound by our indigenous cook's stories of Maximón's outlandish exploits. I did not suspect then the antiquity of his legend or the intricacy of the cofradía that sustains his cult. Maximón incorporates the Catholic apostle San Simón (Simon Peter) and Ma'am, the ancient Mayan Earth Lord.

The two summers I stayed with my family in Panajachel's old Monterey Hotel only a handful of tourists visited the lake. Strawberry and vegetable plantings covered most of the area that is now overrun with ramshackle rooming houses and restaurants named "The Psychedelic" and "The Last Resort." Like other hippie sanctuaries in far-flung corners of the world, Panajachel was reinvented in the late 1950s by international travelers who found the natives disposed to tolerate their freewheeling drug-and-sex culture in exchange for a modest increment to their livelihood. English is the *lingua franca* of Panajachel, and U.S. dollars are more common than the native quetzal. But even in Panajachel ancient rituals persist in the cliffside cave above the town of San Jorge la Laguna. In early morning and again in the evening, an alert tourist looking up from his hotel swimming pool can detect the curling smoke of copal incense burned by shamans performing animal sacrifices and other costumbre inside the cave, just as they have for centuries.

The Sunday in 1943 when my father first took me across the lake to Santiago Atitlán, the six- and seven-year-olds who met our boat had already learned to thrust open palms in visitors' faces and snap, "Gimme fi' sen." Like beggar gypsies, many Atitecos learn that litany in their cradle. Fifty meters from the boat landing, I felt as if I had been dropped on an alien planet. Already dazed by the sun on my head, the slant of light on the crest of San Pedro volcano, and the scroll-like perfection of the fishermen squatting in their dugout canoes, I was not at all prepared for the dark mystery of eight elders in vividly embroidered pants gathered on their benches in the cofradía of Santa Cruz.

They were swathed in clouds of copal incense as the shaman intoned prayers punctuated by repeated rounds of home-brewed aguardiente. Maximón was nowhere to be seen. The wooden effigy representing the pagan deity would be assembled by his guardian the week before his first public appearance in the plaza on Ash Wednesday. But the chief elder of the cofradía, who had an unnerving laugh, encouraged me to climb a stepladder to the rafters, where Maximón was kept. The roof of the chapel hung with ribbons of crepe paper, stringy sausages, sheafs of arum lilies, dry gourds, and fruits.

"Don't be afraid; he doesn't bite," the elder shouted at me, as he clutched the five-quetzal bill my father had slipped him, and which would be spent on more offerings of cheap rum for Maximón and his guardians. "Maximón likes his nips," the elder had told us, with a toothless grin. "And at night he likes to chase after the single women. But he's not a bad sort. He's already had his tobacco and his liquor, and now he's content."

Torn between terror and curiosity, I made my way up the shaky ladder. In the flickering darkness above the roof beams, I made out a dummy dressed in silk kerchiefs and leather shoes. A black Stetson he wore during Holy Week hung on the wall. I groped in the dark with both hands until I felt the wooden mask with its flat Mayan nose and the mouth-hole for the cigar. Instinctively I felt my way down the dummy's spine to his groin. In the place where his sex should be, Maximón wore a lump of coarse rope. My cry of surprise was drowned by the elder's ribald cackle.

Since my first encounter with Maximón, he has survived numerous attempts to suppress his cult by church authorities. In the fifties, a foreign priest confiscated Maximón's mask with the collusion of local ladinos, and it later appeared in Paris's Musée de l'Homme. (The mask has since been returned.) When I visited Atitlán several years ago for a magazine story on the Holy Week celebrations, the elders of Santa Cruz assured me Stan Rother had been the first priest to show respect for Maximón and to make peace with their cofradía. The fully dressed Maximón stands only three-and-one-half-feet tall, complete with several felt hats on his head, scores of bright scarves, and ladino shoes on his stump feet. The mask used for Maximón now, said to be the third one carved since the original was stolen, is made from the sacred *tsaj'tol,* or miche tree, which gave form to the wooden men of the second creation described in the Quiché-Maya *Popol Vuh.* The cigar invariably protruding from Maximón's mouth is as intimately associated with his cult as a half-smoked stogie was with W. C. Fields.

Variants of Maximón's Dionysiac cult are to be found in over a dozen other highland towns and villages, where he goes under the names San Simón, Rijlaj Mam, Ca Tatá, among others. These images, which draw hundreds of pilgrims seeking small and large miracles, are an enduring expression of pre-Columbian costumbres that have not yet been quashed or appropriated by the white man.

After the offerings of lowland fruits and flowers are laid at his feet, Maximón is taken out of the cofradía on Ash Wednesday. He parades across the plaza of Atitlán on the shoulders of his "horse," or *telenel,* a shaman who is chosen as much for his drinking capacity as the strength of his shoulders. A drum and flute add bounce and verve to the idol's accompaniment of drunken elders, their wives, and the town's reprobates. After paying his respects to Atitlán's mayor, and festooning the municipality with fresh flowers, Maximón is hung as a representation of Judas Iscariot from a dahlia tree post in a chapel below the church. Maximón's next and most dramatic appearance, on Good Friday, is timed to the emergence of the Holy Sepulcher procession from the town church. The recumbent wooden Christ is borne aloft by red-shirted devotees who have paid handsomely for the honor. The bier, ornamented with blinking lights, is followed by the generator and a brass band as it winds its way at a snail's pace down the steps of the church and onto a fancy carpet mosaic of flowers and colored sawdust. The catechists swing incense vessels and intone psalms, with responses from the cortege of respected ladino headmen, shawled virgins with tall votive candles, and hundreds of Tz'utujil men and women in fancy headdress and showy Atiteco pants.

As the recumbent Christ emerges from the church, Maximón is taken down and placed on the telenel's shoulders. When the two processions meet in the center of the plaza, spectators size them up to decide which of the two is more magnetic—the flamboyant and unregenerate Maximón, with his long history of debauchery, or the martyred Christ, with his dolorous face and colorful funeral cortege. Anthropologist Michael Mendelson (a.k.a. Nathaniel Tarn), who wrote his doctoral dissertation on Maximón and related cults, depicts him as a Mayan approximation of Osiris. A dry-season deity, Maximón is unsexed every spring by Christ's martyrdom and resurrection, which are followed by the return of the rains and the first corn plantings. The November harvests herald the rebirth of Maximón. His yearly passage from youth to old age is accompanied by cyclical metamorphoses from sterility and hermaphroditism to virile excess and back again.

The cofradías are at a low ebb today, as the rising evangelical tide threatens to sweep them away. In Santiago Atitlán, where the cult of Maximón began, indigenous costumbres are fighting for their lives with a singular tenacity. During Holy Week of 1989, Atitlán's cofradías staged an impressive performance, as if to prove to the evangelicals that they were alive and kicking. Maximón's cortege was the largest and gaudiest in years, and the offerings brought from the coast by Maximón's attendants attained potlatch proportions. On Tuesday evening the Oklahoma mission priest Tom McSherry paid his respects to Maximón in the cofradía of Santa Cruz, a gesture that won him favor among the cofrades.

In the rival cofradía of San Martín, a deer dance was held behind closed doors on the morning of Maundy Thursday, and then the sacred bundle, whose contents no living person has beheld, was taken out of the royal coffer and presented to a select attendance. The consummate delicacy with which the *nebaysil,* or shaman, danced the velvet-covered bundle around the room, bowing first to the four cardinal directions and then to each of us in turn, as in benediction, made Maximón's pageant seem almost brutish by comparison. But then balancing polarities is one of the cofradías' chief functions. The bundle, which is thought to contain old curanderos' tools, ancient parchments, and the magic shirt of the legendary wizard Francisco Sohuel, signifies far more than the sum of its contents. Mendelson described the bundle as an embodiment of the *Popol Vuh's* Gucumatz, or Heart of Heaven, the female principle in the world's creation. To the nebaysil, San Martín is the forever born and forever present, and Atitlán itself is *remeshush kaj, remeshush ruchulev, remeshush munde,* three terms signifying axis mundi, or world's navel. Tapping his fingers on the royal coffer the nebaysil fixes my eye and incants, "Here is not only life without end, the mother and father of corn harvests and abundant rains, here is also the moving star, the airplane, and the helicopter."

The alcalde of cofradía San Martín, Miguel Sohuel, a descendant of the nineteenth-century miracle worker credited by some with giving material form to Maximón, passes copal incense and *kusha,* or home brew, among the elders and visitors. The heavy drinking in the cofradía is not recreational in origin. The *kusha* is meant to irrigate the Maya world tree, a representation of which stands in the form of a corn-sprouting cross on the peak of the highest volcano. Sohuel anoints with kusha three black volcanic stones wrapped in woven shawls. He addresses them reverently as Saint Pedro de Alvarado, Maximón, and La Malinche, Hernán Cortés's much maligned Indian mistress. With sadness in his eyes, Sohuel confesses the cofrades no longer make pilgrimages to mountain shrines to pray to San Martín to save the world from earthquakes and other disasters. "The army is there now. They accuse us of helping the guerrillas and burn our milpas. The earthquakes go out from here and cause destruction around the world. Atitlán is safe because of San Martín." He places his hand on my shoulder. "The presence of you and your friends from abroad is important; it helps to offset the power of the army." And he points to three new saints the nebaysil is anointing with kusha as part of his propitiatory rituals. The three stones, placed in a row next to "Saint" Pedro de Alvarado, are named "private," "sergeant," and "colonel."

2

When Stanley Rother arrived in Santiago in 1968, he was a cautious political conservative. And he proved more adept at handling a plow, repairing a tractor, and erecting a schoolhouse than at inspiring a churchful of Mayas to seek salvation through prayer and self-sacrifice. (The one time I'd met Rother, in 1971, he had struck me as a low-keyed and likable but rather straitlaced country pastor.)

Stan Rother's gift, other than his understated bent for selfless service, was an evidently stubborn instinct for conciliation. During his thirteen years in Santiago he constantly sought a working balance among the influence-seeking ladinos, the earnest catechists of Acción Católica (his favorites), and the *costumbristas* of the town's twelve cofradías. After ORPA guerrillas made their appearance, followed immediately by an army detachment, Father Rother's task would become far more daunting.

Within a year of Rother's arrival in Santiago, Father Ramón Carlin, the new priest's role model and the only one to grasp his potential, became ill and returned to the States. Five of the six other Americans in the mission married and left the church. An American nun who had worked with Rother poked gentle fun at his blindness to the sexual activity going on under his nose and then added: "Father Stan had selective vision, I guess, and that was part of his quiet, unsophisticated nature. He was a farm boy at heart, with a stubborn streak and a large capacity for hard work. His single-minded devotion won over his Indian parishioners, and he became one of them." Six years after his arrival, Stan Rother was named administrator of the Oklahoma mission. Inspired by the erudite Father Carlin, who had translated the New Testament in 1964, Rother acquired sufficient Tz'utujil to converse with his parishioners in their own language.

Rother's gift for conciliation and his capacity for hard work did not prevent his making important enemies in the community. One of these denounced him to the army as "a defender of his people." The Ibsenian irony in this charge bemused Father Stanley, who chose to take it as a compliment. Rother's friends in Santiago included the town's cofrades. He drank with them on occasion, and they named him an elder. A ladino community leader called Rother a saint deserving of canonization; even the evangelicals I spoke with claimed to have been friends of his and invited him to their services.

There have been Protestant churches in Guatemala since before the turn of the century; but it was not until the devastating earthquake of February 1976 that missionaries of U.S. fundamentalist and Pentecostal sects arrived in large numbers. Stan Rother felt secure enough within the Catholic community to take the evangelical invasion in his stride; but his allegiance to his parishioners would be severely tested after ORPA militants made their first appearance in 1980, and the army occupied the town. Several key events had foreshadowed the troubles that lay ahead.

Early in 1978, the Committee for Peasant Unity (CUC) distributed leaflets in town that called for Maya laborers to organize and demand minimum salaries and improved working conditions. The National Indian Beauty Queen of that year (Señorita Rabin Ahau), who came from an impoverished coastal community, was invited to Santiago, where she denounced the army's recent massacre of over one hundred Quekchí Mayas in the plaza of Panzós.

A handful of Atitecos who had studied law in Guatemala's San Carlos University, held, with the mission's backing, open sessions in the town plaza to educate their neighbors about their civil rights. Jude Pansini, an American Benedictine colleague of Stan Rother's, was especially supportive of the town's young militants. Pansini had stayed on in Atitlán after marrying a Spanish woman, and they adopted a Tz'utujil twin girl whom Rother had rescued from an almost certain death of malnutrition. Pansini's collaboration with CUC activists in finca-based health projects was one of the activities that later forced him to leave the country in fear for his life. The Benedictine pastor's militancy and his precipitous flight contributed to Atitlán's reputation as a haven for subversives.

In this atmosphere of rising political ferment the first recruiters for ORPA appeared in town, in June 1980, and received a warm reception. Thousands of Atitecos cast their lot with the guerrillas, and events soon took an irreversible turn, not only for the community but for its Oklahoma pastor. Four months after the ORPA rally, which climaxed with dozens of supporters meeting the guerrillas outside of town to ply them with food and drink, the army moved in and set up its barracks in a coffee grove that belonged in part to the mission's cooperative farm.

Thousands of Atitlán residents became active or tacit supporters of ORPA, the most disciplined of the four guerrilla organizations that make up the Guatemalan National Revolutionary Union (URNG). By carefully screening its Mayan recruits, ORPA had more success than the EGP in training combatants and securing their loyalty. Thirty to forty ORPA guerrillas formed the Xavier Tambriz Front and set up camps in the lower slopes of the two larger volcanoes bordering on the lake, Tolimán and Atitlán. From their entrenched hideouts ORPA struck at army-appointed informers and at landowners who persistently abused their indigenous workers. The army retaliated against all Atitecos suspected of provisioning or otherwise collaborating with the guerrillas.

In his letters home to his family and friends, as well as to his bishop, Stan Rother wrote of the rising incidences of violence. He kept a grim score of his parishioners who disappeared from their homes, never to be seen again. And he also kept meticulous count of the foreign priests killed elsewhere in the highlands. He wrote that only the most disreputable, antisocial Atitecos were picked by the army to be informers and *comisionados,* and they were paid for every "subversive" they added to their list. He added: "The denunciations are sometimes because of envy, vengeance, or just downright greed."

In September 1980, Stan Rother wrote his archbishop in Oklahoma: "The country here is in rebellion and the government is taking it out on the Church. The low wages that are paid, the very few who are excessively rich, the bad distribution of land—these are some of the reasons for the widespread discontent."

A few days later the director of the mission-sponsored radio station, a former deacon, was kidnapped outside the station. The following night the station itself was broken into, and its files were rifled and valuable equipment was removed. Stan Rother remarked pointedly: "Anybody who has made an advancement at all is being pursued." But he then added a characteristic note of cautious regret that the catechists who ran the radio station's "Voice of Atitlán" had allowed

political discourse to supersede their original purpose of promoting
literacy.

In that same letter Stan Rother wrote for the first time of the perils
to his own life, as the army's threats to the mission became more
serious. He wrote that he did not want to abandon his flock when
the wolves were making random attacks. He took the precaution of
sleeping in a different part of the building every night but remained
convinced—despite growing evidence to the contrary—that his U.S.
passport would afford him protection.

Every killing or disappearance in Atitlán deepened Stan Rother's
commitment to the community. His cautious, conservative instincts
gradually yielded to a consuming outrage at the atrocities he was
witnessing. At the end of his letters home he began to append the
phrase, "Please pray that I don't do anything foolish." And he told
friends, "Shaking hands with an Indian has become a political act."

Against the advice of some of his superiors, Father A'plas, as his
Tz'utujil parishioners called him, continued to give shelter in the
mission to anyone who asked for it—although he later confessed that
his even-handedness stopped short of putting up army informers on
the run from guerrillas. And Rother surely knew that many Atiteco
members of his staff were actively supporting ORPA.

Townspeople with grudges against Stan Rother and the mission
started spreading rumors that his periodic trips to the coast—where
he went on contemplative retreats with other priests—were to contact
guerrillas and to collect weapons that he added to a hidden cache
inside the mission.

When the list of parishioners missing and unaccounted for rose to
ten, and the number of foreign clergymen killed or disappeared nationwide had reached a half dozen, Stan Rother still wrote letters
home that wished his father good luck on his fishing expedition; and
he asked his friend Frankie Williams for an insecticide to rid the
mission safe of silverfish.

Rother had assured his family that he would leave the country if
he learned of a direct threat on his life. He did not have long to wait.
Early in January 1981, one of the mission's brightest Tz'utujil catechists, named Diego Quic, was seized from the rectory steps in broad
daylight by four tall masked men. Father Stanley heard Quic's calls
for help and came out in time to see him yanked off the banister and

pushed into a waiting car. Rother looked on in a helpless agony, for he knew he would be killed if he tried to intervene. He waited twenty minutes and radioed the police in San Lucas to intercept the car; instead, the police went into hiding. Witnesses on the road reported that an army jeep and an ambulance escorted the abductors' car with Diego Quic still screaming inside. He was not heard from again.

Rother described the kidnapping in a letter he wrote to an Oklahoma priest, who circulated it in the States. The next to the last paragraph in the letter read: "The whole Central American area is in the process of change, and if the governments don't want to do it peacefully, then it will be done by war."

Two days after Quic's kidnapping sixteen farmworkers were massacred by the army in a coffee plantation outside Atitlán where guerrillas had been active. Five days later Stan Rother was informed by U.S. Embassy sources of a direct threat on his life. On January 28 he flew from Guatemala with his Tz'utujil assistant, Father Pedro Bocel, who had also been threatened. Rother arrived in Oklahoma in midwinter wearing a short-sleeved shirt and carrying a slim attaché case.

Father Stanley remained in Oklahoma for two and a half months and discreetly turned down most speaking engagements and other solidarity activities so as not to endanger his prospects for returning to his parish. He confessed to friends that he no longer felt fully three-dimensional in the States, and his heart was in Atitlán. One of the few addresses he delivered, to the Catholic Congregation in Edmond, Kansas, moved one of the congregants to write the Guatemalan Embassy in Washington that Stan Rother was advocating the overthrow of their government. For all his cautious conservatism, Father Stanley came to be branded a "radical priest" for his opposition to the Guatemalan army's decimation of his parish. President Romeo Lucas García is reported to have shouted, "He's a Communist!" after he was shown the letters denouncing Rother. But none of these continuing signs of the danger to his life deterred Rother from his decision to return to Santiago.

In one of the few letters Stan Rother wrote after his return on the eve of Palm Sunday, he took pains to project a steady calm in the middle of the storm. The army had returned to the coffee farm after vacating it for six weeks and a tense expectancy prevailed. Shortly after his arrival Rother made a point of visiting the base on a practical matter, as he had done on past occasions, but he was told the comandante "was not in." (Later on, some of his catechists would reproach Father Stan for consenting to celebrate mass in the barracks, in keeping with his spirit of conciliation.)

Two more priests and several catechists had been disappeared in the highlands during Stan Rother's absence; he painfully reported the growing number of Atiteco widows and orphans who were left without a breadwinner. Another casualty during Rother's absence was the cooperative farm, which had fallen into disrepair. One of his greatest satisfactions had been experimenting with new vegetable crops; he planted peach and avocado trees, which grew luxuriantly in the fertile volcanic soil. The bumper crops of wheat had contributed substantially to the mission's campaign to reduce the endemic malnutrition, which claimed half the community's children before they reached the age of five. But there were no more threats on Stan Rother's life, and he wrote jocularly of his newfound firmness in setting the catechists to their tasks of administering the sacraments.

Father Stanley's return to Atitlán added a new measure of respect to his growing popularity. He was thrilled to minister to a record 109 marriages in the church, which gave the impression of a Catholic community determined to replace its losses and keep alive its faith. And here was a shepherd who refused to abandon his flock, even after the bishop of neighboring Quiché had withdrawn all clerics from his diocese. Of the two dozen or so foreign priests and nuns, all but a handful had fled the country or gone into hiding. (A friend of Rother's, Father Dave Stewart of Santa Apolonia, was among the last to leave after receiving threats—a fact Father Stan duly reported.) Oddly, Rother does not mention in his letters the widely publicized murder of Archbishop Romero and four North American religious workers in El Salvador; but he pointedly remarked on two Maryknoll nuns who had left Nicaragua during the fighting and returned to meet the reproach of their parishioners who asked, "Where were you when we needed you?"

On July 28, 1981, three and a half months after Stan Rother's return to Atitlán and on one of the last days of celebration for the town's patron saint, several strangers were seen mingling with soldiers near the town plaza. An Atitlán resident described them as "good-looking, strapping fellows, the kind the army recruits in the eastern provinces for the special forces."

Shortly after midnight, as the marimba music and the celebrations in the streets were winding down, three tall masked men broke into the mission. After an unsuccessful search for Father Stanley in his bedroom, the three men grabbed the terrified young deacon—the only other occupant of the mission that night—and ordered him at gunpoint to take them to Rother's hiding place.

"Father, three men have come to look for you," the deacon called outside his door. After a long pause, Stan Rother opened the door. He had evidently debated taking flight and rejected it, knowing the deacon would die in his place.

The three men entered. The deacon heard scuffling, then Father Stanley's shouted plea, "*¡Mátenme aquí!*" (Kill me here!) This was a premeditated decision, backed by Rother's knowledge of the tortures he would be subjected to before death if they got him outside the mission. And he appeared determined that his murderers bear on their souls the additional mortal sin of violating holy sanctuary. Two shots were fired, and the men fled.

The American consular officer who visited Atitlán the following day found thousands of townspeople gathered outside the mission in mourning for their parish priest.

Within days Stan Rother's parents arrived (his father had had a premonition of his death the day of the murder), and a solemn funeral procession in town drew thousands more mourners from every sector of the Atitlán community. Although the family took most of Stan Rother's remains to Oklahoma for burial, by a prior agreement his heart remained in Atitlán. It is buried in the church sanctuary, together with a peanut-butter jar full of his blood. The memorial stone in back of the altar reads (in Spanish):

STANLEY FRANCISCO ROTHER

Martyred Priest
Born March 27 1935 Okarchee Oklahoma
Ordained Priest May 25 1963
Arrived in Diocese June 17 1968
Remained in this parish of Santiago Apostle 13 years

Assassinated July 28 1981
"There is no greater love than this:
To Give One's Life for One's Friends"
Jn 15:13

The murder of Stanley Rother got some fleeting attention in the international press. In the U.S. Congress, Frankie Williams protested the killing of her friend and confidant to the House Committee on Foreign Affairs.

Shortly after Rother's death, his letter describing the abduction of Diego Quic was printed in the *New York Times;* a subsequent article in *Time* magazine, "Requiem for a Priest," speculated that his bishop's circulation of the provocative letter may have cost Rother his life. The *Los Angeles Times* ran an interview they did with Rother a month before his murder, in which he said, "I have found out that I am on a list to be killed. I talked too much when I was in Oklahoma, and some of it got back to Guatemala."

On August 24, 1981, *Time* ran a follow-up article titled "Case not closed—Framing a trio for murder," in which they exposed the cynical mockery of the Guatemalan military after they seized three innocent townspeople to bear the blame for their own dirty work.

Fourteen thousand Oklahomans signed a petition asking President Reagan and Secretary of State Schultz to exert pressure on the Guatemalan government for a thorough investigation of Rother's murder; but the document disappeared from public notice after a few weeks. The chief outcome of the murder was a negative "tourist advisory" published by the U.S. State Department that effectively dried up American vacations in Guatemala for the next three years.

The murder of Stanley Rother went underground, where it spawned a movement to have him canonized as a martyr and saint of the Catholic church. Two years after Rother's death, a school and chapel bearing his name were erected in an outlying neighborhood of Santiago Atitlán.

In the fall of 1982 I spoke in San Francisco with Father Ron Burke, a California missionary who had worked closely with Rother and had been on retreat with him one week before he was murdered. Father Burke had himself fled Guatemala shortly afterward. "All that stuff about his collaborating with the guerrillas is nonsense, although he shared some of their indignation at the military's treatment of the

Indians. Heck, who doesn't? Stan and I had pastoral disagreements about how to deal with Maximón. He was all for joining in and even drinking with the cofradías, whereas I believed they were a corrupting influence and should not be encouraged. No, Stan was no saint," Father Burke concluded. "But I suppose he rose above the ordinary to a quiet kind of heroism. He did not seek out martyrdom, but he did not run away from it either."

3

Three years passed before Catholic priests returned to the Santiago Atitlán mission. In 1983 Father Stanley's parents, Franz and Gertrude Rother, aired out the rectory and spent three weeks there, in the course of which they received numerous visits by Tz'utujil mothers bearing infants they had named "Francisco." (The name Stanley has no direct Spanish equivalent.)

For the long-suffering community of Atitlán, Rother's assassination was to be a prelude to more violence. After 1982 Ríos Montt's civil defense patrols were instituted in Santiago Atitlán as well as throughout the highlands. Poor fishermen and farmworkers were forced to leave their homes and patrol the streets of their town and the outlying villages in search of "subversives." The chief of the comisionados at that time was an especially ruthless and hated toady of the military who was known to press sexual advances on the wives of Atitecos while they were on patrol. And he forced townspeople to provide him with fish, corn, and other fruits of their labor. (The chief, Martínez Ruiz, later died of a stroke said to have been wished on him by an avenging brujo.)

As had been the case in Quiché, large numbers of Catholics continued to convert to one of the evangelical sects, hoping to find a measure of protection from the army or the guerrillas. But those whose names appeared on lists—whether of the left or the right— were marked for death regardless of their religious affiliation. Still, thousands of Atitecos sought relief from the violence in the cathartic transports of the Pentecostal church services and the biblical panaceas of the fundamentalists. The Pentecostal sect Elim, which claims four thousand members, erected a temple that rivals the Catholic church both in size and in its prominent location. In the evenings, the Pentecostals shout their hallelujas through giant loudspeakers, accompanied by organ or electric guitar music. Hundreds of townspeople swing their arms, stamp their feet in exorcistic ecstasy, and respond to their pastor's exhortations in a jumbled outpouring of tongues. The Pentecostals, neo-Pentecostals, and their Catholic brethren, the charismatics, are the fastest-growing religious movements in Guatemala, as well as throughout much of Latin America. Atitlán's Pentecostals like to claim their services generate the highest per capita attendance records in the world. "Our lives are so fragile anyway," a recent convert to Elim confided. "We may as well live out what is left in a way that helps us forget our troubles."

To thousands of Tz'utujils, ecstatic transport, laying on of hands, prophecy, and other gifts of Pentecost, with their roots in poor U.S. rural southern white and black communities of a century ago, proved a more immediate comfort than the Catholic church's five-century-old promise of eternal life in the hereafter.

ORPA guerrillas in the meantime kept up their hit-and-run assaults on the military and continued their executions of comisionados and their lackeys. In 1984 ORPA was apparently responsible for blowing up the town's municipal building, which contained files of Atitecos suspected of subversion. Ten thousand ID cards were also destroyed, which substantially reduced the number of eligible voters for the 1985 presidential elections.

Two weeks before the election, an ORPA hit squad killed the new military comisionado, another civilian appointee named Nicolás Pedro, who was cut from the same cloth as his predecessor. The day after Pedro's assassination his body was found mutilated and his head was "disappeared," apparently by local residents bent on revenge. That same week two more Atitecos disappeared from their homes, as the paramilitary death squads struck back.

In spite of the killings, the townspeople turned out in large numbers on November 3 and again on December 8 to vote in Guatemala's first legitimate election in twenty years. A marimba band played in the background while Atitecos cast their vote in the town plaza. They gave Marco Vinicio Cerezo Arévalo, the forty-year-old Christian Democrat, over 90 percent of their vote—twenty points above the national average. Cerezo had visited Santiago and impressed voters when he warned the local police he would throw them in jail if they abused the townspeople.

The newly elected mayor of Santiago Atitlán was a Tz'utujil Maya and Christian Democrat named Antonio Ixbalán Cuncz. The day after the election Cuncz, a fisherman and carpenter, spoke of modernizing the town's lighting and water plants, paving the road to San Lucas to encourage commerce, and replacing the town hall blown up by ORPA the year before.

Most of the townspeople I talked to were not expecting much from Cerezo's presidency. Hardly anyone thought he would prosecute the army commanders who ordered hundreds of killings in Atitlán nor did they expect him to take on the powerful planters who hold 70 percent of the arable land in the municipality. Mayor Cuncz did say he hoped Cerezo would find a way to curb the inflation that had placed sugar, rice, milk, and other staples beyond the reach of many campesinos. "Otherwise," concluded the mayor, "how will we be able to eat?"

Although three-quarters of the residents of Santiago Atitlán remain illiterate, I discovered the level of sophistication in the town had risen dramatically in the five short years since the murder of Stanley Rother. "From each of the last three elections we have learned something," said Ramiro, a respected artisan and community spokesman. "Even if they were fraudulent, even if the wrong man won, we learned something. The army and the politicians can't take that away from us. Whatever happens to Cerezo during the next few months, we plan to appoint our own council of elders that can do something for the needs of our community."

Such outspokenness has been rare in Atitlán since Arbenz's brief presidency in the 1950s, when Ramiro's uncle was the town delegate to the Agrarian Reform Council.

In April 1986 thousands of people poured into the streets of Atitlán to protest the intolerably high cost of living. Shortly afterward, Atitlán became one of the first towns in the highlands to vote to disband the civil defense patrol.

After he was elected mayor of Santiago Atitlán in December 1985, Antonio Ixbalán Cuncz's first order of business was the construction of a new town hall and municipal building. When I first met with him he was bursting with confidence from all the expressions of support he had received from the community. Cuncz was one of the very few Mayas in the history of Santiago Atitlán—and the first Christian Democrat—to be elected mayor. After a scant six months he discovered that the funds for a new lighting and water plant, and for paving the road to San Lucas, were not so easily obtained. But the work on the new municipality proceeded on schedule, and he remained popular with the townspeople, who staunchly defended him when a new zone commander tried to bend him to his will in order to reinstate the civil patrols.

The last time I met with Mayor Cuncz was in 1988, shortly after the inauguration of the handsome new town hall, which had a prominent plaque on the wall that bore his name. He was only two years into his term, but something had changed drastically. The townspeople I spoke with now complained that Mayor Cuncz no longer had time for them and was consorting exclusively with ladinos. There were rumors of kickbacks for undisclosed favors to unscrupulous entrepreneurs who "planned to take over the town." Ramiro, who had been one of Mayor Cuncz's firmest supporters, claimed he had betrayed the Christian Democrats who elected him. Like Mayors Guzmán of Nebaj and Nicolás Sánchez of Cotzal, whom I interviewed earlier that year, Mayor Cuncz had apparently proven all too vulnerable to the enticements of ladino culture. Through the common practice, dating from colonial times, of extending privileges to Indian officials which they deny to the community at large, powerful ladinos had driven a wedge between Mayor Ixbalán Cuncz and the townspeople who elected him.

A visit to Atitlán on anything other than a two-hour tourist cruise inevitably leads to some reminder of a murder or disappearance. When Atitecos give directions, the signposts are likely to be "the corner where Doña Lucha's son was kidnapped" or "next to the house where the comisionado was found without his head." And the passage of time is apt to be measured similarly: "It was about five months after the sixteen boys were massacred at the Chacayá finca."

During a boat crossing to Atitlán, I engaged in a lively chat with a young Tz'utujil woman about the situation in her town. In a moment of seeming carelessness, she frowned and blurted out that her father, the town pharmacist, had been murdered only three weeks earlier "because of his association with the mission." I visited the drugstore, whose windows were barred shut, and was admitted by the pharmacist's widow and three sons. They formed a circle around me as they pointed out the two bullet holes on the wall, the exact place where he had stood when the first bullet hit him, the time it had happened, and the place where he fell, which was marked with flowers. In the somber gray light of the shuttered pharmacy, they thanked me for coming and sharing their grief, and I realized Atitecos have no one to speak to about these things.

A week after this incident the ladino owner of a fleet of buses who was co-founder of an orphanage for Tz'utujil children was killed in a manner almost identical with the murder of the pharmacist.

During the three days I spent in Santiago Atitlán that summer, the sense of menace that descended after dark was almost palpable. The hours before midnight are still ruled by Atitlán's traditional spooks and necromancers, the antipodes of good shamans known as "Food and Water Men." In hidden grottoes outside town, *aj'itz,* or brujos, are said to practice black magic to cast assorted plagues and mishaps on their enemies. The *characoteles,* who outwardly resemble normal citizens, transform themselves with three backward somersaults into dogs, cats, pigs, or horses—their *nahuals*—who wander around town at midnight and scare their neighbors half to death. On the night of April 1, 1989, Juan Ramírez Zapalo chased down a dog that had been eating his corn and hacked it to pieces with his machete. As it died, the dog turned into Ana Marcelina Hun Piney, a teenaged neighbor of his. At his trial in Sololá the following month, Ramírez Zapalo accused Hun Piney of being a bruja who turned herself into a dog every night to prey on his milpa. The nonplussed ladino municipal judge declared Ramírez Zapalo innocent for reasons of temporary insanity and released him. The story was first told to me by Ramiro, who with most other residents of Santiago, has his own fund of stories to back Ramírez Zapalo's testimony.

The early morning hours in Atitlán belong to the silent death squadrons that visit Tz'utujil communal leaders and ladinos suspected of collaborating with ORPA. An invisible clock with knifeblades for hands ticks away the minutes until the first scream or cough of a Galil rifle shatters the suspense.

I learned that summer that the murder of Stan Rother as well as that of hundreds of innocent Atitecos has fanned a hunger for more martyrs, to alleviate the intolerable tensions. To many Atitecos, death no longer seems so terrible—not even violent death—because it puts an end to torture. I learned of widows who seek out their husband's assassins and beg them to kill them. *"Regaláme un balazo,"* they plead. Let me have a bullet. "I owe no one, therefore I fear no one," is the commonplace boast of a prospective victim. The murder or disappearance of a neighbor is often justified for settling a debt—and incurring another. For other killings, *envidia*—malicious envy—is sufficient explanation. A resident gringa's two neighbors are killed because she pays them a higher price for their woven belts and wristbands, and the additional income has made the two women haughty and adulterous. Envidia often means punishment meted out by the community to those who presume to rise above prescribed standards.

The morning after a killing in Santiago Atitlán there is an eerie sense of buoyancy. Atitecos send their children off to school, wash their clothes in the lake, fish and attend to their cornfields, as always. In the town center the lovely bolts of woven cloth are put on display, and the women don the wraparound *xk'ap* headdress for the tourists who start to arrive shortly after ten. Death is another form of catharsis, as are the heavy drinking and fireworks that accompany costumbre, the convulsive services in the Pentecostal and charismatic temples, the gleeful squeals of kids watching Schwarzenegger or Stallone blast dark-haired foreigners in the town's video parlor. In the Catholic church, I noted the expectant brightness in parishioners' eyes one Sunday morning, when the gringo pastor was an hour late for mass.

In Atitlán, the hunger for martyrs has become an addiction.

10

The Missionaries' Return

"The pot is boiling, friend. You can't believe what will be
coming down in this country. And I expect to be right in the
thick of it."

Father John Vesey

In the summer and fall of 1984, the repeated pleas of Atitlán's parishioners were answered with the arrival of two American parish
priests, Oklahoman Thomas McSherry and John Vesey of the diocese
of Brooklyn, New York. Vesey had recently completed a stormy seven-
year pastoral assignment in Paraguay. The priests arrived during a
period of relative calm when the two chief guerrilla organizations,
EGP and ORPA, were recovering from their setbacks.

They found Stan Rother's cherished farm in a sorry state of abandon, with the army still bivouacked in one corner. Six courageous
Carmelite sisters had kept the mission open and in reasonable working
order. Acción Católica was active again, and the Voice of Atitlán had
returned to the air with religious and self-improvement programs.

The tensions and dissensions that contributed to Stanley Rother's
assassination still simmered under the surface. Although reduced in
numbers, ORPA still found support among the poor and exploited
of the community. From its peak in 1982, when ORPA controlled
large portions of Sololá Department, the group of active militants
had shrunk from about 1,500 to 500 or so. Fifty to one hundred of
them made periodic appearances in Santiago and in the neighboring
town of San Lucas Tolimán. Together, these two towns forge the
main link between the Pacific coast's cotton and sugar plantations,
and the zones of conflict in the western and northern highlands, a
strategic location that has accounted for the continued guerrilla presence in the region and for the army's determination to uproot them.

191

In 1985 a British journalist was invited to visit a rebel camp of the Xavier Tambriz Front on the western slope of Atitlán volcano. Ambrose Evans-Pritchard found about fifty resolute and spirited combatants who stoically weathered the cold and damp winters as well as the heat of the dry summer. The comandante, "Pancho," was a ladino son of former United Fruit employees, and his lieutenant, "Ana," the rebel daughter of a military officer. The guerrillas lived on a diet of beans, rice, and occasional meat, almost all of it provided by Atitecos. In the evenings they liked to read Tolstoy, Dickens, and Shakespeare, whose plays they staged with Coleman lamps and flashlights. The front's Galil rifles and other arms had been confiscated from the army or bought on the international black market. Their most effective weapon by far was the home-made claymore mines they use in ambushes of army patrols. But the mines were indiscriminate and too often victimized innocent farmers and wayfarers who inadvertently stepped on them.

A young Norwegian adventurer who visited the Xavier Tambriz Front two years later found a still resolute but less inspired band of combatants relying on the same guerrilla tactics. They had made no adjustments to new military counterinsurgency strategy and technology, which included bombing raids on their mountain hideouts and a growing—and ecologically heedless—reliance on chemical defoliants. The foreign visitor remarked that rum rations formed part of the guerrillas' basic diet. The Shakespeare plays staged on "cultural evenings" had been replaced by a battery-run television receiver on which wide-eyed Mayan recruits watched Rambo, the helicopter serial "Air Wolf," and other high-tech war films. "We know they are counterrevolutionary propaganda, but they're exciting," a young Tz'utujil guerrilla confessed to the visitor.

In the three years after Rother's murder the evangelical sects had continued to make inroads in the Catholic community, and now claimed over 30 percent of the faithful. The fastest-growing Catholic movement in town was the charismatics, whose members spoke in tongues and practiced laying on of hands and other neo-Pentecostal departures from orthodox Catholic observance. Before the end of the year, many of the charismatics would defect to Elim and other Pentecostal sects.

Father Tom McSherry, who had been Stan Rother's associate,

agreed to help groom John Vesey to take his place. But McSherry's low-key pastoral approach proved to be at variance with Vesey's conception of his role. Vesey had befriended Stan Rother when they were both young seminarians, and he believed Rother to be a misunderstood saint who was cruelly martyred by the Atiteco community.

Father McSherry felt a bilingual school program would be the most fitting memorial to Stan Rother. He supported the Oklahoma-based movement for Rother's canonization, but wondered whether his sanctification by the people of Santiago would not have been more meaningful to him. John Vesey, a pugnacious New York Irishman who favored the Gospel of Confrontation, had his own distinct idea of how best to run the parish. The contrasts in the two churchmen's temperaments and pastoral philosophies virtually guaranteed a standoff.

Shortly after his arrival John Vesey called a meeting of Acción Católica's catechists. He accused them, as well as the cofrades and select members of the ladino community, of sharing responsibility for Stanley Rother's murder. Weeks later Father Vesey claimed to have uncovered a plot by the military, which he reported to the U.S. Embassy. According to Vesey, the townspeople's continuing support for ORPA had confirmed the fears of zone commanders that Santiago Atitlán was hopelessly contaminated. As a result the officers presented to their superiors a plan to execute twelve thousand suspected subversives and to relocate thousands more to a new model village to be erected fifty kilometers north of Atitlán, near Nahualá.

When I visited Atitlán to look into Father Vesey's allegations, I was unable to find any corroboration for the army plot John Vesey reported. And I was equally unable to find any substantiation for his claim that he had been the target of an assassination attempt while driving in the outskirts of town. The incident was alleged to have taken place shortly after All Souls' Day, which is celebrated by the cofradías with abundant drink and loud music, nightlong fireworks and revelry, and the ringing of bells. Vesey, who was recovering from bronchial pneumonia, rose from his sick bed and repaired to the cofradía of Santa Cruz to confiscate the bell rope and ladder. Shouting like a latter-day Diego de Landa, he vowed to put an end to the drinking and "devil worship."

The cofrades I met with confessed their antipathy toward Vesey and said they had reported his assaults on the cofradías to the army,

but they flatly denied conspiring against his life. When I spoke with
the former mayor, a ladino supporter of costumbre, he admitted to
having threatened Vesey with arrest and imprisonment if he violated
the sanctuary of the cofradías again. In November 1984, John Vesey
left the parish of Santiago Atitlán and flew to New York after being
warned by the U.S. Embassy that he was "no longer welcome" in
Atitlán and that his life might be at risk. Five months later he was
summoned by the bishop of Sololá to serve in the neighboring parish
of San Pedro la Laguna.

The controversies Father Vesey stirred up during his four months
in Atitlán left bitter memories. Father McSherry, a quietly flamboyant
urban cowboy who affects a western hat, boots and cords, chose a
low-profile clerical style after he replaced Vesey as Atitlán's parish
priest. When I met with him, he was barely able to conceal his animus
toward Vesey and challenged him to present a deposition with the
names of Atitecos he accused of having plotted Stan Rother's murder.
For all his outward incongruities—he is more adept at water-skiing
than at handling a plow—Father McSherry has effectively continued
the health and education programs that Stan Rother started before
he was murdered; and he courageously supports some of the bold
initiatives by Acción Católica. But McSherry is no martyr and scru-
pulously avoids any confrontation with the cofradías, the ladino community, and the army. On the afternoon we met, four townspeople
who had been killed in a neighboring finca were put on display in
the town square, an event which had visibly shaken McSherry. He
denied being haunted by Stan Rother's memory but admitted that he
froze whenever the lights went out, as they had on the night of the
murder. "This is the most people that have been killed in one day
since I've been here, and I have to ask myself, 'Is history about to
repeat itself?' "

Three other American clergymen who have served in the Sololá
diocese for many years, Fathers Pat Greene of Sololá, Greg Sheaffer
of San Lucas Tolimán, and Jim Hazelton of Santa María Visitación,
were more circumspect in their criticism of Vesey's pastoral methods.
In private, however, they all sided with Father McSherry's view. U.S.
volunteer health workers in Atitlán's hospital viewed Vesey's provo-
cations as desperate attempts to measure up to Stan Rother by joining
him in a violent martyrdom.

The catechists I interviewed in Atitlán told me Father Vesey had reopened all the wounds inflicted on the community by Stan Rother's murder, just as they had begun to heal. Cofrades expressed indignation that Stan Rother, whom they had named an elder of their brotherhood, had been replaced by a man who flung reckless accusations in all directions and whose attitude toward Maximón mirrored the worst intolerances of his Spanish predecessors.

Father Vesey's reputation soon followed him to San Pedro la Laguna, which he found better suited to his temperament. That parish, which has undergone its own periods of strife and upheaval and has an even larger proportion of evangelical converts than Santiago Atitlán, is far better integrated. By presenting a united front, San Pedranos have managed to keep at bay both the military's comisionados and recruiters for ORPA. San Pedro, where Maximón survives more in shadow than in substance, voted out its cofradías in the mid sixties. Nevertheless, after a brief honeymoon with his new parishioners, Father Vesey was soon embroiled in fresh controversy.

In summer of 1987 he closed down the church of San Juan la Laguna, a small town bordering on San Pedro that still had three functioning cofradías. Father Vesey refused to celebrate communion in San Juan's church after a dispute with cofrades and Acción Católica over control of church funds and the ministering of sacraments. The catechists subsequently forced open the church door and invited the notorious Father Andrés Girón, who heads a peasant-based agrarian reform movement, to celebrate mass. Father Girón, whose own reputation for outlandish behavior rivals John Vesey's, roundly denounced the arrogance of "foreign priests" who misappropriated church funds and attempted to abolish a Catholic community's ancestral costumbres. (In a chance encounter with Father Girón in the Guatemala City airport, I learned that Girón had documents proving Father Vesey's "dirty" tactics and that he planned to continue visiting San Juan until Vesey was removed.)

Although John Vesey had made important enemies in Guatemala, the bishop of Sololá, Monsignor Eduardo Fuentes, adamantly supported his efforts to keep a tight leash on his Tz'utujil parishioners and discourage idolatrous costumbres. An admirer of Opus Dei, the ultraconservative ecclesiastical movement based in Spain, Bishop

Fuentes reportedly admitted to a colleague, "Try as I might, I cannot sympathize with the Indians."

I met with Father John Vesey on several occasions in his parish church of San Pedro la Laguna. During our first interview, in December 1986, he spoke glowingly of Stanley Rother's saintly qualities and suggested that no one understood the man's true greatness. "Nobody has read Stan's letters," he said. "They have only looked at the words. Stan Rother knew like no one else did that you cannot understand or perform a spiritual martyrdom until you have accepted the risk of physical extinction."

Vesey blamed the entire community of Santiago Atitlán for Rother's death but felt the time had passed for recriminations. When I asked him about the army plan to eliminate twelve thousand residents of Atitlán and relocate the remainder, he replied, "I have my sources," and said he had been given the information by two highly placed army officers. He said he had prayed for the community after hearing of the plot and suggested that he deserved credit for exposing it in time.

When I next met with John Vesey in August 1987, he seemed a different person altogether. I found him outside the parish church, dressed in a track suit for his morning jog. He was visibly distraught and looked as if he had aged considerably more than the eight months since our first encounter. Vesey bitterly mocked the evangelical sects of San Pedro, which had established seventeen temples and now claimed one-third of the town's faithful. He was contemptuous of the cofrades who clung to their "pagan" practices in neighboring San Juan, and all but accused Acción Católica catechists who opposed his will of criminal activity against the church.

When Stanley Rother's name came up, Vesey immediately accused the defunct military comisionado, Martínez Ruiz, of having turned Rother in to the army and claimed he was also responsible for the attempt on his own life. (In our subsequent meetings he named several other culprits.)

"Father Stan was a good, gentle, and powerful man, but he did not understand the Indian mentality. Stan did not have an analytic gift. He was an innocent who understood justice and holiness, but he could not see into people's motives. There is a great amount of evil in Atitlán, and there were many who wanted to destroy Stan Rother because of his power for good. If he had lived, the evangelicals would not have taken over the parish, and the killings would have stopped.

"Now, the evil is everywhere. There is so much, it is impossible to take it all in." Father Vesey looked up at the sky. "Today is the first day this week the F-14's haven't flown overhead on their way to Atitlán. There is going to be hell to pay in this country, and nobody sees it. Nobody." He emphasized these last words with peals of laughter followed by a disconcerting elfin smile.

2

In October 1987 a delegation of more than a dozen cofrades and Acción Católica catechists of San Juan la Laguna visited the offices of Guatemala City's two major newspapers to demand the resignation of Father John Vesey. Their charges against him included the "sacking" of San Juan's church. The cofrades claimed he had removed and hidden away gold reliquaries, antique wooden images, and other religious objects used in the Eucharist. The catechists accused him of misappropriating over two thousand quetzales (about $800) the community had gathered to renovate the town church. The catechists also claimed that their appeals to the church hierarchy to have the offending foreign priest replaced had been ignored, and they were left with no choice but to make their grievances public.

On October 27 *El Gráfico* printed a letter from Bishop Eduardo Fuentes, who vigorously defended Father Vesey and dismissed as absurd the accusation that a North American priest of Father Vesey's means and probity would lower himself to steal from his own parish. Bishop Fuentes issued a stern call to San Juan's parishioners to repudiate the charges and accept conciliation within the church. Behind the firm, paternalistic tone hung a veiled threat to resort to draconian measures if they persisted in their apostasy.

Disputes of this nature have been familiar to Guatemala's Catholics since the colonial era, as church and civil archives can attest. But the Vesey controversy had an added, surreal mix of violence and psychopathology that is distinctly contemporary.

A few days after the "Yankee priest scandal" made prime time TV news and the front pages, I made a third visit to Father John Vesey in San Pedro. By happenstance, I found him once again wearing his jogging togs and a T-shirt with "Farrell's St. Patrick's Day Brooklyn 1985" emblazoned across the front.

Vesey appeared to be enjoying all the media attention and gave the distinct impression that, like Father Girón, he would rather be vilified than ignored. In an almost cheerful tone, he assured me the worst of the crisis had passed and the situation was well in hand. He said it had been Bishop Fuentes's decision to shut down the church in San Juan because of "rampant immorality."

Vesey denied that there had been any collection of funds for renovating the church and claimed he had left all the treasures and relics intact when he closed it down. He then accused the leaders of the protest of being allied with the same "sinister" factions that had murdered Stan Rother and that had kept close tabs on him in Atitlán, "waiting for the right opportunity." He said Monsignor Fuentes had taken the matter in hand and serious decisions would be made in the next few days. "He is very concerned with holiness, as I am, and as Stan Rother was. I am ready to comply fully with Bishop Fuentes's judgment, in the spirit of conciliation within the church."

As we spoke, an army helicopter flew high overhead, riveting Vesey's attention. "They've been going by every day," he said, "and so have the F-14's. It's all coming to a head." In one of his abrupt turnabouts, he became sarcastic and mocked the parishioners of San Juan for their drinking and blaspheming and again accused them of being in league with sinister reactionary elements that were responsible for the deaths of hundreds of villagers. For the first time, he hinted at having been involved in similar controversies during his seven years in Paraguay, which he said prepared him for his pastoral service in Guatemala. "I am no martyr, friend. I know I have made mistakes, and Bishop Fuentes has at times been very critical of me. But I have his support and that of the other bishops. I believed in what I was doing, and I know that in the end, evil is overcome by grace. I know I am being denounced, just as Stan was, and we both made important enemies. G-2, the army's intelligence unit, is sending agents down here to inquire about me; and the U.S. Embassy decided I was off the wall after I spelled out for them the army's plan for Santiago

Atitlán. They accused me of making it all up and denounced me to the bishop, but I am still here." He burst into laughter and subsided into his unsettling elfin smile.

That afternoon I walked the two kilometers to San Juan la Laguna to interview Vesey's opponents. A right-wing former mayor, Francisco Sumoza, told me Father Vesey had been ushered into town a year before on a carpet of flowers; but he then repaid the parishioners' welcome by exploiting old land disputes between San Pedro and San Juan to sharpen dissensions between the two communities, "exactly as he did in Santiago Atitlán."

Vesey had about 150 followers in town who attended services in the chapel, but at least 1,500 of the town's Catholics had stayed with the reopened church and were calling for Vesey's removal. They had appealed to Bishop Fuentes for a priest from a neighboring town to serve San Juan and asked to be named a separate parish. When the bishop turned down their request, they invited Father Girón to administer the sacraments. Father Girón, who was to have arrived two days earlier, sent a telegram excusing himself because of conflicts with his bishop.

Pedro Cholotio Iquic, an earnest, articulate catechist who heads San Juan's Acción Católica delegation, was most incensed at Father Vesey's demeaning attitude toward catechists and cofrades. He had refused to perform the Eucharist for them, claiming they were unworthy and calling them "imbeciles," "stupid little Indians," and "puppets." Iquic said he was heading the delegation that would visit Archbishop Penados del Barrio in Guatemala City to plead for his intercession.

The following morning I located Monsignor Eduardo Fuentes in the bishopric at Panajachel. He was awaiting the delegation from San Juan, not suspecting that they were on their way to Guatemala City to seek an audience with the archbishop. Monsignor Fuentes, a tall, youthful-looking cleric of about forty with an impressive—and distinctly European—physical presence, preambled our brief interview with a baseball simile. Deploring the laity's attempts to "declericalize" the Catholic church, he likened San Juan's demands for a new priest to outfielders who insist on playing the infield, which "the manager" in Rome had assigned to the clergy. I asked Bishop Fuentes if he had instructed Father Vesey to close down the church in San Juan. He admitted he had, but only after the parishioners had defied his will by rebuffing his conciliatory gestures. "Father Vesey made mistakes when he first arrived in San Juan. He has admitted his errors and asked for the forgiveness of the parishioners, but they have remained obdurate. They have rejected the adjunct priest, an Indian like themselves whom I proposed as Vesey's replacement. But that is not the central issue. I can remove Vesey, and the question of defiance of church authority still remains. Where is their spirit of forgiveness? If I were to give in to their demands, it would be like the tail wagging the dog, or the screw replacing the machine. Disobedience simply cannot be tolerated in the Catholic church, as Pope John Paul II made eminently clear during his pastoral visit here some years ago."

When I brought up my talks with Francisco Sumoza and Pedro Iquic and listed what I thought to be legitimate grievances, Bishop Fuentes appeared to relent. "Yes, I have heard these grievances, and I still pray they can be redressed in a spirit of obedience and forgiveness. This matter has provided ammunition for the evangelicals, who will undoubtedly profit from our internal disputes. Please understand, I do not doubt that many of the parishioners have acted in good faith, but then . . ." He threw up his hands. "Who can say where the truth lies?"

As our interview concluded, Monsignor Fuentes asked me if I was Christian, and I told him I had been born a Sephardi Jew. Placing his hand on my shoulder he alluded to our common roots and traditions and assured me the three religious figures he most admired had been Jews—Mary, Jesus, and the Apostle Paul.

The next day the delegation from San Juan occupied Guatemala City's metropolitan cathedral, requesting an audience with the archbishop. *El Gráfico*'s editorial of November 9 attributed the scandal to a clash between cultures, depicting it as one more instance of a foreign priest failing to understand the "magic-religious" traditions of the indigenous communities. By the end of the day, Archbishop Próspero Penados del Barrio had met with the fifty-four delegates. After some heated exchanges, the archbishop called Bishop Fuentes on the phone. The matter seemed on its way to a resolution, but not before causing acute embarrassment to the Catholic church and to Bishop Fuentes in particular.

In the following days, the press reported the appearance of the missing funds in the bank statements of the Sololá diocese; the confiscated saints and relics showed up in a San Juan basement. In a spirit of reconciliation, Father Vesey was relieved of his duties in San Juan and was to be replaced by a recently ordained Cakchiquel pastor from Panajachel. By the week's end, the church had moved to repair the damage. At an annual gathering of priests and layworkers of the Sololá diocese, Father John Vesey was fully exculpated of any wrongdoing, and the disturbances in San Juan were blamed on a small faction of malcontents.

The "Yankee priest scandal" was not so easily disposed of. When I returned to Santiago Atitlán three months later I learned that Bishop Fuentes had sent threatening letters and telegrams to three American priests in the diocese for failing to properly support John Vesey. In McSherry's case, Fuentes had also sent a letter of reprimand to his bishop in Oklahoma. A furious Tom McSherry suggested Vesey had "programmed" Bishop Fuentes by catering to his intellectual prejudices and his sympathies with Opus Dei. The quarrel, which had uncovered sharp divisions within the church hierarchy, was taking on larger dimensions.

In Atitlán, meanwhile, the climate of violence was reminiscent of the last year of Stan Rother's ministry. After an ex-military comisionado was killed in a guerrilla ambush near Cerro de Oro, the army unfurled a banner across the entrance to the municipality that read: "The Townspeople and the Army of Santiago Atitlán say No to Communism and Yes to Democracy." The army circulated a death list they claimed to have found in the possession of a captured guerrilla. The nearly two hundred names included all the town's Tz'utujil principales and a handful of ladinos who had opposed the civil patrol, but few evangelicals. At least twenty of those listed—including most of the schoolteachers—left town after receiving visits from army officers, who kept up the fiction the list was ORPA's, rather than their own. Ramiro, the community leader who had convened a council of elders to plan Atitlán's future, was informed his name was on the list. Instead of leaving town, he holed up in his bedroom and refused to see anyone. The army's purpose became clearer after they began pressuring evangelical pastors and Mayor Cuncz to reinstate the civil patrol to provide "protection" from the guerrillas. A week after the list appeared, two of those named were taken off a bus by soldiers and were not heard from again. In the weeks that followed, several more townspeople on the list disappeared one by one, and their bodies were later found tortured and mutilated.

A U.S. newspaper reporter who visited Atitlán asked the post commander if two women he claimed to have been murdered by guerrillas had been army informers. The comandante replied, "I don't bother my head with such garbage."

Father McSherry, who admitted to being "scared to death" by the rumors of a separate gringo death list, succumbed to army pressures to the extent of celebrating his first mass inside the barracks. Although he absented himself more and more frequently from Atitlán, he continued to supervise the construction of a new school and orphanage behind the church.

In the course of a conversation with Father McSherry at the mission, he bristled at the mention of Monsignor Fuentes's threatening telegram and vowed to resist the bishop's pressure to force American priests into retirement, so he could replace them with supporters of Opus Dei. The other two dissidents, Fathers Greg Sheaffer of San Lucas and Jim Hazelton of Santa María Visitación, had been serving in the Sololá diocese for years before Fuentes was ordained a priest. (Hazelton has since been reassigned to the diocese of Escuintla, on the Pacific coast.)

"The bishop and Vesey want to divide us, but instead they have united us," McSherry said. He accused John Vesey once again of undoing during his brief tenure in Atitlán the thirteen-year legacy of Stanley Rother. "Humility is not John's strong suit," he said. McSherry smiled at my suggestion that it was as if a weighty moral drama by Ibsen had degenerated into a Luis Buñuel screenplay on the wages of misguided holiness.

"I've done some studies in psychiatry," McSherry responded, "and I've always been intrigued by the fine line that divides madness from saintliness. I give John credit for possessing both qualities in abundance." Father McSherry concluded by saying his stay in Rome had helped him to understand his role in Atitlán, and he felt calmer about the possible consequences. Evidently McSherry, unlike Vesey, had given up all pretensions to a missionary's calling and was content to hold his own as a simple parish priest.

3

I began to see the four American priests in the Sololá diocese as planets orbiting about Stan Rother, the exploding star whom Monsignor Fuentes, with his fondness for extravagant metaphors, was attempting to replace with his own constellation. By 1988 four new Opus Dei supporters had been inducted into the seminary that served Sololá. To the mounting challenge of a well-organized, wholesale evangelical takeover of their flock, the diocese of Sololá had responded atavistically. The entrenched ecclesiasticism of Opus Dei, with its medieval secretiveness and arcane discipline and its doctrinaire anticommunism, fits Guatemala's old-guard ladino priesthood like a glove. Archbishop Penados del Barrio, who on occasion has taken stands to the left of the political center, privately called the Opus Dei movement "dangerous," because of its alliances with powerful mercantile and agrarian interests that have traditionally exploited the poor and the landless Guatemalans. Monsignor Josemaría Escriva de Balaguer, the founder of Opus Dei who died in 1975, was being supported for beatification by Pope John Paul II less than fifty years after the sect's establishment. The archbishop voiced his regret: "The pontiff's undue haste in sanctifying Balaguer has sent ripples through all of Christendom. It reflects the sect's growing influence within the Vatican itself, a development many of us view with alarm." Archbishop Penados del Barrio has earned worldwide recognition as coauthor of "A Clamor for Land," an impassioned pastoral letter by Guatemala's bishops that calls for social justice for Guatemala's poor and landless.

In May 1988 Father John Vesey was relieved of his parish in San Pedro and took up residence in Sololá as Bishop Fuentes's private secretary. When I ran into Tom McSherry in late July during the celebration for Santiago Atitlán's patron saint, he predicted wryly that Vesey "had a great future" in his new post. On the wall of his new quarters Father Vesey had hung a poster, "Modern American Martyrs," which included short biographies of Stan Rother and the four religious women killed in El Salvador.

The violence in Atitlán abated after articles in the U.S. press exposed the army death lists, and McSherry returned from a retreat to serve in his parish full time. Although the army lists had stopped circulating in Atitlán, none of the schoolmasters who fled after receiving death threats had returned as yet. In September 1987, the base comandante had persuaded five hundred Atitecos to form a new civil defense patrol, but compliance was spotty and resistance to the patrols remained high. And although ORPA leaflets had not been seen in town for many months, guerrillas were credited with the continuing executions of former military comisionados, their relatives, and their cohorts. Two men associated with the military were shot through the mouth and dumped in the streets during the week of the fiesta, perpetuating the egregious Atiteco tradition of cathartic bloodletting in times of stress or celebration. But ORPA's obstinate silence regarding the ajusticiamientos eroded some of their support among Atitecos. Ramiro, whom I have consulted regularly for over a dozen years, was of the opinion that recent setbacks had affected the youthful buoyancy and idealism Atitecos associate with "los muchachos," as they like to call the guerrillas.

"Before, they used to have iron discipline and could stay put in their mountain enclaves for months on end, enduring the hunger and cold without complaint. That is how they won the respect of many Atitecos. Now, los muchachos are rotated to Cuba every six months or so, for ideological indoctrination and recreation. As they grow older and their goals fall short of realization, they become soft and cynical, and they lose their common touch with the people." Ramiro added, "Atitecos hate the army as much as they ever did, but this no longer translates automatically into support for the guerrillas."

4

Mayor Antonio Ixbalán Cuncz had completed his two-and-a-half-year term in office with two visible accomplishments: a new municipality and commercial center and a remodeled park. Despite rumors that he had salted away enough money to invest in the town's chief tourist motel, he had come out of an impossible task with his personal integrity more or less intact—no small feat in a town so riven with gossip and suspicion. Even his enemies credited him with *huevos* (balls) for stubbornly resisting the army's pressure to reinstate the civil defense patrol.

Mayor Cuncz's replacement was a ladino Christian Democrat so wary of making promises that he was already being criticized as an ineffective namby-pamby. During his first month in office the water-pumping system broke down, and Mayor Delfino Rodas had to face the indignation of Atitecos without water in the higher cantones.

In a brief interview three months after he took office, I found Mayor Rodas a personable official proud of his mastery of the Tz'utujil language, a factor that contributed to his election by an Atiteco community disenchanted with Ixbalán Cuncz. His overriding concerns, apart from resolving the water crisis, were the purchase of a garbage truck to offset the worsening contamination of the lake with refuse and the construction of a paved road to San Lucas. But he shrugged and smiled even as he spoke, tacitly conceding that a ladino mayor had about as much hope of raising funds for communal improvements as a Maya mayor did.

With Robert Carlsen, a University of Colorado graduate student who is writing his doctoral thesis on the ethnohistorical relations between costumbre and evangelism in Santiago, I visited the three chief cofradías taking part in the July 1988 festivities. On Saturday the saint of each cofradía was marched in procession to the church, where the processioners spent the night. On Monday, July 25, the fiesta climaxed as Santiago, San Martín, San Antonio, and four other saints were carried out of the church by hundreds of cofrades and marched slowly around the four cardinal points in the square. At each of the four stations, the revelers paused to burn incense, drink, chant prayers, and dance their saints in a sustained ceremonial frenzy aimed at restoring equilibrium in the universe.

In April 1989 an added suspense highlighted the Holy Week festivities in Santiago. Before the ceremonies began, an apparently deranged man fired several shots at Maximón's telenel with a pistol, wounding him in the stomach. Two days prior to the procession, the telenel rose from his sick bed and began his preparations. The question in everyone's mind on Good Friday was whether Maximón's bearer would have the strength to lift him aloft and carry him all the way back to the cofradía of Santa Cruz. The bare heads of gringo tourists, anthropologists, journalists—and one or two longhaired "apprentice shamans"—stood out from the sea of straw hats surrounding Maximón's chapel, where he hung as Judas Iscariot. The Antichrist patiently waited with a smoking cigar in his mouth as the Holy Sepulcher made its tortuous way down the church steps. The loud clack clack of wooden noisemakers punctured the lugubrious funeral march played—off key as always—by the brass band accompanying the recumbent Christ. It took over an hour for the bier to reach the flower carpet in the center of the square, as Father McSherry wafted his blessings from the mission's portico. Heads turned expectantly, but Maximón made no move. The tall foreigners in the square, several of them drunk or nursing hangovers, eyed one another, sensing something unusual was about to take place. No one in town could remember the last time the Holy Sepulcher had been allowed free passage across the square, unchallenged by Maximón. At last, a full three hours after the crucified Christ had been lowered from the cross and placed in his bier, a surge of movement was observed in the chapel. Noisemakers exploded as the figure of Maximón disappeared behind a cloud of incense and reappeared on the telenel's shoulders, his tower of Stetsons and fetish cigar visible high above the heads of his followers. The flute and drum eclipsed the brass tubas and trumpets as the musicians, incense bearers, and principal cofrades parted the multitude, making way for the flamboyant idol.

The telenel paused at the foot of the church steps to bow four times and then moved like quicksilver, overtaking the Holy Sepulcher on the edge of the flower carpet. Within seconds, Maximón had descended another flight of steps and disappeared into the crowds below, on his way to Santa Cruz. In the cofradía, Maximón would be dismantled and relegated to the rafters, to await his resurrection in the fall. The telenel had mustered all of his strength for what turned out to be the briefest confrontation ever between the two cults and one of the most dramatic.

After the ceremony I met with a very drunk but still lucid Francisco Sohuel, sprawled on a bench at San Martín. He explained that Maximón had "given his seed" to Christ during their brief encounter. If he had failed to do so, Christ would have remained dead, and there would be no New Year to celebrate. He gripped my arm and whispered, "What you have seen is like a grain of sand, compared to what lies below." With an erratic finger he pointed at his brow, at his heart, and then at the red velvet bundle of San Martín, lying on a bed of rose petals in front of the altar.

Despite the impressive pageantry, Robert Carlsen saw multiple signs of the continuing disintegration of the cofradía belief system. What centuries of persecution by doctrinaire clergy had failed to accomplish—the suppression of the syncretic Catholic-Mayan cults—was now well under way in what Carlsen called a "transfer of magic" from costumbre to the evangelical cults. As a result, the cofradías have become increasingly dependent on outside support, to the extent of training foreigners as full-fledged Tz'utujil shamans. Martín Prechtel, a blond New Mexican of German extraction, became an apprentice to Nicolás Chiveleo, a reknowned Atiteco shaman, and he eventually was named an elder of Santa Cruz cofradía. Prechtel married the daughter of a cofrade after curing her of epilepsy. The worsening violence subsequently drove Prechtel and his wife, Dolores, out of the country. Prechtel, a talented polymath with an authentic spiritual calling, continues to serve as a practising shaman to Anglos and native Americans in Pecos, New Mexico, where he lives with Dolores and their two children.

"Of course," observed Carlsen, a rugged Coloradan with all the earmarks of a potential shaman, "the evangelicals will themselves be supplanted after their miracle-working fails to deliver the goods. The Pentecostals have been promising bumper corn crops and abundant fish harvests through prayer for some years now, with no appreciable results. I think you'll see a movement back toward some new level of nativistic ritual in the next two to three years."

Carlsen agreed that if the cofradías managed to keep a quorum of elders for a few years longer, the wheel could turn and young people might be drawn once again to the core of mystery in their Maya heritage. The cofradía system has teetered on the brink of oblivion before. What brings it back is its capacity to adapt to change, as embodied in the versatile personage of Maximón. I could already visualize a Maximón who speaks in tongues, preaches moderation in drink and sex, and levitates his followers with a Mayanized laying on of hands. By making saints of Pedro de Alvarado and army officers and ceremonializing Maximón's metamorphoses, cofrades strike a durable balance between the light and dark forces that inform their legacy.

For the present, the larger evangelical sects like Assemblies of God and Elim continue to draw hundreds of new converts from the cofradías and the traditional church. Even Reverend Sun Myung Moon's Unification Church has made inroads in Santiago with a community center they have erected behind the innocent-sounding rubric of CARP (Collegiate Association for Research Principles).

On Thursday of Holy Week, the fifty-six-year-old nebaysil of San Juan cofradía, which also houses a San Martín bundle, drank and sang late into the night. He insisted on celebrating the toxic pollution of the lake and the mountains of uncollected garbage that pose a rising health hazard to Santiago. "It is Martín," he sang ecstatically, as he danced with each of the cofrades and the gringo visitors. "It is all San Martín. The killings too are Martín." After all the other revelers had drunk themselves into a stupor and collapsed on the floor in a heap, the nebaysil continued his necromantic dance of celebration.

"Ah, Martín, santo mundo, tit of the world, we are devouring ourselves, we are devouring ourselves. We are devouring the world." Although his words echoed the sentiments of a millenarian Pentecostal, his blazing eyes and fixed, contorted grin more nearly reflected cosmic laughter. "Ah, santo mundo Martín, when all the world is consumed, only you, Martín, the forever present and forever holy, will remain. And you will make the world anew. Ah, Martín."

In his cowboy hat and boots, Father McSherry looked as relaxed as I'd ever seen him. His work on the new schools, the orphanage, and the widows' programs had been well received. The consensus in the religious community was that he had "hit his stride." Tom McSherry moved about Atitlán and its aldeas with relative ease, and he was beginning to enjoy the kind of affection Atitecos lavished on Stan Rother, before the military set up barracks outside town.

Everyone knew the army's low profile was deceptive and that the situation could degenerate overnight if sparked by another guerrilla ambush or a polluting resurgence of envidia.

A civil defense patroller in San Juan Atitán, Huehuetenango.

San Simón in army uniform, Sololá.

Maximón and his *telenel*, or bearer, in Santiago Atitlán.

Assorted "saints" in the San Martín Cofradía, Santiago Atitlán.

Deer dancer, San Martín Cofradía, Santiago Atitlán.

Forensic staff with remains of "Hermano Pedro," San Francisco church, Antigua.

In late April 1989, the murder of Juan Sisay, Santiago's foremost primitivist painter and a figure of international standing, led to a brief resurgence of violence. Four months later, between seventy-five and one hundred militants of the Xavier Tambriz Front, led by the fair-skinned, six-foot-plus Pancho, entered San Lucas Tolimán, apparently with the intention of holding a rally. They were met by a hail of bullets from the police station and a platoon of soldiers bivouacked in back. After a brief but intense skirmish the guerrillas withdrew, leaving one dead behind and taking their wounded with them. Father Greg Sheaffer was intercepted on his way into town from Atitlán and had his jeep confiscated briefly by the guerrillas but was otherwise unharmed. "The boys appear to be losing their touch," he said afterward, in reference to their poor timing and faulty intelligence. Despite their miscalculation, the front's bold incursion was cheered enthusiastically in Atitlán, where supporters spread rumors that the guerrillas had downed two helicopters and inflicted heavy casualties on the army and police.

The next day I visited Ramiro, who had been a good friend of Sisay's, to get a fix on the new wave of killings in Atitlán; but he seemed as mystified as everyone else. "The violence makes no sense any more," he said. "Sisay had many enemies, and he had been the target of envidia ever since the president awarded him the Order of the Quetzal thirty years ago. But no one has taken responsibility. The intention now from both sides seems to be to spread uncertainty by killing at random, with no apparent motive. There are no more lists circulating to warn suspects to leave town. There are only these senseless, casual killings carried out with a cool, impersonal saña. In Atitlán, killing has become a way of life."

Ramiro confessed he had not visited the Sisay home since the murder, for fear of making a slip of the tongue that could provoke a relative or visitor whose political opinions differ from his own.

The calm in Atitlán did not last long. In May and June 1990, while new peace talks were held between guerrilla leaders and government representatives in Madrid, eight Atitecos died violent deaths. The victims included two men hired by Robert Carlsen to collect data for a sociological survey. When the army set up camp in his neighbor's backyard, Carlsen picked up stakes and moved across the lake to

Panajachel. Father Tom McSherry also had to leave town for a time
after receiving a fresh spate of death threats.

Ramiro, who knew several of the victims, speculated that private
vendettas were behind the murders, although the army capitalized on
the situation by calling for the reinstatement of the civil defense
patrols. The week following, two more Atitecos were taken off a bus
and never heard from again. "The guerrillas and the government can
talk peace in Spain, but in Santiago Atitlán nothing has changed,"
said Ramiro, who was as upset as I'd ever seen him. "The violence
we live in is of our creation, and there is no longer the will on anyone's
part to put an end to it. In Atitlán today, people are targeted for
extermination simply because they owe money or boasted about
screwing someone else—or because they are the wrong religion. There
is a woman from San Pedro, a mistress to the comandante, who is
taking revenge on everyone simply because they are Atitecos. People
know she is denouncing them to the comandante, but they are afraid
to speak out. They think their innocence protects them, but most of
them are vulnerable."

For the first time in the years I've known him, Ramiro spoke of
his Protestant faith—he is a third-generation Baptist—as his shield
against malefactors and the hydra-headed monster, envidia. "Sisay was
a devout Catholic, and yet when his time came, his faith could not
save him. As a Christian, I know I carry the true God within me, and
so I am safe. I know the person responsible for Sisay's murder has
denounced me as well, and my name has appeared on death lists.
Whenever I feel personally threatened, I pray with all my soul. Tears
come to my eyes, and I am filled with a warmth that protects me
from harm. In the harder times ahead, only true Christians will be
protected from evil." Under the implacable stress of daily life in Santiago Atitlán, Ramiro had given in and aligned himself with God's
chosen.

When I ran into Father John Vesey in Guatemala City's Central
Park, he appeared startled by our third chance encounter in less than
two years. But he recovered quickly and said he was in town on an
errand for Bishop Fuentes. Father Vesey looked comfortable in his
new role, as he described his work coordinating diocesan activities
for the bishop. His newest project was a human rights office that he
planned to set up in Panajachel. Inevitably, the sinister edge rose to

his voice when we spoke of the continuing violence in the countryside and the threats to Cerezo's presidency. He smiled disdainfully on revealing that his old adversary Father Andrés Girón planned to take a leave from his parish, in preparation—Vesey felt certain—for running for higher office.

"The pot is boiling, friend," he said, looking not the least put out. "You can't believe what will be coming down in this country. And I expect to be right in the thick of it." His explosive laughter reverberated in the park.

5

On midnight of December 2, 1990, approximately twenty-five hundred Atitecos, led by the outgoing mayor, Delfino Rodas, and the mayor-elect, Salvador Ramírez, marched on the army barracks south of Santiago Atitlán and demanded to speak with the comandante. At the mayors' urging, the marchers were unarmed and carried only sticks and white banners. Earlier that evening five plainclothes military, among them the base commander, had harassed several townspeople after drinking heavily in a local cantina. The comandante—who was apparently drunk—had attempted to rob the home of Andrés Sapocu Jabuychan, and neighbors rang the churchbells to summon help. When a young man identified them as soldiers, the commanding officer fired his weapon, wounding a nineteen-year-old Atiteco in the hand and leg. Another youth apparently struck the officer in the face with a stone. The plainclothes soldiers gave themselves away when they had to be rescued by an army patrol, which escorted the officer and his four men back to the barracks.

The marchers were met by the comandante, who told their leaders to turn back and return the following day. According to eyewitnesses, an Atiteco toward the rear threw a stone at the comandante. A soldier fired into the air and a sergeant major manning an automatic weapon opened fire. Witnesses report that a courageous marcher threw himself on the gunner to prevent a slaughter, but it was too late. The soldier continued to strafe the crowd even after everyone fell to the ground or sought cover. When the shooting stopped, eleven men, women, and children lay dead on the ground, and at least twenty-one more were wounded. Two of these later died in the hospital. The final tally revealed most of the dead and wounded were Catholics, among them several catechists with Acción Católica.

The following day a clamor arose for the expulsion of the army garrison from Atitlán. Father Tom McSherry quietly set up microphones in the square, as more than half the town's twenty thousand residents gathered to hear the Attorney for Human Rights and other speakers demand the army's removal. Mayor-elect Ramírez went on national TV to denounce the murder and the disappearance of two thousand Atitecos over the past eleven years. Before thousands of astonished viewers, he laid the blame squarely on the army.

Outgoing President Cerezo and the two leading presidential candidates called for an investigative commission to look into the mayor's charges. A CERJ delegation led by Amílcar Méndez interviewed survivors and pressed for prosecution of the officers and soldiers involved in the shootings. Within twenty-four hours of the massacre, fifteen thousand Atitecos had affixed their thumbprints and signatures to a petition demanding that those responsible for the shooting be tried and punished and that the army base be removed immediately.

The hundreds of foreign visitors who toured Santiago Atitlán every week dropped to a trickle, but even these hardy souls helped focus international attention on the Atitlán Massacre, as it was headlined around the world. For several days, reports of the shooting and the townspeoples' response broke through what had been a virtual news blackout on Central America since the onset of the Persian Gulf Crisis. Human rights organizations in the United States and Europe moved to cut off all aid to Guatemala until the killings were resolved.

By week's end, the army high command, under intense domestic and international pressure, agreed to withdraw its six-hundred-man garrison from Santiago Atitlán. For the first time in living memory, an indigenous community had rid itself of a military occupation. It was a significant victory by all accounts, even before the guilty officers were indicted and prosecuted.

In February 1991 I visited Atitlán and met with Ramiro; one of his nephews had been wounded in the shooting. He showed me two landscape oil paintings he had done in black and white, because, he said, "Since the massacre the colors have fled from Atitlán." But he remarked on the dramatic decline in the violence since the army's departure on December 20. "We are only beginning to understand the full extent of the military's accountability," he said. "It now appears they were responsible for nearly all the murders we attributed to the guerrillas, including the assassination of Juan Sisay."

At Ramiro's suggestion, I went to meet with Mayor Salvador Ramírez, who greeted me in his office with unexpected effusiveness. He had mistaken me for a delegate from Germany's Konrad Adenauer Foundation, which had pledged $3 million to rehabilitate Santiago Atitlán. But although the mayor had already formed a reception committee, no delegation had as yet showed up. "Things are *alegre* here now, since the army decamped," said Mayor Ramírez, a large Tz'utujil Maya with the broad, vivid features of an ancient Olmec. "The townspeople can go gather firewood on the slopes of the volcano once again without fear of running into an army patrol. We are just starting to breathe freely for the first time in eleven years. The muchachos who had gone with the guerrillas have come back and are tilling their milpas and caulking their fishing pirogues. They told us that the Xavier Tambriz Front had vacated the area two years ago and moved to Acatenango volcano, near Antigua. Since the army's departure there has not been a single killing here, although we've had altercations with the National Police. Needless to say, our success in expelling the army has impacted on indigenous communities throughout the altiplano, and this makes the army very anxious."

I asked Mayor Ramírez, an evangelical, how he explained the disproportionate number of Catholics killed in the massacre. "The bullets do not differentiate between Catholics and evangelicals," he said. "The fact is that every sector of our community was represented among those 3,000 marchers, and that is what frightened the soldiers into shooting at us. Our people were fed up. They feel as I do that all men are created alike in God's image, and no one has the right to treat another human being the way we have been for too many years. For now, the eyes of the world are upon us, and the army will not dare retaliate. We have become known worldwide as a community that hates the army. But I know in time they will come back, probably dressed up as guerrillas, and try to reimplant themselves in our community. We will be ready for them. If they show up here again, we will chase them out with sticks and stones."

In summer of 1991 I met with the Auxiliary Attorney for Human Rights, Oscar Henríquez Cifuentes Cabrera, who is based in Santa Cruz del Quiché. He assured me the army had detained and was holding for sentencing both the commander of the Atitlán garrison and the sergeant major who fired the weapon that killed the 13 Atitecos. Several months later the *New York Times* confirmed the arrests. If the officers were tried and found guilty, and then served time in prison, the army's impunity from legal prosecution would be penetrated for the first time in modern Guatemalan history.

As Mayor Ramírez indicated, the army is not likely to loosen its hold on Atitlán indefinitely. Army spokesmen have emphasized their intention to maintain vigilance over the community, which sits inside a Zone of Conflict. In response, Santiago Atitlán has declared itself officially "neutral," and called on both the guerrillas and the army to cease operations within a declared twenty-five-kilometer "security perimeter." In an effort to maintain communal solidarity and forestall the divisions that have invited interference by the army in the past, Mayor Ramírez created a Committee for Security and Development. Every night security patrols made up of representatives from every cantón, church, and local cooperative make the rounds of Atitlán, armed only with whistles and white banners.

On two occasions in May, close to one thousand Atitecos armed with machetes intercepted a thirty-five-man army patrol probing the town's southern border. The soldiers were driven away, "shaking and trembling," after the crowds threatened to lynch them if they dared show their faces in the vicinity again. In July the town council of neighboring San Lucas Tolimán voted to expel the National Police from the community after a shooting incident that wounded a local resident. The town council also filed a request with the army comandante to move out his garrison as soon as possible. Smaller uprisings against military and municipal authorities in Patzún and other highland communities were evidently inspired by the Atitecos' bold example. For the first time in over five centuries, the Tz'utujils, who had been held in such scant regard by the conquistadores as well as by their bellicose Cakchiquel and Quiché neighbors, mounted a successful civil insurrection against an armed oppressor.

I visited Santiago Atitlán soon after the commemoration of the tenth anniversary of Stan Rother's martyrdom. The solemn services, led by Tom McSherry and Oklahoma's bishop, were attended by a huge gathering of Atitecos that included Protestant and evangelical pastors, members of the town's ten cofradías, and Acción Católica catechists. Toward evening I walked past Stan Rother's old farm, where the army had been bivouacked since 1980. Mayor Ramírez had named the old barracks a "Peace Park," and an altar had been erected to commemorate the thirteen Atitecos who died there. In place of former guard posts and gun emplacements neighbors had planted glossy green coffee trees whose branches drooped with crimson berries.

Two men were found guilty of the assassination of twelve Atitecos and injuries to twenty-one others: Sergeant Major Efraín García González, who manned the machine gun, and Lieutenant José Antonio Ortiz Rodríguez, who was the comandante of the Atitlán barracks at the time of massacre. In August 1992, the Guatemalan Ninth Court of Appeals increased the prison sentence of García González from twelve years to twenty, at the request of the Public Ministry. Lieutenant Ortiz Rodríguez was awaiting sentencing.

PART V

El Petén

11

🁢

Saving the Mayas' Rain Forest

"The Petén's humid forest is a tropical ecologist's dream."
James Nations

"The hardwood forests of the Petén are under our sovereignty."
"Juan," a guerrilla with the Rebel Armed Forces

The evening of my arrival in February 1989 at Yaxchilán, the classical Mayan ceremonial center on the Mexican shore of the Usumacinta River, I spotted two men in olive fatigues on the opposite bank. They were walking downriver with submachine guns slung over their shoulders. The Mexican immigration officer in Frontera Echeverría, three miles upriver, had warned me not to camp on the Guatemalan shore because of the dangerous guerrillas lurking there. I did not tell him I was a good deal more apprehensive about running into government troops, Guatemalan or Mexican.

Earlier in the day I had accompanied an international expedition of environmentalists to the top of Shield Jaguar Temple, the highest point in Yaxchilán, from which we gazed across the river at the majestic Sierra del Lacandón, a 2,358-square-mile reserve of dense humid forest containing one of the last large stands of giant hardwoods in Guatemala's northern region of El Petén. The largest of nine sawmills licensed to operate in Petén, the Aserradero del Norte (Sawmill of the North), had already marked one thousand mahoganies for logging in the Sierra by the end of the year. The 150-foot crests of mahoganies and the tallest cedars and ceibas keep in place the tropical forest's closed canopy, while their shallow root systems help bind together the fragile top soil. The logging roads blazed through the forest to reach these last mahoganies are the first stage in an expanding agricultural frontier: the roads bring in milpa farmers whose slash and

219

burn practices clear the forest. After two or three years the top soil gives out; the *milperos* move deeper into the forest, and their cleared lands are taken over by the cattle ranchers. The resultant loss of forest cover eventually leads to ecological dislocations that are already affecting climate and rainfall patterns on the Central American isthmus. The deforestation also contributes additional carbon dioxide to the greenhouse gases in our atmosphere, whose long-term global effects we have only begun to appreciate.

Recent statistics compiled by Guatemala's Commission for the Environment (CONAMA) reveal the country has lost 40 percent of its forest cover during the past thirty years and suffered a concurrent reduction of nearly 50 percent in annual rainfall. Petén, the northern third of Guatemala, has lost well over half of its humid forest to loggers, cattle ranchers, and the still rising influx of new colonists. The calamity gathering behind these statistics could eventually overshadow the human cost of Guatemala's armed conflicts. And it would undermine the slow, agonizing recovery of indigenous populations in army-designated Zones of Conflict, which include portions of northern Petén.

Apart from Petén's immeasurable importance as one of the Western Hemisphere's richest—and most endangered—ecological reserves, other reasons have also drawn me. Starting in 1986 I made repeated visits to investigate the effects on Petén of a decades-old, low-intensity conflict involving the Guatemalan army, a powerful mafia of lumber and drug contraband, transnational oil companies, and guerrilla militants of the Rebel Armed Forces (FAR), the fourth arm of the Guatemalan National Revolutionary Union (URNG). The thousands of homesteaders from the Oriente and the Mayan highlands who arrive in Petén every year participate in this war as army mercenaries, guerrilla recruits, and most prominently, as victims caught in the crossfire.

Petén and its fragile ecosystems are important for other reasons: within its borders are located no fewer than seventy of the most important archaeological sites in Mesoamerica, among them the classical Mayas' oldest and largest city-state, Tikal, and the ceremonial centers of Piedras Negras, Uaxactún, Ceibal, Río Azul, and El Mirador. The magnificent Yaxchilán, on the Mexican bank of the Usumacinta, is still revered by the Mayas' last living descendants, the forest-dwelling Lacandones.

Petén's 36,000 square kilometers of humid forest, savanna, and wetlands are home to six thousand plant species and thirteen mammalian orders; its extensive lagoons and marshes provide nesting sites for hundreds of migratory birds. (Of the fifteen hundred vertebrate species native to Guatemala, forty-five are found nowhere else.) This extraordinary biological diversity could be reduced by half before the end of the century if the current rate of deforestation is not reversed.

Of growing significance are Petén's largely untapped petroleum reserves, which recent estimates place at over 25 million barrels. Only three to four thousand barrels a day are extracted by government-licensed foreign corporations; a steady rise in world oil prices could provide the incentive to expand operations, at the expense of forest conservation.

On the other side of the ledger, the Petén has become a staging area for the Rebel Armed Forces, whose ranks include survivors from the FAR of the 1960s and defectors from the EGP. In the early 1980s the reborn FAR established small enclaves in the western reaches of the Petén, in response to the large peasant migrations there and the land grabs by army generals in the transversal strip below the region. The army and the U.S. Drug Enforcement Agency have repeatedly attempted to link the guerrillas to an expanding marijuana cultivation and export trade in northern Petén, as well as to the trans-shipment of Colombian cocaine to Mexico across Petén's northern borders.

These factors weighed on my mind as we put back into the river at Yaxchilán the morning after we spotted the two armed men. During the remainder of the day we sighted spectacular scarlet macaws, keel-billed toucans, and various large birds of prey on both banks of the river. In early morning and late afternoon we heard the blood-curdling calls of the howler monkey, which sound like jaguars tearing apart the forest. We saw the larger and nimbler spider monkeys only on the densely forested Guatemalan bank, swinging along arboreal highways or hanging on branches by absurdly elongated appendages. The continued presence of the monkeys, and the soft mating calls of a jaguar we'd heard the evening before, gave our spirits a needed lift. By the following morning we were twenty miles downriver from Yaxchilán. The forest cover on the Mexican side was all gone, except along the deep, narrow canyons, where white-water rapids diverted our attention from the devastation. Midafternoon the next day we pulled into the black sand beach at Piedras Negras, the second most important Mayan site on the river, after Yaxchilán. As we anchored our rafts on the Guatemalan bank, two men in olive fatigues came out to meet us, with an M-16 and an AK-47 pointed above our heads. Their tense smiles suggested that news of our arrival had preceded us.

The two men asked our purpose on the river and whether we carried any weapons. After we reassured them on both counts, they introduced themselves as members of FAR. They said they were Cakchiquel Mayas from Chimaltenango who had spent a combined total of thirty years in the Petén forest, both as homesteaders and as combatants. Although they had not seen combat in many months, their eyes shone with dedication to the cause, and they professed themselves ready to die at a moment's notice. The older of the two men, who was about fifty, had not had contact with his family in nine years and was no longer sure whose side they were on. He told us his ancestral lands in Chimaltenango had been taken away by unscrupulous developers because he had no title to them and no money to hire a lawyer. He said he was fighting to eradicate poverty and ensure a more equitable distribution of land. This was a familiar story throughout the altiplano, where poor farmers have been radicalized by the expropriation of their lands.

"We have a right to live and we have a right to our own dignity," he said. Like other indigenous insurgents I had met, he seemed surprisingly gentle and avoided the doctrinal rhetoric of his ladino counterparts. His bright eyes darkened only once, when a member of our group contradicted him. "It is not true that we are trained by Cubans or Nicaraguans," he insisted, "although we have borrowed ideas from their struggle, just as we have learned from your Declaration of Independence. As for trafficking with drugs, that is strictly contrary to our disciplinary code. At bottom, ours is an indigenous movement, and we draw our strength from our Mayan roots."

I liked and instinctively trusted "Juan," as he called himself, so I broached the matter of the Sierra del Lacandón and the mahoganies. "Yes," he assured me, "we control that zone, and the entire river clear to the Mexican border. We are also a dominant presence in eleven departments of Guatemala and are solidly represented in Chiapas and Belize. The sierra and its hardwood forests are under our sovereignty."

Juan's claims echoed a conversation I'd had in Mexico ten years earlier with an EGP leader who claimed the guerrillas controlled eleven municipalities and two hundred fifty villages. Apparently, no one had informed Juan that the URNG's defeats in the past decade had altered Guatemala's geopolitical map in the army's favor. I informed Juan of the Aserradero del Norte and its owner's intention to log a thousand mahoganies in the sierra. In my meeting with Antonio del Cid, the supremely self-assured operator of the sawmill, he had suggested the guerrilla problem in the sierra had been taken care of. Sawmill operators reputedly grease their chainsaws and skidders with periodic payments to guerrilla commanders, who refer to them as "war taxes." With this in mind I challenged Juan, "Are you going to permit such a flagrant violation of your sovereignty?"

"By no means," he said. "Four years ago we chased away some Mexican engineers who came to take a survey for building a dam. And our compañeros to the south are sabotaging your oil companies' explorations in our territory."

He was correct on both counts. One of the deterrents to the construction of a series of dams on the Usumacinta, proposed in an agreement between Guatemala and Mexico, was the guerrillas' threats to sabotage them. And Amoco had recently suspended activities in Guatemala in part because of guerrilla interference in its field operations.

When Juan asked for more specifics on the sierra's mahoganies and the sawmill operator's intentions, I suggested half in jest that the best way to enhance their international reputation was to become known as forest conservators or "green guerrillas." Juan smiled at my little joke but promised to take up the logging matter with his comandante.

The next morning, before we parted, Juan came down to share our breakfast and then presented us with half a *tepeizcuintle*, or paca, he had trapped. The paca is a large rodent native to Central America; when roasted, it is by far the tastiest meat in the forest. "Please extend to your colleagues in North America a warm greeting from the Cakchiquel people," Juan said, waving his weapon as we put back into the river.

Juan's claims to the contrary, there probably are no more than
eight hundred active FAR militants in Petén, and the area they cover
has no major strategic importance. But their presence does act as a
buffer against uncontrolled development, and their activities tie down
growing numbers of military personnel and their equipment. If the
ongoing talks between the army and the URNG collapse, FAR could
turn into a major headache for the army by carrying out coordinated
assaults on military targets with EGP and ORPA. If that happens,
army commanders might revert to their brutally effective Maoist tactic
of "drying the ocean the fish swim in" and go after the guerrillas'
grassroots support bases in Petén.

                                    2

I accompanied to Petén an American anthropologist and tropical ecologist, James Nations, who was on a Fulbright scholarship to study
the impact of deforestation on communities bordering the proposed
Petén Biosphere Reserve. I had met Nations, a tall and energetic Texan
who looks younger than his forty-one years, in southern Mexico's
Lacandón forest, where he was researching his doctoral dissertation
on Mayan agronomy.

In Tikal, Guatemala's oldest national park, we met with Santiago Billy, a slight, intense Frenchman of thirty-one who works with
CONAMA. The conservation of Petén's tropical forest had become
his consuming obsession. Waving his arms over a huge map of the
oddly duck-shaped Petén in his office, Billy exclaimed, "We are going
to propose a conservation plan President Cerezo cannot turn down:
a biosphere reserve that will become a blueprint for tropical forest
conservation throughout Latin America." Billy, who had been born
in Guatemala almost by happenstance, returned at the age of twenty-
one to explore his country of birth. He soon became consumed with
the challenge of saving Petén's unique tropical forests. In a French-
inflected Spanish that appeared to compound his sense of commitment, Billy explained that when combined with proposed forest reserves in Mexico and Belize, the Petén biosphere will become the
largest tropical forest reserve north of the Amazon.

"What we will do," said Billy, sweeping his hand from east to west
across the top of Petén, "is link together a network of national parks

and biotopes, or small reserves, with Tikal at its center. This comprehensive reserve will cover over ten thousand square kilometers of unexploited tropical forest north of parallel 17′ 10″, or roughly one-fourth the surface area of Petén." He explained that another five thousand-plus square kilometers would be put aside as a multiple-use buffer zone for limited harvests of timber, allspice, and chicle gum. "As to the remaining 20,000 or so square kilometers—well, realistically we have to accept that those areas not already being exploited will be colonized, hunted, logged, razed, drilled for oil and other mineral resources, and will be largely lost to conservation in the next two to three years."

"As is happening to Mexico's Chiapas?" interposed Nations. "And as has already happened to Tabasco and Campeche?"

"That's right," Billy said. "The same development and population pressures that have been at work in southern Mexico for the past three decades are operating in Petén today. One crucial difference is that we are starting this project with a prior awareness of the devastating ecological consequences of massive tropical deforestation. And we also have in Guatemala for the first time a civilian head of state—Vinicio Cerezo—who has placed forest conservation near the top of his agenda."

Nations patiently explained how the 6,500-square-kilometer east-west corridor would permit the optimal range for large predators like the jaguar, the mountain lion, and the collared and white-lipped peccaries, as well as for the herbivorous tapir, the largest animal in Petén. But more important, the corridor would assure the conservation of germ plasm for all the endangered plant and animal species. "The corridor is a tropical ecologist's dream," Nations said, in rising excitement. "It provides an ideal crucible for preserving the full variety of Petén's living species. For instance, the jaguar population here has been swelled by the large numbers fleeing deforestation in Mexico. If they fall below a given threshold, they can no longer sustain themselves, because they cannot mutate and diversify. And the same can be said of thousands of other animals and plants that are unique to this area. If we succeed in preserving the east-west belt, Petén will become the second largest natural gene pool for tropical forest species in our hemisphere."

The Petén project received a mixed blessing when the West German

government agreed to construct a paved road to Petén with the pro-
vision—put forth by Germany's Greens—that Guatemala draw up be-
forehand a viable forest conservation plan. President Cerezo had assigned Billy and CONAMA to draft a Petén conservation proposal
within ninety days. If he approved it, a government lawyer would then
redraft the proposal and present it for ratification to the National
Congress.

But the real challenge begins once the project has passed into law,
as Billy and Nations were the first to recognize. The paved road would
bring in thousands of new colonists and place added stresses on an
already threatened and fragile ecosystem. The crucial next stage will
involve allocating funds to hire and train the necessary personnel to
maintain and protect the Petén biosphere reserve. Billy had taken a
step in that direction by securing the support of mayors in Petén's
larger towns.

Still, pledges of support may not mean all that much in the frontier
atmosphere of Petén, a region of rugged individualists who are fa-
mously nimbler with a gun or machete than with a pen. The Maya
Itzá who inhabited Petén when the Spaniards arrived were a combative, proudly independent nation that resisted the conquistadores
until 1697, nearly two centuries after the lower two-thirds of Guatemala was pacified and Christianized. (The only later holdouts were
scattered communities of Lacandones who lived deep in the rain forest
and were not discovered until the twentieth century.)

The fortified capital of the Itzá, Tayasal, was located on an island
in Lake Petén-Itzá, site of the present-day city of Flores. Hernán
Cortés had stumbled on Tayasal during an expedition to Honduras
in 1524. The encounter was peaceful, and Cortés left behind one of
his horses. After it died, the Itzá made a stone effigy of the horse,
which they worshiped as the "thunder tapir," Tizimin Chac. In 1618,
two Franciscan missionaries arrived to convert the Itzá but were
chased away after they destroyed the stone idol of Cortés's horse. A
third Franciscan missionary who arrived in Tayasal four years later
was killed and decapitated by the Itzá together with his escort of
twenty-five Spanish soldiers, whose heads were placed on stakes
around the city. This was the last Spanish contact with the Itzá for
the next seventy-five years.

On March 13, 1697, an expedition of one hundred twenty-eight foot soldiers led by Sergeant Major Urzúa y Arismendi approached the island stronghold on hastily built brigantines and subdued the Itzá with a single volley of gunfire from their matchlock harquebuses. Dozens of Itzá warriors in war paint and feathered headdresses fell dead or wounded from that fusillade, in what was to be the last military engagement of the Spanish Conquest. The terrified survivors flung down their weapons and dived into the lake, where they were easily captured. The once proud and defiant Can-Ek, king of the Itzá, was captured and spent the remainder of his days in prison in Antigua. Today, picturesque Flores, the administrative nerve center for northern Petén, resembles a prosperous Mediterranean or Baltic coastal resort. The descendants of the proud Itzá have become ladinicized, although the Itzá language itself is still spoken in isolated settlements. Large numbers of Mopans, the other sizable Mayan community native to Petén, emigrated a generation ago to Belize, where they form a distinct English- and Maya-speaking subculture. Nearly all the remaining Mayas are Quekchí homesteaders from Alta Verapaz who arrived in the nineteenth century.

After the subjugation of the Itzá, Petén lay practically untouched throughout the remainder of the colonial era. A small enclave of wealthy criollos and less well off ladinos became rooted in and around the lakeside community of Flores. A wave of new colonists toward the close of the nineteenth century was composed largely of outlaws and former convicts, as well as migrants from the Mexican state of Campeche. Many of the new arrivals intermarried with native Mayas to form a hardy breed of mestizo farmers, hunters, and other exploiters of the forest's abundant resources. The systematic harvest of chicle gum from the chicozapote forests got under way in the 1880s, accompanied by contraband trade in plumed birds and animal hides. The first logging concession was granted in 1907 to the U.S.-based Guatemalan Mahogany Company, which worked the length of the Pasión River for twenty-three years.

Beginning in 1958, the government agency FYDEP, in charge of the "fomenting of development in El Petén," issued thousands of land grants to landless Mayan and ladino colonists from Alta Verapaz, the southern coast, and the eastern provinces. Ten years later they licensed the construction of a network of lumber roads that brought in thousands more colonists. The homesteaders were told they had

to clear at least half of their parcels before they could claim legal
title to them; in the process, FYDEP turned the settlers into accomplices in heedless deforestation. In 1988 FYDEP was broken up and
reorganized by President Cerezo, after it was charged with administrative corruption and incompetence.

Thirty years after FYDEP gave out its first land grants, and twenty
years after the construction of access roads to the southern half, the
population of Petén has soared from 26,000 to over 250,000, and
more than 20,000 square kilometers of tropical forest have been converted to pastureland, at the rate of one thousand square kilometers,
or 250,000 acres, per year. Rufino Barrios's drastic reforms of the
1880s bypassed Petén, which remained out of touch with the lower
two-thirds of the country. What Norman Schwartz calls the Second
Conquest of Petén has already proved far more destructive to its rain
forest environment—and to the archaeological monuments and treasures left behind by its original inhabitants—than Spain's conquistadores, who left Petén's forests and monuments largely undisturbed.

3

Tikal National Park, a 576-square-kilometer (222-square-mile) forest
preserve established in 1956, encloses within its borders the famous
classical Mayan ruins of the same name. Tikal, Guatemala's first national park, was declared a World Cultural and Natural Monument
by UNESCO in 1979. Tikal is to serve as a model for the larger Petén
Biosphere Reserve, and the reserve itself will serve as a prototype for
a three-nation "Mayan Peace Park" that will include proposed reserves
in the bordering Yucatán Peninsula and in Belize. Another initiative
called "Ruta Maya," energetically backed by Wilbur Garrett, the
former editor of National Geographic, has been approved by President Cerezo and the Guatemalan congress. Ruta Maya would preserve
for enlightened "ecotourism" the chief archaeological sites in Mesoamerica, together with the web of ancient Mayan roads that connected them. An entrepreneurial counterpart, called "Mundo Maya,"
or Mayan World, has gained ground with tourism ministries in Guatemala, Mexico, El Salvador, Honduras, and Belize. The success of
any one of these three initiatives could mean that the second largest
tropical forest in the Americas can still be substantially salvaged. For

Guatemala's President Cerezo, who was upstaged as Central America's peacemaker by Costa Rica's Nobel Prize winner Oscar Arias, it would mean gaining dual recognition abroad as Central America's environmental president and the protector of priceless Maya sites.

Santiago Billy, who had worked in Tikal as director of flora and fauna, offered to take us on a nature conservation trail he designed to dramatize the wealth and the fragility of Petén's humid forest; and he also wanted us to understand better, in his words, what was at stake.

Before setting out on our walk we paid a brief visit to the Plaza Mayor, the ceremonial center of Tikal, which had been excavated and partially restored in the mid-fifties by archaeologists with the University of Pennsylvania. When I first visited Tikal in 1959, the Great Plaza already looked much as it does today: two large pyramidal structures facing each other across a grassy knoll and a sprawling acropolis to the east. Temple I, also known as the Great Jaguar, rises 44 meters, or 145 feet, and is crested by a chambered platform with a magnificent roof comb. The ceremonial chamber's A-shaped corbeled arches—the only kind designed by Mayan architects—required massive slabs of limestone, which sacrificed interior space for the sake of sturdiness and durability. A nobleman's burial vault and treasure trove were discovered at the foot of the pyramid, together with dozens of limestone stelae with incised glyphs recording dates of royal accession. The North Acropolis, east of the temples, contains shrines, a ball court, and numerous stelae and sculptures; a mound of skulls found nearby suggests that human sacrifice was practiced as routinely in Tikal as in other Maya city-states throughout Mesoamerica. The dates on the stelae range from the third to the ninth century A.D.

Gazing down on the acropolis from the top of Temple I, one could readily visualize a typical market day in, say, 700 A.D.; dozens of tradesmen in cloaks and breechcloths engage in the commerce of animal pelts, salt, spices, shells, jadeite and obsidian, and domestic fowl. From scenes drawn on polychrome Maya pottery, and the uncanny clay figurines found in Jaina, one could picture the *pelota* players in the adjoining ball court, bouncing the black pumpkin-sized rubber sphere off their leather-padded chests, hips, and shoulders. At the game's conclusion the losers—or winners, according to a rival conjecture—would be sacrificed to the gods on a nearby altar.

But these more or less credible invocations lack a historical frame. In fact, what little we know of the classical Mayas' cosmology differs so radically from our own, we have only begun to learn how to compose the proper questions. The modest explosion of new information that resulted from the decoding of Maya glyphs in Palenque, Copán, and elsewhere has not yet elucidated the origins or the principal functions of Tikal's city-state. Evidence has been found of human habitation in Tikal since before the Christian era, but it remains unclear who actually built the majestic structures—whether it was indigenous Mayas or migrants from the north. (We do know that these remarkable stonemasons, sculptors, and carpenters worked without the benefit of the wheel, metal tools, or beasts of burden.) Although trade routes have been uncovered that link Tikal to other city-states as far north as Teotihuacán in central Mexico and as far south as Copán in Honduras, the complex web of these connections has only begun to be unraveled. Nor is it understood by what divine or hereditary authority the Maya elite ruled over court astronomers, architects, and priests, or what rank in the social hierarchy—if any— was held by farmers who enabled the aristocracy to survive. In the last twenty-five years we have learned more of the dynastic succession of Maya kings and other related matters than we have in the four centuries since the infamous bonfire in Yucatán's Plaza of Maní that destroyed possibly hundreds of precious Maya manuscripts. And yet, compared to the fragmentary data we have collected about the Mayas, the lives of Egyptian Pharaohs who ruled three millennia ago read like an open book.

Notwithstanding, numerous clues have surfaced that provide insights into a developed agriculture that included "floating" vegetable and flower gardens and canals stocked with fish—a far more diversified system than the monocultural slash-and-burn agriculture practiced by the Mayas' descendants. A recent study suggests that the protein-rich fruit of the *ramón*, or breadnut tree, which grows in large numbers around Maya sites, may have been cultivated as a supplement to maize, which it rivals in nutritional value. (Today, ramón is used for mule and cattle fodder.) This would help explain how at its height Tikal supported an estimated 70,000 to 100,000 inhabitants, out of a total Petén population that may have reached 1.5 million.

The work of Linda Schele and other archaeologists in the classical site of Palenque, Chiapas, has brought to life a full-dimensional portrait of Pacal the Great, a seventh-century ruler whose fierce ambitions, intrigues, and loves resemble those of powerful kings throughout recorded history. We are discovering that later rulers often altered events and dates to claim fictional victories or obfuscate humiliating defeats. Like any system of writing since Sumerian cuneiform, glyphs could be manipulated to enhance the reputations of the rulers who commissioned them.

All these glimpses into a highly developed civilization leave intact the deepest mystery of all: why were Tikal and other magnificent classical sites abandoned—so abruptly that hundreds of structures were left half finished and blocks of limestone to be shaped into stelae were left partially hewn from their matrix? The latest date found in Tikal is 869 A.D., which roughly approximates the dates when Palenque, Copán, Yaxchilán, and other classical centers were likewise vacated. The considerable distances separating these cities would seem to rule out famine, plague, overpopulation, civil war, or foreign invasion as all-encompassing explanations. A global theory gaining wide acceptance stresses the environmental degradation caused by the constant warring among kings of rival city-states, as dramatized in Linda Schele and Mary Miller's *Blood of Kings*.

In the classical Maya capital of Dos Pilas, a Vanderbilt University dig led by Arthur Demarest uncovered the tomb of Itz K'awil, or "Ruler 2," who reigned over an extensive kingdom from A.D. 698 to 725. Demarest depicts Ruler 2 as a juggernaut perhaps responsible for the collapse of Maya civilization by drastically altering traditional rules of warfare. Early in the eighth century, he launched expansionist wars of conquest that wreaked more havoc on Petén's environment and on its Maya city-states than all the previous dynastic wars put together.

One of the truisms that has endured the current overhaul in our conception of the Maya is that apart from ritual bloodletting, war and captive sacrifice, and a life-long preoccupation with death and the underworld, the classical Mayas were obsessed with recording the passage of time. Time came to be regarded as the sole lasting coinage for all earthly and celestial transactions. The Mayas viewed the uni-

verse as a vast chain of interlinked time segments recurring in predetermined cycles, so that nothing was ever truly lost in their cosmos;
nor, for that matter, was anything finally gained. The great wheel of
time ground all earthly events, great and small, to a fine dust, whose
grains germinated the seeds of the next cycle of creation. In Tikal,
Copán, Chichén Itzá, astronomers represented zero as a seashell that
symbolizes, alternatively, an end with no beginning, or a beginning
without end.

Among other important news not to be found in the Old or New
Testament is the quintessential Maya postulate that time is circular,
so that in our world not only the past is prologue, but the present
and future as well.

4

A short distance from the Great Plaza we encountered bands of wild
turkeys, numerous curassows, and crested guans—all sizable and eminently edible fowl that must have nourished Maya royalty as well as
the lowly peasant. I was struck by their increase in number and vis-
ibility over my three previous visits to Tikal, when most animals were
still wary of humans. We repeatedly stumbled, quite literally, over the
blue-necked, russet-winged ocellated turkeys in our path. The cries
of toucans, chachalacas, and large parrots filled the air. Tikal probably
has as diverse and abundant fauna today as it did at the height of the
Maya era, when much of today's Petén forest was terraced farmland
and savanna, with scattered stands of tall trees. Billy estimates that
more jaguars live inside the park than are left in the whole of Mexico's
once extensive Lacandón forest. But outside the park, I would soon
discover, it is open season on anything that moves. As a result, the
basic stock of nearly every large plumed, scaled, or hair-coated creature is becoming alarmingly depleted.

The nature trail begins near one of the splendidly preserved cause-
ways that link ceremonial sites scattered over the four-kilometer circumference of the excavated portions of Tikal. It was close to 3 P.M.,
and the hordes of mosquitoes, gnats, and chiggers—three of the park's
least endangered species—were near their peak of activity. On the first
bend of the two-mile trail, Billy stopped to point out a cavity beside

an unexcavated ruin, where looters, called *huecheros* or armadillos in the local argot, had burrowed for hidden treasure. Sadly, not all the exposed monuments we encountered were left behind by looters. Guatemalan archaeologist Renaldo Acevedo, who works for the Institute of Anthropology's National Tikal Project, would show me dozens of small structures under which University of Pennsylvania researchers had hastily dug trenches to collect data or rummage for artifacts. None of them had been repaired or covered up, and many showed severe erosion from exposure to the elements. (In Antigua shortly afterward I interviewed Edwin Shook, a retired archaeologist with the Carnegie Institution, who had been hired by the University of Pennsylvania to work in Tikal. He insisted that all of the monuments had been reburied or rebuilt before they left Tikal. He admitted, however, that no such constraints applied during earlier digs by Carnegie and Pennsylvania at Uaxactún and Piedras Negras. They had simply gone in on muleback to retrieve all the treasures they could carry, leaving a mass of rubble behind. "The Guatemalans didn't care," Shook remarked. "They were happy to have us go in there and bring them back the loot.")

I was surprised by the many large gaps in the forest canopy, caused in part by past logging of hardwoods and more recently by blight and drought. Near the end of the trail we would visit a camp of *chicleros*, or chicle gatherers. The crow's-feet slash marks on nearly every chicozapote tree we passed were made to extract the viscous latex that used to form the base for all packaged chewing gum. At its peak during the first half of our century, chicle was known as "white gold." It was Guatemala's third leading export crop after coffee and bananas. Beginning in the 1950s, the U.S. manufacturers Wrigley and American Chicle introduced a cheap petroleum-based gum substitute that did away with chicle altogether. Today, virtually the entire chicle crop is bought by Japan, which also imports—directly or through the intervention of middlemen—the bulk of Petén's hardwood lumber.

Nations pointed out the small Chamaedorea palm, or *xate*, which thrives in the shadow of larger trees and shrubs. Its elegant long leaves are used in flower arrangements by florists and funeral parlors in the United States, where they are known as evergreen fern. (European importers prefer the more delicate *Chamaedorea elegans,* locally known as *hembra*, or female.) Nations pointed out that Chamaedorea palm fronds now bring in the highest returns of any forest product other than hardwoods. Since the 1970s, *xateros* have replaced chicleros as the most ubiquitous foragers of Petén's forests, and they inflict far less environmental damage. They harvest the Chamaedorea fronds every four to six months, leaving one stem on each plant to regenerate. The xateros' trade would be relatively benign and even pro-conservationist were it not for the sad fact that many of them also trap birds, hunt, and trade illegally in precious artifacts to supplement their income.

In August and September many xateros turn to harvesting *pimienta gorda*, allspice, which commands a comparable price to xate. Unfortunately, impatient or hard-up *pimienteros* sometimes chop down allspice trees rather than climb them to collect the ripe fruit and leave the tree to bloom again.

A noisy thrashing of branches high above our heads signaled the proximity of spider monkeys swinging along the tops of arboreal passageways in search of tender leaves, ripe fruits, and nuts. The band of long-limbed, prehensile-tailed simians approached us, and then, quite fearlessly, three large males ganged together to hiss and chatter in orchestrated bellicosity. Their comportment made me feel distinctly unwelcome, but Billy was exultant.

"Excellent, excellent!" he exclaimed, with a broad grin. "These monkeys are neither intimidated nor tame. Look how well they protect their territory!" The spiders were doing very well, Billy informed us; there were many hundreds in the park, and they are prolific breeders. But the howler monkeys, a shier species despite their aggressive yells and roars, were nearly wiped out some thirty years ago by an epidemic of yellow fever. (When I visited the Director of Fauna and Flora, Fernando Lanza, he performed a riveting impersonation of the ailing howlers' moans and the sickening thud of their bodies as they fell from the trees, stone dead.)

Howlers and spider monkeys often mingle and feed in the same trees, but they are easily distinguishable. The howlers have larger heads in relation to their compact bodies, much shorter limbs and tails, and the whiskers under their chin give them an ancient and wise appearance; by contrast, the small-headed spiders look—and act—like perennial adolescents.

Despite the howlers' present scarcity, Billy is confident that they are in no danger of becoming extinct. His optimism was borne out by the healthy, forest-shaking roars we would hear later that evening and again the following morning.

After another half-hour we reached our first destination, the giant mahogany the trail is named after; the largest in Tikal, it measures about twenty-five feet in circumference, which rivals in girth California's centenarian redwoods. A typical hectare of rain forest can sustain only one or two mahoganies of comparable size. Like any forest giant, the mahogany fills a virtually complete ecological niche. Tiny white orchids populated its lower and middle branches, repaying their inoffensive tenancy with gorgeous bloom. Choker and wickerwork vines wound themselves in tight coils around the upper trunk. The tree's thick, shallow roots serpentined into the forest in a widening radius, disappearing in the underbrush. This mahogany was too large to be threatened by the strangler fig, or *matapalo*, a killer tree that sprouts from a sticky seed dropped by a bird on the lower branches of a hardwood or smaller tree. The fast-growing *Ficus* sends a tangle of roots down to the ground to buttress its often mortal embrace on its unlucky host. During our walk we would encounter a number of cedars, ceibas, and chicozapotes whose life was being systematically extinguished by the octopus-like embrace of the matapalo. The strangler fig's inventiveness in shoring itself to the ground in order to shut out its host's access to sunlight and soil nutrients has a creepy and almost *willed* quality that suggests an invasion of tree-snatchers from a distant planet.

Billy vented his amusement at my consternation over what increasingly looked like a Daliesque charnel house. With his infectious grin, he pointed to the flexible spiny palm, his favorite, which like the proverbial willow before the storm, bends away from the strangler's grasp by contracting the vascular bundles in its flexible trunk and then growing anew in ladderlike stages.

I soon learned that the tropical forest has as efficient a system of checks and balances as a working constitutional government. Every form of aggression has an answering defense—and vice versa. Even the most destructive-seeming trait or mechanism has a beneficial side. The matapalo, whose roots can split a limestone stela into fragments, also helps to conserve the Mayan temples by wrapping its limbs around them like strapping tape. And the strangler fig creates a hospitable habitat for numerous birds and small animals that feed on its abundant fruit.

Nations bent down to pick up the shard of a pre-classic ceramic pot, smoothed and lovingly rounded by a nimble artisan's hands. (On another trail he would find a slender obsidian blade, so finely worked it resembled tinted glass.) Many of Tikal's treasures still lie under the ground, buried in vaults or hidden in underground caches. Many—far too many—of the painted ceramic pots and vases that describe in vivid detail the daily life of Tikal's former residents have been plundered by amateur or professional looters and scattered to the four corners of the globe. Only a meager portion of the unearthed treasures remains in Guatemalan hands, poorly displayed in dimly lighted regional museums or stored away in the basement of the National Museum of Anthropology. As a result, only a shattered reflection of the story of Tikal is ever likely to become available to us.

Until the present decade, the excavations by Guatemala's Institute of Anthropology and History—which took over from the University of Pennsylvania in 1968—proceeded at a snail's pace, as its austere yearly budgets permitted. At first, the bulk of the institute's revenues went into repairing the damage done to Tikal's chief monuments. A rising sensitivity to "tampering with the national patrimony" has brought unhelpful controversy to restoration work in Tikal. Renaldo Acevedo angrily complains of self-serving politicians who trumpet the Great Jaguar's imminent collapse, while ignoring the institute's crucial salvage work on the far more imperiled Temple V, which lies off the beaten path.

The chicleros were the ruggedly independent pioneers of the selvatic frontier. Their camp resembled a forest version of a fugitive cowpoke's or horse rustler's hideout. Scattered about the palm-thatched lean-tos and bunk beds were rusted coffee pots, a manual corn grinder, imported liquor and medicine bottles, and discarded tobacco pouches. The chicleros were the first to bring back news of archaeological treasures, of exotic new medicinal plants and rare animal species. They were also the first hunters of these rare species, the first looters of the Mayan sites, the first to bring hard liquor and disease to the aboriginal communities such as the Lacandones. The romance that grew up about the chicleros' trade is strikingly similar to that of the Wild West in the United States—and it sprouted a comparable number of tall tales, books, and ballads, if not an entire film genre.

Like the cowboys, chicleros also earned their macho reputation the hard way. The forest they opened up to the outside world teemed with malaria and yellow fever, among other plagues. Chicleros fell prey to jaguars, poisonous snakes and the caiman, or tropical crocodile, which is every bit as ravenous as its northern and Old World cousins. They were blinded or disfigured by the *chechem* and other poisonous plants, and they even had one scourge named after them: the *mosca chiclera,* a fly which carries a deadly protozoa—*Leishmania*—that eats and digests human cartilage in the first available orifice it can call home.

The two chicleros we found whittling sticks in the camp hardly fit the prototype of wild frontiersmen. The decline in the chicle market worldwide (except for Japan) had tamed them into part-time scouts, cooks, tourist guides, and soft-drink peddlers. They patiently explained the complex process of gathering the white latex from the chicozapote tree, boiling it in huge vats, stirring endlessly to remove the moisture, then setting the dry latex into molds. The hardened blocks of chicle were then carefully packed and sent for grading and crating to middlemen, who skimmed off the larger share of the profits before the chicle reached the processing plants of Wrigley and the American Chicle Company. As was the case with bananas and lumber, the lion's share of the profits from chicle extraction traveled abroad.

Today, a modest resurgence in demand from Japanese and other importers keeps about four thousand chicleros operating in the northern wilderness. But the chiclero frontier romance ended in the mid-fifties, on the day a Tikal park guard, acting on explicit instructions, shot a chiclero dead off the top of a chicozapote tree.

At the end of our tour, we stopped for a sunset view of the park from the roof comb of Temple IV. At 270 feet, it was the tallest known pre-Columbian structure until the discovery of pre-classic pyramids in El Mirador, which are eighteen stories high. It was from the top of Temple IV that the scenes of the rebel base in *Star Wars* were shot by director George Lucas, who was evidently drawn to the site by its enveloping aura of mystery. In the soft light of sunset, the sweep of pristine forest with the tops of temples poking through the canopy evoked a painting by Henri Rousseau. Near the crests of the trees below us, six or seven large keel-billed toucans hopped from branch to branch. The cries of the crested guan were accompanied by spectacular flights of the purple and brown forest fowl as they skimmed above the forest canopy. Bands of large parrots flew past, nearly at eye level, creating a racket out of proportion to their numbers.

The canopy below us teemed with animal and floral life, far beyond what had been visible from the forest floor. From this height, the canopy's role in the forest's life cycle was more readily apparent. While the roots of giant hardwoods hold together the forest's top soil and help maintain the water table, the canopy intercepts nine-tenths of the sunlight that converts carbon dioxide into oxygen and carbon. The trees store the converted CO_2 in their trunks, leaves, and roots. The forest's role as the "lungs of the world," although significant, has been unfortunately exaggerated. Over 90 percent of our biosphere's oxygen is generated by oceanic plant life or exists as a stable supply already in the atmosphere. Far more important is the canopy's role in generating the vapor that condenses into rain clouds. Tropical forests generate as much as half of the world's rainfall. Among the major contributors to drought are the huge gaps created in the forest canopy by fire or indiscriminate logging. Selective logging does not cause nearly as much havoc to the environment as clear-cutting and slash-and-burn agriculture. The carbon stored in the trees is released by fire and converts back into CO_2. As yet no one has accurately determined the amount of carbon dioxide released into the atmosphere by the burning of tropical forests; educated guesses place it at between 10 and 20 percent of the global output. If accurate, this figure means that the contribution of deforestation to the greenhouse effect is second only to the still rising emanations of CO_2 caused by our runaway consumption of fossil fuels.

As dusk descended, the royal chamber behind us sank into shadow. I pictured a Maya lord seated at his throne, surveying his kingdom with satisfaction. A sudden clatter of wings startled us, as two large *zopilotes* glided down from the top of the roof-comb to the tallest tree nearby, where they would roost for the night.

5

My visit to Petén with Billy and Nations had instilled in me by turns feelings of hopefulness and despair. Too many of the forces I had watched destroy Chiapas's Lacandón forest within the past decade were already ganging up on Petén, and the time left to gather the will and the resources to oppose them was fast running out.

Virtually none of the foresters, congressmen, conservationists I would interview in coming weeks held any realistic hope that a substantial fraction of the remaining Petén forest could be saved, much less two-fifths of it. Guatemala's annual population growth of 3.2 percent, the highest in Central America after Nicaragua's, will bring added pressures, compounded by the estimate that 75 to 80 percent of Guatemalans live in extreme poverty. The same percentage of the population utilizes forest products for lumber and firewood. Hundreds of thousands of these landless and dispossessed Guatemalans are moving steadily north in search of a plot of earth for their milpas.

Another cause for alarm is the Landsat photographs commissioned by NASA, which reveal the penetration of Mexican loggers into northern areas of Petén. The infrared satellite photographs show the lumber poachers have built a web of roads and are clearing out stands of hardwoods inside the proposed reserves. At the same time Mexican cattle ranchers, in apparent collusion with Guatemalan homesteaders, have been moving their herds of zebu cattle into border areas cleared for grazing. Starting in the late eighties an illegal influx of Salvadorans and Nicaraguans entered Petén, many of whom cultivate marijuana. Instead of helping to safeguard the borders, Guatemalan army officers and treasury police continue to collect bribes from the Mexican intruders, as well as from the Central American refugees.

My visit to the military base in Flores had deepened my apprehensions, as platoons of kaibiles in red berets calling themselves "Kaibil Balam" (Jaguar Kaibiles) shouted defiance at the enemy as they marched past us in close-order drill. It did not surprise me to hear stories of kaibiles who, in idle moments during patrol, would shoot their Galil rifles at forest animals, purely for sport. In the spectacular lagoon and classical Maya site of Yaxhá, near the Belizean border, residents recall with horror the war exercises that brought helicopter loads of kaibiles from the nearby base in Melchor de

Mencos. Trees were used as blinds, plants were flattened, and loose bricks and mortar flew as the helicopters landed next to the pyramids in the ceremonial plaza. (The kaibiles, who were taking a jungle survival course, were dropped in the forest with their knives and a dog as their sole companion. At the end of the training course, according to the testimony of former kaibiles, they are required to butcher and devour their pet dogs.)

Too much of the Petén conservation project's chances for survival will rest on the good will of the military, which has the final jurisdiction over any civilian undertaking, particularly in Zones of Conflict. When huge scattered fires apparently caused by loggers and slash-and-burn farmers destroyed fifteen hundred square kilometers of Petén forest in 1987, rumors circulated that the army had dropped napalm near guerrilla-controlled enclaves in order to smoke them out. And the press carried persistent reports that the U.S. Drug Enforcement Agency's spraying of glyphosphate on marijuana plantations was coordinated with the army's counterinsurgency operations. Given the military's track record in the highlands, these rumors have been difficult to dismiss.

The Maya rulers of Tikal and Piedras Negras also denuded the great mahogany forests of their day, converting them to terraced corn and vegetable fields and their fish-stocked floating gardens. But they left behind enough seeds and germ plasm so they could regenerate, within half a millennium, into the dense, majestic climax forests found by the Spaniards. Between 1900 and 1956, approximately eighty thousand prime hardwood trees were logged, according to information gathered for a national seminar on the economic development of Petén. From 1979 to 1987 FYDEP reported the logging of 103,544 mahoganies, cedars, and other hardwoods. In 1987 alone, the most recent year for which statistics are available, nine sawmills logged 18,000 mahoganies and cedars, or nearly a fourth of the total taken out in the first half of the century. At that rate, the mahoganies and cedars will entirely disappear within five years. This time, it is not at all certain whether sufficient cones and germ plasm will remain to begin another cycle of regeneration. In a few years, the "land of quetzales" will have no quetzales left, and its original Nahuatl name, Quauhtemalan, "Place of Forests," will become a cruel misnomer.

Although the blame for the degradation of Guatemala's tropical forests—and of the environment as a whole—is shared by a wide range of social and economic sectors inside the country and abroad, the bulk of accountability must once again fall on Guatemala's ladino officer class. The same army officers who see a potential subversive in every Mayan child and adult, regard trees as enemies in league with ambush-minded guerrillas. Cornfields are the guerrillas' food supply, to be burned down along with thatched huts, which are their hide-outs. Tropical and cloud forests are part of the spoils of conquest, to be felled for lumber and sold to the highest bidder. Macaws and toucans are feathered price tags, more lucrative when taken alive—as opposed to jaguars, ocelots, and caimans. Monkeys are useful mainly for target practice. All of nature is suspect, or at best expendable, if it does not yield a material return or cooperate with the military's strategies.

If the military's atrocities against its citizens should one day hold them to account in a Guatemalan court of law, their crimes against the environment should put them on trial in a world tribunal. In the unlikely event such an "Ecological Court" were ever to be named, it could never hold the millions of witnesses for the prosecution or the military's legions of accomplices.

The new "democratized" army under Defense Minister Gramajo likes to call itself a partner in forest conservation, but individual officers are continuing the contraband of hardwood lumber. Much of the deforestation of lower Petén by land-hungry campesinos was actively encouraged by military and other large landowners; after the colonists cut and burned clearings in the forest, the landowners moved in their cattle and pushed the homesteaders further north, to start the cycle over again. Although exploration by foreign companies has uncovered scattered pockets of recoverable petroleum, the vast oil fields the generals hoped to find beneath their property have not materialized. The exploitable crude in Petén is only a tiny fraction of southern Mexico's abundant reserves, but there is enough to make Guatemala self-sufficient in oil for decades to come. Basic Resources International, a Bahamas-based consortium licensed to carry out explorations in Petén, has completed a 4,000-barrel-a-day oil refinery in La Libertad. If the guerrillas permit petroleum extraction and processing to proceed uninterrupted, the military's upper echelons are certain to get their cut of the revenues; and more than likely, the guerrillas will also get theirs in the form of "war taxes."

As I sat in the gathering dusk atop Temple IV, I took pleasure in visualizing an avenging forest seizing its human despoilers in a stranglehold; a similar fate befell the wooden men of the second creation in the *Popol Vuh*, a scenario described repeatedly in Miguel Angel Asturias's "magic realist" novels. And yet to a forest creature humans may seem like just another aberrant intruder to be assimilated and ignored, rather like an unarmed scuba diver is viewed by a coral-reef dweller. In that case, the forest creatures ignore us at their peril. A tropical forest's internal checks and balances have produced no durable defense against the ravening efficacy of human technology.

Every year it becomes increasingly evident that nothing short of worldwide alarm can prevent the destruction of the large majority of our remaining tropical forests by the end of the century. And still, developed countries like Japan, West Germany, and the United States, and international institutions like the World Bank continue to invest their cash overflow in tropical deforestation under the rubric of Third World Economic Development.

One of the few positive initiatives to emerge in the past years has been the debt-for-nature swaps proposed by international banks and private agencies. Bolivia has committed itself to protect more than 4 million acres of rich forest and grasslands in the Amazonian lowlands of the Beni River in return for a substantial relief of its foreign debt. Similar swaps are under way in Ecuador and Costa Rica, and the World Bank has increased its environmental staff to work out similar exchanges involving other debtor nations with extensive tropical forests. One key question yet to be resolved is what incentives the debt relief from these swaps will provide the millions of hungry colonists who cause the bulk of the deforestation. In the case of Guatemala, which has been regularly servicing its relatively modest foreign debt of $2.5 billion, the debt-for-nature swaps would prove prohibitively costly unless its secondary bond market prices are revised downward.

In the meantime, Antonio del Cid and his Aserradero del Norte are going ahead with the logging of Sierra del Lacandón. Following a week-long exploration of the Sierra in July, Santiago Billy calculated that the sawmill had felled up to 2,000 mahogany and cedar. The trucks and tractors awaited the end of the rains before moving the lumber out. If the remaining hardwoods of Sierra del Lacandón are logged to extinction, the proposed Petén Biosphere Reserve will risk exposure as a toothless paper document, or worse, a cynical smoke-screen for runaway exploitation.

The destruction of the Petén's humid forest would be as calamitous, in its way, as the burning of the Mayan codices in Yucatán nearly five hundred years ago. Jim Nations compares the resultant loss of germ plasm to the burning of manuscripts in the Plaza of Maní by Bishop Diego de Landa; and he predicts future generations will look back at the eradication of millions of species in our forests as "A Great Dying," surpassed only by the disappearance of the great dinosaurs 65 million years ago.

The defeat of conservation in the Petén would also contribute to the almost certain erosion of conservation plans for Belize and other Mesoamerican forests, in an ecological "domino effect" that began with Tabasco and Chiapas. And, like the looting of Mayan tombs, deforestation and its concomitant vandalizing of archaeological sites will cause a further fragmenting of the images of ourselves reflected in the Mayan cosmos. As these other mirrors into our origins that are the tropical forests recede from the surface of our planet, the few islands of green left standing in the guise of biospheric reserves and national parks will represent less a refuge than a reproach.

12

The Battle Is Joined

"In Eastern Europe, communism may be going out of
fashion, but here in Guatemala we have no perestroika."
Colonel Guillermo Portillo Gómez,
Santa Elena garrison, Petén

"The teaching of environmental science, whose natural laws
take precedence over the military's code, is at the heart of
what we are trying to accomplish."
Román Carrera, environmentalist with CONAP

In the fall of 1990 I find myself beside the lovely lagoon of Yaxhá
in eastern Petén, standing atop a hundred-foot Mayan pyramid located inside one of the newly designated Protected Areas. As sunset
approaches, two howler monkeys engage in an ear-splitting court-
ship on the upper branches of neighboring breadnut trees, and farther off a band of blue-crowned parrots conducts a seminar on the
day's activities. About five miles away, on a barely visible ridge that
is unapproachable by road during the rains, sits Yaxhá's sister city
of Nakum, where, in the evenings, archaeologists listen to the soft
moans of mating jaguars. Across the lagoon, a small boat has just
left the island of Topoxté with staff members of Project Tikal who
are restoring the island's spectacular but frail post-classical Mayan
monuments. Even the unsightly cattle ranch to the east of the island
cannot spoil the wild, pristine beauty of this place. Large crocodiles
still lurk along the lakeshore, and the encroaching forest is home
to tapirs, deer, and wild boar, as well as a runaway band of feral
cattle. Although I am the only privileged guest here today, Yaxhá
and Nakum have been selected as future meccas for ecotourism.
The Maya sites and their natural wonders are expected to draw
revenues for restoring ancient monuments at the same time that
they educate visitors on the fundamentals of tropical forest conservation. Archaeologist Renaldo Acevedo, my guide here, is not sold

on the blessings of ecotourism. That morning he had shown me Topoxté's tallest pyramid and demonstrated how a single boatload of tourists standing at the crest could cause the structure's upper story to collapse in a cloud of dust and flying mortar. "What we really need," Acevedo remarked, only half in jest, "are ecovisionaries who fund our work while appreciating these treasures from afar."

In the past month, the Environmental Commission has posted ten youthful *guardarecursos,* or resource monitors, in Yaxhá; among their many responsibilities, they are here to prevent the cattle rancher from denuding any more forest for pasture and to put an end to the local practice of hunting alligators by torchlight.

As the sun sets behind Topoxté, a soft breeze rises from the lagoon, redolent with jungle scents and the faint musk of orchids. My chest expands, and tears rise to my eyes.

In late February 1989 President Vinicio Cerezo signed into law a Protected Areas proposal that converted close to 15 percent of Guatemala's territory into a system of ecological parks, biotopes, and biosphere reserves. The law also created a National Council of Protected Areas (CONAP) to administer the fifty parks and reserves. Approximately a third of Petén's humid forest and northern wetlands are included in the resolution. The loggers' and landowners' lobby immediately circulated a dissenting opinion. They deplored the quixotic impracticality of placing such a vast expanse of forest in the hands of a handful of environmentalists who didn't appreciate the needs of the common folk. Their solution was to allow private enterprise in the region to pursue its own enlightened interests. In so doing, the loggers, oil drillers, and cattle ranchers would magnanimously safeguard the exotic fauna and the Mayan archaeological sites, since they generate foreign revenue by attracting tourism.

President Cerezo named a twenty-nine-year-old architect, Andreas Lehnhoff, to head CONAP. With the collaboration of select conservationists, a green band was drawn across the top of Petén and named the Maya Biosphere Reserve. The reserve, which covers a surface area of nearly 1.7 million hectares (4 million acres), features seven inviolate "nuclear" zones bordered by extensive buffer, multiple use, and "recovery" areas. The strictly protected nuclear zones include the partially excavated remains of Mayan civilization in Tikal, Uaxactún, El Mirador, and Río Azul; the marshlands of Laguna del Tigre that provide nesting sites for thousands of migratory birds; the Sierra del Lacandón National Park, and three biotopes administered by San Carlos University's Conservation Studies Center (CECON). The outside financing needed to turn this "tropical ecologist's dream" into working reality was soon forthcoming. Within months of the passage of the Protected Areas Laws, U.S. AID, Nature Conservancy, Conservation International, and the World Wildlife Fund offered to match the Guatemalan government's $7.1 million outlay with combined grants of $15 million to help manage and maintain the Maya Biosphere Reserve.

As soon as the first allocations from Nature Conservancy were approved, Andreas Lehnhoff and his staff began filling the first seventy-two positions for resource monitors and supervisors. I met with Lehnhoff, who admits to a "madness for the trees," at an ecology congress in the capital. At 6'2", CONAP's young executive secretary is unusually tall and lean for a Guatemalan, even for one with Lehnhoff's distinctively European features. "Our first job in Petén will be to make our presence felt," he said. "Once we have laid down precedents for a strict protection of the nuclear zones, then we can negotiate with interested parties for a limited exploitation of the secondary areas." The questionnaire he drew up for aspiring resource monitors included questions such as: Have you contracted malaria? How have you overcome it? Have you been bitten by a poisonous reptile? How did you survive? How do you orient yourself in the forest? The most experienced applicants turned out to be former chicleros, who form part of a nonliterate "forest society" that can treat a snake bite in seconds and read true north by the way a vine twists around a tree. Still, the majority of the guards hired were students, agriculturists, and fledgling professionals in their early and middle twenties. Lehnhoff summed up, "The first qualities we look for are high moral standards and an unshakable commitment to forest conservation."

In this next, crucial chapter of the drama to save the Mayas' forest, the financial backing is largely foreign, but the will and motivation as well as the bodies to be put on the line, are Guatemalan.

In May 1989 President Cerezo barely survived a second coup attempt in less than a year, which seriously curtailed his executive prerogatives. As his power declined, his support for the Protected Areas Laws became increasingly symbolic. If he had been unseated before his term ended, the Maya Biosphere Reserve would likely have gone out the window with him. In July I questioned President Cerezo regarding the runaway logging of Sierra del Lacandón and the uncontrolled incursions of Mexican loggers and cattle ranchers inside the northern Petén border. He replied that agreements had been reached with Mexico to provide tighter border controls and that the army and the treasury police—notoriously the most venal of the public law enforcement agencies—were being assigned to patrol the borders against further incursions. He added that he had proposed legislation to rescind all logging permits in the newly designated protected areas. President Cerezo concluded that he planned to dedicate himself to promoting forest conservation and ecotourism upon his retirement, because the issues "fascinated" him.

A good piece of news on the Petén conservation front broke in spring of 1989. A nationwide publicity campaign and a timely international response prevented Exxon from drilling exploratory wells within the newly protected park boundaries of El Ceibal, one of Petén's key classical Maya sites as well as an important forest and wildlife reserve nearly two thousand hectares in area. The extensive press coverage given the Ceibal controversy placed the words "ecology" and "biosphere reserve" in Guatemala's public domain, if not yet on the public's conscience. The dispute also pitted CONAMA and the Ministry of Culture against the Ministry of Energy and Mines, which projected the drilling could yield $100 million in oil revenues. Staff members with the Ministry of Culture formed a human blockade to prevent Exxon from moving equipment into the park.

On the international front, the issue alerted influential lobbyists like the Audubon Society and Germany's Green Party, which had been among the first to propose the Maya Biosphere Reserve. The Greens' demand for an environmental impact report before going ahead with construction of a road to Flores effectively scuttled that project, and Germany diverted the allocated funds to a census of Petén's flora. Exxon, still smarting from the furor over the massive oil spill in the Straits of Valdez, bowed to the mounting pressures and announced the suspension of a $40 million oil exploration contract with the Guatemalan government. But the suspension proved to be temporary, as the rise in oil prices provoked by the Persian Gulf crisis made Guatemala's reserves increasingly attractive.

The emerging "ecoarchaeologists" had won only the first round in the protracted contest yet to come between conservationists and the powerful oil and lumber interests. To no one's surprise, President Cerezo immediately claimed credit for stopping the drilling in Ceibal; but the massive logging by nine major sawmills continued unchecked throughout northern Petén, as did the border invasions by Mexican loggers and cattle ranchers.

Following passage of the Protected Areas Statutes, Jim Nations and Santiago Billy went on the environmental lecture circuit—which appears to expand as the environment itself dwindles—with the sensible postulate that tropical forests return more profit per hectare when they are left standing. Taking the lead from Brazil's rubber tappers, Nations actively promoted huge extractive reserves that would harvest xate, allspice, and chicle under the shadow of unmolested stands of giant cedar and mahogany. Nations's optimal-returns proposal appeared to impress a handful of liberal Guatemalan congressmen and businessmen, but no grassroots movement of xate or chicle harvesters arose to match the 500,000-strong rubber tappers' movement in Amazonia. The risks of taking on the powerful landowners and the army, which tend to look on any grassroots movement with murderous suspicion, remained prohibitive.

2

I returned to Petén to check on the protected areas and to interview some of the seventy-two park guards hired and trained by Lehnhoff and his staff. In Guatemala City I had met with the Maya Biosphere Reserve's coordinator, Hilda Rivera. She impressed me as a consummate conservationist who leavens her fierce commitment to principle with a healthy dose of pragmatism. Rivera, a chemical biologist by profession, had been a disciple of Mario Dary, the father of Guatemala's environmental movement. Beginning in the late 1960s, Dary had pioneered integrated ecological reserves such as the admirable

Quetzal Biotope. Dary was murdered in 1981 after he tried to stem the spread of drugs in San Carlos University, where he was rector. But he could as easily have been killed by any of a host of other enemies of his environmental initiatives.

"If Mario Dary had lived," conjectured Rivera, "the passage of the Protected Areas Statutes, for which he laid the groundwork, would have been his proudest achievement. I regard myself as one of several pygmy Mario Darys he left behind to carry on his work." Rivera's assignment to Petén, an area she has known since childhood, was preceded by research and field experience in Costa Rica, in sea turtle reserves on Guatemala's Pacific coast, and in the manatee conservation biotope on Lake Izabal, another of Mario Dary's brainchildren. Rivera, who is twenty-eight and single, admitted she would probably have turned down the job if she'd had a family to raise, because of the hazards involved. She clearly shared her boss Andreas Lehnhoff's wholehearted dedication and is more than his match in audacity. But whereas Lehnhoff is given to drawing up elaborate outlines and diagrams and approaches a tree as a marvel of architectonics, Rivera's eyes light up at the mention of a nesting leatherback turtle or the discovery of a quetzal nest. During her first three months on the job she had snatched protected birds and other fauna from the clutches of high officials attempting to smuggle them out of Petén. The wife of the chief of National Police had become so enamoured of a blue-crowned parrot she'd bought from an illegal trapper, she offered Rivera a trip to Europe if she were allowed to keep it.

"Obviously," remarked Rivera, "I had to put my foot down and say no. Predictably, she threatened to raise a big fuss, but to have given in would have set the worst kind of precedent. The next time I got into hot water was after a treasury police official refused to turn over a macaw chick and two toucans he'd taken from a protected area. I immediately faxed a letter to the head of the treasury police in the capital, and the birds were returned a few days later. I guess these two incidents may account in part for my 'iron lady' reputation."

At another CONAP checkpoint, Rivera intercepted seven trailers loaded with forty-eight thousand cubic feet of board lumber. The falsified logging permit bore an authorization from the government's forestry department (DIGEBOS), which has offices inside the military garrison of Santa Elena, near Flores. She confiscated the contraband mahogany and filed a complaint in court.

"Several days later," recalled Rivera, "President Cerezo called me up about the death threats coming through his office. He asked if I wanted a bodyguard, and I said absolutely not!" Her large dark eyes spark with indignation. "What would I say to my eighteen-year-old unarmed monitors, who stare down smugglers with guns pointed at their heads, if I were to show up with an armed bodyguard? It is out of the question!" Two months later, two loggers with links to the army were found guilty of using false permits to violate the Protected Areas Act and spent time in jail. The death threats continued.

Despite CONAP's decision against the use of guns by resource monitors, a sensitive ruling in Petén's wild west atmosphere, Rivera insisted she is not a "pure" conservationist. "I know I am not hired to train Gandhis, but the first time one of my monitors uses a gun, all the ethical guidelines we are trying to lay down will immediately be compromised. That is the risk you have to take when you pioneer legal conservation in what remains a lawless, open frontier. In Petén, we have to work with the realities of hunger as well as with the institutionalized privileges of the army and the powerful lumber barons." Rivera boasted that she had good working relations with the comandante of the Santa Elena base, as well as with the lumber operators whom CONAP is inviting to become partners as forest stewards in a balanced conservation policy.

She said, "I do not believe in an absolute preservation of Petén's parks and reserves, because that is simply not feasible. Logging, farming, hunting, and oil exploration will go on in the multiple-use zones and outside the park boundaries; but I am committed to protect unconditionally the designated nuclear zones like Tikal and Uaxactún and to promote well-managed, sustainable use of the buffer areas neighboring them."

3

In the absence of Hilda Rivera, who was invited to an environmental conference in the States, I was met at the Flores airport by her assistant, Román Carrera, a twenty-three-year-old Petén native and undergraduate student assigned to be my guide. Only toward the end of my visit did I learn this thoughtful young conservationist was CONAP's acting coordinator of reserve posts in Uaxactún, Dos Aguadas, Laguna del Tigre, and two other remote areas. The future of the Maya Biosphere Reserve was in the hands of an ecological youth corps with a median age of around twenty-two.

In the Santa Elena offices of CONAP two gringo Yale graduates, Robert Heinzman and Conrad Reining, were completing a study on sustainable harvesting of xate, chicle, and allspice. The project was sponsored by Jim Nations, who has since taken a vice-presidential post with Conservation International in Washington. Heinzman and Reining, who also served as CONAP consultants, had recently returned from an expedition to El Mirador. Atop the 220-feet-tall Danta Temple, the tallest known Maya structure, Robert, the more extroverted half of the team, had experienced the grandeur of the universe and the puniness of human endeavor. ("We are but a grain of sand in a big beach, and an eyeblink in time.") In no way had this bittersweet epiphany dented his enthusiasm for forest conservation. Heinzman's upbeat attitude translates into sweeping assertions like, "The eyes of the world are on Petén. If we play our cards right, the Maya Biosphere Reserve will be the flagship for Latin American tropical forest conservation."

Conrad Reining, the more introverted and studious partner, worked away at the office computer, loaded with data on the nutritional value of breadnut, the feasibility of breeding paca, and xate extractive reserves. The ambiance in the offices of CONAP fairly crackled with a New Frontier energy and resolve. At dinner, Heinzman and Reining counseled me to visit Dos Aguadas and Uaxactún before going on to Yaxhá, which Rivera had recommended as an ecoarchaeological showcase. Andreas Lehnhoff supports ecotourism as "a necessary evil" only so long as it encourages local communities to safeguard the forest; Lehnhoff held fast against the government Tourism Institute's plans to put up a large hotel in Yaxhá and promote package tours inside the fragile reserve.

4

The road to Dos Aguadas took us around Lake Petén-Itzá, past the sawmills at San Andrés and a prosperous-looking orphanage funded and managed by a U.S. Protestant mission. The family of towheaded Midwesterners who started "Children's Ranch" appears to be sincere and hard-working, without the proselytizing fervor of the more militant evangelical sects. But their tenure in Petén was jeopardized in September 1990, when URNG guerrillas evicted Elam Stoltzfus and his family from their New Life Protestant mission on the Pasión River on charges of collaborating with the military.

In a full-page letter published in the Guatemalan press, the Stoltzfus family accused URNG commander Pablo Monsanto of having destroyed nineteen years of selfless service to the poor and disadvantaged communities of southern Petén. In a stirring and at times bizarre plea, Elam Stoltzfus forgave Monsanto his errors after asking him to publicly acknowledge them and repent. At the airport, Stoltzfus pledged to come back and rebuild their mission the moment the death sentence against him was lifted.

Exactly one week after the Stoltzfus family boarded a plane for Pennsylvania, President Cerezo admitted to U.S. officials that the military was "probably" involved in the torture and murder of another long-term North American resident in southern Petén. Michael DeVine, a former poultry rancher who had run tours in and around Poptún since the early seventies, was the victim in June 1990 of a kaibil-type execution—his head was nearly severed from his body— that the army tried, unconvincingly, to pin on the guerrillas. U.S. Ambassador Stroock had to press for an investigation after the army stonewalled his inquiries, giving rise to suspicions that DeVine might have stumbled on arms- or drug-trafficking connections involving high-echelon military officers. In response to the army's continued obduracy, U.S. threats to reduce military aid—reported in the *New York Times*—finally forced Cerezo's hand. At the risk of provoking a military coup a scarce four months from the end of his term, Cerezo removed army post commanders from Poptún and Santa Elena and called for the arrest and prosecution of the killers. Eight persons, including five soldiers, were charged and arrested. Efforts continued to track down and indict the high-ranking military and intelligence officers who gave the orders.

In spite of Cerezo's efforts, the U.S. Congress stopped all military aid to Guatemala in December 1990 because of ongoing human rights abuses.

5

Five park monitors greeted us at Dos Aguadas, a CONAP station located in a populated buffer zone between Tikal and the Biotope of San Miguel la Palotada. Twelve other guards were currently on patrol or on leave. The station's log, which I was asked to sign, kept a record of logging, hunting, and other violations, as well as the contraband in birds and hides. The animals shot by hunters included wild boar, deer, and tepeizcuintle. CONAP monitors had made a population census of the area; they noted encounters with xate and chicle harvesters and recorded the eviction of several maize farmers. Significantly, most of the violations were registered during the station's first two months of operations.

The head resource guardian at the post, twenty-four-year-old Hugo Aguilar, is a college graduate whose family owns a lumberyard in Poptún. He admitted right off that this was the most "delicate" job he'd had but that he liked the satisfaction of setting a precedent for those who came after. A robust six-footer with a shock of curly black hair, Aguilar smiled uneasily when I inquired if "delicate" was code for "life-threatening."

"When we first got here, many residents as much as dared us to interfere with their illegal trade in lumber and animals. If they pulled a gun on us, we had to bite our tongues and give them right of way. What alternative did we have? We learned of entrepreneurs who offered chainsaws and pickups to colonists in exchange for logging hardwood trees, only a fraction of which they could keep. When they slacked off, the owners took back the chainsaws and trucks and passed them on to more aggressive depredators. This is one way they create a rising spiral of despoliation. We have also had to face G-2 army officers in loaded lumber trucks who threatened to make mincemeat of us if we tried to stop or denounce them. The army fuels local residents' fears that we are taking away their livelihood. 'These are your lands,' they tell them; 'no one can take them away from you.' That is a call for defiance of the rule of law. As the colonists have come to realize that we are here to stay and that we cannot be scared away, much of the contraband has moved north toward Naranjo, and there have been fewer confrontations. Still, a local candidate for mayor is running on the pledge to rid Dos Aguadas of all environmentalists.

"Right now, the hardest part of our job is that the reserve's borders are not yet firm, and this makes law enforcement a delicate matter. I don't mind facing up to armed smugglers, but I hate kicking out a poor milpa farmer from a contested area."

I expressed curiosity about a silver Star of David Aguilar wore around his neck, and he said his Jewish brother-in-law had given it to him for protection. I asked him, "How do you feel about the ban on guns?"

The nervous smile reappeared on his face. "I am not a Gandhi. I know how to handle weapons and would use one strictly for self-defense. To be frank, I would feel safer having a low-caliber rifle, but Hilda has convinced us that the precedent we set here is absolutely predicated on rational persuasion and renouncing the use of force. So we abide by her ruling."

Aguilar and two of his guards showed me around the post, which outwardly resembled a chiclero camp, minus the female cook or helper. The guards admitted to long, lonely nights of beer drinking and hankering after distant girlfriends or hanging out with the few single women in Dos Aguadas. (In Yaxhá, where CONAP and Project Tikal had a total of ninety male employees and not a single woman, the head archaeologist confessed, "After two or three tours of duty here most of the men turn to alcohol, dope, or gay sex, or they discover the True Religion.")

On a tree branch above us sat one of two toucans that, together with the now famous blue-crowned parrot confiscated from the wife of the chief of police, were waiting to be returned to the wild. Neighbors had clipped the toucans' wings to prevent their flying into their yards to pilfer eggs and grain. The black keel-billed toucan, with its handsome yellow collar, bright red tail coverts, and motley eight-inch-long beak, is a true oddity. Even the normally sober Roger Tory Peterson is baffled by the bird's ax-handle beak, whose function he dubs "mysterious." An unwieldy rebuke to Darwin's theory of survival adaptation, the toucan's beak would pitch its owner to the ground head first, were it made of solider stuff than spongy tissue. Nattering away interminably with its froglike croak, the toucan gazed dolefully at us from its low perch, as preposterous a spectacle as a New Year's reveler wearing a lampshade or a prankster with a Jimmy Durante schnozzola.

6

On the drive back toward Santa Elena, conversation turned once again to the resource monitors' ethical dilemmas. Román, who like Hugo is a native Petenero, addressed one of these contradictions head-on: "Andreas and Hilda have their principles and convictions, just as we do," he began, "but they are intellectuals who have been brought up in an urban middle-class environment. Most of us here have at one time or another survived as corn farmers, loggers, hunters, xate or chicle harvesters, the same as those whose infractions we are paid to report. How can I order Hugo to impound a sack of corn from a poor milpa farmer, even if he happens to be inside a nuclear zone? The fact of hunger is an imperative here. When we look an armed soldier in the eye, we know that he may have worked his fingers to the bone in his father's milpa or picked coffee in a wealthy landowner's finca; but army officers, who like to complain of the 'ignorance' of their recruits, have usually had a privileged upbringing and are dissociated from contact with the earth and manual labor. The peasant/soldier can be taught to understand the importance of maintaining the water table or the value of extractive reserves. Military officers live according to their own laws, which they learned in the Politécnica and refined during postgraduate training abroad. The teaching of environmental science, whose natural laws take precedence over the military's code, is at the heart of what we are trying to accomplish." After a moment's silence, Román concluded, "If our work is to bear fruit, we must first raise our own consciousness before pretending to be examples for others."

My admiration for Román Carrera and the resource monitors rose several notches as I accompanied them on their hazardous beats. A nimble mestizo, Román combines the instincts of a forest-dwelling Maya with the analytic detachment of a student of Western philosophy. Román needs both faculties to survive in Petén, where "delicate encounters" are everyday occurrences.

On the road to Tikal the next day, we spied two men who scurried like shadows into the forest. We parked the jeep over a rise one hundred yards ahead and walked back to find two hooded long-haired men staring at us from the thickets. Román hesitated, taking a step back.

"Are those guerrillas?" I inquired, as my legs began to buckle.

"Hard to say, but they are probably armed," Román said. Without venturing any farther, we climbed back into the vehicle and reported the sighting to the administrator in Tikal, who guessed they were illegal xate harvesters waiting for a pickup. Román thought it likelier they were huecheros, or looters, on the lookout for their fence. Another monitor later reported seeing a band of ten to twelve men in that very spot. The administrator reported the two sightings to the army, as a matter of routine. And there, as a matter of routine, the matter rested, until the next encounter.

In Tikal Park we flagged down a truckload of archaeological guardians returning from the Laguna del Tigre Reserve, near the northwest border with Mexico. CONAP has also posted guards there to monitor game hunters and assess the potential damage to the lagoon's wetlands and bird-nesting sites from oil explorations under way by Basic Resources International. Thus far, hard lobbying by ecologists Jim Nations and Paul Dulan, who prepared critical environmental impact reports, have prevented Basic Resources from putting up a refinery in Laguna del Tigre. But they have already drilled two of the seven projected wells, whose combined output may eventually account for as much as 40 percent of Guatemala's oil production. As we spoke, the driver took out a polychrome vase that showed two dancing figures in animal pelts, with their heads cut off. He said he had found it near an abandoned campfire whose embers were still warm. The vase was classical Maya and its blue and ocher colors were preserved intact, except that its upper half had apparently broken off during removal, causing the looters to abandon it. How many hundreds of unbroken vases had looters absconded with, for each damaged one they left behind? The archaeologists with Project Tikal would not even hazard a guess.

Halfway between Tikal and Uaxactún, the driver slammed on the brakes to avoid running over a snake. It was a *barba amarilla*, or fer-de-lance, with the characteristic velvet diamond pattern and the squarish pit viper head. Although this one was less than two feet long, even the youngest of Central America's deadliest serpent can unhinge its jaws wide and inject enough poison to kill a grown man in a matter of hours. Most Peteneros kill the barba amarilla on sight as a matter of course, particularly during the summer moulting season when they are most aggressive. The Maya kings were in such awe of the *nauyaca,* as it is called to this day, they sculpted it on their stelae and temples in the form of Kukulcán, the feathered serpent god known to the Aztecs as Quetzalcoatl.

"Goodbye, Mr. Snake, be thankful that we are conservationists," Román called to the fer-de-lance, after it had safely crossed the road. During the remainder of the afternoon, Román and Carlos the driver regaled us with accounts of the grisly deaths suffered by dozens of their friends and acquaintances who had fallen victim to barba amarilla.

In San Andrés we stopped to visit the Aserradero del Norte and its owner, Antonio del Cid. When I first met him two years earlier, he had been preparing to send skidders and tractors into the Sierra del Lacandón. Stacked in the yard were approximately 3 million board feet of mahogany and cedar, ready for shipment. And yet, compared to the hub of activity that had greeted me on my previous visit, the sawmill seemed half deserted.

Don Antonio met us in his office, looking bowed with fatigue and years older than his fifty-three or four. In August 1988 he had looked every bit the lumber tycoon, as he showed me around his pet tree-nursery; he had planted several rows of wilting mahogany and cedar saplings four to five feet apart, which virtually guaranteed they would never mature. When I asked if he planned to transplant ten mahoganies and cedars to the deforested areas for every one he had taken out, as the forestry laws stipulate, he laughed in my face and said the grove was a "little park" for his employees' amusement. As for the guerrillas he knew to be active in the Sierra, he had shrugged and remarked, "We will deal with that problem in its proper time."

It had not turned out quite as planned. In a lugubrious voice, Don Antonio described the large group of armed men in olive fatigues who invaded his logging camp in La Lucha, or The Struggle, as that sector of the Sierra is known. "I don't know if they were guerrillas or common delinquents, but they gave my men five hours to get out and forced them to leave the trees and our equipment behind." Don Antonio slapped his hand on the table. "Two years' work gone, just like that. We were working against the clock, because the new forestry laws would come into effect this past June, and our concession would be revoked. As a result, we were only able to take out two hundred mahoganies."

"What happened to the remainder?" I asked, incredulous.

"The guerrillas kept them. Apparently, they were in league with a group of refugees who had formed a cooperative near La Lucha and who kept them informed of our activities."

Don Antonio confessed he had "nearly fainted" when he first read the new Protected Areas Statutes. "The hardship is not for me alone, but for the dozens of workers I had to fire for lack of work. Now, we have to wait and see if we will be permitted limited logging in the multiple-use areas. Otherwise, we might as well fire everybody and shut the mill down."

The hint of sanctimoniousness behind this remark erupted into full bloom moments later, when he proposed that loggers defray the cost of reforestation out of their own pockets. "As it stands, the new forestry laws are worthless, because they are impossible to enforce. Given a chance, private entrepreneurs could solve this problem among ourselves. Last year, I planted a large grove of pine trees near Poptún, all of it with my own money." Román, who had not spoken a word, barely contained himself. This "deathbed conversion" was clearly intended for his benefit. Some of Román's relatives worked for Don Antonio, and he was well informed of the logger baron's real views on environmentalists, journalists, and all other "communists." "A logger is like the barba amarilla," Román warned us afterward. "He is most dangerous when his back is to the wall."

Don Antonio's wounded pride and twisted self-justifications were not nearly as remarkable as the inadvertent convergence of interests that made allies of President Cerezo and the URNG, who delivered a one-two punch for conservation.

My euphoria was short-lived. On my return to the capital Santiago Billy corroborated that the Aserradero del Norte had taken out all of the approximately two thousand trees they felled before they were stopped by the revocation of their license. And a CONAP officer informed me the URNG commanders, in common with some army officers, were known to be selling contraband lumber to Mexican dealers. The Mexicans in turn resold the lumber at much higher profits to the Japanese, who already import approximately 45 percent of the world's rain forest hardwoods. One way or another, the depredation of Sierra del Lacandón would continue, and very little of the profits would be likely to filter down to Juan or his fellow indigenous combatants.

7

In the garrison of Santa Elena I interviewed Colonel Guillermo Portillo Gómez, an imposing figure at around 6'1" and 250 pounds, with arresting blue eyes. Colonel Portillo Gómez was born and raised in Cobán, a highland region dominated until the Second World War by German coffee planters, many of whom fathered children with the local Quekchí women. The colonel speaks an excellent English, learned while doing postgraduate training in Fort Bragg, Fort Benning, and Fort Leavenworth.

The colonel apologized that the post commander, Mario Roberto García Catalán, whom Hilda had recommended as a straight-talking officer with a nascent environmental conscience, could not see me because he "had contracted malaria." (Two weeks later I learned Comandante García Catalán had been removed by order of President Cerezo, apparently to protect him from fallout from the investigation into Michael DeVine's murder.)

The new posters in Colonel Portillo Gómez's office reflected the army's public sensitivity to environmental issues. One showed a cat in army fatigues planting trees with peasants under the legend "the army and the people are one big family."

Colonel Portillo Gómez insisted on taking me around the base to show me the two hundred saplings they had planted in conformity with the new laws. But first, he aired some misgivings about CONAP. "We are a consultative member of CONAP and are doing our share to protect our patrimony. But questions have risen about the agency's affiliations. We work closely with the forestry department's DIGEBOS, whose offices you can see from here, next to this barracks. Who is CONAP allied with?" I assumed he was referring to the delicate matter of the confiscated lumber shipments and decided not to press the issue. Instead, I tried a legalistic approach.

"According to the CONAP charter, Colonel Portillo Gómez, part of the military's responsibility in this regard is the protection of borders against illegal contraband and other depredation."

"Yes, but where are those borders? They have never been clearly defined. How can I deploy my men along hundreds of kilometers of borders that don't exist?"

"I believe they show up quite clearly in the Landsat photographs," I said. "They show incursions by Mexicans into northern Petén to log, hunt, and cut clearings for their cattle."

"I have patrolled those areas myself," Colonel Portillo Gómez said. "I found no loggers and no herds of cattle. A few fields of marijuana, yes, and we are dealing with those in collaboration with the U.S. Drug Enforcement Agency." (Comandante García Catalán had warned Hilda Rivera, "If you see marijuana fields, check with me first. Chances are they may belong to Influential Families and are therefore out of bounds.")

"And what of the traffic in rare birds and animal skins?" I asked him.

Colonel Portillo Gómez smiled frostily. "Well, friends are always after me to get them a baby macaw, but I haven't been able to find one. I did get my mother a pair of fine parrots, however."

I stared at the colonel in astonishment, detecting no sign that he recognized his gaffe. Instead, he spoke affably of how he "had a way" with parrots and other animals. He had evidently misunderstood my question. For the first time since my evening with the comandante of Nebaj, I felt a chill up my spine. There is a cobra-like fascination about persons in high rank like Colonel Portillo Gómez. During the Vietnam War, when the colonel would have been training in U.S. bases, the appropriate appellative was, "Strangelovian." I was in this man's grasp and would not leave before he was ready to let me go.

As we waited for a jeep to take us on a tour of the base, I perused several other framed legends on the wall: "Victory in war depends on the combative spirit of the troops, on the will of the commanders, and on civilian support." "Combatant! You must have patience and dedication in study, and decisiveness and initiative in action. Col. Portillo Gómez." In substance, these slogans were unexceptional and could as readily have been applied to forest conservation. In the artillery range shortly afterward I would read another slogan apparently intended for new recruits, which also bore Colonel Portillo Gómez's imprint: "The enemy is not defeated in battle. You win over him by destroying his mind, his intelligence, and his will."

Colonel Portillo Gómez was intent on showing me every single tree planted by his men in the farthest corner of the huge base. Most of the saplings were already engulfed by weeds, and no attempt had been made to camouflage the giant felled trees in zones of new construction. The air force base at Santa Elena is one of the largest garrisons in the country, and Petén now has the largest military presence of any Guatemalan department. Although Colonel Portillo Gómez's expected promotion to base commander was by no means certain, one would not have known it by the crisp, bug-eyed salutes that greeted his every move among his soldiers and inferior officers. If it was his intention to keep me off balance by impressing me with his authority, he eminently succeeded. The colonel mouthed his words slowly, with painstaking care, as if he feared that—like Doctor Strangelove's dummy right arm—they might rise up of their own accord and give away his game. And yet his tone would at times become almost pleading, as though he sincerely wanted me to sympathize with his position.

"These are my corps of engineers," he said, pointing to a construction crew working on a new road. "Before this, they were working on the transversal highway out of Cobán. You may have heard about it. The project had to be abandoned after guerrillas killed 60 percent of the engineers in repeated assaults. Do you see what happens when we attempt to introduce civic improvements and modernize our homeland? In Eastern Europe, communism may be going out of fashion, but here in Guatemala we have no perestroika. Brigandage and vandalism are the modus vivendi, and the guerrillas have become past masters at it. How can they be expected to change now, after all these years, and seek gainful employment?"

Colonel Portillo Gómez neglected to add that the infamous "transversal highway" had long before been exposed as a huge money-making scam and was never meant to be completed. In common with the Chixoy hydroelectric plant and the CELGUSA papermill deal with Spain that would have devoured Guatemala's pine forests within a decade, all of these grandiose projects had helped sink Guatemala's economy and undermine its fledgling democracy. In the end, they were left half finished or were scuttled altogether after hundreds of millions of dollars had been skimmed off the top by military and civilian contractors.

An hour later we had reached the furthest outpost of the base,

by which time we had counted more than one hundred saplings in
varying stages of decline. In this tour of inspection we had also encountered a World-War-II-vintage Pershing tank in military maneu-
vers, a grounded Grumman jet fighter placed on display, monuments
to heroic combatants and to twelve artists killed in an air crash after
the army invited them to Petén. We also met dozens of uniformed
men who sprang to attention and barked out their name, rank, and
assignment as though their lives depended on it. As it happened,
Colonel Portillo Gómez had one more surprise in store.

On turning a corner we came upon fifty youngsters in light khakis
who were rolling on the ground, their faces and uniforms layered
with dust. When the sergeant in charge barked at them to get out
of the way of the jeep, fifty bodies jumped as one, with wooden
cudgels clasped between their thighs, like the monkey men in Maya
scripture.

"Colonel, sir!" yelled the sergeant, with a stiff-armed salute. "These
are new recruits receiving their punishment." None of the Mayan
and ladino recruits looked older than seventeen or eighteen, and yet
the exhaustion and terror disfiguring their faces likened them to the
ageless creatures in Goya's sketches on the horrors of war.

"Carry on!" snapped Colonel Portillo Gómez. I turned to catch a
glimpse of the recruits groveling in the dust once again, with the
cudgels clasped between their thighs. The very light around them
appeared leached and unforgiving.

"Isn't that punishment a bit harsh?" I suggested, ingenuously.

Colonel Portillo Gómez smiled. "Of course. Otherwise, they
would go bad on us."

Six months after our meeting, Colonel Guillermo Portillo Gómez
was indicted with thirteen other officers in a suit filed against the
army by the widow of Michael DeVine. Colonel Portillo Gómez was
named as one of two officers responsible for the orders to kidnap
and murder Michael Vernon DeVine. Colonel Portillo Gómez, who
was relieved of his post in preparation for trial in a military court,
denied any complicity in DeVine's murder, alleging he had been away
from Petén at the time. Former Post Commander Mario Roberto
García Catalán, who many believe to have been the "intellectual author" of Michael DeVine's assassination, has not been indicted. In
September 1991, the military tribunal released on their own recog-

nizance Captain Hugo Contreras Alvarado and Private Fabián Arévalo. Colonel Portillo Gómez was freed without conditions. The military prosecutor appealed the tribunal's decisions.

Eight soldiers of the twelve military still under indictment for DeVine's murder were in prison, awaiting sentencing. In August 1992 one of these soldiers, Rafael Tiul Cucul, openly accused Captain Hugo Contreras, Colonel Portillo Gómez, and two other officers of having given the orders for DeVine's assassination. Tiul Cucul also named six soldiers and low-echelon officers, who he claimed carried out the orders.

On September 29 six soldiers, including Tiul Cucul, were given thirty-year prison sentences for the assassination of Michael DeVine. The charges against Captain Hugo Contreras were dropped because of "insufficient evidence." The dismissal of the charges against Contreras has been appealed by the Public Ministry.

8

At dinner with Román, Robert, and Conrad that evening, we went over the encounters with Antonio del Cid and Colonel Portillo Gómez. I was feeling discouraged by the entrenched prejudices of these two men who personified opposition to forest conservation. Who was to say the next president would not be cut out of the same cloth and would not kill the Maya Biosphere Reserve with deliberate neglect?

Román refused to be taken in. "The struggle to save this forest is a race against time, admittedly. We have to stay one step ahead of the forces that have always conspired to cut, burn, bleed, and otherwise destroy the forest. To military men like Colonel Portillo Gómez a tree is either an enemy or a product to be cut up and sold for profit. But for the first time, we are putting these men on the defensive. We are telling them that it is in their own best interest, in the long run, to see that this forest is not destroyed; and that they have as much of a stake in its survival as the maize farmer, the chiclero, or the xate harvester. There are powerful international forces on our side, and they are being brought to bear on these two men and on hundreds of others who still think as they do. We of CONAP and the other conservation agencies working here are young and determined, and we have time to learn from our mistakes, to grow and develop as environmentalists. We are the first. Working together, we can help to educate a new generation of soldiers and young army officers who respect the new laws and who are sensitive to the importance of protecting our natural resources. We have the necessary patience, because we know we are doing the right thing."

For the first time since my travels to Chiapas and Petén began three decades before, I felt the battle lines had been clearly drawn.

9

After his election in January 1991, President Jorge Elías Serrano replaced the Environmental Commission's director, Jorge Cabrera, with Antonio Ferraté, an engineer whose brother was a cofounder of CONAMA. Before leaving office, Cabrera counseled Serrano to strike a deal with the loggers and grant them limited concessions inside the reserve.

At a meeting with his officers in February, Ferraté disregarded his predecessor's advice and enforced the ban on all logging in the biosphere's nuclear zones.

"If we give in to the loggers and grant concessions," he reasoned, "the colonists will have all the excuse they need to burn down protected forest for their milpas. And the cattle ranchers and oil drillers will be right behind them."

In private, Ferraté acknowledged that his firm stand would be taken as a declaration of war by the powerful loggers' lobby.

Even before the reversal on logging concessions was made public, loggers in Naranjo, near the reserve's northwest border, retaliated against CONAP's confiscation of contraband lumber shipments by inciting settlers to set fire to CONAP and CECON stations. CONAP's four resource monitors in Naranjo had to flee for their lives. Inevitably, this assault affected the morale of resource monitors in other checkpoints, as the contrabandists intended. Within six months, the army began removing large quantities of mahogany and cedar from the vicinity of El Perú, on the road to Naranjo, with licenses issued by DIGEBOS.

In February I met with Hilda Rivera and Santiago Billy, who with Ferraté, Andreas Lehnhoff, and Román Carrera had become the loggers' lobby's chief targets. (During a field visit to Guatemala in February, Jim Nations hailed them as "the finest forest conservationists in Latin America.") Hilda told me guards in Dos Aguadas and other stations had vacated their posts after the Naranjo incident and had to be reassured of their safety before they agreed to go back. In Uaxactún, chicleros and maize farmers threatened to "burn down the mountain" if the loggers were allowed to fell trees in their area. In the nuclear zone of Sotz, according to Billy, a logger named Federico Juan had marked fifteen hundred mahoganies in anticipation of the lifting of the ban. There were growing signs that large concerns like Aserradero del Norte might simply ignore the ban and go ahead with logging inside the nuclear zones.

Hilda had received so many death threats since the arrest of the army-linked contrabandists, she was persuaded to stay out of Petén for varying intervals. She now routinely sent photocopies of all her directives, not only to top government officials but also to representatives of international environmental agencies active in Petén. "That way, they will not think I am just a small fish who can be easily got rid of without anyone noticing." Hilda was in the gunsights of both the army and the loggers, whose network of friends in high places made her self-protective measures provisional, at best. The afternoon we met, she spoke of the branch of G-2 that specialized in assassinations that looked like accidents.

Within six months of taking his position, Antonio Ferraté's firm stand appeared to wilt under the relentless pressure; increasingly, CONAP turned a blind eye on the army's illicit contraband trade, both within the nuclear zones and in the neighboring buffer areas. In March, Hilda Rivera left her post at CONAP to work as coordinator for a private conservation agency in Sierra de las Minas, a Protected Area in the Oriente. Six months later she accepted an administrative position with CARE, the international relief agency.

As the crisis in the Persian Gulf intensified, U.S. funding for forest conservation projects fell by the wayside. AID dragged its feet on allocating funds for the Mayarema (Mayan Resource Management) project. Alfred Nakamura, the prime mover behind AID's forest management program, assured me the first million was in the pipeline and the agency's commitment remained firm. After fielding several tough questions, he confided, "I'll tell you the truth. Some of the support is softening, but I still think a good chunk of the nuclear zones can be saved."

Early in 1991, Conservation International, Nature Conservancy, and the Audubon Society were awarded AID's $5 million package bid to create extractive reserves in the Petén for the sustainable exploitation of rain forest products such as chicle, allspice, and xate. Robert Heinzman and Conrad Reining were hired by CI to continue their work on Petén's renewable resources.

In January 1992, the Audubon Society denounced the transshipment of Guatemalan lumber through Belize, en route to Mexico. The story raised a brief stir in the Belizean and international press, but the contraband continued. The shipping documents bore the DIGEBOS rubber stamp. In August, an environmental impact report funded by Germany estimated that all mahogany and cedar outside the protected areas would be gone within two years. Even more alarmingly, the study concluded the protected areas themselves would be denuded of hardwoods within six years, and Petén would have no forest to speak of by the year 2012. A Conservation International volunteer working with chicleros and xateros compared the rampant anarchy in Petén to "a supermarket without a checkout counter."

In quick succession, Andreas Lehnhoff and Román Carrera quit their posts, alleging personal differences with the new director of CONAMA and his officers. (Carrera and Hugo Aguilar were immediately hired by Conservation International.) Lehnhoff's replacement, Marco Palacios, is a conscientious environmentalist who confessed shortly after he took the job, "I will do my best to protect the Biosphere Reserve, but where the army's activities are concerned, you must remember that I have a wife and children." Byron Milián, the young ecologist who replaced Román Carrera, places both hands over his ears and declares, "I have the ears of a fish." In February 1992, Santiago Billy announced he would resign his post with CONAMA by the end of the year. All the staff members named by Vinicio Cerezo were now gone, and a new chapter opened in the campaign to save Petén's Maya Biosphere Reserve.

CONAP was put to a severe test on December 2 and 3, in northwest Petén's wildest frontier. Two CONAP officers, an archaeologist, a *Siglo XXI* correspondent, and three plainclothes treasury police were assaulted by residents of Naranjo after they came upon a logging camp in Paso Caballos, inside a Protected Area of the Reserve. The reporter, Omar Cano, photographed the logging activities and the dozens of boats loaded with contraband lumber heading for the Mexican border.

Uniformed soldiers from the local garrison joined residents in the attack on Spencer Ortiz, director of the Maya Biosphere Reserve, archaeologist Obed Galvez, and the three treasury police, who were threatened with hand grenades. The five men were removed from the CONAP truck, tied up and beaten, and taken to the military base, where they received no first aid for broken ribs and multiple cuts and bruises. The following morning, after the five men were forced to spend the night in the open during a thunderstorm, the Naranjo residents returned to the base and beat up the men once again in front of the military.

Omar Cano and Rafael Luna, who heads CONAP's Protected Areas in Petén, had fled the attackers and reached the river, hiding in water up to their necks until the next morning, when they too were caught and beaten by the local residents. The two men were tied up and delivered to the army base with the message, "Tell the lieutenant we have carried out the order."

The following day, CONAP informed Petén Governor Carlos Asturias of the assault, and a helicopter was dispatched to retrieve the seven men. Omar Cano broke the story from his hospital bed in Flores, blaming the Naranjo military garrison for the attack. Cano also accused the zone commander, Lieutenant Otoniel Ramos Carranza, of illegally trafficking in hardwoods from Petén's Protected Areas. (A month later, the threats on his life drove Omar Cano out of Guatemala.)

The military spokesman's cynical disclaimers that the beaten men had been mistaken for guerrillas were overwhelmed by the outcry in the national and international press. CONAP officer Armando Ozaeta told *Crónica* of the agency's powerlessness to stop the massive contraband by army officers in league with local and Mexican loggers. "You can count the mahoganies and cedars that remain standing in the reserve," he told interviewers.

The mounting evidence against the army took on the appearance of a "smoking gun." The U.S. State Department sent a representative to investigate the charges, and President Serrano's office was flooded with protests from abroad. Still, there was little CONAP could do to capitalize on the tide of condemnation. With a staff of 220 monitors to cover the Biosphere Reserve's 1.5 million square hectares, and a yearly budget stripped to $200,000 that barely covered staff salaries, CONAP's role was reduced to that of a helpless eyewitness to runaway depredation.

Early in 1993, the ongoing investigation into Michael DeVine's murder concentrated on Captain Hugo Contreras Alvarado, who was flatly accused by four soldiers serving sentences of having issued the orders for DeVine's assassination.

On February 28 lawyer Gonzales Rodríguez, the attorney for DeVine's widow, Carol DeVine, was driven off a road in Guatemala City by an unmarked car. Rodríguez suffered a skull fracture and was taken to a hospital in a semi-comatose condition. Although the U.S. Embassy has continued to press for prosecution of all those involved in DeVine's murder, Captain Hugo Contreras has yet to be arrested and tried.

PART VI

13

Unfinished Conquest

"They say the earthquake is a punishment from God."

"But why then were so many *naturales* killed, and so few ladinos?"

"Ah, in that case, it must have been a punishment from the devil."

Conversation between Cakchiquel Mayas
in Chimaltenango, 1976.

THE QUETZAL

The quetzal, Guatemala's once-proud currency, which maintained parity with the dollar until the mid-eighties, is still impressive for its graphics. In her as yet unpublished thesis on Guatemalan iconography, art historian Anna Blume discovers hidden meanings in the one-quetzal bill. Its face depicts a Mayan woman on her knees offering copal incense to a ladino general whose patrician features are framed by a Mayan pyramid. To the left of the kneeling woman, a resplendent quetzal with long green tail feathers and crimson breast floats above a blank space. When held against the light, the blank space resolves into the stern visage of Tecún Umán, the Quiché chieftain slain by Pedro de Alvarado in one of the epic engagements of the Conquest of Guatemala. Legend has it that as Tecún Umán lay dying, the quetzal dipped its chest in his blood before expiring alongside its master.

The ladino artist who designed the quetzal bill evidently knew his semiotics. Tecún Umán, the part mythic, part historical shadow figure still revered by his Mayan heirs and long reviled by his conquerors, has been resurrected on Guatemala's legal tender, and the irony seems appropriate; just as the huge tracts of land seized by the conquistadores were worthless without Indian slaves to work them, and just as the coffee barons would never have made their millions without the thousands of Mayan harvesters, so Guatemala's currency is null

and void without the Tecún Umán watermark. Both in symbols and
in fact, the culture of the conquerors continues to draw legitimacy
from the culture of the conquered, on whose myths and descendance
it nourishes itself. (Since 1990, the quetzal bills printed by the Guatemalan treasury no longer bear the Tecún Umán watermark.)

2   EARTHQUAKE

Two of the five chief factors behind the transformation of Guatemala's indigenous culture since the mid 1970s have been violent ones;
the first was the major earthquake that convulsed the Mayan highlands
in February 1976; the second is the war of counterinsurgency that
threatens to implant itself in the country's soul. The other three
factors, evangelical conversion, the population explosion and the ex-
patriation of approximately 1 million Mayas, are closely linked to the
first two.

I flew to Guatemala immediately after the earthquake and traveled
throughout the highlands for two weeks, as volunteer relief worker
and reporter. It was my first contact with many of the Mayan villages
and hamlets I visited, some of which had never seen a foreigner. To
many of these devastated communities in remote corners of the altiplano, the generosity of European and North American volunteers
who came to offer housing and provisions was a revelation. Here were
white-skinned "ladinos" speaking in a strange tongue who offered aid
and comfort and asked for nothing in return. (In many cases, of
course, the *quid pro quo* would be exacted later on in the form of
evangelical conversion.)

Some of the hardest hit areas in Chimaltenango and Quiché would
also suffer the brunt of the military's retaliations in the early eighties,
after the Guerrilla Army of the Poor and ORPA gained hundreds of
converts there. Everywhere I went, I heard praise for the gringos who
brought medicine, wooden sidings, tin roofs, poultry, and second-
hand clothes. It did not matter that most families rebuilt their adobe
homes as soon as the gringos departed and used their prefabricated
earthquake-proof dwellings for their chickens and pigs.

In the plaza of Chimaltenango I witnessed a group marriage of a
dozen couples, the younger kin or offspring of husbands and wives
buried under tile roofs while they slept. "To recover the departed,"

the relatives and in-laws whispered again and again, as the young couples marched through town in their colorful ceremonial finery, the shock still fresh on their faces.

In the town of Patzún I had my first look at a nascent form of village democracy in a traditional Mayan context. I arrived with a Dutch engineer who had collected funds in Holland for the town's restoration. A dozen elders of the Cakchiquel community awaited us in a lot behind the municipality, whose ladino officers had ignored the townspeople's pleas for a new water-pumping system. "The hand pump broke," the village headman explained, "and two of our upper cantones are totally dry."

When the Dutchman began to explain the obstacles to installing an electric pumping system from scratch, he discovered that the elders had made a thorough examination of the problem. Each of the twelve elders had undertaken the mastering of a different phase of the construction, according to his skills and experience. Among them were a carpenter, a mason, an apprentice engineer. They discussed the project at length, inviting me to chime in with suggestions although I had no expertise to contribute. The eldest among them, a curandero who had taken it upon himself to lay down the water pipes, traced long serpentine lines on the ground with a stick, concentrating on his design with such intensity I half expected it to spring to life and begin spouting water. Another elder discussed the pumping mechanism with broad, lively gestures; when words failed him, he mimed the rising and falling motions with his shoulders and hips, in the manner of a village storyteller.

The months passed, and life in the villages slowly recovered an outward normalcy; beneath the surface, however, many highland communities had suffered a radical alteration. Two hundred fifty thousand Mayas, many from remote aldeas, made their way to the slums of Guatemala City, in desperate search of work and a new start. Traditional Catholics began speaking of an "Indian earthquake," a punishment from God—or the devil—that spared devout ladinos. To many of the victims, the retributive or Satanic explanations they heard in church sermons were no longer good enough. The old Catholic churches in many communities had been leveled or irreparably damaged, while the newer temples of evangelical worship, and the cement block shrines of cult figures like San Andrés Itzapa's "San Simón" survived unharmed.

The third major factor behind the Mayas' cultural transformation was the fundamentalist and Pentecostal missionaries who came to aid and comfort the afflicted. At first, many of these missions overwhelmed their new converts with a freewheeling largesse, which the beleaguered Catholic parishes could not match. Despite the good work done by charities like Caritas, the Protestants outspent the Catholics many times over, even as their promises of salvation through hard work, abstention from liquor, and strict marital fidelity multiplied exponentially. The evangelicals brought with them a puritanical yet pragmatic Christianity that assured its followers they did not have to wait for the afterlife to attain personal redemption. In effect, they could reap the benefits of the ladino and gringo ways of life without having to forfeit their "Indianness."

The savvy new recruiters for the Guerrilla Army of the Poor—the other beneficiaries of the 1976 earthquake—promised the Mayan communities much the same thing, under the raised standard of armed revolution. In the Catholic church, only the proponents of Liberation Theology and the catechists of Acción Católica, with their emphasis on attainable social justice, attempted to match the reformist agendas of the evangelicals and the Marxist-Leninist guerrillas.

The earthquake and its aftermath did modify the ingrained prejudices of many ladinos toward the Maya communities, at least for a time. One heard fewer references to Indians as beasts of burden or as subhuman robots. Although they had been the hardest hit by the quake, Mayan communities recovered much sooner than the city dwellers, most of whom had suffered nothing worse than a bad jolt and some broken crockery; and yet, for many months afterward, the sale of Valium and Librium broke records in the capital, as psychiatrists did a booming business.

Accustomed over the centuries to nature's cycles of decay and regeneration, the Maya communities stoically absorbed the new calamity, without ignoring the opportunities offered by the evangelical missions, Acción Católica, and the two guerrilla organizations, EGP and ORPA.

In 1976, highland Maya villagers affected by the earthquake were exposed to white people who did not treat them with disdain, and they bared open their lives to accept their assistance. This was the start of a shift in outlook that would put an end—for better or worse—to the isolation of these communities from the outside world.

The violence visited on the leaders of earthquake-reconstruction committees by Lucas García's regime two years later led to the first mass migrations across the border into Mexico. The counterinsurgency also provoked the first massive displacement of internal refugees, beginning in the Ixil Triangle, where the majority of the population supported the EGP.

3 UNFINISHED CONQUEST

By the end of the eighties, even the most triumphalist army officers would admit that the Mayan communities of the altiplano had survived the third cycle of conquest, variously known in military circles as "Plan Victoria" or "Operación Ixil" and some of whose civilian components went under the rubrics "Castellanización," "Integración Social," or, simply, "Ladinización." What was yet to be assessed was the cost to all sides in the conflict and to the Mayan communities in particular.

Each of the indigenous communities located in a Zone of Conflict was victimized to a greater or lesser degree by the military's grim determination to *vencer* by eliminating the guerrillas' popular support base. And the cost of survival for many of these communities has been a profound dislocation in their traditional structures of subsistence. The character and extent of this transformation are as peculiar to each region as the idiosyncrasy of its geography, its customs, its language, and its history. Communities that attempted to "Mayanize" the violence by framing it within a familiar context of ancient myths and prophecies or by attributing it simply to envidia—that is, a rootless ladino culture bent on destroying a deep-rooted indigenous one—suffered radical disfigurements in their self-perception as Mayas. In too many highland communities, the unimagined scale and brutality of the violence—inflamed by an endemic *mala saña*—overwhelmed traditional rationalizations.

The children of San Martín Jilotepeque, Comalapa, and other towns of Chimaltenango located near the epicenter of the 1976 earthquake would later suffer the brunt of the military's violence in that province. U.S. linguist Julia Becker Richards found that children in these and neighboring towns tended to identify the Cakchiquel language with the term "victim" and turned away from their language and customs in greater numbers than anywhere else in the altiplano. In the outlying aldeas, Cakchiquel usage and costumbre have declined at significantly lower rates, even in places that suffered more devastation than did the towns and provincial capital. It is too soon to speculate whether Cakchiquel language and culture can regenerate once again from the more remote rural outposts, as they have after previous upheavals since the Conquest.

Paradoxically, Chimaltenango province is also known for hardworking, progressive communities: Tecpán, Patzún, Comalapa are cradles of Mayan linguists, anthropologists, teachers, artists, computer programmers, and labor leaders. Chimaltenango itself has been the focal center of rural health, native craft and agricultural cooperatives, as well as a stronghold of the durable Committee for Peasant Unity (CUC). Chimaltenango has also suffered the greatest losses of Maya labor organizers, rural health promoters, and leaders of earthquake reconstruction. One of the most publicized massacres of civilians during Cerezo's presidency took place in the Chimaltenango aldea of Aguacate, where twenty-two residents were killed by unknown assailants in the fall of 1988. Although Defense Minister Gramajo insisted the murders were committed by a "rogue" unit of ORPA, a half dozen separate investigations have yet to determine culpability. This failure damaged not only Cerezo but the democratic process as a whole. (The latest investigations have uncovered a possible drug connection to a local army commander who cultivated opium poppies in the vicinity.)

In the summer of 1989, a column of more than a hundred guerrillas—including women and children—descended from Acatenango Volcano into the town of San Miguel Dueñas, sixty kilometers from Guatemala City and less than ten from the safe haven of heavily touristed Antigua. The rebels rounded up the town's policemen, confiscated their weapons, and held a rally in the square. Similar actions took place in Escuintla and other coastal towns in 1990 and summer of 1991. These shows of strength by guerrilla units were attributed by Defense Minister Gramajo to the Xavier Tambriz Front of ORPA that had been active for years in the Lake Atitlán region and the coastal piedmont, or *bocacosta*. Gramajo also made the ominous statement that the guerrillas had again become "an ethnic problem," because of the number of Mayas observed at the head of the column. Their unchallenged operations in heavily populated regions of Escuintla, Sacatepéquez, and Chimaltenango obliged army spokesmen to raise their estimates of active guerrillas from 700 to over 1,000 and to upgrade their belligerency status from "nuisance" to "resurgent."

14

🔳

Profiles and Portents

"What I can say, after this terrible and fecund experience of
six years, during which I have peered into the abyss of this
comedy of man against man, is that democracy today is
headed precipitously toward a doctrine that is at once
Hitlerian and Phoenician."

President Juan José Arévalo's valedictory address,
March 1951

DOC BEHRHORST

"He was the father of us all."
Cakchiquel nurse, Behrhorst clinic

Doctor Carroll Behrhorst, the Kansas missionary whose hospital in
Chimaltenango was filled to bursting for months after the big quake,
estimated that more bones were broken during the minute or so of
the earthquake's duration than in any single calamity in the Western
world's recorded history. Although he had come to Guatemala with
a Lutheran mission, Doctor Behrhorst became a convert to Maya
culture and married one of his Cakchiquel nurses shortly after di-
vorcing his Midwestern wife. In the following years, Behrhorst learned
about the Mayas' reliance on herbal medicines, prayer ceremonies,
and other costumbre to maintain their balance with nature.

Behrhorst introduced a rural extension program in the Cakchiquel
communities of Chimaltenango that would become a model for third
world countries as far away as New Guinea. He was among the first
to see the deep-seated linkage between land tenancy and health statistics. He found that landless peasants suffer from far higher infant
mortality rates, and he actively promoted agricultural cooperatives as
part of holistic preventive medicine. Doc Behrhorst and his beneficiaries were to pay dearly for his foresight.

After Lucas García became president in 1978, the clinic's ambitious community extension program, which trained dozens of Maya health promoters from remote aldeas, provoked a violent response from the government. Lucas's military officers were suspicious of any communal organizations that led to the campesinos' betterment. The most outspoken and effective health promoters were the first to disappear. In 1982 a Guatemalan intern who worked closely with Doctor Behrhorst was seized by armed soldiers and dragged screaming out of the clinic as the doctor looked on helplessly. The intern was never seen again. As had been the case with Stan Rother in Santiago Atitlán, the murder of his co-workers stiffened Carroll Behrhorst's determination to stay on.

Thirteen Maya health promoters were disappeared from their aldeas between 1980 and 1983, either by the army or by army-sponsored death squadrons, which accused them of being in league with guerrillas. The victims included Behrhorst's brother-in-law and a Guatemalan physician Doc was training to be his successor. In private, Behrhorst denounced the assassinations as an assault on his own person as well as on his progressive rural health program. In spite of continued threats, he refused to leave the country because, he said, his life was with the Cakchiquel community.

And yet when Ríos Montt seized the presidency in March 1982, Doc Behrhorst welcomed the evangelical preacher as the savior of his people. They became friends, and Behrhorst collaborated with the civic action and "Love Lift" phase of Ríos Montt's strategy in the Ixil Triangle, while turning a blind eye on his scorched-earth policies. After Ríos Montt was unseated by Mejía Víctores in 1983, Doctor Behrhorst's spirit finally broke and morale in the clinic declined, practically overnight.

When I visited Behrhorst in 1983, he confirmed that one-third of his health promoters had been killed in the aldeas. But now he blamed the guerrillas exclusively for provoking the army's reprisals. And he insisted that Mayas were as distrustful of the ladino guerrilla commanders as they were of the ladino military. In the depths of his consternation Doc Behrhorst, the good paternalistic country doctor who prided himself on his horse sense, appeared to have fallen prey to Ríos Montt's messianic delusions. With an unblinking eye he told me, "A lot of folks are saying that I work hand in glove with the military. Nothing could be farther from the truth. Why, I had lunch with Ríos Montt just the other day, and he promised to speak with Mejía Víctores about raising one million quetzales for our clinic."

A number of courageous Cakchiquel midwives, nurses, and health promoters who were devoted to Behrhorst expressed confusion and dismay at his change of heart. "I no longer know what to think," said Hortensia, a midwife from Comalapa who had worked with the hospital from its inception in 1964. "Doc's friendship with Ríos Montt seems to be taking him away from us. Without steady direction from Doctor Behrhorst we have become like orphaned children, and our hearts are no longer in our work."

After the ouster of Ríos Montt, Doc Behrhorst phased himself out of his medical post in the clinic, and he trained a Guatemalan staff to replace him. He told me that he did not care to be referred to as the "Guatemalan Albert Schweitzer," as I had titled an admiring op-ed piece published in the *New York Times*. "These people don't need that kind of paternalism. They can stand on their own two feet." But Doc retained the presidency of the Behrhorst Foundation, the international body in charge of fund-raising and the overall administration of the project. By then, the Behrhorst paramedic and preventive-medicine programs had become prototypes for rural health promotion throughout the third world. It was Doc's fate that admiration for his pioneering achievement would peak just as the clinic and its rural extension program were disintegrating, first from the army's unrelenting assaults and then from internal demoralization and collapse. An old friend of Behrhorst's compared the clinic's decline to a healthy plant that curls inward and dies after releasing its spores.

In 1985 the Virginia-based Christian Children's Fund, whose chairman sits on the Behrhorst Foundation's board of directors, named a Guatemalan surgeon to head the clinic. The new director proceeded to place his ladino associates in management positions, while attempting to discredit and expel the indigenous staff members who had been with Doc Behrhorst from the beginning. By 1987 Guatemalans had taken over management of the clinic, which was rife with favoritism, kickbacks, absenteeism, and the other forms of internal corruption that overtake too many Guatemalan institutions.

Hospital attendance dropped by two-thirds; the rural extension and preventive-medicine programs were eliminated. In the spring of 1989, the parish priest of Chimaltenango proposed a street march to protest the corruption and mismanagement of the clinic. But Doc advised against it, arguing that he did not want the clinic's internal squabbles aired in the press.

When I ran into Doc Behrhorst in Antigua that summer, he appeared to be his normal rubicund self and spoke with his accustomed aplomb. He had been teaching rural health at Tulane for two years, but his heart remained in Guatemala's highlands. With a saddened countenance, he said he intended to dissociate his name from the clinic because it no longer served its founding purpose. Instead, he was starting a new community health program in the altiplano, to be called the New Dawn.

On May 6, 1990, Doc Behrhorst returned to Chimaltenango to get his new health project off the ground. He had told friends he felt full of renewed energy and planned to live another twenty-five years. That same afternoon he suffered a massive heart attack. He died in the hospital later that night.

I attended the funeral services at his hilltop home in Chimaltenango, which was packed with hundreds of his hospital staff and former patients, nearly all of them Cakchiquel Mayas. Doc's loyal assistants, Margarita and Hortensia, keened and mourned aloud, repeating over and over, "He is gone, the father of us all is gone." The few dozen pale faces belonged to gringo friends and to members of Doc's extended family that included ten children by his two wives. Among the handful of ladinos present was a pastor with Ríos Montt's Church of the Word. Doc's Cakchiquel widow, Alicia, an evangelical convert, had invited him to deliver the eulogy. The preacher praised Doc as a great champion and public servant who would be triumphantly resurrected during the Last Days.

After the service, and before the long funeral cortege left for Doc's final resting place, whispered rumors circulated about Doc's heavy drinking in the past years and about his heartbreak over hundreds of thousands of dollars that vanished from the ledgers of the clinic that still bears his name. Perhaps the heaviest blow had been the death of his close friend and former chief health promoter, Pedro Chacaj, killed in a freak accident two months earlier. Hortensia confided that his enemies in the clinic had paid a brujo two hundred quetzales to put a curse on Chacaj, and she suggested they were capable of doing the same to Doc Behrhorst.

When the violence came to Chimaltenango, Carroll Behrhorst had chosen silence and by his own admission sacrificed principle in order to remain at his post. By doing so, he may have shielded members of his staff who would otherwise have been killed. And yet in the end he was shut out of the institution he had created and to which he dedicated his life. The ladinos he disdained had seized on his mistakes in their efforts to break him, while the Cakchiquel community forgave him all his contradictions, only to perpetuate them after his death. Doc's departure from this world was attended by the paternalism and superstition he had deplored. As a final irony, his funeral service was conducted by evangelical missionaries associated with those he had turned his back on when he married into the Cakchiquel community, and before Ríos Montt came on the scene.

VINICIO CEREZO

"What we'd give to have an Arbenz now. We are going
to have to invent one, but all the candidates are dead."
A State Department official, 1979

"A government that does not abuse does not govern."
*Attributed to an army officer involved in the
overthrow of Ríos Montt, 1983*

Juan José Arévalo, Guatemala's Spiritual Socialist, is now praised as its greatest modern president by military officers and conservative politicians, whose predecessors attempted no less than twenty-seven coups d'état against his civilian government between 1945 and 1951. (He was rescued by loyal officers, among them his Minister of Defense Jacobo Arbenz Guzmán, who would succeed him as president.) After leaving office, Arévalo wrote that Guatemala is governed by two chief executives, one of whom holds a gun to the head of the other.

In 1986, shortly after he was elected president, Vinicio Cerezo expanded on Arévalo's apothegm. He said, "If we institute reform measures that affect private enterprise and don't take the army into account, we shall be overthrown; and if we attack the army without having the business sector on our side, the result would be the same." As it happened, Cerezo had already decided where to throw in his lot.

Two years before, in a pamphlet titled "The Army and the Christian Democrats: An Alternative," Cerezo had set out to neutralize the gun he knew would be pointed at his temple. The pamphlet set down guidelines for a political alignment between moderate elements within the army and his Christian Democratic party. The opponents were the right-wing bankers, industrialists, and latifundistas who had been the bane of his candidacy, working in tandem with unnamed "foreign interests." After a year in office, Cerezo pushed through as Army Chief of Staff General Héctor Alejandro Gramajo, a moderate who kept his pledge to uphold at least the outward forms of a constitutional democracy. Gramajo, who was later named Minister of Defense, twice saved Cerezo's office—and his own—by putting down the *cuartelazos,* or barracks coups, mounted by dissatisfied midlevel officers on May 11, 1988, and again on May 9, 1989. But each of the coup attempts resulted in concessions by Cerezo to the hard-line military, which allowed him to remain in office only at the price of crippling reductions in the democratic political space.

Cerezo's presidency appeared to have a more auspicious beginning than that of Julio César Méndez Montenegro, the only other popularly elected civilian president since Arévalo. In 1966, Méndez Montenegro was permitted to assume the office he won at the polls only after signing an eight-point agreement with an officer corps that was armed, trained, and advised by the U.S. military. The secret pact, which has since become public, gave the military authority to appoint their own minister of defense and chief of staff and to carry on the war against the leftist insurgency as they saw fit.

Immediately after his election, Cerezo assured a gathering of journalists, at which I was present, that he would never submit to a similar humiliation; and that he would rather resign to expose the army's hollow pledges—and provoke a popular uprising—than remain in office as the military's stooge. In two interviews I've had with Cerezo since then, he sounded considerably more cautious. Cerezo, I discovered, has the chameleon's ability to alter his coloration to suit the political moment. And he is also endowed with the supple politician's instinct for playing to the prejudices of his interlocutors.

During his presidential campaign, Cerezo banked on the respect he had gained by surviving three attempts on his life. "A Democrat does not have the right to be naive," he told Harry Reasoner on "60 Minutes," to explain why he travels with a heavy escort and a small arsenal of weapons. He subscribes to *Soldier of Fortune* magazine and practices martial arts, including karate, in which he is a black belt. (In the summer of 1988 a rumor circulated that he had shot and wounded—or killed—an intruder in his presidential study who fired at him at point-blank range and somehow missed.)

At the opportune moment, Cerezo has proven adept at exchanging the macho warrior and ladies' man reputations for that of the paternalistic conciliator. His favorite political term is *concertación*: government by consensus. In a sense, Cerezo attempted to cheat Arévalo's formula by splitting himself into two mandatories, the democratic statesman and the president who holds the gun.

Cerezo, a pro-labor lawyer and civil rights advocate, was forty-three when he became president of Guatemala in 1986 with close to a 70 percent majority over the center-right candidate of the Union of the National Center (UCN), Jorge Carpio Nicolle. Cerezo was only twelve when the CIA organized the invasion from Honduras that replaced Jacobo Arbenz with the first of nine repressive military regimes. "I was leaning against a tree watching and crying as the planes circled over the capital," he told an interviewer prior to the election. "I did not have a clear idea of what was happening but felt we were losing our sense of freedom and human rights, and I decided then that we would have to struggle in order to get them back."

Cerezo's inauguration speech on January 14 was high-minded and eloquent. He talked of the deep-seated corruption and the violence that afflicts the country's 4 million Mayas. He also complained of having inherited an empty treasury. Without spelling out specific reforms, he pleaded for time and understanding to help him reestablish civilian authority after thirty years of military rule.

The limits placed on his office by the military he courted became evident during his first six months in office, when he allowed to stand a number of decrees passed by Mejía Víctores shortly before he stepped down. They provided for the continuation of the civilian defense patrols to assure military control in the countryside and amnesty from prosecution for all crimes committed by both sides in the military conflict. And although Cerezo disbanded the Department of Special Investigations (DIT), which was most likely involved in the early attempts on his life, he never moved against the military's own formidable intelligence apparatus. The dreaded G-2 is held accountable for widespread assassinations of political and trade union leaders, university professors and students, journalists and priests—in short, the full spectrum of the military's opponents.

Despite an unrelenting campaign from the Group of Mutual Support (GAM), Cerezo never yielded to its demands to prosecute three high-echelon army officers whom they accused of masterminding the disappearances of their relatives and loved ones. And neither the Supreme Court nor any of the Human Rights Commissions appointed by the government acted on a single one of over fifteen hundred writs of habeas corpus presented by GAM and other advocacy groups in the names of the disappeared.

Nineth García, the only founding member of GAM who has not been murdered or driven into exile, is a young schoolteacher whose husband, a university student and union leader, was "disappeared" in 1984. García proved herself to be Cerezo's match in both eloquence and courage. She requested that distinguished international figures like Adolfo Pérez Esquivel, the Argentine winner of the Nobel Peace Prize, head a commission to investigate the military's role in thousands of murders and disappearances. And she embarrassed Cerezo by dismissing some of his democratic initiatives, such as his dissolution of DIT, as a "diversionary tactic that changes nothing." In April 1986, when GAM members held their weekly vigil in front of the National Palace, Cerezo shouted from the balcony, "I am with the people, and GAM does not represent the people of Guatemala." But GAM has refused to go away, and its international reputation grew to the point that a British parliamentary group nominated GAM for the Nobel Peace Prize. (Since then, Rigoberta Menchú has also been nominated and was awarded the Nobel Peace Prize in 1992.) In his attempt to distance GAM from the political center, Cerezo seriously underestimated its strength.

In his inauguration and in several subsequent statements, Cerezo emphasized that his five-year presidency was a transition toward effective democracy and that it would only begin to deal with Guatemala's deeply rooted problems. After the dust raised by campaign promises settled, he confessed that he did not expect to hold more than 30 percent of actual power during his first two years in office and 70 percent by the end of his term. The reverse now appears to have been closer to the mark.

On human rights issues, the conservation of energy resources, education, and the environment, Cerezo's record has been a checkered one, at best. Although political crimes declined during his first two years in office, delinquency and drug-related offenses rose calamitously. Vigilante death squadrons such as the Avenging Jaguar and the Secret Anticommunist Army returned to threaten prominent civil rights activists like Nineth García and Amílcar Méndez and to spread terror in the countryside. Although the far right remained divided, its proponents managed to keep Cerezo and the democratic opening off balance by invoking the communist menace and mounting repeated coup attempts. In August 1989, Cerezo accused the far right of the assassination of his Christian Democrat ally, Danilo Barillas. Anonymous callers claimed Barillas was killed for having organized the talks in Madrid between guerrilla commanders and government officials, when he was ambassador to Spain. In the following weeks ten university student leaders disappeared, and their bodies began appearing in the streets, horribly mutilated. Shortly after that, visiting Salvadoran socialist Héctor Oquelí and Guatemalan Social Democrat Gilda Flores were killed in a death squad operation that may have involved collusion between Salvadoran and Guatemalan intelligence services. As a result of these and a rising number of other political murders, the U.S. State Department issued a negative travel advisory for the first time during Cerezo's presidency.

After his election, Cerezo had dragged his heels in naming an Attorney for Human Rights, or ombudsman, as he had pledged to do. Part of the problem, unquestionably, was the ombudsman's short life expectancy, which discouraged many qualified candidates from applying for the job. In August 1987, he finally appointed the seemingly inoffensive octogenarian lawyer and Christian Democrat, Gonzalo Menéndez de la Riva. Less than a year later, he stung the president by siding with private enterprise in denouncing Cerezo's proposed tax increases as a human rights violation. Menéndez de la Riva was understandably slow to investigate the killings in Aguacate and hundreds of other murders and disappearances, a task that would require cool nerves as well as determined legwork. Menéndez de la Riva resigned from his post in October 1989, after charging that he had not received the government support he required to carry out his official functions. He was replaced by Ramiro de León Carpio, a much younger attorney who pursued human rights violations with a more visible energy and perseverance. Although de León Carpio gained credibility as an advocate for the rights of Guatemala's disadvantaged, his hands were tied when he was confronted with major crimes such as the Aguacate massacre or the death squads' kidnapping and assassination of dozens of prominent Guatemalans.

Among his unquestioned accomplishments, Cerezo deserves credit for proposing and backing the Protected Areas Statutes. One of the more effective lobbyists for environmental protection happens to be his eldest son, Marco Vinicio Cerezo Blandón, a law school graduate on the President's National Reconstruction Committee who pressed Congress for the passage of wider legislation to protect the nation's forests. (Since his father left office, Cerezo Blandón has been involved in corruption charges of his own.)

Despite his laudable Protected Areas initiative, Cerezo was unable to prevent the depletion of basic energy resources, notably firewood and water, which has reached crisis proportions in many highland areas. He appeared helpless in the face of the $1 billion disaster known as the Chixoy Hydroelectric Project, a massive dam on the Río Negro built during Lucas García's presidency that ended up costing Guatemala nearly the equivalent of its foreign debt. The construction of Chixoy involved extensive high-level defalcations and outright incompetence that spanned three military governments. The plant's cement tunnel is so porously constructed, millions of dollars are spent to repair it every two years. Deforestation of the river basin where the dam is located is causing severe siltation and other ecological problems that further impair the plant's efficiency. Even if the dam is kept from collapsing altogether, its working life will be a fraction of what its designers projected.

Cerezo's record on public health support was abysmal. His health minister, Gehlert Mata, arguably the most incompetent and corrupt member of his cabinet, virtually ignored the scandalous paucity of health services in the Mayan highland communities. In 1990 only a small number of the 540 rural health posts were functional, and nearly 20,000 communities had no health services of any kind.

Cerezo's alignment with Gramajo and other moderate officers enabled him to survive a full term in office. But political attrition prevented him from pushing through his package of social and economic reforms. During his last year in office, Cerezo often behaved like a lame-duck president, upstaged and outmaneuvered by presidential hopefuls from his own party, among them his politically savvy first lady, Raquel Blandón de Cerezo. Her bold but ill-fated feminist campaign ended when she was constitutionally disqualified from running. René de León Schlotter, the Christian Democrats' patriarch, left the party to ally himself with the struggling Social Democrats, the only left-of-center party participating in the elections. During his unsuccessful campaign, de León Schlotter excoriated Cerezo and his economic policies, insisting that lust for power had blinded his former protégé to social injustices. Toward the end of his term, Cerezo unexpectedly came out swinging against the ten opposition candidates, challenging the leaders to television debates as though he rather than his hapless heir apparent, ex-Foreign Minister Alfonso Cabrera Hidalgo, was running for office.

For all his frustrations in the domestic arena, Cerezo had one notable triumph on the international stage. He initiated the regional peace negotiations that came to be known as Esquipulas I and II. To Cerezo's chagrin, his Costa Rican colleague Oscar Arias would receive most of the credit for the forum's partial success.

Although the member nations' slack compliance with the peace resolutions—including Guatemala's—are a matter of record, the accords defused rising tensions in the region, at least temporarily. And they produced one significant symbolic achievement: for the first time in history, five Central American presidents had met and defied the will of the colossus to the north. Their unanimous vote to demobilize the Contras in August 1989 was a slap in the face to U.S. hegemony in the region dating from the Monroe Doctrine. Cerezo's endorsement of active neutrality, a policy he inherited from his predecessor's foreign minister, Andrade Durán, kept Guatemala from becoming entangled in other Central American conflicts. It also enabled Cerezo to stay at arm's length from President Reagan's anti-Sandinista game plan in Nicaragua, although the country ultimately paid the price in sharply diminished military and economic aid from Washington.

Cerezo's enhanced stature in Europe and Latin America in the early stages of his presidency helped him ride out assaults on his domestic program; but it did not procure him the major foreign assistance he hoped for to stabilize the economy. And Arias's Nobel Peace Prize eclipsed his ambitions to become known as Central America's peacemaker.

Cerezo passed legislature to erect new rural municipalities and marketplaces and lay down hundreds of paved streets in remote villages that asked instead for medicines and schools. He signed laws that created a standard alphabet for the twenty-one Maya-speaking communities and protected their rights to a bilingual education. But Cerezo's attempts to ingratiate himself with the indigenous majority and the labor unions were undermined by his mismanagement of the economy and by the widespread corruption that marked the second half of his administration—two scandals that were skillfully exploited by his enemies in the private sector.

Ironically, one of the developments that temporarily saved Guatemala's economy from a crippling recession was the millions of U.S. dollars sent back yearly by the thousands of displaced campesinos who had made their way—like the ill-starred brother and sister in the film *El Norte*—to the industrial cities of the north. The dollar sign that had symbolized the oppression of Guatemala's indigenous majority became the hallmark of the Mayas' newfound economic power. But even they could not prevent the collapse of the quetzal by the autumn of 1990, when its worth against the dollar plummeted by two-thirds. Inflation soared to an unprecedented 50 percent, matching the country's rate of unemployment.

By 1987, 68 percent of Guatemala's population had fallen below the poverty line, as defined by United Nations guidelines. In 1990, estimates rose to 73 percent, making Guatemala's poor majority the largest in Central America. Conversely, 67 percent of Guatemalans polled in July 1989 voiced support for the democratic process; one year later, the figure had dropped to a dismal 23 percent approval rate. Opposition leaders began speaking of the eighties as "the lost decade."

Guatemalans' disenchantment with democracy was fueled in about equal measure by the economic collapse, administrative corruption, and the explosive political violence. International condemnation of Guatemala's human rights violations has been unequivocally harsh. Costa Rica's Human Rights Commission and Americas Watch reported over four hundred extrajudicial executions in 1988 and again in 1989 and hundreds of unsolved disappearances. In 1990 these figures rose even higher. The usually circumspect U.S. State Department wrote in its 1990 report on Guatemala that "there continued to be credible reports of security force personnel and political extremists engaging in extrajudicial killings, disappearances, and other serious abuses."

Perhaps only history can judge if Cerezo let slip a golden opportunity when he was elected president by a convincing majority, the largest of any president since Arévalo. He chose an alliance with a more accommodating sector of the army, rather than forge his millions of dispossessed and hungry supporters into the populist presidency he had projected in his campaign. (It may also never be known whether he could have driven a wedge between the retrograde chambers of commerce and agriculture and the more flexible younger entrepreneurs.) At the end of Cerezo's third year in office, attrition had exposed the sad deficiency of talent in his cabinet and government bureaucracy. Too many Christian Democrat mayors, cabinet officers, and congressmen had fallen victim to the violence in the past two decades. This fatally damaged grassroots infrastructure only served to highlight Cerezo's personal shortcomings.

Like his fellow Christian Democrat Napoleón Duarte, Cerezo may have raised expectations too high before taking office. The decline of Duarte's fortunes in El Salvador had inevitable repercussions on Cerezo's presidency. Both seemed men with strong convictions, a stubborn will, and a charisma that gave the appearance of power but lacked the substance. The defeated center-right candidate, Jorge Carpio Nicolle of UCN, who publishes the influential daily *El Gráfico*, regained some support from the traditional right by linking Cerezo's policies to Duarte's political and economic failures. But these attacks did not compensate for an insubstantial, wilting candidacy, and Carpio lost the 1990 runoff election by a landslide to evangelical Jorge Serrano Elías.

During his last eighteen months in office, Cerezo's often brittle sense of humor showed signs of cracking. He was jeered for dubbing himself, only half in jest, the best president in Guatemala's history; and he hinted he would not be adverse to reforming the Constitution in order to run for a second term.

Like other decent but underendowed public servants before him, Cerezo ended by covering up his failures and disappointments with unseemly bluster and vainglory. And, in sharp contrast to his model and mentor Juan José Arévalo, Cerezo left office vastly enriched and hounded by scandal over extravagances like his luxurious thirty-five-foot yacht, *Odysseus,* and his rumored multimillion-dollar island retreat in the Mediterranean, for which he reportedly outbid Julio Iglesias. Suspicions of possible links to the international mafia were fanned by Cerezo's dogged promotion—against nearly unanimous opposition—of a multimillion-dollar race track and casino complex to be erected next to the international airport. The initiative faded away after the outbreak of the Persian Gulf crisis.

Toward the end of his term even Cerezo's bolder measures backfired. His call for a ten-quetzal ($2) minimum daily wage so incensed plantation owners and industrialists, they resorted to mass firings rather than pay their workers the equivalent of an additional forty U.S. cents a day. At the behest of Alfonso Cabrera, Cerezo named a tough new chief of police, Julio Caballeros, in an attempt to stem the spiral of violence. It was a case of locking the barn door after the horse has bolted. In spite of tightened police controls, political killings during Cerezo's final weeks rose to their highest levels since the early eighties. Among the death squad victims were an independent news agency director and his wife, two congressmen, a social science investigator, a radio interviewer and commentator. Even Sandoval Alarcón, the godfather of death squadrons, came back into the picture when his politician son Fernando Sandoval and a friend shot and killed two supposed assailants on a motorcycle. Police Chief Caballeros abruptly dropped his investigation when Sandoval Alarcón rose to his son's defense, growling menacingly, "Do not mess with God or the Christ of Esquipulas." This last was a reference to the patron saint of his home district, whose handwoven likeness Sandoval had presented to a guerrilla commander in Madrid.

In late July 1989, President Cerezo granted me an hour-long interview I had requested a month before, to discuss the Petén conservation statutes and his presidential legacy. Forty thousand underpaid schoolteachers nationwide were in the seventh week of a dangerously volatile strike, and the postal workers, who had also walked out to demand pay raises, had been joined by three other government dependencies. The MLN (Movement for National Liberation) was calling for Cerezo's resignation six weeks after the latest military coup attempt, and the threat of anarchy hung in the air. On entering the president's study in the National Palace I found him jarringly buoyant, almost euphoric.

Cerezo began by spelling out his accomplishments, ranging from his role as architect and host of the Esquipulas Peace Accords, to his creditable contributions to a climate propitious for the democratic process. He assured me that Gramajo's successors as Army Chief of Staff and Minister of Defense would be just as firm in their commitment to constitutional government. The president expressed particular satisfaction about the Protected Areas Statutes and his revocation of logging licenses in the Petén. Clearly, he was enjoying his self-investiture as Central America's "Green President."

On the touchy subject of drug trafficking, Cerezo grudgingly acknowledged the Colombian cartels were using Guatemala as a cocaine bridgehead to Mexico and the United States. He took credit for recent seizures of huge cocaine and heroin shipments by an expanded treasury police but admitted the problem threatened to grow out of control. At the time, the U.S. Drug Enforcement Agency estimated that 4,500 acres of Guatemalan territory were being used for poppy cultivation, which would convert to a $2 to $5 billion heroin trade on U.S. streets. In response to the charges of indiscriminate herbicide spraying in marijuana and poppy-growing regions of Petén and San Marcos, Cerezo assured me the DEA operations were being carefully monitored to prevent further destruction of fruit and vegetable orchards. A report in *Newsweek* claimed hundreds of peasants had turned to poppy cultivation after their tomato crops were contaminated by the DEA's excessive application of glyphosphate.

In an abrupt shift, Cerezo deplored the Bush administration's delay in extending a long-promised $80 million loan to help balance Guatemala's payments and the servicing of its foreign debt. "We are only now receiving the 20,000 M-16 rifles that were contracted for a decade ago and a few helicopter replacement parts that are equally overdue. These delays appear to be related to U.S. dissatisfaction with policies we've inherited from previous Guatemalan governments. Only last week, a U.S. intelligence service attempted to implicate my foreign minister, Alfonso Cabrera, in an alleged heroin drop with one of his brothers." President Cerezo paused, and lowered his voice to a confidential tone. "This is an obvious attempt to keep us off balance and damage our international prestige. Another consequence is a growing impatience within regressive elements of the army, which have twice attempted to overturn our emerging democracy." Cerezo shrugged his shoulders and smiled. "You have to understand that if I don't keep the generals happy, I will be overthrown."

President Cerezo's jauntiness took on an eerie air. Surrounded by the symbols of high office, his vulnerabilities had made him a captive of his own army and of the U.S. government's perceived interests. For all his claims to the contrary, Cerezo had fallen into the very trap a younger and brasher candidate Cerezo had promised to avoid at all costs.

President Cerezo's decline, and Washington's evident distaste for Alfonso Cabrera, persuaded George Bush's handpicked ambassador to Guatemala, his old Yale crony and fellow oilman Thomas F. Stroock, that the Guatemalan military was the only credible guarantor of Guatemala's frail democracy. Ambassador Stroock also regarded the generals as the most effective deterrent against a massive penetration by the Medellín drug cartel.

(When the dynamic leader of CERJ, Amílcar Méndez, questioned Ambassador Stroock on U.S. support for the unconstitutional civil patrols, he replied that "we" intend to keep the patrols until after the elections, to ensure an orderly transition. A testy Ambassador Stroock pointedly suggested to Méndez, who has since been awarded both the Jimmy Carter and Robert Kennedy citations for his human rights monitoring work, that he should be thankful General Gramajo was the Minister of Defense.)

General Gramajo's replacement as Minister of Defense, General Juan Leonel Bolaños Chávez, seemed perfectly cut out for both of Ambassador Stroock's assignments. Bolaños descends from a moderate wing of the army that dates back to Arévalo, and his pledge to support Gramajo's democratic renovation played well in Washington. Ambassador Stroock congratulated Cerezo and the army when they indicted five soldiers for the murder of U.S. national Michael DeVine. But as the case wore on, it became apparent that the murder and subsequent cover-up involved officers at the highest levels of the military. These new revelations added fuel to the accusations made in June 1990 by a cashiered army official, José Fernando Minera Navas, who implicated high-ranking army and police officers in the traffic of cocaine and heroin. Although Minera Navas's countersuit was dropped when the courts cleared him of drug-connected charges, Ambassador Stroock's decisive tilt toward the army—a throwback to U.S. complicity in military takeovers in Guatemala—still threatened to blow up in his face.

A noteworthy result of Cerezo's democratic opening was the slow, painful rehabilitation of Jacobo Arbenz Guzmán. The ten-year "Guatemalan Spring" of 1944–1954 returned to haunt the country with visions of what might have been if Arbenz's agrarian revolution had been permitted to run its course. For the first time since his overthrow in 1954, the press portrayed Arbenz as a patriotic and "correct" military officer and president whose worst mistake had been to underestimate his enemies. A new centrist daily, *Siglo XXI* (Twenty-first Century), ran two series of articles downplaying the long-standing charge that Arbenz harbored communists in his government. And yet the record stands that Arbenz relied on his communist ministers and other members of the Guatemalan Workers Party (PGT) to implement his agrarian reform. (Arbenz's Agrarian Reform Agency distributed parcels of public and private lands to 500,000 campesinos in a little over eighteen months, a remarkable feat by any measure.) Guatemalan historian Eduardo Weymann Fuentes argued persuasively that Arévalo's and Arbenz's reforms were far closer in spirit to Franklin Roosevelt's New Deal than they were to the socialist revolutions of Salvador Allende and Fidel Castro. However, these nationalist historians tend to overlook the internal opposition to Arévalo's and Arbenz's reform programs, which was as determined as that of the United Fruit Company and the CIA. Arbenz's role in the unintended 1949 assassination of popular conservative Major Francisco Javier Arana, who was his chief rival for the presidency, caused deep cleavages in the military high command and may have doomed Arbenz's presidency even before he took office.

On October 8, 1990, three months before the end of Cerezo's term, Juan José Arévalo died of a heart attack at the age of eighty-six. Thousands of Guatemalans filed past his bier as he lay in state in the presidential chapel of the National Palace, fifty yards from Cerezo's study. Although he lived his final years in semiobscure retirement enforced by his nearly total deafness, Arévalo was often seen walking the streets of the capital without the obligatory armed escort, and his lifestyle remained simple and frugal. To his last days, Arévalo appeared the dignified, classically handsome figure I had looked up to in my roller skates on the day of his inauguration, as he addressed cheering crowds from the palace balcony. Although I was barely ten at the time, I sensed I was in the presence of a great man.

Arévalo's death led to an outpouring of praise by the heirs of politicians, generals, and newspaper columnists who had reviled him when he was president and who used his newfound virtues to berate Cerezo. Arévalo's speeches and writings, reprinted in the press for the first time since the early 1950s, revealed a statesman of global stature as well as an orator and writer of distinction. In his valedictory address of 1951, which overnight has become required reading in schools and universities, Arévalo spoke in elegiac tones of his "terrible and fecund" six years as president. Arévalo made no bones about his animosity toward the United Fruit Company and its Praetorian guards, Eisenhower's Secretary of State John Foster Dulles and his brother Allen, who had been the company's attorney before taking over the CIA. Arévalo lamented that Hitler's ideology had survived his military defeat and denounced the "little Hitlers" who were assuming power throughout the world, in league with the New Carthaginians whose greed-driven machinations threatened democratic institutions he had fought to preserve. Arévalo's uncanny foreshadowing of Eisenhower's speech warning of the military/industrial complex spared Eisenhower himself, even though he gave the order for the overthrow of Arévalo's elected successor. Arévalo, the "spiritual socialist" who fathered most of Guatemala's surviving social and political reforms, would later praise Eisenhower as "the pacifist general" who was ill-served by his cabinet.

After standing watch beside Arévalo's bier, Cerezo lauded him as an exemplary public servant whose life should serve as a model for the country's youth. The ill-timed eulogy drew derisive jeers from mourners gathered outside the palace. Stung by the crowd's reaction, Cerezo chose not to attend Arévalo's funeral and sent his wife, Raquel Blandón, in his place.

In July 1991, seven months into Jorge Serrano's troubled presidency, Cerezo's Christian Democrats gathered for a weekend convention at the Belén Convent in Antigua, where I happened to be on a month-long retreat to complete this manuscript. The mood of the gathering was unexpectedly jovial as the Christian Democrats, who still enjoyed a dominant presence in Congress, exulted over the persisting spiral of violence and the sputtering economic performance that had Serrano's administration off balance and increasingly divided.

Vinicio Cerezo looked every inch the fat-cat elder statesman. He had put on weight, and the sheen of comfortable prosperity replaced the aura of presidential power. Cerezo seemed untroubled by the charges of corruption that had stained his last years in office and that led to ongoing legal suits against him and several of his cohorts. And he looked equally untouched by the burgeoning scandal of his administration's dubious transactions with the Bank of Credit and Commerce International. Anson Ng, a free-lance correspondent for London's *Financial Times* investigating Guatemala's shady links to the BCCI, had been murdered ten days before, and U.S. Senator Alan Cranston suggested on the Senate floor that the two events were interrelated. Meanwhile, a report in *Time* magazine directly implicated Vinicio Cerezo, his brother Milton, former Defense Minister Gramajo, and two other military officers in a highly questionable deal involving the purchase of three helicopters from Jordan. The middleman in the negotiations, Munther Bilbeisi, a notorious Jordanian arms dealer and contrabandist, had been named in an indictment by Guatemala's Interior Ministry. Bilbeisi was charged with bribing government officials in connection with a $4 million coffee contraband operation financed in part by the BCCI. The suit had been abruptly dropped, without explanation, while Cerezo was still president.

Overcoming his visible discomfiture at our unplanned encounter in such an unlikely setting, Cerezo parried my questions with his customary dexterity. I reminded him of his boast during our interview two years earlier that his government was diversifying its arms imports with the purchase of three helicopters from Jordan.

"Wasn't that purchase negotiated with Mr. Munther Bilbeisi?" I queried Cerezo. "And did it not result in handsome commissions for you and several military officers?"

Ex-president Cerezo did not blink an eye. "Oh yes, the notorious

Mr. Bilbeisi. He was our initial contact, but that is all. We bought the three Sikorsky helicopters directly from Jordan."

According to *Time,* I reminded him, the deal had been financed through the BCCI.

"Absolutely not. I am writing to one of your senators, who has made baseless accusations linking me to illicit deals, to emphasize that our negotiations with BCCI involved financing for agricultural projects and other nonmilitary initiatives. This has all been duly documented and forms part of the public record." As a smiling Mother Superior approached to greet the former president, he laughed out loud and congratulated me on not having lost my journalistic acumen.

"President Cerezo," I got in, hearing my voice break, "I believed you five years ago when you said yours would be a government of transition; but I thought you meant transition toward democracy, not to uncontrolled corruption and disintegration."

Slipping an arm around the beaming Mother Superior, Vinicio Cerezo introduced me—straightfaced—as an old chum with whom he was carrying on a lifelong, open-ended debate.

Subsequent articles in *Time, Crónica,* and other publications verified that Munther Bilbeisi, President of Mura International, and the BCCI were directly involved in the Guatemalan government's purchase of two executive-type Sikorsky helicopters and one ambulance. The transaction allegedly resulted in commissions of $400,000 for agents of BCCI, $270,000 for Milton Cerezo, and $150,000 for Generals Roberto Mata Gálvez and Edgar Godoy Gaitán.

15

Profiles and Portents II

FATHER GIRÓN

"For God's sake, tell your countrymen not to send us
these lethal pesticides. Tell them to send us tractors
instead, and farm tools instead of M-16's."

Father Andrés Girón

Early in May 1986, a corpulent priest in white cassock, white straw
hat, and dark glasses led sixteen thousand landless campesinos on a
147-kilometer march from the coastal town of Nueva Concepción
to the National Palace. As they entered Guatemala City, the lines of
Mayan and ladino peasant marchers in straw hats stretched one kilometer behind. The normally unexcitable spectators on the formerly
posh Sexta Avenida, who had not seen anything like this since the
Arbenz era, erupted in spontaneous applause. President Vinicio Cerezo and Raquel Blandón appeared on the palace balcony to greet the
marchers. In a brief address, the president pledged to study their
demands for cultivable farmlands and give them a reply within a
month.

The man at the head of the march was Father Andrés Girón de
León, who founded the first Guatemalan agrarian movement of any
consequence since the overthrow of Jacobo Arbenz three decades
earlier.

In the weeks following the dramatic march, spokesmen for the bankers' and landowners' lobbies attempted to paint Father Girón with a red brush. They accused him of being secretly in league with Cerezo to stir up discontent and reawaken the specter of agrarian reform. Undaunted, Girón responded that he was not interested in invasions or appropriations of private lands; he intended to purchase fallow nationalized or bank-mortgaged farms on credit, as was the right of any citizen under the new Constitution.

From his parish in Nueva Concepción and Tiquisate, near the heart of banana, sugar, and cotton-growing country, Father Girón founded in February 1986 the National Peasant Association Pro Lands. Within a few months, to Father Girón's gratified surprise, enrollment skyrocketed to thirty-five thousand members. More than a quarter of the recruits were indigenous campesinos from the highlands, and the rest, ladinos from the Oriente and the coast. Although evangelicals were welcome, about 85 percent of the membership was Catholic.

In July, Father Girón delivered a sermon to five thousand campesinos in Nueva Concepción, in which he spoke out for the acquisition of government lands. Sitting in the audience was Raquel Blandón de Cerezo, who as a self-proclaimed "Advocate of the Poor" had helped draft a secret land-redistribution resolution for the Christian Democrats in 1984.

Only days after Girón delivered his sermon, assassination threats were scrawled on the walls of his parish church and the neighboring hospital. A nasty smear campaign was launched by the right-wing media, linking Raquel "Evita" Blandón and Andrés "the Red Priest" Girón to the communist underground and to one another. In response to the unrelenting bombardment from the press and the far right, the first lady drastically lowered her public profile; Girón for his part reluctantly acquiesced to President Cerezo's offer of armed bodyguards.

Several months after making his pledge to Girón, Cerezo paved the way for the transfer to the Peasant Association of the first of several government-administered fincas. The agreement stipulated that the campesinos would work the lands communally and repay their assessed value, interest-free, with the fruits of their labor.

In August I made my way to Nueva Concepción to track down Father Girón. The steamy, lowland ladino town looked like a front lot for a seedy western. In mid-afternoon, I passed a dozen brothels already open for business and half as many evangelical temples. On the wall of the town's most prominent whorehouse, next to a provocatively seated hooker, a sign read, "Entra y eleva tu vida." (Enter and elevate your life.) The sign could have as aptly hung on Father Girón's door.

In the parish sacristy, a young seminarist led me to Father Girón's study, guarded by two impassive security agents. Directly inside the door sat a Belgian nun of about seventy who has worked with Father Girón for years and another older woman, calmly embroidering a colored cloth, who turned out to be his mother.

"Spanish or English?" exclaimed Father Girón, rising to his feet and shaking my hand energetically. He is a tallish, rotund man with thinning, tousled hair and a sparse mustache. I knew from a recently published book on Girón (see Cambranes: *Agrarismo en Guatemala*, 1986) that he had passed his novitiate in a La Salle Seminary in Glencoe, Missouri, and became a lay brother in the order. He had also marched in Memphis with Coretta and Martin Luther King, Jr., an event that sealed his commitment to nonviolent resistance.

Our interview switched back and forth between the two languages, according to the setting and the sensitivity of the topic. Father Girón began with pungent reminiscences of his experiences in the States, first as novice in Missouri—his happiest years—and later on as parish priest for two years in Oakland, California, and most recently as fundraiser for his association. Father Girón's story was fascinating, and he delivered it with a riveting, theatrical flair. He is an unabashed showman as well as an accomplished raconteur.

Andrés Girón comes of a criollo landowning family in Tecpán, a short distance from the ancient seat of the Cakchiquel nation, Iximché. The "place of corn trees," as its name translates, had served briefly as the quarters for the first Spanish colony on the Central American isthmus.

The Girón family records in the church of Tecpán date from the first years of the Conquest and include a number of cavaliers and missionaries. Father Girón vividly portrayed his formidable grandfather, the patriarch who amassed the family's landed properties. Girón credited his father, a former three-term mayor of Tecpán, with passing on to him his political ambitions, while his pious great aunt and a Belgian missionary who served in China were the inspirations for his religious vocation. Girón remembered playing the role of conquistador with a Cakchiquel classmate, Narciso, who acted the warrior chief in a game of king of the mountain on the ruins of Iximché. In school pageants Andrés was invariably given the part of the priest, and he enjoyed administering the sacraments to his classmates.

Upon his return from the States, Girón chose to remain with the La Salle order, inspired by the French founder's dedication to communal enterprise to benefit the poor. One of his teachers at Glencoe had been a radical cleric named "Joe," who propounded Marxist theology while sporting a black beret, like Che Guevara's. Following an alienating experience in a Mexican seminary, Brother Andrés returned once more to Guatemala and was put to work with poor ladino communities in the Oriente.

His attempts at starting livestock cooperatives in Chiquimula proved a disaster, and he was assigned to head a La Salle school for seven hundred privileged youths in Zacapa. At twenty-four, Brother Girón's future in the order seemed secure. But his admitted repugnance against pandering to the landowners' pampered offspring led to his first confrontation with authority. When he offered fellowships to 240 poor peasants, his superiors countered by closing down the school. For the first time, Girón received anonymous death threats calling him an extremist and a communist subversive. He quit the La Salle order soon after, charging that its founding principles had been compromised by elitism.

"I knew then that I was a revolutionary, in the sense that Jesus was a revolutionary. In Glencoe I was taught that Christ was an ample, many-faceted figure, who could be worshiped as a saint and also emulated as a social reformer. The belief that Jesus converted the fish into loaves of bread by divine dispensation is pure crap. The miracle was that he convinced the wealthy who had bread to share it with the poor."

From that point on, Andrés Girón's story plays like a medieval morality tale in contemporary trappings, culminating with the march to the National Palace that made him a controversial international figure.

On Good Friday in 1974, he was invited to celebrate communion

in the highland town of Comalapa. Girón nearly fainted when the hy-
drocephalic infant of a Maya woman praying at the foot of the crucified Christ suddenly laughed at him. The strange laughter of the
emaciated infant with the grotesquely enlarged head caused something to snap inside Father Girón. He fell to his knees and shook
with spasms of weeping and moaning that frightened worshipers and
alarmed his superiors. "That pitiful infant's laughter burned through
my complacent sense of superiority and let me know I was nothing
but offal, a cipher, in comparison with what he endured every moment of his life. It was then I decided to accept my sacerdotal calling.
I knelt and asked forgiveness of Christ our Lord and pledged to heed
his summons and dedicate my life to the poor and the invalid."

Two years later, the massive earthquake of February 4, 1976, leveled Tecpán. Father Girón drove down from his seminary in Huehuetenango to find hundreds of dead and broken bodies blocking
the entrance to the town. He found his parents alive, but their home
was rubble, and all their possessions had been sacked, including his
precious library of two thousand books. The sixteenth-century
church that had housed the family records was a skeleton of broken
pilasters and twisted girders. Father Girón spent a week burning
corpses to prevent epidemic and burying the remains in a common
grave.

In 1980, as General Romeo Lucas García was stealing the presidency in a fraudulent election, Girón was ordained a priest in the
seminary at Chiantla. Weeks later he organized a religious protest
march with hundreds of faithful incensed by the murders of two U.S.
priests who had worked with the landless poor. Maryknoll Father
Bill Woods, who began a land cooperative movement in the Ixcán,
died in a mysterious plane crash that Girón and others have denounced as a veiled assassination. Father Charles Stetter, who replaced Woods in Huehuetenango, was killed by a death squad, in a
manner similar to the murder of Stan Rother. As a consequence of
that march, whose message got back to Lucas García, Father Girón
had to flee for his life, together with a third Maryknoll father who
had also been threatened.

As Father Girón made his preparations to leave Guatemala, his
father was assassinated in Tecpán. He recalled that weeks earlier,
Mayor Jorge Girón's life had been threatened by a group of Mayas

allied with Lucas García's interior minister, a murderous extortionist. When Andrés's mother began receiving death threats, the family sold its remaining goods and flew to Italy, leaving their ancestral home in Tecpán forever.

Father Girón found no solace being an intern in a parish in Rome, where he felt isolated and remote from his life's work in Guatemala. He applied to the diocese of Oakland, California, and was assigned a parish filled with Chicanos and Latino immigrants. He soon became a popular father confessor, and by his own account, made pots of money from generous parishioners and pilgrims who traveled long distances to be confessed by the *"padre chapín."*

In March 1982, Ríos Montt replaced Lucas García. Father Girón packed his bags and returned to Guatemala, but his political activities put an end to his welcome in the conservative diocese of Huehue-tenango. When he threatened to return to the States, a well-placed friend in the church interceded on his behalf. Girón was given the parish of Tiquisate, the banana-growing province where the United Fruit Company had been headquartered for over half a century, until a U.S. court's antitrust ruling drove them out of the country. And that is where Girón launched his career as agrarian leader and revo-lutionary priest.

Capping off his autobiographical ramble, Father Girón confessed that procuring lands for his thousands of followers was only the springboard for his life's work, which contemplated larger ambitions. "There are 500,000 peasant families in desperate need of land in this country. President Cerezo has promised to make available at most a half-dozen fincas. Apart from that, there are a little over a hundred fincas entering the market, at prices that landowners have artificially inflated in order to sabotage our movement and 'screw the priest and the president too.' Altogether, these fincas add up to less than 50,000 hectares. Even if we could buy all those lands and settle 5,000 fam-ilies a year in them, at an average of 7 hectares per family, it would be at least seventy-five years before we acquired enough lands to accommodate the remaining 495,000 families.

"Our first priority is to bring about profound structural changes in land tenure in this country, but without resorting to violent land invasions, or the large-scale appropriations that brought about Arbenz's downfall. So we are starting with a handful of farms and 35,000 hungry peasants to create viable models for an eventual over-haul of the entire system.

"We will work these lands communally and plant only export crops that bring in the largest returns, beginning with coffee, bananas, and going on to nontraditional crops like cardamom, sorghum, snow peas, cashews—whatever the market demands. I want to move these peasant farmers toward a growing independence from the traditional corn-based milpa. To the Mayas, corn has a sacramental value that is increasingly at variance with its economic worth. At present, we can import corn from Iowa cheaper than we can grow it. The fact is, as our lands become leached, poisoned, and exhausted by our abuse of pesticides and chemical fertilizers, there will not be enough lands for peasant farmers, whose numbers are multiplying at an alarming rate. Come see the thousands of farm laborers who are dying of cancer, right here in my parish, because the water they drink is contaminated by the cotton planters' pesticides. Your country shares responsibility for dumping on us lethal poisons that your own farmers are forbidden from using." Father Girón's voice rose, as he shook with anger. Shaken myself, I asked what could be done.

"Go back and tell your countrymen not to send us these lethal pesticides. Tell them to send tractors instead, and farm tools instead of M-16's. Some of your right-wing congressmen would call me a communist for suggesting this. But I told your Senator Pat Leahy in Vermont, your former ambassador to El Salvador Robert White, and anyone else who would listen, that by helping us provide land and tools to hungry peasants you will be preventing the spread of com-munism, which feeds on hunger and discontent. Tell them to send us agricultural advisers, the latest technology in irrigation, and fer-tilizers. And for God's sake, stop sending us your poisons and weapons!"

By the end of that remarkable interview, I felt that I was in the presence of a charismatic grassroots reformer on the order of India's Vinobe Bhave or Italy's Danilo Dolci, who surface once in a gen-eration. Father's Girón's agrarian reforms would probably have been applauded by Friar Bartolomé de las Casas; and they would likely have goaded into a homicidal rage not only Liberal Reformer Justo

Rufino Barrios, but all his presidential successors until Arévalo. Earlier, I had asked Father Girón if he did not fear the potentially fatal consequences of his radical ideas, given the realities in Guatemala. He told me, as he has reiterated many times since, that his fate was in God's hands.

Just before the end of our interview, a firecracker went off in the church courtyard. Father Girón leapt to his feet. For just an instant, I saw terror in his eyes. It was the same fear I saw reflected in Doctor Behrhorst's face as he described the abduction of his most trusted intern; and that I imagined in Stan Rother's eyes when his favorite catechist was torn off the bannister of the mission church, screaming for help.

Several months later I accepted Father Girón's invitation to visit Málaga, a 2,700-hectare finca Cerezo had promised to the Peasant Association. The transfer of title had dragged for months in the courts, and Father Girón had decided to take action. When I got to the huge farm, at the end of a long, dusty ride that skirted Agua and Fuego volcanoes, I found that several hundred families from Sololá, Totonicapán, and the Oriente had already pitched their tents in one corner. Newspaper headlines would proclaim the following day that Father Girón had broken his pledge and mounted his first land invasion. But President Cerezo immediately scotched the accusations by pointing out that only a technicality stood in the way of a legal transfer, which would be finalized in a matter of days.

I spoke with several of the highland Maya families, whose elders had spent their savings on membership dues and transportation to the finca. They were all eager to get down to work. Sorghum, soya, and cashew were the export crops to be grown in Málaga, followed by watermelon and coffee. The highland farmers had already assessed the optimal yields to be expected, based on their experience with small orchards back home. Their high spirits reminded me of the peasant rallies I had attended in the capital's Parque Central in 1953, when land titles were handed out by officers of Arbenz's Agrarian Reform Agency. The sense of déjà vu sent a chill up my spine.

Father Girón was surrounded by dozens of the new landowners, who peppered him with questions and then listened raptly to his replies. Their affection for him and trust in his judgment were palpable, irrespective of Girón's admission that he had practically no farming experience. I would hear often from campesinos, both Mayas and ladinos, that Father Girón's blunt, earthy vocabulary was the only kind that made any sense to them.

During the few moments I managed to snatch him away, Girón explained that the Maya farmers had taken to communal land cultivation far more readily than the ladinos, who preferred to work their own individual parcels, even when experience showed this to be counterproductive. "The Indian farmer is communalist by nature," he said, "while the ladino is a potential capitalist. What has brought them together here is a common need. But I will keep them in separate fincas, so they can experiment in the methods that are most natural to each."

Another large finca, not far from Chimaltenango, passed into the association's hands several weeks later, and two more fincas were lined up in Escuintla, for banana cultivation. The protests from landowners abated after a meeting between Girón and representatives of the Agriculturalists' Association, UNAGRO, whom he presented with a turkey. But the truce was a fragile one. Toward the end of 1987 UNAGRO began criminal proceedings against Girón. It accused him of inciting thousands of campesinos from the south coast to usurp lands. The suit could have resulted in a six-year sentence for Girón, but UNAGRO never gathered enough evidence to make their legal action stick.

Father Girón distanced himself increasingly from Cerezo, whom he accused of dragging his feet on the title transfers under pressure from landowners. In any event, there was not enough land to meet the demands of association members, whose numbers Girón claimed had risen to nearly 150,000 heads of families. In his sermons and at other public appearances, he talked increasingly of the need for a restructuring of Guatemalan society top to bottom that included health, housing, education, and taxation, as well as land tenure. To many of his followers, and to his enemies, he began to sound like a presidential hopeful.

In July 1987, he became involved in a controversy with Father John Vesey when the cofrades of San Juan la Laguna invited him to celebrate mass at their church. Bishop Fuentes of Sololá complained to Girón's superiors about this breach of clerical protocol, and he was dressed down by his bishop in Escuintla. Rumors circulated in Nueva Concepción that Father Girón was about to be defrocked.

Father Girón continued to make frequent fundraising trips to the States and to Europe, where he was well received by church groups and farmers' associations. In June 1988, he made one of the serious blunders of his career. The newspapers had a field day with Father Girón's investment in 100,000 pairs of inexpensive jeans, which he expected to sell at a profit for the benefit of the association. Shortly after the purchase it was discovered that the EPS label in the back pockets of the jeans stood for "*Ejército Popular Sandinista*" (Popular Sandinista Army). The jeans sat unsold in a warehouse; although Father Girón later recouped a part of his financial losses, he had to absorb the jeers and humiliation in silence.

In village pageants throughout the country, Father Girón began to be represented as a buffoon. The university students' annual *marche macabre* portrayed Father Girón clutching fistfuls of dollars as he sucks up to a papier-mâché Uncle Sam. Nineth García, the head of GAM, lampooned Father Girón's presidential ambitions, referring to him contemptuously as "*el padrecito.*"

In September 1988, several weeks after Father Girón's aunt was intercepted on her way to visit him and killed—the fifth member of his family to die assassinated—he narrowly survived an attempt on his own life. He was driving his white jeep on a back road of Chimaltenango when—according to Girón's account—about twenty-five men in olive fatigues blocked the road. Without saying a word, one of the soldiers shot Girón's bodyguard in the neck and wounded the young seminarist traveling with him. The bodyguard, a family man assigned to Girón by Cerezo, died at the scene. The seminarist, whom Father Girón cared for as an adopted son, recovered quickly from a superficial wound. Father Girón himself was unharmed, a fact that remains at the center of a persisting controversy.

The press, as usual, published conflicting versions, each according to its political slant. *La Prensa* insinuated the assassins were guerrillas whom Father Girón had double-crossed. Another, more credible, version placed the responsibility on hired killers for UNAGRO. A third account had Girón engineering the attempt on his life to gain sympathy, in furtherance of his presidential aspirations. Father Girón disappeared from public view for several months, apparently under instructions from his superiors.

Girón's withdrawal did not slow the growing demands for cultivable lands. Over a dozen pro-land groups surfaced in the Oriente and the highlands, the majority under the auspices of the troubled INTA, the government's National Institute for Agrarian Transformation. A group headed by Carlos Dubón García claimed thirty thousand members. After securing one finca, Dubón García became embroiled in charges of corruption. Commentators wrote that agrarian movements had preceded Father Girón, and they would long outlive him. And so would the entrenched latifundistas and their private death squads. To the proliferating bands of hungry peasants that threatened to invade abandoned or fallow lands, Father Girón served more as a stalking-horse than a spiritual leader.

Despite Girón's mounting troubles, the three fincas acquired by the association prospered. German capital and Belgian agronomists helped to train the peasants and provided the latest fertilizers and irrigation techniques. A small crop-diversified finca near Escuintla was the most successful, earning each of seven homesteading families a handsome yearly profit of nearly $2,000. But the sum total of association members who were awarded lands still added up to less than a thousand. As the government balked at turning over additional farmlands, Father Girón grew increasingly irascible and unpredictable. His enemies had uncovered Father Girón's Achilles' heel and began to drive a wedge between the man of God who consecrated his life to the landless poor and the presidential aspirant driven by unhallowed political ambition. In Girón's memoir, the pious aunt who inspired his religious mission competes for his soul with his father, the three-time mayor of Tecpán who thought priests were lacking in manhood and who wanted Andrés to pursue a legal career.

In May 1989, Father Girón appeared subdued and even somber on a television interview in which he bragged of the $6.5 million dollars contributed to his movement by the European Economic Community. He reminded viewers that he could gather fifty thousand marchers at a moment's notice, and criticized a recent pastoral letter by Guatemala's bishops, "A Clamor for Land," for not going far enough in responding to peasants' needs. When asked if he still harbored presidential ambitions, he told of the recent murder of the administrator of one of the association's fincas. He hinted that if Cerezo made good on the ten fincas he had promised to hand over, he would withdraw his candidacy. And then he said, "The land movement is my child, but the church is my mother, and my first loyalties are to her. I will do as she commands me." Nevertheless, the rumors of growing discontent with Father Girón among Guatemala's bishops and in the Vatican gained wider currency as the elections grew nearer.

In Tecpán, stories surfaced of the Girón family's long history of exploiting the poor. Father Girón's claim to the contrary, his family retained properties in Tecpán, and his brother continued to manage a prosperous hardware store until 1987, when he moved it to Antigua. A Cakchiquel linguist from Tecpán, coincidentally named Narciso, presented testimony that directly contradicted Father Girón's version of his father's murder. Narciso Cojtí claimed that Jorge Girón had used the mayor's office to enrich himself at the expense of the native community. His most outrageous scam was the massive logging of the hillsides above Iximché and his sale of the lumber for private profit. The first voice raised in protest against the logging had been that of the supervisor of schools, a respected member of Tecpán's Maya community. When threats failed to silence him, Mayor Girón had the supervisor killed. According to Cojtí, the assassination of Jorge Girón was an *ajusticiamiento* carried out by the supervisor's Cakchiquel relatives and allies.

"The Girón family prospered from exploiting my people from the very start," claimed Narciso Cojtí. "And Andrés Girón, behind his sacerdotal frock, is an opportunistic exploiter just as his father was. Instead of helping to preserve Maya culture on his fincas, as he claims, he mixes together communities of different backgrounds and attempts to sever their ancestral attachments to Mother Corn. Like other self-styled 'protectors of the Indians' dating from colonial times, Girón's paternalism ultimately promotes the eradication of our ethnic identity."

My interviews in Tecpán's Cakchiquel community produced widespread support for Cojtí's viewpoint. In the lowlands, however,

Girón's popularity among landless campesinos held firm, so long as
he remained on the cutting edge of the agrarian movement.

Shortly before the attempt on his life, I ran into Father Girón at
Guatemala City's airport. He was returning from a fund-raising tour
in the western United States.

We met in the baggage room at 5 A.M., after a night flight from
Los Angeles. Father Girón looked groggy from lack of sleep, but he
perked up as soon as we began talking of his controversies with
John Vesey. Girón claimed to have proof that Vesey was working
hand in glove with a right-wing evangelical conspiracy to take over
Guatemala.

When I brought up his current relations with Cerezo, Father
Girón's indignation rose another notch. "That man has defrauded
all Guatemalans!" he shouted. "He has allied himself with the military to save his ass and sold us all down the river. But we are going
to do something about it. I intend to mount my own radical candidacy!" Father Girón's jowls shook as he slammed his fist down on
a rail. Then he unbuttoned his suit jacket to reveal stacks of U.S.
bills stuffed in both inside pockets. "This is how I intend to start,
with the generosity of my supporters abroad."

He blinked, in apparent response to the astonishment on my face.
"But of course," he said, in a lowered tone, "this money is not for
me. It is for the children of God."

When I spoke of this encounter with a priest who has known
Father Girón and his family for many years, he smiled and remarked:
"Andrés Girón may be a fool, but the forces that shaped him make
him a peculiarly Guatemalan fool, and he cannot be disregarded. The
truth is, he embodies all our contradictions, and that is a cross he
has chosen to carry all the way to Calvary."

In May 1990, Guatemala's Episcopal Conference ruled against
Girón's petition for permission to run for political office. On May
15 he surrendered his parish of Nueva Concepción and Tiquisate and
launched his campaign as congressional candidate on the Christian
Democratic ticket. He told supporters he had hung up his frock to
serve social justice but that he would continue to proclaim the word
of God as a lay preacher. Rumors circulated of a secret deal worked

out between Father Girón and the Christian Democratic presidential candidate, Alfonso Cabrera Hidalgo, who trailed badly in the polls. In exchange for turning over his large following to the Christian Democrats, Cabrera would name Girón the party's leader in Congress immediately following his election.

As expected, Girón won a congressional seat as Christian Democrat candidate for Tiquisate. The Christian Democratic party, which came in a strong second in Congress despite Cabrera's dismal showing in the presidential vote, named Girón to head Congress's Human Rights Commission. That post assured he would not stray far from fresh controversy in this new stage of his career.

After six months, Girón found that his new political clout had not brought him the broad-based political support he was after. Although he continued to speak out against social injustice and periodically called for land invasions by peasant groups, Girón found that political office removed him from the cutting edge of the agrarian reform movement, where he was most effective. His thousands of peasant followers began to grumble that he was enriching himself at their expense.

"The sad truth is, Guatemalans are an ungrateful people," Girón complained to a colleague.

At the July 1991 Christian Democratic convention in the Belén Convent, which Girón did not attend, rumors circulated of his reiterated threats to leave the party, quit his congressional seat, and return to his parish in Nueva Concepción.

"We managed to talk him out of it, but Andrés has become deeply depressed," I was told by the Christian Democrat deputy from Puerto Barrios, who is Girón's close friend.

On March 2, 1992, Andrés Girón reported an attempt on his life the previous night at his home in Nueva Concepción. *Siglo XXI* ran a front-page photograph of the portly congressman as he pointed to automatic rifle bullet holes on his front door. Congressional leaders and the president's public relations office repudiated this latest aggression against Girón. From his old parish office Girón assured the press that his would-be assassins would not prevent him from carrying out his duties as protector of the poor. "Human rights in this country are a farce," he said. "A cloak of impunity shields the assassins of Guatemalans who clamor for social justice." Father Girón was back in business. He fired several more broadsides at Guatemala's impotent criminal justice system and the Ministries of Education and Housing and denounced local military commissioners who had threatened his life. He ended the press conference by announcing that he was taking seriously the advice of members of his association to spend a few months in a friendly country away from Guatemala.

Two days later Archbishop Penados del Barrio denounced the attempt on Girón's life, while regretting at the same time that he had not troubled to report it to the church's human rights office. He repeated that Father Girón's clerical status would remain in suspension so long as he engaged in political activities. Before he could gain reinstatement, Girón would have to cease all participation in government and ask forgiveness from the curia in person.

In the summer of 1992 a scandal erupted when several deputies were found to be abusing congressional immunity and privileged license plates to carry on a thriving contraband trade in hard drugs and stolen luxury cars. When a majority of congressmen refused to indict their colleagues in closed pretrial hearings called *antejuicios,* an outraged press and public called for a radical reform of Congress. An equally vocal faction called for the outright dissolution of Congress, a la Fujimori in Peru. No one denounced the rampant corruption louder than Congressman Andrés Girón, who vowed to take to the mountains and join the URNG after the legislative body was dissolved.

16

The New Indian
versus the New Maya

"We are the result of the sexual violence of the Spanish
conquistador against the Maya woman."

A ladino anthropologist

"I do not expect to live very long."

Calixta Canek

In a forest clearing near the Lacantún river in Chiapas, Mexico, a
Lacandón boy returning from the hunt spies a newly pitched camp
of Guatemalan refugees. They are Kanjobal Mayas in flight from
immigration authorities. The boy knits his brows in a gesture of distaste. He doesn't want these people there, in his community's hunting
preserve. They look like Chamulas, the highland Mayas who are the
Lacandones' traditional enemies. Only these people are dressed in
rags and don't look nearly as fierce as the Chamulas he has heard so
much about. Moving toward the edge of the clearing, the youth picks
out three barefoot boys kicking around a deflated plastic ball. Two
of them cough spasmodically between yells of excitement. The other
has the swollen belly he recognizes as a sign of acute malnutrition.

"Where are you from?" the youth asks the three boys, who stop
to stare at him in astonishment. The youth's shoulder-length hair,
long white tunic, and .22 rifle evoke a welter of confused emotions.
Although their parents had told them they were in the country of
Lacandones, their forest-dwelling kin who lived like hunters and still
kept the ancient ways, they had no idea what a Lacandón looked like.

"Venimos de la montaña," the biggest boy replies at last, in Spanish.
He points across the Lacantún river, in the direction of Huehuetenango. "We come from the mountains in Guatemala."

The Lacandón youth nods. His parents have told him of the refugees from Guatemala. His grandfather had once gone to Guatemala

"*de paseo*," on a stroll. He had found good hunting there, but the people spoke a strange language.

A spark of recognition has passed between the Lacandón youth and the three boys. Although the youth's family converted to Protestant Christianity a decade ago, he is closer to his Maya ancestors than the Guatemalan boys, who are Catholic, and whose forebears intermarried with ladinos centuries before.

This encounter would have taken place in the vicinity of the southern Lacandón community of Lacanjá Chan Sayab. In 1982, several hundred Guatemalan refugees were permitted to camp on the Lacantún river, after they had asked permission of the Lacandón president of Lacanjá, José Pepe Chan Bor.

The interactions between highland and lowland Mayas have brought to the fore complex questions of Maya identity. Until the early fifties, when a U.S. missionary for the Summer Institute of Linguistics succeeded in converting the southern Lacandones to Baptism, they had lived for centuries as traditional Maya communities in a direct, if degenerated, line of descent from the classical Mayas. What, in essence, are the bonds that tie the Lacandones and the highland communities to their Maya ancestors?

When the loggers' road came through his forest, Chan K'in of Nahá—one of the last traditional Lacandón spiritual leaders—abandoned his home and milpa and started new ones by the side of the road. In doing so he was challenging the white man's technology with "Lacandón magic." Ten years later, Chan K'in's corn and tobacco plants finally grew to a respectable size, and he announced that Lacandón ways had survived. Chan K'in, a stooped, shaggy-haired elder of ninety-four, says that Akyanthó, the god of foreigners, has taken over the sun from Hachakyum, the traditional Lacandón solar deity. "But he is not so bad," he has decided, although the *xu'tan*, or world's end, is inevitable. Chan K'in points to the sky. "Look! The sun is still shining." Wisely, Chan K'in has chosen to live one day at a time.

Chan K'in's buoyant fatalism contrasts with the grim outlook of native Americans who seek him out with growing frequency in his jungle sanctuary. In spring of 1989, I served as translator when Leon Shenandoah, the seventy-one-year-old Onondaga chief who heads the Iroquois Confederacy of Six Nations, found his way to Nahá. He had come to consult with Chan K'in about "the great punishment" that Iroquois elders forecasted for humankind in the first decade of the twenty-first century. Shenandoah believed that traditional peoples were turning away from their ancient teachings, and this has given the white man license to ride roughshod over Mother Earth. As custodian of the "fire that never dies," passed down through generations from the first Iroquois Peacemaker, Chief Shenandoah is seeking out leaders of other traditional cultures, among them Nicaragua's Miskitos, Australia's Aborigines, and Tibet's Dalai Lama.

In anticipation of the prophesied cataclysm, the Iroquois are removing their children from reservation schools, taking up arms against desecrators of their ancestral burial grounds, and practicing other forms of "spiritual preparation." To Chan K'in, who expects the xu'tan around the year 2008, opposition to the inevitable is simply irrelevant. World's ends are in the natural order of things, a way for the gods to cleanse and renew their creation. Chan K'in has lived through so many death/rebirth cycles he cannot recall them all. He does, however, remember the 1902 eruption of Guatemala's Santa María volcano when he was a small boy and clouds of ash and cinder "covered the sun and turned day into night." That, Chan K'in says, was his first xu'tan.

"Let go of the world," Chan K'in admonishes visitors. "It is so old and tired it is moaning and groaning all the time. The world wants to die, so the new one can be born in its place." In summer and fall of 1991, following the solar eclipse of July 11, Chan K'in and three of his sons discarded their old copal-blackened incense burners. As the culmination to an exacting ritual that lasted sixty-eight days, Chan K'in and his helpers fashioned thirty-six new incense burners embodying the full spectrum of the Lacandón Mayas' major and minor gods. The previous incense-burner renewal ceremony had been held in Nahá in 1970.

Chan K'in would laugh if you asked him how he "knows" he is a descendant of the ancient Maya. It is not, to him, a matter open to conjecture. He tells foreigners that they can live like a Maya— work the fields, hunt, even pray in the Godhouse and drink their ceremonial liquor *balché*—but that will not confer Mayanness. His son K'ayum bares his arm and points to his veins. "My blood is red," he says, simply. "The blood of the foreigners and the ladinos has a

, mixed, darker color." In the Lacandón canon, Shenandoah qualifies
as *winik*, or person, which puts him several notches above ladinos
and foreigners; but only the Lacandones are *hach winik*, true
persons.

Chan K'in is confident that the northern Lacandones will survive
the white man's xu'tan, even if they are reduced to one family clinging
to a hillside too steep for logging, drinking balché from a mahogany
canoe, and worshiping the traditional Mayan gods in a thatch-roofed
temple. If the Lacandón Mayas can regenerate from one family in a
patch of forest, can highland Mayas likewise maintain their culture
with one cluster of adobe huts on a Cuchumatán mountaintop too
isolated for the army or the guerrillas to bother with?

Demetrio Cojtí Cuxil (no relation to Narciso), a Guatemalan highland Maya who is a professor of communications at San Carlos University, has done a thorough investigation of the elements of ethnic
identity. Step by step, he refutes widely accepted ladino theories that
claim the present-day Indians are at best a transculturated "residue"
of a Mayan civilization that was all but defunct at the time of the
Conquest. Professor Cojtí's personal contradictions perhaps enhance
rather than detract from his qualifications for addressing this complex
issue. A native of Tecpán, Cojtí commands two European languages,
Spanish and French; in pursuit of his doctorate, Cojtí mastered the
Western academician's analytic cast of mind to a degree most Maya-
speakers cannot even conceive of.

Four years ago, when he returned from Belgium with his Ph.D.—
one of a handful of doctorates obtained by Maya-born Guatemalans—
Cojtí was thrust toward the forefront of a resurgent indigenous movement. Two testing grounds have been the government and missionary
schools that promote bilingual education as a bridge toward the "social integration" of Maya children into ladino society.

"The Mayan linguistic communities are the victims of an internal
colonialism," Cojtí wrote in an opening salvo in the *Boletín de Lingüística*. "The dominant ladino culture presses them to abandon their
native language and replace it with Spanish. For this reason, there
cannot be a bilingual education that is not assimilationist." Demetrio
Cojtí notes acerbically that a viable Mayan culture appears to have

survived all attempts by ladino and foreign academicians to explain it away. Dialectical materialism, socioeconomic, linguistic, or evolutionist theories do not take into account the Maya's stubborn spiritual devotion to his ancestors.

Inoffensive and technical as these remarks sound today, it would have been worth Cojtí's life to profess them as recently as 1985; to the generals who ruled Guatemala for the better part of three decades, the very idea of an "Indian professor" aroused murderous suspicion. And that same lethal envidia is certain to arise once again.

The first indigenous revivals date from the early colonial era, when educable "savages" were taken to Europe to be turned out as proper linguists, musicians, and darlings of cultural soirees. These early minions of the colonial society would sometimes return as Mayan nationalists, with a revived appreciation for their cultural origins. The revolts against colonial authority ignited by Atanasio Tzul in Totonicapán and by Jacinto Canek in Yucatán were as much about restoring a Mayan sense of pride as they were a revulsion against intolerable servitude and social injustice. Today's indigenous revival is in a direct line of descent from those movements and from the uprising of Rafael Carrera and his Maya hordes in the mid-nineteenth century. Today's rebels, however, are more likely to wield a computer or mimeograph machine than to strike out with a machete.

When asked what lies behind the Guatemalan establishment's obsession with ladinicizing the Maya, Cojtí points out that most ladinos unconsciously regard Mayas as their shadows. They are constant reminders of a reality they find too painful to confront. In an essay he contributed to the Pacific News Service via journalist Mary Jo McConahay, Cojtí quotes a ladino anthropologist who confessed, "We are the result of the sexual violence of the Spanish conquistador against the Maya woman." Cojtí comments, "Nobody wants to dig into this kind of beginning; there is a profound resistance against studying and accepting it. The ladinos say to us: 'You must forget your language. You must abandon your culture. You have to become like us to release us from the responsibility of discriminating against you.' This is the way it is, from the legislators to the intellectuals to the teachers in the children's schools."

I first met Demetrio Cojtí at a Maya languages workshop in Quezaltenango, where he took on the Summer Institute of Linguistics.
He and three other native Maya speakers denounced the SIL/WBT
missionaries as parasites who tried to rob native Mayas of their culture
to fulfill their own warped evangelical and geopolitical agendas. "The
time has come," Cojtí declared, "for Mayas to reclaim their own
languages as well as the distinct cultural vision they sustain. We have
no more need of foreign excavators and interpreters of our Maya
heritage." At the end of the session I spoke with Cojtí about the
implications of their frontal assault. What began as a scholarly encounter between native and non-Maya linguists had verged on a declaration of war against all ladino and foreign Mayanists.

Cojtí recognized the paradox of his assuming so militant a posture
in a forum planned and subsidized by a ladino university. As a foreign-
trained Ph.D., he has clout on both sides of the cultural divide. But
he also has two sets of vulnerabilities. Why was he biting the hand
that feeds him? "For better or worse, I have been placed in a position
of leadership. The questions of Maya identity invite confrontation by
their very nature. I am being pushed from behind." Cojtí's dilemma
bears comparison to that of mayors Guzmán, Ixbalán Cuncz, and
Nicolás Sánchez, as well as to Congressman Diego Velasco Brito's.
But whereas these New Indians exchanged a part of their identity for
a place in the ladino political landscape, Cojtí heads a small intellectual Maya elite that refuses to compromise. This adherence to principle carries a high price, as Cojtí is well aware; if he slackens his
assaults on the ladino establishment, his supporters will accuse him
of betrayal. If he stays the course, he becomes a target for the death
squads.

Since the mid seventies, the number of educated Mayas who conserve their native traditions has risen substantially. Linguist Nora England, in an article published in *Mesoamérica* in 1991, points out that
there were no more than thirty Mayan university students fifteen years
ago. Now there are more than five hundred. From a few dozen, the
number of Maya teachers has burgeoned to three hundred with paid
positions and hundreds more without. The number of Mayas with
university degrees has multiplied from fifteen to seventy with a B.A.
equivalent, ten with Master's degrees, and a handful of Ph.D.'s.

During this same period, seven organizations and university programs have come into being for the purpose of preserving Mayan languages and culture. They are almost entirely run by native Maya-speakers. They include the Academy of Mayan Languages, which only recently received official recognition by the state, the Association of Maya Writers, and the National Program for Bilingual Education (PRONEBI). Each of these groups has been accused by more militant indigenists of serving colonial interests by including ladino advisers or soliciting outside funding.

The weight of responsibility on the hundred or so university-trained Maya leaders is enormous. Not only must they deal with a five-hundred-year-legacy of suspicion of educated Mayas by their own community; they have to define a space on the margins of ladino society that is incorruptibly Maya, without provoking violent reprisals. In the persisting climate of "permanent counterinsurgency," to borrow the phrase coined by Ken Anderson and Jean-Marie Simon, any above-ground indigenous movement can survive only at the sufferance of the military.

2

In the past ten years I have met more than a dozen Mayas who immersed themselves in the dominant culture or who traveled abroad and returned to their ancestral traditions with a renewed sense of purpose. The following profile of one such "new Maya" has been altered somewhat to protect her privacy.

I first met Calixta Canek under the name Eugenia Gonzales in 1982, in the San Francisco parish of Father Cuchulan Moriarty. We had been invited to meet with Rigoberta Menchú, who told of her austere childhood working the milpa alongside her father in an aldea of Uspantán. When Vicente Menchú organized the first peasant rallies that contributed to the formation of CUC, his daughter Rigoberta was invariably by his side. In her flawless, cadenced Spanish, she described how each of her family members were tortured, burned, and killed. She concluded with a few words about her political formation and her commitment to social struggle.

Rigoberta's presentation left most of us stunned and filled with wordless admiration. The first to speak up was another woman in

Maya traje, who introduced herself as a Cakchiquel schoolteacher from Chimaltenango. She too had a story to tell and she had rendered it in poems, which she proceeded to read aloud. They told of the violent death of her three brothers, the torching of her village and her father's fields by the army, their desperate flight to safety in the middle of the night. Her last poem was an impassioned appeal to an international tribunal to restore justice and dignity to her homeland.

The contrasts in the two women's presentations were as striking as the parallels in their lives. Rigoberta's subdued, matter-of-fact delivery magnified the horror of the events she described, without sensationalizing them. She was a practiced speaker who wove into her narrative, ever so subtly, the socialist philosophy she absorbed during her years with CUC. As Rigoberta admitted afterward, the underground had taken the place of her family. Eugenia declaimed her stories in a torrent of furious energy, as if she were bent on sweeping away the darkness with the idiosyncratic power of her voice.

In the following months I met with Eugenia as we traveled the Guatemala lecture circuit, and I pieced together prominent features of her story.

Eugenia had lost her three brothers in 1981, after the guerrillas showed up in the village outside Chimaltenango where her family had lived for generations. (Eugenia was the first girl in her aldea to graduate from primary school.) Her oldest brother had been a policeman and warned his younger brothers not to be taken in by the promises of the guerrillas. But after a band of FAR militants came into the aldea to hold a consciousness-raising rally, the middle brother disregarded his older brother's advice and decided to collaborate with them.

Some weeks later, the policeman was found dead by Eugenia's father. He was one of several army collaborators executed by the guerrillas. When the army moved into the aldea, the family thought their deceased son's membership in the National Police would protect them from Lucas García's brutal reprisals. But soldiers burned down their house and killed all their farm animals except for their horse, which Eugenia's father had managed to hide. Eugenia showed me a poem she'd written about that period, which she called "The Killing Goes On":

> In March of 1982
> 200 soldiers came to our village

> to burn down our homes;
> they massacred 35 campesinos
> burned 60 homes
> and thousands of *quintales* of beans and corn.
> Today the hunger continues
> thousands go on dying
> but millions of seeds are born
> of the children of the Maya people.

Eugenia told me what happened when the army apprehended her seventeen-year-old younger brother. First they removed his fingernails and applied electric shock to his genitals to make him confess his ties to the guerrillas. Her father found his half-incinerated body in the village square. That is when they decided to leave.

"What about the third brother?" I asked her.

"My middle brother left for Mexico and disappeared on the journey home. We hear rumors from people who saw him, but we don't know who killed him."

Soon after she arrived in California as an undocumented refugee Eugenia moved in with a group of indigenous religious women and priests who were affiliated with the peasant labor movement. She became a spokesperson for Maya refugees and later collaborated with the sanctuary movement to bring persecuted Guatemalans to the States. Eugenia, who in her village had belonged to a Catholic *comunidad de base* that worked for social justice, became close friends with one of the religious women and considered joining the Sacred Heart order. During the day she worked in a rubber factory with Mexican migrant workers, most of them women. The conditions of work were unsanitary and harsh, and Eugenia organized the women in a protest to demand improved health facilities. Later she worked in an auto parts assembly plant, where she met for the first time with members of the North American Indian movement.

At fundraisers for Guatemalan refugees, Eugenia would sing her own songs, accompanying herself on the guitar, and speak about the murder of her brothers in a tradition of bearing witness that is older than the Mayan pyramids. She found college audiences particularly responsive and took in her stride the occasional insensitive questioners, like the woman who asked her why she did not jump off the Golden Gate Bridge.

As she approached her thirtieth birthday, Eugenia fell into a deep despondency. All seemed dark and hopeless; she was unmarried, her three brothers were dead, and her parents were far away. She borrowed her roommate Deborah's car keys, intending to drive to the bridge and jump into the bay so that it would seem somehow like an accident. Deborah reminded her that a call was expected from a close friend in Guatemala. Mindful of the trouble her friend would go to in placing a call to California, she decided to wait. By evening the crisis had passed; Eugenia resolved to accept her destiny and go on with her life. The call from Guatemala never came.

Eugenia started meeting with Navajos and Hopis who introduced her to sweat lodges and peyote ceremonies. For the first time, she was able to share her sense of pain and loss with native Americans like herself. A Hopi elder, Henry Tyler, suggested she return to Guatemala and become a Mayan priestess.

As invitations to speak took her farther afield, Eugenia became more outspoken. At an Oregon seminar attended by Frederick Chapin, the former U.S. ambassador to Guatemala, she accused him of deliberately downplaying the Guatemalan army's massacres of Maya peasants and of lying about the extent of U.S. involvement. She then told those in attendance: "I see the same forces building here that are destroying my country. Your great wealth and your culture will not protect you from the disintegration of this society, which is hastened by the greed and blindness of the people who lead you. The harm your State Department and your Pentagon and your presidents have done to our small, unprotected communities will also be done to you."

After four years in California, Eugenia had grown increasingly restless. Although she had been told her name was still on army death lists, the election of civilian President Cerezo in 1985 persuaded her that it was time to go home. In 1986 she returned to Guatemala unannounced to visit her parents, who had begun their lives anew in the municipal capital of Chimaltenango.

The killings of dissidents by death squadrons declined during the first year of Cerezo's presidency; but Eugenia had to endure the suspicion of neighbors who felt threatened by her new ways and by the pale-faced gringos who on occasion visited her home.

After six months, Eugenia met a Quiché priestess who told her she had accumulated too much "darkness" during the violence. She also revealed that she had lived a former life as a California Indian who met a violent death. The years abroad had enabled her to make peace with her past and present lives and to move beyond them. She then told Eugenia that her return to her home village was the start of her rebirth as a Maya woman. Eugenia became a disciple to the Quiché priestess under the Mayan name Calixta, which she has since used exclusively.

Through a mutual friend I made contact with Calixta in the summer of 1988, and she came to meet me at the Guatemala City airport.

I hardly recognized the militant feminist. In her blue wraparound corte and bright red huipil, Calixta glowed. Eugenia's furious, unkempt energy appeared to have become internalized, and a more serene, spiritual Calixta had emerged. She had been the priestess's apprentice for over a year and was soon to receive her investiture. She told me she had found her calling and understood she was not meant to marry or bear children. It was the same message Rigoberta Menchú had relayed in Father Moriarty's parish house six years earlier, after she pledged to carry on her father's work.

Before we parted, I asked Calixta if she felt she was part of a Maya religious revival.

"Oh no," she said. "You don't revive something that has never died. We have practiced our religion and observed our calendar without interruption since the time of the Conquest. But we have kept it hidden from outsiders. Now, after the destruction of many of our communities and the scattering of thousands of our people across the face of the earth, the time for secrecy has passed. Our elders have decided to make available our teachings to those few non-Mayas who are capable of understanding and who can become our allies against the powers of darkness that are taking over the world."

On my return to Guatemala a year later I met with Calixta in Antigua, where she had embarked on a university career in social work. In the afternoon we took the bus to Chimaltenango to meet her family. She was now a practicing Maya priestess, although she confessed she had not yet mastered the Maya calendar. Each of the twenty Mayan name days is endowed with healing or negative properties to be conjured or warded off—a task only a skilled shaman can accomplish. On the way, Calixta also informed me her political action group had fragmented, and the more extreme faction was accusing her of "not having definition."

Her father, Antonio, met us at the bus stop and accompanied us to their home on the outskirts of town. Nearly a decade had passed since they had left their village, and he had saved enough to open a small bakery and general store.

"It is *alegre* (cheerful) now that we have enough to eat once more," he said. "But I miss my fields and my animals. We still have enemies in the aldea who would report us if we tried to rebuild our home there. But a relative keeps an eye on our cornfields, and we go back twice a year for the harvest. We work at night, so the neighbors won't see us." Don Antonio, tall for a Cakchiquel, still wears his traditional woolen apron and sandals. In his youth, Calixta's father had lived as a traditional Maya. After he married a Catholic, he joined Acción Católica, and became mayor of his aldea, La Estancia. By enemies, I discovered, Don Antonio meant the EGP guerrillas who remain a presence in the outlying aldeas. He told me it was they who were responsible for the death of his eldest son, the policeman. And he insisted they had tortured and killed his youngest son and probably his middle son as well.

"My father and I do not see eye to eye on that subject," Calixta explained later. "He is unable to comprehend that the army could commit such atrocities. When the guerrillas killed Paco, who had been his pride and joy, father simply shut his eyes. Now he blames the guerrillas for everything."

"The enemy burned all our possessions, even our corn and beans," said Don Antonio, when we gathered for dinner. "Only my poncho survived, and our horse, which I kept hidden in a neighbor's field. When they burned down the house and our fields, my wife wanted to give up. 'They have killed our sons and burned our home, let us stay and die here as well,' she said. But I thought about it and decided we would not give our enemy the satisfaction of seeing us die of sorrow. So we gathered our belongings and walked all the way here, in the dead of night. A cousin had set apart a few *cuerdas* of land for us. Although it was not planting season, we scattered a few kernels, and the corn grew by itself, in abundance. So we knew we had made the right decision. Now we have a pen in back for a few chickens and pigs, and even our horse seems contented enough, although he hardly has room to ramble."

Calixta's mother, Felipa, wears the traje of her village and only reluctantly speaks a few words in Spanish. During the hours I spent in her home, I never once saw her idle. The lunch she and Calixta prepared included herbs they picked in the campo and corn tamales with *chipilín*, a native herb, Cakchiquel style. Late in the evening I learned Felipa had recently joined the charismatic renovation movement as a lay healer. She was among the first Catholic charismatics in the town, and neighbors viewed her activities with distrust. When she was seen laying hands on an ailing child who lived two houses away, his aunt threatened to report her to the army as a subversive. Calixta said her mother supports her vocation as a Maya priestess, but she would not enter her altar because charismatics do not approve of saints or idols.

After dinner Calixta took me in back of the house to her altar. In the center of the small dark prayer room she had laid a circle of ten large pumice stones, with an old stone cross in the center. A large copal brazier was set to one side. Bunches of rue and other herbs were stacked by the side of the door and hung from the ceiling. A wooden San Simón figure with one leg sat in back. The altar itself was covered with small talismanic objects and letters from close friends abroad.

Calixta had offered to do a *limpia,* or cleansing, ceremony for me in preparation for my planned journey to Nebaj. She lit candles of different colors and recited prayers in Cakchiquel. She had looked up my date in the calendar but was not entirely certain she had found the right attributes to correspond with my Gregorian birthdate. (Some time ago in Chiapas, a Maya day keeper had read my birthdate as 13 Ahau, which corresponds in their calendar to a period of calamity and Christian conversion. He told me, "Your birthdate has destined you to be a witness to endings as well as to new beginnings.") Calixta burned copal incense and intoned more prayers, which mentioned my travels and various guardian saints, both Christian and Cakchiquel. The black candles, she told me, were meant to propitiate the dark forces, and the shot of kusha she gave me was to dispel cobwebs that obscured my spirit. At the end, she rubbed a poultice of herbs on my forehead and intoned a final benediction.

Afterward she told me, "You are a typical Occidental in that your head is cluttered with too many thoughts; they create confusion, and trap the good spirits so they cannot work for you as they should. But the road ahead for you is a positive one."

Several months later, Calixta was run over by a car as she was stepping down from a bus near Tecpán. The car's driver, who happened to be the wife of an army officer, stopped only because two policemen were present at the scene. Calixta was taken to the local hospital with a concussion, a nasty cranial wound, and internal injuries. The ladino doctor did not bother to take X-rays, and Calixta refused to have her head wound stitched. ("I was half-unconscious, seeing lights in front of my eyes; but I still knew enough not to let myself be stitched up in that filthy place.") Eventually, Calixta settled with the colonel's wife for a sum that would appear negligible in any court of law outside Guatemala; but it did at least cover her hospital costs. Calixta suffered from headaches and dizzy spells for months afterward, and her internal injuries later developed into endometriosis. The experience left her, in her words, "with a taste of ashes in my mouth."

Several months after her accident Calixta went to a curandera to receive treatments for her persistent headaches and depression. The curandera passed three candles and a raw egg over Calixta's body while reciting incantations to rid her of the *aires*, or cold humors, that had invaded her head and her womb. After cracking the egg open to examine its contents, the curandera lit the candles to propitiate each of the three "angels" invoked to cure her of her ailments. After three treatments Calixta's depression lifted, although the headaches persisted. The curandera told her the only lasting cure for her condition was to become pregnant.

Calixta was now a fully empowered Maya priestess with a crowded religious and political calendar. She took part in mass ceremonies in Iximché, Utatlán, and other holy Mayan sites, where Cakchiquel and Quiché priests burned incense, performed sacrifices, and prayed for the healing of the earth. At the same time, she found work with a government ministry that sponsored agricultural cooperatives in the altiplano.

Her restless spirit continues to involve her in confrontations with the authorities. Like Father Andrés Girón, she is torn between the demands of her religious vocation and her longstanding political commitments. But as a Maya woman, the stigma she bears for defying her community's norms of marriage and child-bearing is beyond the comprehension of a ladino. With the return of the violence, the political and personal spaces she fought for have begun to close around her, and she feels increasingly isolated.

Calixta continues to travel abroad. At a congress of native Americans in Vancouver, an Iroquois told her the Mayas had the best chance of surviving the approaching "punishment" because they had learned over centuries to survive under the harshest conditions imaginable. Calixta agreed and told him the thousands of displaced Ixils who scratch out a meager existence in the mountains were precursors of the post-apocalyptic Maya.

As the 1990 elections approached, the killings of dissident Mayas accelerated. In June Calixta traveled to Norway to meet with Sameis and Laplanders from three Scandinavian countries who share a passionate interest in the plight of the Mayas. She is becoming part of a worldwide network of traditional leaders who come together to prepare their communities against the calamities their seers prophesy for the start of the new millennium.

When she returns from abroad, Calixta finds envidia roaming the streets of her town with one hundred eyes that never shut. "My travels and my foreign connections create too much resentment in my community," she says. She is saddened by the growing distance between herself and her mother, whose charismatic church discourages political activity. "My parents won't say so aloud, but they fear I am traveling the same road as my dear brothers." She wants to believe her teacher's assurances that she is safe so long as she keeps faith with her Maya gods, but the last time we met she told me that she does not expect to live a long time.

In 1991 Calixta reneged on her pledge and married a sorcerer's apprentice from a village in Huehuetenango. On October 12, Calixta and her husband joined thousands of Mayas to protest the celebration of Columbus Day. She added her voice to a proclamation by The New Dawn (*Majawal Q'ij*), which calls for "a just and humane society in which we are no longer treated as objects, but take part as equal subjects in reconstructing the political, economic, and social life of our country."

In October 1992, Calixta took part in ceremonies in Iximché on the five hundredth anniversary of the "discovery" of America. She joined hundreds of thousands of other protesters from indigenous communities who took part in similar demonstrations throughout the Western Hemisphere. They called their healing ceremonies "Returning the Gift."

17

⬚

The Evangelical Presidents

"The Guatemalan people know who I am and what I stand for."

Efraín Ríos Montt

"I am not a man of a soft hand."

Jorge Serrano Elías

Two weeks prior to the 1990 presidential elections, Efraín Ríos Montt finally exhausted his last legal recourse against the constitutional ban that prohibits the election of any candidate who previously seized the presidency by force. Although the strain of his lengthy and frustrated campaign had slowed his momentum, Ríos Montt remained a force to contend with. During his legal battles in the courts his lead in the polls had continued to widen. On November 11, however, his millions of followers failed to heed his call to invalidate the elections by voiding their ballots. Instead, most of them voted for the other evangelical candidate, Jorge Serrano Elías, a former protégé of Ríos Montt who had headed his Council of State in 1982. Serrano came in second behind centrist UCN candidate Jorge Carpio Nicolle, who had lost the runoff to Cerezo in 1985. Serrano confidently assured supporters he would win the second round against Carpio by a wide margin.

To many of his nonevangelical supporters, Ríos Montt had blown a golden opportunity as president by blatantly favoring his Word Church and naming two of its religious counselors to head his staff. Mejía Víctores invoked constitutional grounds for unseating Ríos Montt in August 1983, denouncing the Word Church as a "fanatical and aggressive religious group" that abused its insiders' ties to the presidency and "ignored the fundamental principle of the separation of church and state." Behind this lofty-sounding justification for the coup lay baser motives: Ríos Montt's strict anticorruption stand—he demanded that government officials sign a pledge never to steal, lie, or abuse—got in the way of the military officers' perks and privileges.

Many Christian Democrats who voted for Ríos Montt in 1974 still resent his unseemly supineness after he was hustled out of the presidency by strong-man Arana Osorio and his protégé Kjell Laugerud. But short of calling for outright revolution, there was little Ríos Montt could have done. Archbishop Penados del Barrio confided to me in an interview that the day after the elections Ríos Montt had appealed to his old friend Cardinal Mario Casariego to intercede on his behalf. The ultraconservative cardinal, who maintained excellent relations with the army, turned him down cold. Discouraged, Ríos Montt gave up his electoral victory without a fight and, fearing an assassination attempt, he accepted the post of ambassador to Spain.

Ríos Montt's rebirth in Christ began in California one year later when he met Jim Durkin, a recovering alcoholic and former "Jesus freak." The head of Gospel Outreach put the crestfallen general through a disciplinary regimen exactly suited to his military temperament. Ríos Montt is fond of boasting that he purged his soul of old grudges by cleaning toilets in the Eureka-based mission. During his teens he had performed similar menial chores for a U.S. Maryknoll mission in Huehuetenango. Years later, as a training officer at the Politécnica he issued strict orders to all his cadets, Protestants included, to attend Catholic services in the chapel. Ríos Montt would prove to be equally doctrinaire as an evangelical Protestant.

These alternating episodes of ascetic self-abnegation and arrogant self-assertiveness appear to have tempered Ríos Montt's peculiar charisma. (His 1982 "beans and rifles" campaign sums up best the contradictions between the philanthropic evangelical and the draconian anticommunist general. His field officers as much as warned the highland Maya communities: "If you are with us, we will feed you. If you are against us, we will kill you.") At the core of Ríos Montt's evangelical conversion was the army man's determination to *vencer,* not merely by winning hearts and minds, but by destroying the adversary's mind, his intelligence, and his will.

By his very presence, Ríos Montt polarizes Guatemala's political and religious institutions. Although the approximately 2 million new Protestant converts are by no means unanimous in glorifying him, he has legitimized evangelical conversion as an instrument for waging military as well as ideological war. In villages and towns where militant sects like the Word Church have converted 50 percent or more of the population, the potential for explosive "little Belfasts" persists. Evangelical pastors in aldeas such as Lemoa, outside Chichicastenango, succeeded in purging minority Catholics from municipal office by denouncing them as communists. (In summer of 1992, Guatemalan and foreign forensic experts exhumed twenty bodies from a clandestine cemetery in an aldea of Lemoa. All of them showed bullet perforations and evidence of torture. The survivors who identified the bodies blamed the civil patrol for the torture and execution of their relatives.) Should religious conflict break out into the open, evangelized civil defense patrols could rise up as so many avenging "swords of God" to strike down the spawn of the Pope or the communist devil.

To millions of ladinos and Mayas disenchanted with democracy's unkept promises, Ríos Montt's mix of selective generosity and iron-fisted authoritarianism still packs a powerful message. Older Mayas hear echoes of paternalistic dictator "Tata Ubico," who instilled in them an unquestioning subservience. But then, obeisance to a beneficent yet cruel despot has marked the peasant farmer since the dawn of the Ahauob, or Maya kings.

The downtrodden ladinos recognize in Ríos Montt a fellow sufferer who transforms defeat and humiliation into an irresistible will to power. And Pentecostals welcome his fiery-eyed, eschatological pronouncements as signs that he is indeed the Chosen One to carry out God's design. Whether or not he eventually reclaims the presidency, Ríos Montt has placed his indelible stamp on the closing decades of Guatemala's twentieth century.

2

Alarmed by the evangelical ascendancy, the archdiocese responded with aggressive measures of its own. After Jorge Serrano Elías's strong showing in the first electoral round, Penados del Barrio called for a massive outpouring of Catholic voters to deny him the presidency. Fliers put out by Catholic civic committees linked Serrano to diabolical plots hatched in Los Angeles and Amsterdam to use Guatemala as a beachhead for an evangelical Protestant invasion of Latin Amer-

ica. Serrano's election posters were defaced with a "666"—the sign
of the Antichrist—scrawled across his forehead.

But the Catholic backlash fell far short of the archdiocese's expectations. Serrano won the second round handily over Carpio, a
traditional Catholic. Although Serrano garnered a majority of the
Catholic vote, a "pox on both your houses" sentiment prevailed as
less than one-third of registered voters bothered to vote in the runoffs.

Serrano Elías, an elder and preacher with the neo-Pentecostal Shaddai church, became the first elected civilian president in Guatemala's
history to succeed another elected civilian president. Taking his cue
from his former mentor, Serrano declared shortly before casting his
vote, "I am not a man of a soft hand." Like Ríos Montt, Serrano
seems unfazed by the incongruities of "seizing the highest public office
to carry out God's designs," as he announced in a religious pamphlet
he published in Miami.

For ten years after his rebirth as a Baptist in 1975, "Brother Elías"
had been a member of Ríos Montt's Pentecostal Word Church. And
he had also been associated with Elim, where he rose to the rank of
"prophet," a notch below Ríos Montt's "ancient." From the start,
Brother Elías felt more at ease with charismatic ritual and personal
testimony than with theological issues. When his bid to challenge
Cerezo for the presidency in 1985 fell short, a disappointed Prophet
Elías departed Elim for his present church, Shaddai. (Disgruntled
Elim brethren characterized him as "undeniably charismatic and
intolerant.")

Shaddai, founded by a U.S. missionary who arrived in Guatemala
after the 1976 earthquake, has a core of five hundred adepts who
receive televised instruction by satellite from the mother church in
California. In Guatemala, Shaddai's services are notorious for one
peculiarity: Congregants spend many hours ecstatically chanting the
phrase "Jesús es el Señor"—Jesus is the Lord—in order to exorcize
the demons left behind by the Mayas during the Conquest.

For all his quirky metaphysics, Serrano's presidency began on a
pragmatic note when he named talented opposition leaders to head
his cabinet. Critics were quick to point out he had little choice, since
the slender coalition he rode into office had been drastically short on
talent and experience. His inaugural address called for a "Social Pact"
that united private business and industry with labor unions and pop-

ular organizations to get the country back on its feet. But no mention was made of the poorest sector of all, the majority Mayan communities; and although Serrano struck a lofty stance with his pledge to uphold and protect civil rights, he pointedly did not include freedom of the press.

Within a month of taking office, Serrano revealed his thin skin and quick temper when he condoned the arrest of columnist Hugo Arce, who vigorously lampooned Serrano in *Siglo XXI*. Arce was arrested on charges of "plotting to overthrow the government." The evidence against him amounted to several ounces of cocaine and three sticks of dynamite purportedly found in the trunk of his car. The apparent plant by police was so clumsily executed, the case was thrown out of court—although not before Arce had languished in prison for nearly a week. Serrano badly underestimated the response by Guatemala's young but determined human rights lobby to this bungled exercise in strong-arm tactics.

Six months into his presidency, Serrano Elías's Social Pact began to fall apart as labor unions and popular organizations walked out, complaining of unkept promises to halt the spiraling rise in the cost of living. Serrano's insistence that his government by consensus would survive after "structural adjustments" had a hollow ring, as his energy minister raised electricity rates by nearly 100 percent. Former labor militant Miguel Albizures wrote that the poor were being asked to pay for the horrendous imperfections built into the Chixoy hydro-electric plant by unscrupulous contractors.

To compound Serrano's problems, in the summer of 1991 La Violencia in Guatemala reached levels unknown since Lucas García's presidency. Consecutive massacres on the coast and in the highlands of Alta Verapaz made Serrano vulnerable to charges that he was losing control of the country's security apparatus. Serrano's pledge to call an end to the "culture of impunity" that shields high-placed criminals was undermined by the assassination in broad daylight, only fifty meters from the capital's National Police headquarters, of the chief investigator assigned to the assassinations of Myrna Mack Chang and Michael DeVine.

Serrano, who had participated in the early rounds of talks with the URNG as a member of the National Committee of Reconciliation, hopes to gain credit for negotiating a lasting peace with the guerrillas. The end of the cold war and the United States' decision to end conflicts in Central America it had previously inspired and heavily subsidized appear to work in favor of Serrano's ambitions.

Even Guatemala's private sector, represented by CACIF, expressed its vested interest in putting an end to the three-decade-old conflict. But Guatemala's internal war is the oldest in Latin America and is stubbornly impervious to geopolitical shifts elsewhere in the hemisphere. The peace treaty signed in El Salvador between the Farabundo Martí National Liberation Front and the government had no immediate impact on Guatemala. For all the cordial meetings between URNG commanders and military, civilian and church officials, the war in the countryside has shown no signs of abating.

A breakthrough appeared in the offing during the summer 1992 peace talks in Mexico City. The army agreed in principle to suspend all new recruitment for the civil defense patrols and to freeze their numbers at current levels. But the ground gained appeared to evaporate when the talks turned to the harder issue of accountability for human rights violations. The meeting concluded abruptly, with both sides hurling accusations at one another. In the following days, Defense Minister José Domingo García Samayoa presented to the press three young men and women he claimed were guerrillas seeking government amnesty because of the harsh treatment they endured from their commanders. He called on other rank-and-file combatants to disarm and turn in their commanders. And he said that all good citizens should express gratitude to their soldiers, for without them "Guatemalans would be licking the boots of Marxism-Leninism today."

In August, a rash of bombs and death threats were laid at the doorsteps of nearly every major national and international news agency operating in Guatemala. Amílcar Méndez, head of CERJ, was given ten days to leave the country by *Jaguar Justiciero,* Avenging Jaguar, a death squadron known for making good on its threats.

An outbreak of cholera undermined Serrano's attempts to promote tourism as a way of easing the government's balance of payments.

But the thousands of deaths predicted by the press did not materialize, and tourism revenues remained at near-record levels.

By 1992, heroin and cocaine traffickers had established durable enclaves in Guatemala. They were now operating with impunity even in former tourist havens like Antigua, where crack and marijuana have become readily available on the street. The combined specters of uncontrolled drugs, "El cólera," and "La cólera"—the rage of millions of hungry Guatemalans no longer able to make ends meet—threatened to tear apart the country's social fabric.

3

With the ratification of the Academy of Mayan Languages by Congress in October 1990, the Mayan nationalist movement took on a new impetus. The five-million-quetzal subsidy would finance the academy's founding mission of introducing the new standard alphabet in all twenty-one Mayan linguistic communities. The veteran SIL/WBT missionaries who had fought the new alphabet tooth and nail remained adamant in opposition. But time appeared to be on the Mayas' side.

Despite the increase in political violence and the resurgence of the war in the northern and western highlands, other voices arose in protest. Spokespersons for the Communities of Population in Resistance in the Sierra (CPR) courageously backed the thousands of Ixils, Quichés, Kanjobals, and Mams still holding out in the northernmost reaches of Chajul and the Ixcán. In March, CPR published full-page ads in the papers that placed the blame for the persecution of their fellow Mayas squarely on the army. They called for an immediate cessation of military actions against the Communities of Population in Resistance and for a withdrawal of the six army garrisons in the area. The announcement also called for an accounting of eight thousand members of CPR who had been disappeared by the army over the past decade. This bold overture was endorsed by the National Coordinating Committee of Guatemalan Widows (CONAVIGUA), whose seven thousand-plus survivors of the violence are primarily Mayas. By focusing attention on these groups as well as on the better known GAM and CERJ, U.S. and European human rights organizations gave them legitimacy as well as a certain measure of protection.

In February 1991 the office of the Attorney for Human Rights flew their regional director, Alvarez Guadamuz, to the mountains of northern Chajul, where as many as fifteen thousand Mayas remain in hiding. These communities have managed to survive by growing two corn crops a year, scattered for protection and camouflage under stands of tall trees. A truce had to be called between the army and the URNG to permit the helicopter to navigate safely the highland's most embattled Zone of Conflict. About seven hundred Mayas, most of them Ixils, awaited the helicopter in a clearing at the edge of dense mountain forest.

"How can we describe to you in one day ten years of suffering?" a CPR spokesman declared in greeting the human rights attorney and his delegation. The leaders of Xeputul's closely knit community assured Alvarez Guadamuz that they were victims of a conflict not of their making and that they owed neither the army, which continues to strafe and bomb their homes and fields, nor the URNG, which had strained their loyalties in recent years. Still, their years of indoctrination by the guerrillas became evident when they raised clenched fists and shouted slogans of liberation.

"We are not animals," they stressed repeatedly. "We have a right to our dignity." One after the other, the mothers presented their children to the human rights attorney, who placed his hand on their heads to ward off the evil eye.

The displaced Mayas of Xeputul, who are governed by a highly disciplined and egalitarian peasant council, consider themselves "persecuted but not isolated." These fifteen thousand Mayas live in circumstances not very different from those their ancestors knew for centuries before the arrival of Columbus. At the same time, the communities in resistance have organized health brigades and literacy corps, and they keep informed of national and world developments. In the evenings, they gather around their short-wave radio to get news from Havana and Mexico City as well as from BBC's Spanish-language newscast.

When asked why they do not turn themselves in to the army or to the United Nations Refugee Relief Agency, a Quiché woman from Sacapulas replied, "Are we not Guatemalans? Is Xemamatzé to be our tribunal? If we have committed a crime, why are we not given recourse to a justice of the peace?"

Early in 1992, the army's bombing raids on the Communities of Population in Resistance diminished, and word went out that they were no longer considered willing or unwilling collaborators with the URNG. The CPR's public relations campaign was reaping benefits abroad and at home. Rigoberta Menchú's Nobel Peace Prize also affected the power balances in the elaborate chess game played by military leaders and Guatemala's insurgents. The announcement from Oslo in October provoked an immediate outcry from army spokesmen, who insisted Menchú was a member of the insurgency who had caused irreparable harm to Guatemala. Menchú, who was in Guatemala at the time of the announcement, pledged to continue working to protect Guatemala's ethnic pluralism. And she said she would use her $1.2 million prize to set up a foundation in her father's name to protect the rights of indigenous peoples.

4

Country-wide human rights violations continued into summer and fall of 1992, although death-squad activity diminished and observers recorded a modest drop in extra-judicial executions and disappearances, the first in several years. The press and human rights monitoring agencies kept the spotlight on continuing investigations into the murders of Myrna Mack Chang and Michael DeVine and the abduction of Sister Dianna Ortiz.

The resurgence of the press helped create a climate of opinion propitious to Guatemala's emerging democracy. Not since the halcyon years of the *Imparcial* and of crusading journalists Clemente Marroquín Rojas and Isidoro Zarco had Guatemala's newspapers so tenaciously exposed criminal activity and corruption in high places.

In July 1992 close to five hundred campesinos from the aldea of Cajolá, outside Quezaltenango, marched to the National Palace to press their claim to ancestral lands they had received title to in 1910, during Estrada Cabrera's administration. The Cajoleños protested that their lands had been illegally expropriated by latifundista Mariano Arévalo Bermejo, a brother of the former president, Juan José Arévalo Bermejo. When the campesinos squatted in the Plaza Mayor, Interior

Minister Fernando Hurtado Prem sent in riot-control units to remove
them forcibly, even as campesino delegates met with government officials across the street in the National Palace. Twenty campesinos
were injured in the ensuing melee by the club-swinging police units,
which had been trained by Chilean carabiniers. Images of the brutal
beatings were flashed on TV screens and splashed across the front
pages of newspapers. Minister Hurtado Prem fanned the public outrage when he backed his officer's insistence that the campesinos "had
sought out the police clubs with their heads." The Interior Minister's
endorsement of that egregious assertion led to his resignation several
days later. The archdiocese's human rights office immediately filed a
suit against Hurtado Prem and the officers responsible for the un-
provoked assault on the Cajolá delegates.

There was a generalized and almost palpable sense in the summer
of 1992 that the media, human rights groups, and a public fed up
with thirty years of uncontrolled violence and corruption were at last
beginning to flex their muscles. *Siglo XXI, Prensa Libre,* and *Crónica*
kicked off a campaign against congressional and military impunity.
They called for prosecution of criminals in high places, regardless of
their military rank or their privileges of immunity. As recently as two
years earlier, a similar campaign would have unleashed the death
squads and led to the elimination of key journalists, churchmen,
Mayan nationalists, and judicial and human rights investigators. On
the surface, the *coyuntura,* or historical convergence, appeared un-
favorable to the powerful elites that ordered the murders of Myrna
Mack Chang and Michael DeVine and threatened the lives of Byron
Barrera, Amílcar Méndez, Nineth García, and hundreds of others who
worked to preserve Guatemala's vulnerable democratic institutions.

The end of the cold war did not deter army officers from proclaiming themselves the nation's defenders against the international
communist conspiracy. Defense Minister García Samayoa was greeted
with a deafening silence when he asserted, following the collapse of
the peace talks in Mexico, that the military was the sole guarantor
of Guatemala's democracy against the Marxist-Leninist guerrillas who
were bent on tearing it down. The defense minister was particularly
nettled by "dupes of communism" who denounced continued army
abuses against the Communities of Population in Resistance. In August, he lashed out at a multipartite human rights commission made

up of Danish, German, Guatemalan, and North American delegates
who repudiated the military's renewed bombing raids on the CPR in
the Ixcán and northern Quiché. Citing "foreign interference in Guatemala's internal affairs," Defense Minister García Samayoa burst into
a new round of attacks on the CPR; spiking his sarcasm with mixed
metaphor, he averred they are "nothing but the sombrero the guerrillas wear to conceal their true actions" and "the oxygen they require
to survive in order to go on attacking villagers and army patrols as
well as the voluntary civil committees of self-defense"—the army's
euphemism for the compulsory civil defense patrols.

Given the army's inflexible posture, it surprised no one when the
latest rounds of talks between the government and the URNG in
Mexico City ended abruptly. The negotiations stalled over the sensitive issue of who was to blame for human rights violations against
the civilian population. Near the top of the military's "enemies list"
is the International Red Cross, whose potential role as arbitrator in
the peace talks would prove embarrassing to the army. The URNG
as well as human rights lobbies have repeatedly called for the International Red Cross to assess the violations against civilians by all
parties in the conflict and to assign reparations prior to the signing
of a peace accord. Given the military's abysmal human rights record,
particularly in the Zones of Conflict, it is unlikely they will ever agree
to independent arbitration, such as the U.N.'s Truth Commission in
El Salvador.

The suspension of the peace talks was followed by a public relations war between the two sides. Of the young people the army presented to the press as repentant guerrillas, the most controversial by
far was Maritza Urrutia, a thirty-year-old schoolteacher and single
mother who disappeared from her home after she admitted to being
a member of the EGP. Several days later she appeared in a videotape
on two local TV news stations. In the tape a tense, pale Maritza
Urrutia testified she had defected from the EGP and sought amnesty
from the government so she could live at peace with her young son.

The following day Urrutia's father and brother insisted Maritza
had been kidnapped and coerced into making a confession. They
pointed to a shoe she had left behind at the scene of the abduction,
to the uncharacteristic make-up she wore in her taped testimony, and

other glaring inconsistencies. The family's repudiation of Urrutia's "confession" made headlines across the country and set off reverberations in Washington, D.C. This was the first time in memory the family of a confessed guerrilla had challenged an army officer's accusations.

When Urrutia reappeared, she at first corroborated the army's version, but then abruptly changed her mind and sought protection from the archbishop's human rights office, rather than from her putative military liberators. A week after her reappearance, Maritza Urrutia got on a plane and departed unannounced for the United States with her small son. Archbishop Penados del Barrio hinted that his office was no longer able to protect her from a military command infuriated by Urrutia's recantation and betrayal.

On August 11 a political affairs officer in the U.S. Embassy, George Chester, held the army responsible for the abduction of Maritza Urrutia and her coerced confession. When President Serrano was informed that Chester had additionally helped Urrutia slip out of the country, he became incensed. Serrano called for the immediate removal of Chester and of a Minnesota lawyer with the archdiocese's human rights office, Daniel Saxon, whom he accused of "obfuscating" the facts in the Urrutia case. Meantime, four U.S. senators who sided with Chester's account of Urrutia's disappearance wrote President Serrano to request an explanation.

The following week a conciliatory meeting took place between Ambassador Thomas Stroock and Jorge Serrano. The president backed away from his threats to declare Chester persona non grata; instead, he gave him ninety days to collect his belongings and vacate the premises. *Crónica* reported that both parties concluded that the joint antinarcotic operations by the Guatemalan Army and the U.S. DEA were too important to be endangered by an isolated incident such as that of Maritza Urrutia.

The message was clear: stopping the spread of drugs had replaced counterinsurgency as the top priority in Washington's agenda for Guatemala.

In October Maritza Urrutia wrote a letter to United Nations Special Envoy Christian Tomuschat, who often visits Guatemala. She described in detail her abduction by plainclothesmen who interrogated her about her activities with the EGP. Before releasing her, the men, who claimed to be members of army intelligence, threatened the safety of Urrutia's son and family if she denounced the kidnapping.

Guatemalan army spokesmen denied Urrutia's charges, but they became an immediate embarrassment to President Serrano, who was accused of abdicating all control over his army officers. The published charges also embarrassed Attorney of Human Rights Ramiro de León Carpio, who admitted he had been pressured by the army to publicly deny Urrutia's abduction.

The Urrutia case gave fresh ammunition to human rights agencies in Europe and the United States, which inculpated the Guatemalan army in continuing violations against its citizens behind a shield of governmental impunity.

It was evident by the end of the summer that the campaign against government and military impunity could go only so far. Although indictments had been issued against top-echelon officers in both the DeVine and Myrna Mack Chang cases, none of them had led to convictions. The prosecution of Army High Command specialist Noel de Jesús Beteta Alvarez by Myrna Mack's sister, Helen Mack Chang, dragged on in the courts; in July, a somber Archbishop Penados del Barrio predicted that none of the "intellectual authors" named in the pending cases would ever be tried in a military or civilian court.

Guatemala's widening democratic *apertura* appeared to be on a collision course with reactionary hard-liners bent on closing the political space. Following the assassination of the chief investigator in the Myrna Mack case, his replacements have either been shifted to other jobs or they have resigned under pressure, as have judges who showed signs of undertaking a serious investigation. One of these conscientious justices, Leticia Secaira, was transferred to a remote coastal province after she refused to follow unspecified directives from her superiors. Secaira resigned her judgeship and accepted a position with the Public Ministry. On the day she was sworn into her new post, Leticia Secaira accused the office of Supreme Court President Juan José Rodil Peralta of placing telephone calls to herself and her colleagues. Secaira characterized these calls as flagrant attempts to influence or alter judges' rulings in cases that implicated top civilian and military officials.

The persistence against all odds of Helen Mack Chang—who called for the maximum thirty-year sentence against Beteta Alvarez—threatened the military's shield of impunity. Helen Mack, a government clerk with no previous legal experience, vowed to fight until a guilty verdict was brought against Beteta Alvarez and against the high-level officers who ordered her sister's assassination.

On October 8, 1992, a week before the announcement of Rigoberta Menchú's Nobel Peace Prize, the Swedish Right Livelihood Foundation awarded its prize, known as the Alternative Nobel, to Helen Mack Chang. The foundation cited her courageous stand in the face of government and military opposition. Helen Mack declared she would use the $37,000 prize to establish the Myrna Mack Chang Foundation, in defense of citizens' freedom of expression.

In November the Attorney for Human Rights, Ramiro de León Carpio, issued a resolution placing the blame for Myrna Mack Chang's murder on the government of Vinicio Cerezo. On February 12, 1993, Noel de Jesús Beteta Alvarez was sentenced to serve 25 years for the assassination of Myrna Mack Chang and five more years for injuries to Herbert Emilio Ramírez, a minor who was present at the scene. Beteta Alvarez's lawyer immediately appealed the sentence, and a new stage opened in Helen Mack Chang's efforts to bring her sister's murderers to justice. During the following weeks Clara Arenas, co-founder of AVANCSO with Myrna Mack, became the target of death threats in her offices.

On March 21, Helen Mack initiated a legal process against Beteta Alvarez's superior officers, among them General Edgar Godoy Gaitán, who headed the Presidential High Command in 1990. The Public Ministry, which had gathered evidence against Beteta Alvarez before Acisclo Valladares was ousted from office, now ruled that the charges against Beteta's superiors lacked supporting evidence and threw them out of court. Helen Mack Chang appealed the ruling.

When I interviewed Helen Mack several days later, she spoke of growing pressures from army intelligence to assure that Beteta Alvarez did not serve his sentence. She also cited the recent intervention by G-2 in the Guatemalan post office, President Serrano's threat to muzzle the press, and most particularly the death list faxed to the Guatemala Journalists' Association containing twenty-four critics of the government, including labor and civic leaders, as well as nine journalists. She said, "Our efforts to safeguard the democratic apertura are now in a direct confrontation with the government's determination to shut it down." She concluded, "Our main objective is to lay down a juridical foundation to prosecute military officers who order the assassination of their opponents, confident that they are beyond the reach of the law. We want to assure that the murder of my sister is the last to be committed by the military with that arrogant sense of their own impunity." If Sergeant Major Beteta Alvarez's sentence is upheld, he will become the highest ranking officer in modern Guatemalan history to have been convicted, sentenced, and jailed for a capital offense.

5

In early September, President Serrano Elías approved a binational Guatemalan/Panamanian initiative to install a race track and casino in the old hippodrome near Aurora International Airport. This was the same project that Vinicio Cerezo was prevented from pushing through two years earlier, after congressional leaders—Jorge Serrano among them—linked it to Panamanian drug traffickers. The president's critics had a field day two days later when *Siglo XXI* carried photographs of Serrano's private stable of eight polo ponies and four thoroughbred race horses. Jorge Serrano Elías, an evangelical preacher and elder, had pitched headlong into a trap of his own devising.

The hippodrome scandal threatened to do considerably more harm to Serrano than former President Cerezo suffered from all the publicity surrounding his secret liaisons and luxurious island retreats. Congressional and labor union leaders attacked the hippodrome initiative as an undercover money-laundering operation meant to garner huge revenues for government fat cats and the Colombian cartels. The most damaging charges underscored the hypocrisy of an evangelical preacher who planned to enrich himself by promoting gambling and alcohol- and drug-consumption.

Serrano shrugged off the accusations, insisting the hippodrome was a civic undertaking that did not compromise in any way his religious convictions. But the accusations stuck and raised the question, was Serrano's membership in four evangelical churches no more than a convenient springboard to the presidency?

A fresh spate of rumors was ignited by the revelation that Serrano belonged to the Full Gospel Businessmen's Fellowship, an influential

organization composed of wealthy charismatic Catholics and evangelicals. The members meet regularly in various hotels of the capital
for spiritual communion and to plan ambitious undertakings. Columnist Hugo Arce among others linked FGBF to Serrano's presidency,
hinting darkly that he was part of a global evangelical strategy for
the coming millennium. According to the latest rumors, FGBF was
already grooming the next president-elect, a charismatic evangelical
who would usher in the Second Kingdom in the year 2000.

Catholic spokesmen dusted off charges that foreign evangelicals
were on the march, attempting to wrest control of Guatemala's destiny. They fueled speculation about the satellite hook-up between
Guatemala's Shaddai congregation and the Mother Church in California. Was Serrano, like his former mentor Ríos Montt, an instrument of the anticommunist, pre-millenarial U.S. Protestant agenda for
Latin America? Or was Serrano, after all, just another pawn of the
military? This latter suspicion was lent substance by a *Crónica* profile
of Presidential High Command Chief Francisco Ortega Menaldo.

Serrano's right-hand military man, a former head of G-2, is in
charge of monitoring all information entering and leaving the National Palace. As Ortega's influence has grown he has catapulted himself, according to *Crónica,* from the shadow at Serrano's back to the
shadow president who makes the important decisions and, in effect,
runs the government.

To add to Serrano's problems, in late October the head of the
Public Ministry, Acisclo Valladares Molina, was tried for corruption
and influence-peddling, forcing him to resign his office. Similar charges
were filed against another Serrano appointee, Supreme Court President
Juan José Rodil Peralta. Emboldened by the impeachment of President Collor de Mello in Brazil, Serrano's opponents joined forces to
drive him out of office.

Three full-blown interrelated demonologies vied for the citizens'
credence. Serrano was variously depicted as a pawn of the military, a
stooge of the Colombian drug cartel, or a stand-in for the U.S. evangelical conspiracy. The only transparent fact in the murk of conjecture
and gossip that invariably swirls around a Guatemalan president, iso-
lating him from his constituents, was that Jorge Serrano Elías, a bour-
geois technocrat of limited talents and boundless ambition, had
brought most of his troubles down on his own head.

By the end of the year, even Serrano's diplomatic successes were
being turned against him. His recognition of the independence of

Belize in September 1991 ended a long-simmering dispute with Great Britain over this former colony, which Guatemala's presidents since 1821 have claimed under their own national sovereignty. The benefits Serrano expected to reap in improved relations with Great Britain and the Caribbean Commonwealth nations were overshadowed by a rising chorus of condemnation. Ultranationalist politicians and army officers accused Serrano of treason for selling out Belize. One of the chief destabilizers was none other than Serrano's fellow evangelical elder, Ríos Montt, who seized on the Belize controversy and Serrano's other vulnerabilities to drum up support among disaffected military officers. In the provinces, Ríos Montt's faithful began collecting votes for the 1993 municipal elections, hoping to place Riosmontistas in key local offices for a frontal challenge to Serrano's authority. The charismatic former general appeared determined to regain the presidency, either by constitutional means or via the tried and tested resort to a military coup.

Less than two years into Serrano's five-year presidency, the mounting charges and countercharges undermined his ability to govern a fractious and bedeviled nation obsessed with the approach of the new millennium.

In late May, Serrano's mounting frustrations led him to stage a self-coup. He dissolved Congress and the Supreme Court, muzzled the press, suspended part of the constitution, and resolved to rule by decree. Once again, Serrano seriously misjudged his opposition. The United States and many European countries suspended all aid at once, and the Organization of American States, threatening sanctions, called for an immediate restoration of constitutional guarantees. By week's end, Rigoberta Menchú—in Guatemala to preside over the World Indigenous Congress—and other popular leaders took to the streets with thousands of protesters to demand Serrano's resignation. Censored newspapers ran condemnations of Serrano's power grab in defiance of the new restrictions. The intense national and international outcry caused a divided military high command to back away from unconditional support of Serrano.

On June 2, after Serrano's last-ditch attempt to bribe lawmakers fell through, he was escorted from the National Palace by Defense Minister García Samayoa and put on a plane to San Salvador. Several days later Vice President Gustavo Espina was likewise removed from office, following an aborted attempt to take over the presidency with García Samayoa's backing.

Showing surprising resilience, Guatemala's eight-year-old democratic apertura rebounded from its most serious setback. On June 5 the reinstated Congress elected Attorney of Human Rights Ramiro de León Carpio, who enjoyed broad popular support, to fill the presidency vacated by Serrano and complete the remaining two and a half years of his term. On his first day as president, de León Carpio moved to replace Defense Minister García Samayoa and other hardliners in the army high command.

Epilogue

In the fall of 1990, the country seemed to be turning into a setting for an unpublished story by Miguel Angel Asturias. The magic realism that always threatens to erupt from the cobblestones of Antigua took to the streets in the frail, attenuated skeleton of the saintly Hermano Pedro; his glass coffin was led in solemn procession from one holy site to another, as a prelude to his reinterment in the grand new crypt at San Francisco. Friar Demian, the Italian-born Franciscan in charge of the ceremonial transfer, evidently hoped for a certifiable miracle that would cinch Hermano Pedro's claim to sainthood.

In the pre-electoral climate, the Franciscans were not the only ones hoping for a miracle. A pre-millenarial fever burned in the charismatics and Pentecostals who have breached Guatemala's last stronghold of medieval Catholicism. In their separate sanctums, they held continuous ecstatic services to hasten Christ's Second Kingdom. In Guatemala City, thousands of adepts of the Word Church kept up all-night prayer vigils for their anointed crusader, Efraín Ríos Montt.

But the violence that is as endemic to Guatemala as miracles and earthquakes would not be prayed away. In the summer of 1990, the war in the altiplano had crept ever closer to Antigua, threatening to turn the tourist resort into another Zone of Conflict. The guerrillas entrenched in neighboring volcanoes began making incursions into Dueñas, Santa María, Alotenango, and even Ciudad Vieja, the former colonial capital a scarce two miles from Antigua. Army patrols and blue-uniformed tactical police units became common sights in town, as violent crimes rose dramatically. My haven in Hotel Aurora was no longer safe.

Two weeks prior to the elections, six nuns disappeared as they drove out of Antigua, recalling the nightmare of Sister Dianna Ortiz's abduction and torture. The nuns appeared in the capital two days later, dazed and unhurt but without their van; it had been taken at gunpoint by three kidnappers, who may have been guerrillas, right-wing extremists, or common delinquents.

The following evening the Mother Superior of Antigua's Belén Convent, visibly shaken, recalled the day two burly men came for Sister Dianna Ortiz. "They found her in the garden and warned her that if she attempted to resist, they would blow up the convent. After the two men took her away we found Sister Dianna's necklace on the grass. The following day she called from a telephone, very distraught, and exclaimed in her broken Spanish that she had had a horrible experience. In the afternoon, a visiting priest found Sister Dianna's Bible in the branches of an apple tree."

The pattern of killings and abductions had a distressing familiarity. I had lived through periods like this in 1971 and again in 1981. Perhaps a fourth-century Maya calendrist would have detected a historical parallel or cosmic symmetry in these recurring cycles. Lesser mortals trapped in the present like flies on flypaper are denied the privilege of the astronomer's remove. Experience has conditioned me to sleep through tremors that register less than 3.5 on the Richter scale; but events in Guatemala on any given day can deaden other important thresholds.

A former classmate, photographer Ricardo Mata, presented a slide show about Hermano Pedro's birthplace on the afternoon the saint's bones made the rounds of Antigua. Earlier that day two men on a motorcycle had shot our colleague, publisher Byron Barrera, in his car and mortally wounded his wife, Refugio. Barrera, whose news-weekly *Epoca* was firebombed by unidentified agents in 1988, had called President Cerezo's press secretary to report he was being shad-owed. (The press secretary gave him an appointment for the following

Tuesday.) Although wounded in the neck and chest, Barrera's life was saved by the bulletproof vest his wife had insisted he wear, never suspecting she would become a target of assassination herself. The death squad's pinpointing of Barrera was intended to silence independent journalism, just as the assassination of anthropologist Myrna Mack Chang a few weeks earlier had been aimed at independent social science investigators and human rights monitors.

(Barrera returned to Guatemala a year later, under heavy escort, to name the army intelligence officer he accused of ordering the assassination attempt that resulted in the death of his wife. The officer has not been charged.)

After his slide presentation, Ricardo Mata told me of another classmate of ours, my boyhood tormentor Frederick Murga, who had grown up to become Guatemala's leading cardiologist. Recently, Murga had died of the very heart condition that had been his specialty, one that no other cardiologist in Guatemala was qualified to treat. As we parted, Mata said he was traveling to Quezaltenango to attend funeral services for three Swiss friends who had been incinerated by a cloud of live ash and cinder from Santiaguito volcano, one of the most active in Guatemala. Both Mata and his wife, Elena, had smiled inadvertently when we spoke of Barrera—a smile of resigned helplessness I had grown familiar with over the years—and they did not explain why their friends had chosen to climb an erupting volcano, nor did it cross my mind to inquire.

In the following morning's newspaper a third former schoolmate, columnist Carlos Rafael Soto, closed a moving elegy to Myrna Mack Chang and Refugio Barrera with the announcement that the same two men who killed Barrera—he called them "bikers of the apocalypse"—had been parked outside his home. That night I slept through a tremor of about 3.5 on the Richter scale, the third of comparable intensity in as many days.

The night before my departure a knock on my door startled me awake. With my heart pounding in my ears, I could *see* as clearly as if I had X-ray vision the two men behind the door, standing astride their motorcycle. The knocking was not repeated, but I stayed awake the rest of the night. Early in the morning I found under my door the letter I had agreed to post in Miami for a friend. Back home, I had to be held close for many a dreamless night before I could allow enough oxygen into my lungs to breathe properly.

After the victory of Tikal's rulers over Uaxactún in the fourth century, hundreds of nobles and warriors were taken captive. Gazing down on the plaza from his high perch, did the astronomer acknowledge the torture and humiliation of the captive lords? Did he flinch as the chests of one defeated warrior after the other were cut open to expose their hearts and offer them in sacrifice? (Archaeologists tell us the victims made no sound as their hearts were ripped out of their chests.) Perhaps the astronomer had become inured to blood by the penis-perforation rituals he had performed on himself to summon forth the vision serpent. Was the blood soaked into the earth from the Maya kings' unending wars destined to arise and flow from other severed veins centuries later to placate bloodthirsty gods? Self-sacrifice and blood offerings are rooted in the collective memory of descendants of the Mayas. But to the uninitiated there is no solace in the Maya calendrist's vision of the universe as interrelated cycles of millennia when one's whole life may be encapsulated in twenty-four hours and rolled down a precipice.

2

In August 1992 Guatemala's Conference of Bishops issued a historic pastoral letter, "500 Years of Sowing the Gospel." Despite the letter's conservative title, Guatemala's sixteen bishops aligned themselves as a body for the first time with Guatemala's long-suffering Mayan majority. The bishops' letter picks up where their 1988 pastoral message, "A Clamor for Land," left off, vigorously denouncing five centuries of unjust and inhuman exploitation of the Mayan communities. This time, Catholic missionaries are singled out for particular condemnation: "It cannot be denied that the missionary activity was used as a means for territorial expansion. Unfortunately the alliance of Church and State was a natural thing. . . . Although there have been exemplary bishops and missionaries, there have also been errors and contradictions in the comportment of members of the church, which have impacted unjustly on the indigenous communities. We who are the present pastors of the church, ask your forgiveness."

In a further conciliatory gesture, the bishops chose to speak for millions of dispossessed Mayas who deplore "the usurpation and theft of Mother Earth, degraded into a whore, provider of venality, egoism, and profit by encomenderos, landowners, Spanish conquistadores and colonizers, criollos, Germans, French, North Americans" and, by implication, corrupt churchmen as well. In ringing tones, the letter decries the scandal of the 231,000 hectares of fallow national lands still denied to the millions of landless and hungry Guatemalans, who now comprise 84 percent of the population. The letter stops short, although just barely, of endorsing a sweeping program of land reform.

In this document, Guatemala's bishops reached nearly five centuries into the past to invoke Bishop Bartolomé de las Casas. By pledging to respect the Mayas' autochthonous beliefs and customs, as las Casas had done, the bishops broke at last with generations of reactionary churchmen who equated their own and the Vatican's interests with oppressive authoritarian regimes.

The bishops' avowed aim to infuse rather than replace Mayan beliefs with Christ's mystery, validates the life work of Stanley Rother, who honored religious syncretism by learning Tz'utujil and incorporating costumbre into Catholic liturgy. The letter's explicit denunciation of ethnocide by the military also supports—without endorsing outright—the pastoral commitments of Xavier Gurriarán and other priests who joined the indigenous insurgency. Conservative bishops like Eduardo Fuentes of Sololá also have their say in a section devoted to the proposition that evangelization and conversion remain the ultimate objectives of the church's solidarity with the Mayas. One of the surprising results of the Protestant challenge to the Catholic church's hegemony in Latin America is a generation of bishops determined to make common cause with the indigenous communities and to combat together the root causes of their alienation.

The new spirit of tolerance espoused by Guatemala's bishops was echoed by Pope John Paul II's pronouncements on the rights of indigenous peoples during his visit to the Dominican Republic on October 12.

Demetrio Cojtí Cuxil, the first Mayan spokesperson to respond to the pastoral letter, lamented the bishops' reluctance to address the Mayas' needs outside of a missionary context. And he berated the bishops for making no mention of the Mayan resistance movements. This criticism was shared tacitly by the progressive bishop of Quiché, Monsignor Julio Cabrera Ovalle, who was one of the letter's authors. Cabrera, a staunch defender of the CPR and former counselor to Myrna Mack Chang, is believed by Archbishop Penados del Barrio to have been the "intellectual target" of Myrna Mack's assassins.

In February 1993, the first twenty-five hundred of the forty thousand Guatemalan refugees living in Mexico entered Guatemala in accordance with a negotiated agreement among the refugees' Permanent Commission, the U.N. High Commission for Refugees, and the Guatemalan government. The returnees entered along the Pan-American highway and headed directly to the capital, where a festive reception awaited them in front of the National Palace. The following day they set out for the Ixcán, where they were to resettle on lands set aside by the government.

Observers with the Archdiocese's Human Rights Office who visited the Ixcán in mid-March reported the returnees' close-knit organization enabled them to weather the inhospitable conditions they encountered on arrival. The first provisions of corn and beans supplied by the U.N.-sponsored Special Commission for Aid to Refugees (CEAR) were spoiled, and five children had died of gastrointestinal and respiratory ailments.

At night, army helicopters overflew the camps with their lights out, and army patrols had been sighted in the vicinity. (The nearest army garrison, at Playa Grande, is three hours away by foot.) In spite of the military's close monitoring of their activities, morale among the repatriated Guatemalans remained high, and they were determined to stay put until conditions improved.

Another three hours' walk to the west are the nearest settlements of the Ixcán's Communities of Population in Resistance. The returnees and the CPR share a long history of victimization by the army. That shared experience and their highly disciplined organization virtually assure a rapprochement between the two communities, and this is likely to provoke the military's efforts to control and isolate them.

The next group of one thousand refugees was scheduled to arrive in Huehuetenango in May.

3

On August 15 I attended a *fiesta patronal* in a village in southern Quiché. Joyabaj is among the few highland communities in a Zone of Conflict that have managed to conserve their feast day celebrations almost intact.

For the first time since my early childhood, I marveled at the *ángeles,* or fliers, in pink winged costumes who climb a hundred-foot pine pole with a capstan at the top. The pole represents the Mayan world tree, with its crest in the heavens and its base in the underworld. At a signal the ángeles fling themselves into space, clinging to the end of their ropes and shaking tiny gourd rattles as they descend head down in slowly widening circles. Two monkey-masked figures at the top strike sculpted poses as they pay out the rope. At the very last moment, just as their heads graze the ground, the ángeles lurch upright and land on their feet, running. For all the pageant's syncretic mix of Mayan and Christian symbolism, there is no mistaking the two fliers as anything but the fabled twins of the Popol Vuh, Hunahpú and Xbalanqué, whose descent into Xibalbá to defeat the Lords of Death is as seminal an event in the Mayas' cosmology as Moses's ascent of Sinai is to Western religion.

Below, the traditional masked dancers impersonating Spaniards, Mexican charros, and bull calves swirled around the pine pole, pressed so close together by the milling crowds, they could hardly perform their gyrations. Joyabaj has not yet been discovered by tourists, and not a single blond head bobbed above the sea of brown faces. The crush of elbows and shoulders against the small of my back, the cascades of huipil-clad women holding on to their drunken men were exactly as I remembered. But there was a variation in the monotonous Dance of the Conquest that I have observed elsewhere in the highlands over the past years.

When a dancer wearing burgundy velvet finery and a bearded cream-and-rose mask lifted his sword to smite a brown-masked dancer, he lashed back with his chain, and seizing the conquistador by the beard, the Mayan warrior forced him to his knees.

Afterword

In mid-March of 1995 I found Jennifer Harbury, a 43-year-old Harvard-trained lawyer, sitting in LaFayette Park across from the White House. She was in the sixth day of a fast to press the government to reveal the fate of her husband, a Mayan guerrilla *comandante* who had been captured by the Guatemalan army in March 1992. I had met Harbury five years earlier, when we drove together from Chiapas to northern Guatemala, where she was gathering evidence of human rights abuses to assist Guatemalans applying for asylum in the U.S. Harbury, who had recently worked in El Salvador, told a hair-raising story of two masked Salvadorans who had tried to abduct her as she clung to a lamppost, screaming at the top of her lungs until the abductors released her and drove away. Her tenacity had saved her life, at the cost of a dislocated shoulder and a fright that would have traumatized most people for life.

In Huehuetenango, Harbury stepped down from the car and walked alone into the Cuchumatán foothills, without looking back. Two years later she met Efraín Bámaca Velasquez, known by his comrades in the Organization of People in Arms as Comandante Everardo, and in 1992 they had flown to Texas to be married. Everardo was captured by the army shortly after his return to Guatemala, and Harbury set out on a solitary, tortuous journey to find him.

In Guatemala, Harbury was led from one burial site to another by army officials who claimed Everardo had been killed in combat, but none of the bodies they exhumed were her husband's. Shortly afterward, a guerrilla who escaped from military detention reported having seen Everardo alive, undergoing brutal torture. Harbury, who claimed the army was attempting to undermine her sanity, filed a suit to determine the fate of Everardo, and drew headlines with her fasts in front of the National Palace and the Politécnica Academy. As her enemies in the Guatemalan military and the C.I.A would learn to their regret, Harbury's drive and tenacity were exceptional even among the hardy breed of human rights investigators working in Central America.

During her month-long fast in Guatemala, Harbury was savagely attacked in the media, which depicted her as a pawn of the subversives attempting to take over the country. As the anti-Harbury hysteria mounted, and death threats hounded her every step, the indigenous Maya movement stood solidly behind the savvy, determined gringa who had married one of their own.

On the twelfth day of Harbury's fast in LaFayette Park, New Jersey Representative Robert G. Torricelli, a Democrat with the House Intelligence Committee, announced that a Guatemalan colonel on the C.I.A. payroll, Julio Roberto Alpírez, had directed the torture and execution, not only of Comandante Everardo, but also of Michael DeVine, the North American hotelier from Petén who was found nearly decapitated outside his restaurant in 1990. Torricelli revealed that the C.I.A. had funnelled five to seven million dollars into the Guatemalan army in 1992, after President Bush had cut off military aid to Guatemala in retaliation for the execution of DeVine. Forty-one years after the C.I.A. had engineered the overthrow of Jacobo Arbenz Guzmán, the intelligence agency was accused of conspiring in criminal activities against its own citizens.

In Guatemala, President Ramiro de León Carpio vigorously backed Colonel Alpírez, who denied any complicity in the torture and executions of Everardo and DeVine. De León Carpio, the former human rights ombudsman, had been named by congress to close out Jorge Serrano's presidential term in 1993. He has been hamstrung by the military since civil defense patrolers under army guidance assassinated his cousin, the centrist publisher and presidential candidate Jorge Carpio Nicolle. But former Guatemalan generals Efraín Ríos Montt

and Héctor Gramajo freely admitted having close relations with
C.I.A. station chiefs in Guatemala.

In their obsession with containing a three-decade-old insurgency,
the C.I.A. had funded two generations of officers trained in counterinsurgency by cold warriors in Fort Benning's notorious School of
the Americas. And it had actively collaborated with at least three
heads of the dreaded G-2, whose death squads were responsible for
the assassination of thousands of opponents of the government.

In addition, the U.S. Intelligence Service's efforts to maintain lever-
age over the army have raised the specter of C.I.A. collusion with officers enriching themselves from the contraband traffic of precious
hardwoods to Mexico and the transshipment of Colombian cocaine
to the U.S. The U.S. Drug Enforcement Agency, which estimates the
flow of cocaine through Guatemala at 70 tons a year, has identified
ten current and former officers who worked with narcotics smugglers.
In March 1994, Epaminondas Gonzáles Dubón, the highest ranking
Guatemalan justice, was assassinated after he approved the extradition to the U.S. of Colonel Carlos Ochoa Ruiz, who had been indicted
in Florida on charges of smuggling from Guatemala more than 1,000
pounds of Colombian cocaine. In 1995 a former DEA agent also implicated Colonel Alpírez as a drug-trafficker.

As news of C.I.A. interventions in Guatemala continued to generate headlines, President Clinton directed the Intelligence Oversight
Board to investigate a possible C.I.A. role in the assassination of U.S.
citizens there. The independent Oversight Board was given a broad
mandate to examine "any intelligence that may bear on the facts surrounding the torture, disappearance, or death of U.S. citizens in Guatemala since 1984" and to determine if there were patterns of human
rights abuse by U.S. intelligence assets, and if so whether these patterns were identified within the intelligence community and explained
to policymakers. The board consisted of four members headed by
Washington attorney Anthony S. Harrington, who was to present to
President Clinton within ninety days the board's preliminary findings
in the executions of Michael DeVine and Bámaca Velásquez. This
panel was also instructed to investigate the 1989 abduction and torture of Ursuline Sister Dianna Ortiz, and the 1985 murders of Nicholas
Blake and Griffith Davis.

Human rights groups pressed for a wider investigation to include the 1990 assassination of Guatemalan social science investigator Myrna Mack Chang, who had close ties with U.S. universities, and the murder of Epaminondas Gonzáles Dubón, the courageous Chief Justice of the Constitutional Court. Gonzáles Dubón not only stood up to drug traffickers in the army, but was virtually alone in enforcing the constitutional safeguards that prevented Jorge Serrano from pulling off his self-coup in May 1993.

The curtain of silence that had hung over Guatemala throughout the thirty-four-year war of counterinsurgency appeared to be lifting. And the catalyst had been a solitary, tenacious widow who fasted in front of the White House with a photograph of her husband over the legend: "President Clinton, in the name of God, save my husband from the Guatemalan death squads."

The day the news broke that Everardo had been tortured and executed by a colonel on the C.I.A. payroll, Harbury called for the immediate declassification of documents connecting the U.S. government to her husband's death; and she reiterated that she spoke for tens of thousands of Guatemalans when she demanded "the right to know what happened to our sons, our daughters, our loved ones, our husbands." But the Guatemalan press had a field day with the announcement that Harbury had signed a million-dollar movie deal with Ted Turner and CNN for her story.

When I interviewed Jennifer Harbury on March 29 1995 in Washington, she was accompanied by her father, Henry Harbury, a Holocaust survivor and Dartmouth Professor, and her mother Dorothy. Jennifer was an overnight media star, granting a dozen interviews a day to the national and foreign media. Harbury said she was thrilled by the movie contract, because it would keep the spotlight on human rights abuses in Guatemala. And she planned to use the revenues to establish a fund—in Everardo's name—to aid Mayan widows and other victims of the war. When Harbury mentioned her plans to return to Guatemala to reclaim her husband's remains and pursue her lawsuit, I reminded her of the dozens of Guatemalans who threatened to strangle her with their own hands. Harbury's large blue eyes, which had a soft, almost mystical glow during her fast, turned ice cold, and she clenched her teeth in a Clint Eastwood grimace. "I am going back there, and they can make my day."

On May 29, Jennifer Harbury returned to Guatemala, accompanied by one of Torricelli's aides, to continue her search for her husband's remains. A former high-placed G-2 official has revealed that the army deliberately misled Harbury in the previous exhumation.

2

In Guatemala, the revelation of criminal C.I.A. collusion with Guatemala's military had an immediate impact: a fire in the Aurora army base aroused suspicions that they were burning incriminating documents. And President de León Carpio, who accused Harbury of having close ties with the URNG, advised Roberto Alpírez to file a character-defamation suit against Representative Torricelli. This was evidently an attempt to head off an expected suit against Alpírez and any other Guatemalans who may have conspired in the murder of DeVine. According to a 1986 Omnibus Diplomatic Security and Antiterrorism Act, foreign agents implicated in the assassination of a U.S. national abroad are now subject to prosecution and trial in the United States.

In the wake of the bombing of the Alfred Murrah Federal building in Oklahoma City, President Clinton pressed for a revision of the bill to facilitate the extradition of foreign agents accused of capital crimes against U.S. citizens.

In late April Colonel Alpírez and another officer were suspended from active duty. A soldier imprisoned for assassinating DeVine finally confirmed suspicions that Alpírez was the one who actually oversaw the execution.

3

The news of the Zapatista uprising in Chiapas on January 1 1994 exploded like a bombshell in Guatemala's ladino power centers and in the Maya communities. The army of ski-masked rebels was composed primarily of indigenous groups—Tzeltals, Tzotzils, Tojolabals —with close cultural and historical ties to Guatemala's Mayas. Even the wooden rifles carried by some of the rebels reminded Mayas in Guatemala of their five centuries of humiliation by European conquistadors and their colonial successors, who had reduced them to the *Popol Vuh's* equivalent of soulless men of wood. To the military, who saw the hand of Guatemalan guerrillas in the uprising, the

Zapatista insurgency was a perfect excuse to maintain their troops at full strength. And they also used it to justify a crackdown on Guatemalans returning from Mexican refugee camps, many of whom settled in border areas close to the Zapatistas' base of operations.

In March of 1995 when Mexican President Ernesto Zedillo sent his army into the Zapatistas' Lacandon jungle stronghold, the Guatemalan army rushed 6,000 Kaibil troops to the border to cut off the Zapatistas' escape. One plausible justification for the coordinated deployment of Guatemalan and Mexican troops could have been to protect untapped petroleum reserves in the region, as well as to safeguard a lucrative traffic in contraband lumber to Chiapas.

4

In spring of 1994, government and guerrilla representatives signed a Human Rights Accord that was greeted as the first major breakthrough in the six-year-old negotiations. The terms of the accord called for a United Nations-sponsored investigative commission to gather evidence of human rights violations in Guatemala. This Verification Commission was authorized to set up offices throughout the country and to inspect military garrisons and guerrilla enclaves in the zones of conflict. To many human rights observers, the accord was hobbled from the start by a clause inserted by government negotiators that protected individuals from prosecution for the crimes uncovered by the Commission.

When I arrived in Guatemala in June 1994, over 200 U.N. monitors had begun their investigations. Forensic teams from Argentina and the U.S. joined Guatemalans in exhuming hundreds of corpses from clandestine burial sites in Rabinal's Río Negro, Coatepeque, the Petén, and other lowland and highland regions affected by the war. In the Capital's literary cafes, writers, professors, and former student activists exchanged stories of their years in the undergound behind curtains of cigarette smoke; some had composed elegiac poems and begun writing memoirs about shattered utopian dreams and the loss of compañeros; others accused triumphalist URNG comandantes of duping the rank and file and their Mayan supporters by nursing their impossible hopes of an early victory over their oppressors.

As in Argentina at the end of the *guerra sucia*, and more recently in El Salvador, the post-war years in Guatemala promised to be bitter ones, marked by post-traumatic crises, disillusionment and mutual recriminations. In chance encounters at social gatherings, former torturers avoided the probing gazes of their victims. But torture specialists have never lacked employment by Guatemala's army and paramilitary death squads, and new ones are being recruited today.

The ultraright's attempts to obstruct the Verification Commission and derail the peace talks went to murderous lengths in spring of 1994 with the assassination of Chief Justice Epaminondas Gonzáles Dubón. In the following weeks two U.S. women were attacked by mobs in remote regions of the country, suspected of kidnapping children for organ transplants abroad. June Weinstock, an Alaska resident, was savagely beaten in San Cristóbal Verapaz after a mother accused her falsely of kidnaping her 8-year-old son.

The rumors of gringas stealing children, which were fanned by government provocateurs, served the dual purpose of impeding the work of foreign human rights investigators and diverting attention from government officials who reaped enormous profits from the illegal traffic of children for adoption abroad.

Human rights abuses continued to mount in de León Carpio's second year, as he openly supported the army and civil defense patrols. Lost opportunites by three civilian presidents came back to haunt Guatemala in the post-war era. Even as the forensic teams unearthed hundreds of bodies, most of them showing evidence of torture, tens of thousands of other victims would remain sealed in the memory of survivors who feared bearing witness to the disappearance of their loved ones.

In March 1995 the United Nations' Verification Commission issued its initial report. The Commission recorded 22 political assassinations, 10 attempted assassinations and 68 death threats against political activists and human rights monitors. Well over 90 percent of these and lesser abuses were attributed to the military, the army-controlled civil defense patrols and police agencies. On March 15, peace talks between the government and the URNG resumed in Mexico. After two weeks, negotiators finally broke a months-long deadlock with a seven-point agreement that recognized the Mayan majority's ethnic

rights and identity. The agreement promotes bilingual education and
grants other cultural and religious safeguards to the indigenous communities, as well as laying the foundations for a limited political
autonomy. But sticky issues remained to be ironed out on civilian
power and the role of the army; the reintegration of the guerrillas into
civilian life; constitutional reforms and a schedule for implementation and verification of the accord. On an official visit to Guatemala,
U.N. Secretary Boutros Boutros-Ghali extended the Commission's
mandate for another six months, and pressed for a comprehensive
peace agreement by the end of August.

Recently Archbishop Penados del Barrio's human rights office
established its own Truth Commission with offices throughout Guatemala. Unlike the U.N. Verification Commission, the diocese commission will name and indict individual human rights offenders.

5

In summer of 1994 the Guatemalan Republican Front, the political
party headed by Efraín Ríos Montt, won 32 of the 80 seats in the reduced "reform congress" elected to replace the Serrano congress until
the November 1995 elections.

The congressional plurality won by the evangelical preacher and
former army officer was capped in January by his election to the presidency of the new congress. His new post positioned Ríos Montt to
amend the constitutional clause that prevented coup leaders from
seeking a second presidential term. The vote appeared to confirm
Ríos Montt's undimmed popularity. His drive to reclaim the presidency acquired an aura of inevitability, underscored by the millions
of Guatemalans who were sick unto death of the violence, and who
wanted their "human rights" enforced by a charismatic caudillo with
a velvet-lined iron fist. In his opening speech as Congress President,
Ríos Montt addressed his evangelical supporters by urging Guatemalans to adopt "the principles of Christian civilization, converting
good behavior into a way of life."

Early in 1995 a "Broad Democratic Front" mobilized to forge an
alliance among liberal sectors of the Catholic Church, the indigenous
and labor union movements, and the URNG. Alarmed by Ríos Montt's

resurgence, the guerrillas announced their intention to participate in the November presidential elections even if a peace accord had not been signed by the August deadline. Rumors of a candidacy by Nobel winner Rigoberta Menchú, and a bid to draft the Catholic church's former peace negotiator Monsignor Rodolfo Quezada Toruño, waxed and waned during the spring. Héctor Gramajo, the former Defense Minister, became the second announced candidate, as the Broad Front continued its search for a national figure to match Ríos Montt's popularity. In April the Christian Democrats, the centrist UCN, and the Social Democratic Party formed their own United Front and named Fernando Andrade Durán, a centrist businessman, as their presidential candidate. As the numbers of death squad killings rose out of control, rumors resurfaced that the army was preparing to stage a coup and cancel the elections.

The Republican sweep in the U.S. gubernatorial and congressional elections infused new energy into Ríos Montt's flagging presidential campaign, as his old backers in the U.S. Christian Right—among them Pat Robertson and Jerry Falwell—moved to remake the Republican party in their own image, a move that sent shock waves throughout the Americas.

In late May Ríos Montt held a twenty-point lead in the polls over his nearest rival, former Guatemala City Mayor Alvaro Arzú of the conservative Party for National Advancement (PAN). And Ríos Montt warned that if his candidacy was denied in the courts, he would mount a campaign of civil resistance and seize the presidency by popular mandate.

Ríos Montt's evangelical supporters remained confident that nothing would deter their anointed from his appointed destiny, and that he would be seated in the presidential chair to welcome the Second Coming of Christ at the end of the Millenium. This time around, the iron-fisted caudillo would also wear the mantle of messianic prophet.

6

In mid-April 1995 the bombing of the Oklahoma City Federal building by rightwing anti-government terrorists pushed the C.I.A. hearings on Guatemala off the front pages. President Clinton's nominee to head the C.I.A., Deputy Defense Secretary John M. Deutsch, pledged to sweep away a generation of cold warriors and change the intelligence service "all the way down to the bare bones."

But in Guatemala the cold war remained very much alive, as new reports surfaced of decades-old collaboration between veteran C.I.A. station chiefs and old-guard Guatemalan generals. By late April, Clinton was backpedaling from a pledge to pursue the investigation into C.I.A. activities in Guatemala wherever they might lead, and to push for legislation to downsize the agency.

In Congress, Republican House leader Newt Gingrinch pressed for Torricelli's resignation from the House Intelligence Committee on the grounds that he had violated the house rules of secrecy by divulging confidential information. But congressmen backed away from voting for Torricelli's resignation for fear of making him a martyr, and the issue was referred instead to the House Ethics Committee. Wasting no time, Torricelli dispatched a letter to the Committee, Jeffersonian in tone and content, claiming the constitutional issues behind the alleged C.I.A. crimes in Guatemala outweighed the breach of secrecy rules.

As the Intelligence Oversight Board continued its investigations, Gingrich and his allies succeeded in turning the spotlight away from the hearings to Torricelli's breach of the House secrecy rules.

Once again, the curtain of silence appeared to come down on Guatemala, as it had many times before following a shortlived *apertura*. Hanging in the balance was a historic opportunity to end a 35-year-old war of counterinsurgency funded and directed by the C.I.A., and to lay to rest at last an artificially prolonged cold war that has been the chief sustenance of corrupt, murderous regimes at war with their own citizens, not only in Guatemala, but throughout the Americas.

Bibliography

This select bibliography focuses on sources relevant to the highland Mayan communities and the Petén. Key magazine and scholarly articles are included. Other relevant articles and journals, background material, and secondary sources are referred to in the text or in the essay below.

For the European perspective on the Conquest and early colonial history, I relied on the standard sources: Diego de Landa (1566), Bernal Díaz del Castillo (1575), Llorente (1552), Fuentes y Guzmán (1643), and Ximénez (1722). As one of the very few sixteenth-century Spaniards sympathetic to the Mayas, las Casas (1552) duly chronicled their subjugation and the many outrages committed against them by the conquistadores. Still, as a one-time *encomendero* and a royal subject answerable to his sovereign as well as to God, Bishop las Casas is as vulnerable to charges of willful distortion as any other historian of that period. However well intentioned, las Casas's inflated estimates of the numbers of Indians exterminated under Pedro de Alvarado appear to have no objective foundation. As Lovell (1992) and MacLeod (1973) persuasively argue, Old World diseases introduced by the Spaniards killed hundreds of thousands more Mayas than the most ruthless conquistador even dreamed of. (MacLeod aptly calls the epidemics of smallpox and measles "shock troops of the Conquest.")

Among modern historians, Robert Hill's book (1991) is particularly useful on the Cakchiquel revolt against the Spaniards, and Grant Jones (1989) is the best on the Itzá resistance in Petén. Martínez Peláez (1971) captures the power feuds between peninsular and colonial authorities—that is, between Audiencia and Cabildo—and skillfully dissects the *mestizaje* from which ladino culture emerged. Martínez, a Marxist militant, is doctrinaire and therefore less reliable on the post-Conquest Mayas, whom he dismisses as deculturated "indios" and colonial by-products, a stereotype that is ironically convenient to Guatemala's criollo elite and to ladinos as a whole. (This is one of countless instances in which a leftist interpretation of events in Guatemala has been adopted by the right. One by-product of the contradictions inherent in the conquest and subjugation of one culture by another appears to be a mutual cannibalization by the heirs of the conquerors.)

For the perspective of the conquered, I turned to the *Annals of the Cakchiquels* (Recinos 1980), the *Popol Vuh,* and the *Chilam Balam of Chumayel* (Roys, 1967), the last a Yucatec book of prophecy founded on the Mayan calendar. The *Chilam Balam* chillingly portrays the calamities to befall the peninsular Mayas on the eve of the Conquest and Christianization. More than any other extant Mayan chronicle, the Cakchiquel *Annals* spell out the horrors of the Conquest as it was lived by its victims. Each of these documents contains invaluable—albeit fragmentary—images and reflections of Maya cultures prior to first contact with Europeans. I used Edmonson's (1971) verse translation of the *Popol Vuh* into English from the original Quiché; Recinos's remains the standard rendering into Spanish (Goetz, 1950). Barbara Tedlock (1982) and Dennis Tedlock (1985) excel on the *Popol Vuh*'s relevance to living Mayas, but the latter's translation is rather wooden. There is a tacit understanding among the translators that the *Popol Vuh*'s subtle intricacies will elude those who read it simply as a resource. Highland Mayas regard it as their Bible and approach it with the humility and reverence due a sacred text.

The British Dominican friar and traveler Thomas Gage (1648) proved a helpful chronicler on conditions in Guatemala in the 1630s, particularly on the abuses of *encomienda.* John Lloyd Stephens (1841), writing in the mid-nineteenth century, occupies a place by himself. Armed with an insatiable curiosity, a clear, dispassionate eye, and a fine writing style—not to mention the invaluable services of his artist companion Catherwood—he raised travel writing on Mesoamerica, and on Guatemala in particular, to a high art. The multilayered format of *Unfinished Conquest* is inspired in part by Stephens's judicious approach.

Among the moderns, Ralph Lee Woodward, Jr. (1976) is excellent on the Carrera and Rufino Barrios era, viewed within a larger Central American context. LaFeber (1983) has the clearest regional perspective on twentieth-century Guatemala. I read the Guatemalan social scientists Cambranes (1986) for contemporary agrarian movements—Father Girón's, in particular—and Monteforte Toledo (1959) for sociological analysis. Of the North Americans, I turned to Thomas Melville and Marjorie Melville (1971) for their study of the politics of land tenure and to David McCreery (1988) for his scholarly studies of land-centered conflict in the highlands.

Two prescient writers prefigured Guatemala's civil wars. In his lyrical essay "Guatemala: Las Líneas de Su Mano," Luis Cardoza y Aragón (1955) foreshadows the end of the "Guatemalan Spring" of 1944–54 even as he celebrates it. His subsequent exile turned out to be permanent. Miguel Angel Asturias's *El Señor Presidente* (1940, 1983) captures the cruelly surreal era of Estrada Cabrera and the early years of Ubico's reign. His polemical and flawed *El Papa Verde (The Green Pope)* (1951, 1988), the second volume of his "United Fruit Trilogy," weaves a magic realist setting for the 1954 overthrow of Arbenz by a coalition that included the CIA, the United Fruit Company, Guatemala's right-wing officers, and landowning interests. Kinzer and Schlesinger's *Bitter Fruit* (1981) remains the most thorough study of that period, although some of their conclusions are questionable. Richard Immerman's book (1982) oversimplifies the CIA's role. Piero Gleijeses's study (1991) is solid and up to date on the impact of U.S. anticommunist policy on Arbenz, whom he praises as Guatemala's best modern president because of his courageous agrarian reform. Gleijeses devotes a full chapter to a generally overlooked key figure in the 1954 overthrow of Arbenz: Major Francisco Arana, the ambitious Chief of the Armed Forces who was killed in a shoot-out in 1946 after Arévalo gave the orders for his capture. Jim Handy, author of the useful contemporary history *Gift of the Devil* (1984), proposes in an as yet unpublished study (*Revolution in the Countryside: Guatemala, 1944–1954*) that Arbenz was overthrown because army officers became increasingly concerned about peasant organization around the agrarian reform and their own loss of power and influence in Guatemalan society. According to Handy, the CIA's clumsy undercover operations were a lucky catalyst rather than the decisive factor in Arbenz's downfall. Gleijeses, on the other hand, attributes the Guatemalan officers' passive collusion with the CIA to their fear of direct U.S. intervention. José Manuel Fortuny, a former communist and close associate of Arbenz's, may have summed it up best when he assured Gleijeses, "They would have overthrown us even if we had grown no bananas."

The two most eloquent indigenous accounts of the war to date are Rigoberta Menchú's *I, Rigoberta Menchú* (1984) and Victor Montejo's *Testimony: The Death of a Guatemalan Village* (1987). Montejo's description of brutish army officers who tortured innocent villagers and used civil defense patrols as execution squads applied throughout the highlands. Menchú's account is fuller and more harrowing than Montejo's, and more problematic. Marc Zimmerman (1991) and David Stoll point out inconsistencies in her eyewitness account, which is also at odds with Payeras's testimony of the Chajul massacre (1987); there are also problems with the translation into European languages of a "testimonio" whose oral tradition favors a communal perspective over verifiable, firsthand observation. In "Rigoberta's Secrets," Doris Sommer (1991) highlights Menchú's admission, "I'm still keeping secret what I think no one should know. Not even anthropologists and intellectuals, no matter how many books they have, can find out all our secrets." Although her book should be as subject to objective scrutiny as any other published account, the force of Menchú's intelligence and personal integrity, and her almost miraculous survival, render her testimony unique and, to an extent, impervious to critical analysis.

The most thorough and balanced presentation of human rights abuses in Guatemala since 1985 are found in the Americas Watch reports, several of them written by Jean-Marie Simon and others more recently by Jemara Rone and Ann Manuel. In tandem with Simon's book *Guatemala: Eternal Spring, Eternal Tyranny* (1987), the reports exposed the whitewashing of military regimes by the State Department during the Reagan era, a policy that has been partially reversed under George Bush. Amnesty International, the Washington Office on Latin America, and Cultural Survival have also turned out well researched, periodic reports on Guatemala. The biennial Report on Guatemala by the Guatemala News and Information Bureau (GNIB), now published in conjunction with NISGUA, has been particularly helpful in keeping track of refugees who fled to Mexico and in monitoring the incursions of U.S. evangelicals in the Maya highlands. The Guatemalan Church in Exile issues periodic reports filled with first-person testimony from the Maya Communities of Population in Resistance (CPR) and the refugee enclaves abroad. EPOCA has concentrated on ecological abuses by the Guatemalan military, most notably their use of defoliants and other toxic chemicals in counterinsurgency. Their early reports have been faulted for relying on hearsay and unconfirmed sources. Their 1990 report, researched and written by Florence Gardner, is the most solid to date and may have been the last, as EPOCA has become inactive. The occasional reports on Guatemala from Nature Conservancy, Conservation International, and US AID have helped to focus world attention on the plight of Petén's rain forests.

Of the Guatemalan news agencies, the best by far in political and socioeconomic analysis has been Inforpress, and I have consistently relied on their weekly newsletters and yearly reports. No other news agency has monitored as carefully the rise and fall of Vinicio Cerezo or presented more credible evidence of the military's unwillingness to yield even a modicum of authority to a civilian. Another excellent resource is AVANCSO, whose in-depth reports are painstakingly researched by professional investigators. The most incisive—and controversial—was anthropologist Myrna Mack Chang's report on Guatemala's displaced Maya communities and on the army's persecution of internal refugees (1990); the publication of that report may have cost Chang her life. The Centro de Investigaciones Regionales de Mesoamérica (CIRMA), in whose Antigua offices I wrote the bulk of this manuscript, publishes outstanding social science articles in its quarterly publication, *Mesoamérica*. The more pertinent ones are listed below, by author. Human rights reports by the Archdiocese of Guatemala and by the Attorney for Human Rights, appearing irregularly since 1988, have been more courageous than thoroughgoing, owing to the military's unrelenting vigilance. The legal and investigative work by Minnesota lawyer Daniel Saxon, particularly on the Myrna Mack Chang and Maritza Urrutia cases, riled President Serrano to the extent of threatening to remove Saxon from the Archdiocese's Human Rights Office and expel him from Guatemala. (Saxon left of his own accord in November 1992.)

I know of no authoritative history of Guatemala's guerrilla movement from its beginnings in the late fifties to the end of the cold war, culminating in the present peace negotiations. Mario Payeras has written the most compelling testimony by a former guerrilla commander. *Days of the Jungle* (1983) and *El Trueno en la Ciudad* (1987) cover his trajectory from the years of unswerving commitment to armed revolution to his more critical posture following his resignation from the EGP in 1984. Various aspects of the guerrilla movement have been addressed in Adams (1974), Galeano (1969), Handy (1984), Evans-Pritchard (1985), Schwartz (1991), and in the chief news agencies. The defunct Guatemalan daily, *Imparcial*, and Costa Rica's *Polémica* reported on the early stages of FAR, the EGP, and ORPA. *Otra Guatemala*, a quarterly magazine based in Mexico, is erratic but useful as an unofficial mouthpiece of the URNG, as is the EGP's official organ, *Compañero*.

Penny Lernoux (1980), Susanne Jonas and David Tobis (1974), Michael McClintock (1985), and George Black (1984) have traced the military's ascendancy since 1954. Anderson and Simon (1987), Allan Nairn and Simon (1986), George Lovell (1988), and more recently Michael Massing (1990) have presented helpful but inconclusive reports on the new public-relations-conscious army introduced by Héctor Gramajo. Coverage of Guatemala's civil war as a whole in the U.S. and international press has been shamefully scanty, with some improvement during the Cerezo years when news sources became more accessible.

In regional coverage, starting with the Cuchumatanes, I have relied in particular on the scholarly writings of Lovell, MacLeod and Wasserstrom (1983), Stoll (1992), and Colby and van der Berghe (1969). Lovell and MacLeod are outstanding on the northern Cuchumatanes, with significant contributions by La Farge (1947), Davis (1982), Brintnall (1979), and McCreery (1988) on San Juan Ixcoy. Lovell, whose landmark *Conquest and Survival* recently appeared in Spanish (1990) and revised English (1992) editions, is among the proponents of the three cycles of Conquest. On Todos Santos Cuchumatán, I found no more reliable guide to the customs and practices of the Mam of that region than Maud Oakes (1951), whose two studies are discussed at length in the chapters on Todos Santos. Colby and Colby (1981) and Colby and van der Berghe (1969) are most helpful on the Ixil Triangle, particularly in ethnography and folk customs; David Stoll's essay in *Harvest of Violence* (Carmack, 1988) is illuminating on the rise of the evangelicals in Nebaj. Stoll's doctoral dissertation, *Between Two Fires* (1992), is the most thorough scholarly study of Ixil country I have seen to date. However, Stoll's conclusion that Ixils and ladinos have made common cause against both the army and the guerrillas could prove ephemeral, as the power equations in the Ixil Triangle shift once again and the evangelical tide recedes. Montejo's is the most eloquent testimony on Northwest Huehuetenango, Menchú's on Uspantán, Brintnall's on Aguacatán, Melville and Melville's on land tenure in the highlands, and Ricardo Falla's on the massacres at Finca San Francisco (1983) and the Ixcán (1992). I have also drawn from Beatriz Manz's articles on the Ixcán and Playa Grande, and on her study (1989) of refugees from the Mam area.

Carmack is the most thorough on southern Quiché, both as editor of *Harvest of Violence* (1988) and as scholarly writer of several books and monographs (1973, 1981); Carol Smith (1991), Nora England (1991), Victoria Bricker (1981), and McCreery (see Smith, ed., 1991) are useful on the "New Maya," among whose spokespersons Demetrio Cojtí (1990, 1991) and Narciso Cojtí and Margarita López Raquec (1988) stand out. Annis (1987) is often incisive but inconsistent in his use of sources on the Cakchiquel community of San Antonio Aguas Calientes, outside of Antigua.

On Santiago Atitlán, I have relied on diverse sources. I read Hinshaw (1975) and Tax and Hinshaw (1968) on the Cakchiquels of Panajachel; Paul (1959) on San Pedro la Laguna; I relied on Lothrop (1928) and Orellana (1984) for Tz'utujil history, and on Loucky and Carlsen (1991), Mendelson [AKA Tarn] (1965), and Tarn and Prechtel (1990) for ethnography. Carlsen is outstanding on the role of evangelicals. Rother's published letters (1984) are more helpful by far in understanding him, his work, and his martyrdom than any of the proliferating books, articles, and videotapes spurred by the movement for his canonization.

On Petén, I used both foreign and Guatemalan sources. Although Morley and Brainerd's (1983) and Thompson's (1966) views of Mayas as peace-loving, stargazing philosopher-kings are now discredited, their archaeological spadework remains invaluable. Monteforte Toledo's (1948) and Macal's (1969) novels and the Soza monograph (1970) are helpful on the logging history of Petén. Schwartz's book (1991) is the most complete on *la chiclería* and on Petén's social history to the present. It includes a helpful sketch on the rise of FAR in Petén. Schele and Miller's *Blood of Kings* (1986) remains in the forefront of the recent archaeological works, together with epigraphers Knorozov (1962) and Houston and Stuart (1989), as well as Mayanists Coe (1966) and Demarest (1976), among others; however, Schele's conclusion that implacable Maya warrior kings may account for that civilization's collapse is likely to be revised by future investigators.

I read Caulfield (1986), Forsyth and Miyata (1984), and Nations (1988) for the ecology of the Mesoamerican rain forest. Edith Alicia Erazo and María del Carmen Erazo (1991) have contributed an authoritative study on the scavenger society of Guatemala City's municipal dump. Finally, Tozzer (1978) and Bruce (1974) remain the standard sources on Lacandón culture and its links to the Mayan highland communities.

NEWS SERVICES

Central American Report. Guatemala City: Guatemalan Inforpress Centro-american.
Guatemalan News in Brief. New York: Americas Watch Committee.
Latin American Regional Report. London: Latin American Newsletters.
Report on the Americas. New York: North American Congress on Latin America (NACLA).
Report on Guatemala. Oakland, Calif.: National Network in Solidarity with the People of Guatemala (NISGUA).
This Week: Central America and Panama. A Report on Business and Politics. Guatemala.

REPORTS

Americas Watch Committee, New York:
Guatemalan Refugees in Mexico, 1980–84.
Guatemala: A Nation of Prisoners, 1984.
Guatemala: The Group for Mutual Support, 1985.
Civil Patrols in Guatemala, 1986.
Human Rights in Guatemala during President Cerezo's First Year, 1986.
Closing the Space: Human Rights in Guatemala, 1988.
Persecuting Human Rights Monitors: The CERJ in Guatemala, 1989.
Messengers of Death: Human Rights in Guatemala, 1990.
Guatemala: Getting Away with Murder, 1991.
Amnesty International, London:
Testimony in Guatemala, 1982.
Guatemala: Massive Extrajudicial Executions in Rural Areas under the Government of General Efraín Ríos Montt, 1983.

Disappearances in Guatemala under the Government of General Oscar Humberto Mejía Víctores, 1985.

Report on Guatemala, 1988.

Asociación Para el Avance de Las Ciencias Sociales en Guatemala (AVANCSO), Guatemala:

La Política de Desarrollo del Estado Guatemalteco, no. 2, 1986–87.

Por Si Mismos: Un Estudio Preliminar de las "Maras" en la Ciudad de Guatemala, no. 4, 1988.

Política Institucional hacia el Desplazado Interno en Guatemala, no. 6, 1990.

¿Donde Está el Futuro?: Procesos de Reintegración en Comunidades de Retornados, no. 8, 1992.

Cultural Survival Quarterly, Cambridge, Mass.:

Death and Disorder in Guatemala, Jason Clay, ed., 1983.

"Guatemalan Refugees in Chiapas," Christian García, 1983.

"Guatemalan Refugees in Mexico," Daniel Conde, 1983.

"Observations from Guatemala," Wade Davis, 1983.

"From Conquest to Counterinsurgency," George Lovell, 1985.

Counterinsurgency and the Development Pole Strategy in Guatemala, Jason Clay, ed., 1989.

" 'The Land No Longer Gives': Land Reform in Nebaj," David Stoll, 1990.

"Maya Survival in Ixil Country, Guatemala," George Lovell, 1990.

The Environmental Project on Central America (EPOCA), Earth Island Institute, San Francisco, Calif.:

EPOCA Update: Politics Meets Ecology in Guatemala, Florence Gardner, 1990.

Guatemalan Church in Exile (IGE), Managua, Nicaragua:

Guatemala, "A New Way of Life," The Development Poles, 1984.

Development: The New Face of War.

Documentos Oficiales de Las Comunidades de Población en Resistencia, 1989.

Guatemala: Security, Development, and Democracy, 1989.

"Ofensiva del Pueblo": Campesino Contra Campesino, 1989.

Diez Años de Pacificación Contrainsurgente, July 1990.

Guatemala's Guerrilla Army of the Poor (EGP), San Francisco, Calif.:

Compañero. Vols. 1–4, 1982–88.

Guatemala Scholars Network, Houston, Texas:

Response to the Report by the National Bipartisan Commission on Central America, 1984.

Reports from the Network, 1987–91.

Inforpress Centroamericana, Guatemala City:

Guatemala, 1986: El Año de las Promesas, 1987.

Guatemala, 1989: El Año de los Tropiezos, 1990.

Survival International, London:

Nelson, C. W., and K. I. Taylor. Witness to Genocide: The Present Situation of Indians in Guatemala, 1983.

U.S. State Department, Washington, D.C.:

Yearly country reports on the state of human rights in Guatemala, 1979–91.

Washington Office on Latin America, Washington, D.C.:
  Booth, J. A. The 1985 Guatemalan Elections: Will the Military Relinquish
    Power? 1985.
  Krueger, C. The Guatemalan Highlands: Democratic Transition or the Con-
    tinuation of War? 1987.
  The Administration of Injustice: Military Accountability in Guatemala, 1989.

BOOKS AND ARTICLES

Adams, Richard N. Crucifixion by Power: Essays on Guatemalan National So-
    cial Structure, 1944–1966. Austin: University of Texas Press, 1970.
———. Political Changes in Guatemalan Indian Communities: A Symposium.
    Middle America Research Institute, vol. 24. New Orleans, La.: Tulane Uni-
    versity, 1974.
Anderson, Ken, and Jean-Marie Simon. "Permanent Counter-Insurgency in Gua-
    temala." Telos, no. 73, Fall 1987.
Anderson, Marilyn (photos) and Jonathan Garlock (text). Granddaughters of
    Corn: Portraits of Guatemalan Women. Willimantic, Conn.: Curbstone Press,
    1988.
Annis, Sheldon. God and Production in a Guatemalan Town. Austin: University
    of Texas Press, 1987.
Asturias, Miguel Angel. Hombres de Maíz. Guatemala: Editorial Piedra Santa,
    1991.
———. Leyendas de Guatemala. Madrid: Alonzo/Losada, 1985.
———. El Papa Verde. Madrid: Alonzo/Losada, [1951] 1988.
———. El Señor Presidente. San José, Costa Rica: Editorial Universitaria Cen-
    troamericana, [1940] 1983.
Barry, Tom. Guatemala: A Country Guide. Albuquerque, N.M.: The Inter-
    Hemispheric Education Resource Center, 1989.
Black, George, with Milton Jamail and Norma Stoltz Chinchilla. Garrison Gua-
    temala. New York: Monthly Review Press, 1984.
Borges, Alfredo Guerra, "Guatemala 1986/89: Transición a la Incertidumbre,"
    Polémica (San José, Costa Rica), January/April 1990.
Bricker, Victoria R. The Indian Christ, the Indian King. Austin: University of
    Texas Press, 1981.
Brintnall, Douglas E. Revolt Against the Dead: The Modernization of a Mayan
    Community in the Highlands of Guatemala. New York: Gordon and Breach,
    1979.
Bruce, Robert D. El Libro de Chan K'in. Mexico City: Instituto Nacional de
    Antropología e Historia, 1974.
Burgos-Debray, Elisabeth, ed. I, Rigoberta Menchú: An Indian Woman in Gua-
    temala. London: Verso Editions, 1984.
Cambranes, J. C. Agrarismo en Guatemala. Guatemala: Serviprensa Centro-
    americana, 1986.
———. Coffee and Peasants in Guatemala: The Origins of the Modern Plan-
    tation Economy in Guatemala, 1853–1897. Indianapolis, Ind.: Plumsock
    Foundation, 1985.

Canby, Peter. *Heart of the Sky.* New York: HarperCollins, 1992.

Cardoza y Aragón, Luis. *Guatemala, Las Líneas de Su Mano.* Mexico City: Fondo de Cultura Económica, 1955.

———. *Guatemala con una Piedra Adentro.* Mexico City: Editorial Nueva Imagen, 1983.

Carmack, Robert M. *Quichean Civilization: The Ethnohistoric, Ethnographic, and Archaeological Sources.* Berkeley: University of California Press, 1973.

———. *The Quiché Mayas of Utatlán: The Evolution of a Highland Guatemala Kingdom.* Norman: University of Oklahoma Press, 1981.

———, ed. *Harvest of Violence: The Maya Indians and the Guatemalan Crisis.* Norman: University of Oklahoma Press, 1988.

Carpenter, Betsy, "Faces in the Forest." *U.S. News & World Report,* June 4, 1990.

Caulfield, Catherine. *In the Rain Forest.* London: Pan Books, 1986.

Coe, Michael. *Breaking the Maya Code.* New York: Thames and Hudson, 1992.

———. *The Maya.* London: Thames and Hudson, 1966.

———. "A Triumph of Spirit: How Yuri Knorozov Cracked the Maya Hieroglyphic Code from Far-off Leningrad." *Archaeology,* vol. 44, no. 5, September/October 1991.

Cojtí Cuxil, Demetrio. "Lingüística e Idiomas Mayas en Guatemala." In *Lecturas Sobre la Lingüística Maya.* Nora England and Stephen Elliott, eds. Guatemala: CIRMA, 1990, pp. 1–25.

———. *Configuración del Pensamiento Político del Pueblo Maya.* Quezaltenango: Asociación de Escritores Mayances de Guatemala, 1991.

Cojtí, Narciso, and Margarita López Raquec. *Idiomas de Guatemala y Belice.* Guatemala: Editorial Piedra Santa, 1988.

Colby, Benjamin N., and Lore M. Colby. *The Daykeeper: The Life and Discourse of an Ixil Diviner.* Cambridge, Mass.: Harvard University Press, 1981.

Colby, Benjamin N., and Pierre L. van der Berghe. *Ixil Country: A Plural Society in Highland Guatemala.* Berkeley: University of California Press, 1969.

Davis, Shelton H., and J. Hodson. *Witnesses to Political Violence in Guatemala: The Suppression of a Rural Development Movement.* Boston: Oxfam America, 1982.

Demarest, Arthur Andrew. "A Critical Analysis of Yuri Knorozov's Decipherment of the Maya Hieroglyphics." Middle America Research Institute, Tulane University. No. 22, part 3, pp. 53–73, 1976.

Díaz del Castillo, Bernal. *The Conquest of New Spain.* J. M. Cohen, trans. Baltimore, Md.: Penguin Books, 1983.

———. *Historia Verdadera de la Conquista de la Nueva España.* Mexico City: Editorial Porrúa, 1955.

Earle, Duncan. "Mayas in Refuge." *Vanderbilt Review,* vol. 4, Spring 1988.

Eberwine, Donna. "To Ríos Montt, with Love Lift." *The Nation,* February 26, 1983.

Edmonson, Munro S., trans. *The Book of Counsel: The Popol Vuh of the Quiché Maya of Guatemala.* New Orleans, La.: Tulane University Press, 1971.

Ejército de Guatemala (Guatemalan Army). *Polos de Desarrollo y Servicios: Política Desarrollista.* Guatemala: Editorial del Ejército, 1984.

England, Nora. "Lengua y Definición Etnica entre los Mayas de Guatemala," *Mesoamérica,* no. 22, 1991.

Erazo, Edith Alicia, and María del Carmen Erazo. "Los Guajeros del Basurero Municipal," *Cultura de Guatemala*, no. 12, vol. 1, January–April 1991.

Evans-Pritchard, Ambrose. "Inside a Guerrilla Command," *Sacramento Bee*, March 11, 1985.

Falla, Ricardo. *Voices of the Survivors: The Massacre at Finca San Francisco, Guatemala*. Cambridge, Mass.: Cultural Survival and Anthropology Resource Center, 1983.

————. *Masacres de la Selva: Ixcán, Guatemala (1975–1982)*. Guatemala: Editorial Universitaria, 1992.

Farriss, Nancy M. *Maya Society under Spanish Rule: The Collective Enterprise of Survival*. Princeton, N.J.: Princeton University Press, 1984.

Forsyth, Adrian, and Ken Miyata. *Tropical Nature*. New York: Charles Scribner's Sons, 1984.

Fuentes y Guzmán, Francisco Antonio de. *Historia de Guatemala; o, Recordación Florida, 1643*. Parts 1, 2, and 3. Madrid: L. Navarro, 1882–83.

Gage, Thomas. *The English-American: A New Survey of the West Indies, 1648*. London and Guatemala City: Routledge/El Patio, 1946.

————. *Los Viajes de Tomás Gage en la Nueva España*. Part 3, vol. 7. Guatemala: Editorial José de Pineda Ibarra, 1967.

Galeano, Eduardo. *Guatemala: Occupied Country*. New York: Monthly Review Press, 1969.

Galich, Manuel. *Del Pánico al Ataque*. Guatemala City: Tipografía Nacional, 1949.

García Escobar, Carlos René. "Breves Notas Sobre Las Danzas Tradicionales de Guatemala," *Folklore Americano*, no. 47. Guatemala: Instituto Panamericano de Geografía e Historia, 1989.

————. "La Danza Tradicional del Palo Volador en Guatemala," *Folklore Americano*, no. 49. Guatemala: Instituto Panamericano de Geografía e Historia, 1990.

Gleijeses, Piero. *Shattered Hope: The Guatemalan Revolution and the U.S., 1944–54*. Princeton, N.J.: Princeton University Press, 1991.

Godoy, Julio. "Unlike East Europe, Fear Without Hope." *The Nation*, March 5, 1990.

Goetz, Delia, and Sylvanus G. Morley, trans. *Popol Vuh: The Sacred Book of the Ancient Quiché Maya*. From the Spanish translation of Adrián Recinos. Norman: University of Oklahoma Press, 1950.

Goldman, Francisco. *The Long Night of White Chickens* (novel). New York: Atlantic Monthly Press, 1992.

Graham, Ian, ed. *Corpus of Maya Hieroglyphic Inscriptions*. Cambridge, Mass.: Harvard University Peabody Museum of Archeology and Ethnology, 1982.

Handy, Jim. *Gift of the Devil: A History of Guatemala*. Boston: South End Press, 1984.

Heinzman, R., and C. Reining. "Sustained Rural Development: Extractive Forest Reserves in the Northern Petén of Guatemala." Guatemala: US AID, 1988.

Hill, Robert M. *Colonial Cakchiquels: Highland Maya Adaptations to Spanish Rule, 1600–1700*. New York: Harcourt Brace Jovanovich, 1991.

Hinshaw, Robert. *Panajachel: A Guatemalan Town in Thirty-Year Perspective*. Pittsburgh, Penn.: University of Pittsburgh Press, 1975.

Houseal, Brian. " 'Maya Riches': Guatemala's Biosphere Reserve," *Nature Conservancy Magazine,* May/June 1990.

Houston, Stephen D., and David Stuart. "The Way Glyph: Evidence of 'Co-Essences' Among the Classical Maya." Research Reports on Ancient Mayan Writing. Washington, D.C.: Center for Mayan Research, 1989.

Huxley, Aldous. *Beyond the Mexique Bay.* London: Triad/Paladin, 1934.

Immerman, Richard. *The C.I.A. in Guatemala: The Foreign Policy of Intervention.* Austin: University of Texas Press, 1982.

Jonas, Susanne. *The Battle for Guatemala: Rebels, Death Squads and U.S. Power.* Boulder, Colo.: Westview Press, 1991.

Jonas, Susanne, and David Tobis, eds. *Guatemala.* Berkeley, Calif.: North American Congress on Latin America, 1974.

Jones, Grant. *Maya Resistance to Spanish Rule: Time and History on a Colonial Frontier.* Albuquerque: University of New Mexico Press, 1989.

Kinzer, Stephen, and Stephen Schlesinger. *Bitter Fruit: The Untold Story of the American Coup in Guatemala.* Garden City, N.Y.: Doubleday, 1981.

Knorozov, Yuri. *Maya Hieroglyphic Codices.* Translated from the Russian by Sophie D. Coe. Albany: State University of New York Institute for Mesoamerican Studies, 1962.

La Farge, Oliver. *Santa Eulalia: The Religion of a Cuchumatán Indian Town.* Chicago: University of Chicago Press, 1947.

LaFeber, Walter. *Inevitable Revolutions: The United States in Central America.* New York: W. W. Norton, 1983.

Landa, Diego de. *Relación de las Cosas de Yucatán, 1566.* Mexico City: Editorial Porrúa, 1982.

Las Casas, Bartolomé de. *Brevísima Relación de la Destrucción de las Indias, 1552.* Mexico City: Editorial Fontamara, 1984.

Lernoux, Penny. *Cry of the People.* New York: Doubleday, 1980.

Llorente, J. A. "Vida de Fray Bartolomé de Las Casas, Obispo de Chiapa, en América." In *Brevísima Relación de la Destruccíon de las Indias.* See las Casas 1984, pp. 123-200.

Lothrop, S. K. "Santiago Atitlán, Guatemala." *Indian Notes,* vol. 5, no. 4, October 1928.

Loucky, James, and Robert Carlsen, "Massacre in Santiago Atitlán," *Cultural Survival Quarterly,* Summer 1991.

Lovell, W. George. *Conquest and Survival in Colonial Guatemala: A Historical Geography of the Cuchumatán Highlands, 1500-1821.* Revised ed. Kingston, Ont.: McGill-Queen's University Press, 1992.

———. *Conquista y Cambio Cultural: La Sierra de los Cuchumatanes de Guatemala, 1500-1821.* Antigua, Guatemala: CIRMA, 1990.

———. "Surviving Conquest: The Maya of Guatemala in Historical Perspective." *Latin American Research Review,* 23, no. 2:5-27, 1988.

Luján Muñoz, Jorge, ed. *Historia y Antropología de Guatemala.* Guatemala: Universidad de San Carlos, 1982.

Macal, Virgilio Rodríguez. *Guayacán* (novel). Guatemala: Editorial Piedra Santa, 1969.

McClintock, Michael. *The American Connection, Volume Two: State Terror and Popular Resistance in Guatemala.* London: Zed Books, 1985.

McCreery, David. *Desarrollo Económico y Política Nacional: El Ministerio de Fomento de Guatemala*. Guatemala: CIRMA, 1981.

———. "Land, Labor and Violence in Highland Guatemala: San Juan Ixcoy (Huehuetenango), 1893–1945." *The Americas*, 45:2, October 1988.

MacLeod, M. J. *Spanish Central America: A Socioeconomic History. 1520–1720*. Berkeley: University of California Press, 1973.

MacLeod, M. J., and Robert Wassestrom, eds. *Spaniards and Indians in Southeastern Mesoamerica*. Lincoln: University of Nebraska Press, 1983.

Manz, Beatriz. *Refugees of a Hidden War: The Aftermath of the Counterinsurgency War in Guatemala*. Albany, N.Y.: SUNY Press, 1989.

Martínez Peláez, Severo. *La Patria del Criollo*. San José, Costa Rica: Editorial Universitaria Centroamericana, 1971.

Massing, Michael. "The New Game in Guatemala." *New York Review of Books*, October 25, 1990.

Melville, Thomas, and Marjorie Melville. *Guatemala: The Politics of Land Ownership*. New York: Free Press, 1971.

Menchú, Rigoberta. *Me Llamo Rigoberta Menchú y Así Me Nació La Conciencia*. Elisabeth Burgos, ed. Mexico City: Siglo XXI, 1985.

Mendelson, E. Michael [AKA Nathaniel Tarn]. *Los Escándalos de Maximón*. Guatemala: Ministerio de Educación, 1965.

Molina, Diego F., and Luis Alfredo Arango. *Las Confesiones de Maximón*. Guatemala: Artemis y Edinter, 1983.

Monteforte Toledo, Mario. *Anaité* (novel). 1948. Guatemala: Editorial Piedra Santa, 1988.

———. *Guatemala: Monografía Sociológica*. Mexico City: Instituto de Investigaciones Sociales de la Universidad Autónoma de Mexico, 1959.

Montejo, Victor. *Testimony: Death of a Guatemalan Village*. Victor Perera, trans. Willimantic, Conn.: Curbstone Press, 1987.

Morley, Sylvanus G., and George W. Brainerd; rev. by Robert J. Sharer. *The Ancient Maya*. Stanford: Stanford University Press, 1983.

Nairn, Allan, and Jean-Marie Simon, "Bureaucracy of Death." *The New Republic*, 194, no. 26:13–17, 1986.

Nations, James D. *Tropical Rainforests: Endangered Environment*. New York: F. Watts, 1988.

Nations, J., and R. Nigh, "The Evolutionary Potential of Lacandón Maya Sustained-Yield Tropical Forest Agriculture." *Journal of Anthropological Research*, 36:1–30, 1980.

Navarrete, Carlos. "Otra Vez Modesto Méndez, Ambrosio Tut, y el Moderno Descubrimiento de Tikal." In *Historia y Antropología de Guatemala*, pp. 155–70. See Luján 1982.

Oakes, Maud. *Beyond the Windy Place: Life in the Guatemalan Highlands*. New York: Farrar, Straus and Young, 1951.

———. *The Two Crosses of Todos Santos: Survivals of Mayan Religious Rituals*. New York: Pantheon Books, 1951.

Orellana, Sandra L. *The Tzutujil Maya: Continuity and Change, 1250–1630*. Norman: University of Oklahoma Press, 1984.

Painter, James. *Guatemala: False Hope, False Freedom*. London: Latin American Bureau, 1987.

Pansini, Joseph Jude. "Situación de los Trabajadores de las Fincas en Guatemala." *Mesoamérica*, vol. 1, no. 1, January 1980.

Paul, Benjamin. *La Vida de un Pueblo Indígena de Guatemala*. Guatemala: Editorial José de Pineda Ibarra, 1959.

Payeras, Mario. *Days of the Jungle: The Testimony of a Guatemalan Guerrillero, 1972–1976*. George Black, trans. New York: Monthly Review Press, 1983.

———. *Latitud de la Flor y el Granizo*. Mexico: Joan Boldó i Clement, 1988.

———. *El Trueno en la Ciudad: Episodios de la Lucha Armada Urbana de 1981 en Guatemala*. Mexico: Juan Pablos Editor, 1987.

Perera, Victor. "Can Guatemala Change?" *New York Review of Books*, August 14, 1986.

———. "An Ecological Catastrophe: A Forest Dies in Guatemala." *The Nation*, November 6, 1989.

———. "Guatemala: Always La Violencia," *New York Times Magazine*, June 13, 1971.

———. "Guatemalan Refugees: A Political Dilemma for Mexico," *The Nation*, September 8, 1984.

———. "Hot Spots: War on Words," *Mother Jones*, February/March 1989.

———. "The Last Preserve: Guatemala Guards Its Rain Forests." *The Nation*, July 8, 1991.

———. "The Long Journey Home: Pablo Fernández and the Discovery of La Rochela," *Grassroots Development*, vol. 13, no. 2, 1989.

———. [AKA Jaime Nissen]. "Night Visitors: The Murder of a Guatemalan Town," *The Nation*, May 9, 1981.

———. *Rites: A Guatemalan Boyhood*. New York: Harcourt Brace Jovanovich, 1986.

———. "Some Call Him the Schweitzer of Guatemala," *New York Times*, April 16, 1977.

———. "Uzi Diplomacy: How Israel Makes Friends and Enemies Around the World," *Mother Jones*, July 1985.

———. "Vida Cotidiana Después del Terremoto," *Crisis* (Buenos Aires), May/June 1976.

Perera, Victor, and Robert D. Bruce. *The Last Lords of Palenque: The Lacandón Mayas of the Mexican Rain Forest*. Berkeley: University of California Press, 1985.

Petersen, Kurt. *The Maquiladora Revolution in Guatemala*. Yale Law School, New Haven, Conn.: Schell Center for International Human Rights, 1992.

Plant, Roger. *Guatemala: Unnatural Disaster*. London: Latin American Bureau, 1978.

Recinos, Adrián, trans. *Memorial de Sololá, Anales de los Cakchiqueles*. Guatemala: Editorial Piedra Santa, 1980.

Recinos, Adrián, trans. and ed. *Popol-Vuh: Las Antiguas Historias del Quiché*. Mexico City: Biblioteca Americana, 1947.

Recinos, Adrián, Delia Goetz, and Dionisio José Chona, trans. *The Annals of the Cakchiquels*. Norman: University of Oklahoma Press, 1958.

Richards, Julia Becker. *Programa de Desarrollo Integral de la Población Maya*. Guatemala: Universidad Rafael Landívar, 1989.

Richards, Michael Finn. "Cosmopolitan World View and Counterinsurgency in Guatemala." *Anthropological Quarterly,* 3:90–107, 1986.

Rother, Stanley Francis. *The Shepherd Cannot Run: Letters of Stanley Rother, Missionary and Martyr.* Archdiocese of Oklahoma City, 1984.

Roys, Ralph L. *The Book of Chilam Balam of Chumayel.* Norman: University of Oklahoma Press, 1967.

Schele, Linda, and Mary Ellen Miller. *The Blood of Kings.* New York: George Braziller, 1986.

Schwartz, Norman. *Forest Society: A Social History of Petén, Guatemala.* Pittsburgh: University of Pennsylvania Press, 1991.

Sexton, James D., ed. and trans. *Mayan Folktales: Folklore from Lake Atitlán.* New York: Doubleday, 1992.

Sheehan, Edward R. F. *Agony in the Garden: A Stranger in Central America.* Boston: Houghton-Mifflin, 1989.

Simon, Jean-Marie. *Guatemala: Eternal Spring, Eternal Tyranny.* New York: W. W. Norton, 1987.

Smith, Carol, ed. *Guatemalan Indians and the State: 1540 to 1988.* Austin: University of Texas Press, 1990.

Smith, Carol. "Mayan Nationalism." NACLA Report on the Americas, 25:3 28–33, December 1991.

Sommer, Doris. "Rigoberta's Secrets." *Latin American Perspectives,* 70:18 no. 3, 32–50, Summer 1991.

Soza, José María. *Monografía del Departamento de El Petén.* Guatemala: Editorial José de Pineda Ibarra, 1970.

Stephens, John L. *Incidents of Travel in Central America, Chiapas, and Yucatan,* vols. 1 and 2. London: John Murray, 1841.

Stoll, David. *Between Two Fires: Dual Violence and the Reassertion of Civil Society in Nebaj, Guatemala.* Ph.D. dissertation, Stanford University, 1992.

———. "Evangelicals, Guerrillas and the Army: The Ixil Triangle under Ríos Montt." In *Harvest of Violence,* pp. 90–116. *See* Carmack 1988.

———. *Is Latin America Turning Protestant?: The Politics of Evangelical Growth.* Berkeley: University of California Press, 1990.

———. *Fishers of Men or Founders of Empire?: The Wycliffe Bible Translators in Latin America.* Cambridge, Mass.: Cultural Survival, 1982.

Tarn, Nathaniel [AKA Michael Mendelson], and Martín Prechtel. " 'Eating the Fruit': Sexual Metaphor and Initiation in Santiago Atitlán." *Mesoamérica,* vol. 11, no. 19, June 1990.

Tax, Sol. *Penny Capitalism: A Guatemalan Indian Economy.* Washington, D.C.: Smithsonian Institute of Social Anthropology, no. 16, 1953.

Tax, Sol, and Robert Hinshaw. *Los Pueblos del Lago de Atitlán. Seminario de Integración Social Guatemalteca.* Guatemala City: Tipografía Nacional, 1968.

Tedlock, Barbara. *Time and the Highland Maya.* Albuquerque: University of New Mexico Press, 1982.

Tedlock, Dennis, trans. *Popol Vuh: The Definitive Edition of the Mayan Book of the Dawn of Life and the Glories of Gods and Kings.* New York: Simon and Schuster, 1985.

Thompson, J. Eric. *The Rise and Fall of Maya Civilization.* 2d ed. Norman: University of Oklahoma Press, 1966.

Tozzer, Alfred M. *A Comparative Study of the Mayas and the Lacandones*. New York: Macmillan [AMS reprint, New York, 1978].

Warren, Kay B. *The Symbolism of Subordination: Indian Identity in a Guatemalan Town*. Austin: University of Texas Press, 1978.

Watanabe, John M. *Maya Saints and Souls in a Changing World*. Austin: University of Texas Press, 1992.

Webster, Katharine. "Deception in Guatemala: How the U.S. Media Bought a Cover-up," *The Progressive*, February 1990.

Wolf, Eric. *Sons of the Shaking Earth*. Chicago: University of Chicago Press, 1959.

Woodward, Ralph Lee, Jr. *Central America: A Nation Divided*. New York: Oxford University Press, 1976.

———. *Rafael Carrera and the Emergence of the Republic of Guatemala, 1821–1871*. Atlanta: University of Georgia Press, 1993.

Wright, Ronald. *Time Among the Maya*. New York: Weidenfeld & Nicolson, 1989.

Ximénez, Francisco. *Historia Nacional del Reino de Guatemala (1722)*. Guatemala City: Editorial José de Pineda Ibarra, 1967.

Zimmerman, Marc. "Testimonio in Guatemala: Payeras, Rigoberta and Beyond," *Latin American Perspectives*, 71:18 no. 4, 22–47, Fall 1991.

Index

Academy of Mayan Languages, 13, 99, 335
Acevedo, Renaldo, 233, 236, 244–45
Acción Católica: in Ixil Triangle, 66–67, 86, 95, 124–25; in San Juan la Laguna, 195, 196, 197, 199; in Santiago Atitlán, 172, 177, 193, 194, 212, 215; in Todos Santos, 139
Agency for International Development (AID), 42, 246, 265
Agricultural laborers: and debt-peonage system, 8–9, 65, 69, 159; health conditions of, 278, 304; and Spanish-colonial system, 6, 8, 65, 171; and vagrancy laws, 9, 65; wages of, 68, 70, 91, 159. *See also* Foragers; Migrant laborers
Agriculture, 67, 148; chemical fertilizers used in, 20, 304; and exports, 7, 9, 164, 233, 237; in Mayan empire, 230, 240; pesticides used in, 68, 304; in Spanish colonial period, 6, 7–8, 63, 171. *See also* Land tenure; Milpas; *names of specific crops*
Aguilar, Hugo, 253–55
Allende, Salvador, 294
Allspice, harvesting of, 234, 248, 266
Alvarado, Pedro de: and conquest of Mayan Empire, 1–4, 12, 62, 105, 271; in Mayan religion, 170, 178–79, 208
Americas Watch, 49, 62, 75, 92, 108, 289
Amnesty International, 25, 62, 69

Anthropologists, 175, 176, 205, 207, 209, 224, 236
Anticommunism, 40, 338; of Catholic church, 66, 162, 203; of evangelical movement, 11, 12, 73, 87–88, 128, 331, 344
Antigua, xii–xiv, 6, 165–66, 335, 347–48
Arana, Francisco Javier, 294
Arana Osorio, Carlos, 38, 330; Pacification Campaigns of, xi, 41–42, 49, 68
Arbenz Guzmán, Jacobo, 9, 11, 40–41, 45, 163, 282, 284, 294
Archaeology, Mayan, 1, 61, 143, 165–66, 169, 170, 220, 233; looting of, 236, 243, 256; and protective legislation, 244–45; at Tikal, 1, 165–66, 220, 224–25, 228–31, 233, 236–37
Arenas, Clara, 342
Arenas, Enrique, 73–74
Arenas, Luis, execution of, 69, 71, 72, 73
Arenas, Ricardo, 73–74
Arévalo, Juan José, 9, 41, 46, 282, 283, 291, 294–95
Argentina: arms imports from, 11, 82; disappeared persons in, 48–49
Arias, Oscar, 10, 229, 288, 289
Arms, importation of, 11, 82, 108–9
Assassinations, 39, 41, 45–47, 186, 265, 286, 294, 302, 309, 333; of Myrna Mack Chang, 47, 333, 337, 338, 341–42, 349; of Michael DeVine, 47,

and unemployment, 289. *See also* Income levels; Land tenure; Poverty

Ecosystems, conservation of, 224–26, 240; and Cerezo government, 224, 225, 226, 228–29, 245, 247, 258, 287; and Environmental Commission, 220, 224, 226, 245, 264, 266; foreign aid for, 246, 247, 251, 265–66; and Maya Biosphere Reserve, 224–26, 243, 245–48, 251, 263, 266–68; and Protected Areas legislation, 245–51; and Serrano government, 264, 268. *See also* Tikal National Park

Ecosystems, destruction of: and chemical defoliants, 192; and chemical fertilizers, 20; and contraband lumber trade, 258, 265, 266, 267; and deforestation, 154, 224–25, 228, 238, 241, 242, 267; and endangered species, 165, 232, 234–35; and greenhouse effect, 220, 238; military's role in, 239–41, 259–60, 263–64, 265, 267

Ecotourism, 228, 244–45, 247, 251

Education: and literacy levels, 91, 101; and Mayan languages, 91, 101, 289, 316, 319; and social identity, 145, 149, 316–19; and U.S. scholarships, 140

EGP. *See* Guerrilla Army of the Poor

Eisenhower, Dwight D., 295

El Salvador, 45, 228, 286, 290; ARENA party in, 45; peace negotiations in, 10, 334; U.S. aid to, 109

Elites. *See* Business elite; Landowning elite; Military

Emigration, 155–58

Encomienda system, 6, 8, 65, 171

Environmentalism. *See* Ecosystems, conservation of

Esquipulas Peace Accords, 10, 50, 109, 116, 288

Estrada Cabrera, Manuel, 39, 337

Evangelical movement: anticommunism of, 11, 12, 73, 87–88, 128, 331, 344; and Cerezo government, 89; and competition with Catholicism, 11, 79, 85, 121, 125–26, 139, 172, 185, 331–32, 351; and competition with Mayan religion, 175, 205, 207–8; and 1976 earthquake, 11–12, 86, 272, 273–74; relief projects of, 12, 88, 91, 272, 274; and Ríos Montt, 12, 86–89, 91, 279, 329–31, 332, 347; and Serrano government, 331–32, 343

Evangelical movement, by district: in Guatemala City, 28; in Ixcán, 73; in

Ixil Triangle, 73, 79, 84–89, 121; in Lacandón, 314; in San Pedro la Laguna, 195, 196; in Santiago Atitlán, 171, 172, 175, 178, 185–86, 192, 205, 207–8, 215; in Todos Santos, 139, 144

Executions, by government forces: in Huehuetenango region, 55–56; in Ixil Triangle, 66, 105, 106–7; in Lemoa, 331; in Todos Santos, 137, 144

Executions, by guerrillas: in Chimaltenango, 320; in Huehuetenango region, 145, 162; in Ixil Triangle, 64, 69, 70, 71, 72, 73; in Santiago Atitlán, 204

Exports, agricultural, 7, 9, 164, 233, 237, 258, 304

Falla, Ricardo, 161–62

Family relations, 23, 155

FAR. *See* Rebel Armed Forces

Farabundo Martí National Liberation Front, 10, 334

Fascism, 36, 45, 295

Fatalism, 23, 43–44

Ferraté, Antonio, 264, 265

Feudalism, 6, 7, 72, 171

Flores, Mario Aquino, 83

Flores (town in El Petén), 227, 239, 247

Foragers, in tropical forests, 233–34, 236–37, 248

Fuentes, Eduardo, 195–96, 197, 198–201, 202, 203, 210, 306, 351

Fuentes Mohr, Alberto, 46

Gage, Thomas, 8

GAM. *See* Group of Mutual Support

García, Nineth, 285, 286, 307, 338

García Samayoa, José Domingo, 334, 338–39

Girón, Andrés: attempted assassination of, 307–8, 311–12; biography of, 300–303; and controversy with Father Vesey, 195, 199, 211, 306, 310; and corruption charges, 308–9; elected to Congress, 310–11; peasant associations organized by, 299, 303–6; presidential aspirations of, 306, 307, 308, 309; and relations with Cerezo, 298, 299, 303, 306, 310

Godoy Gaitán, Edgar, 342

Gonzales, Eugenia (Calixta Canek), 319–28

Good Neighbor Policy, 41

Gorbachev, Mikhail, 128

Gramajo, Héctor, 46, 53, 58, 128, 163, 241, 276, 283, 292, 296